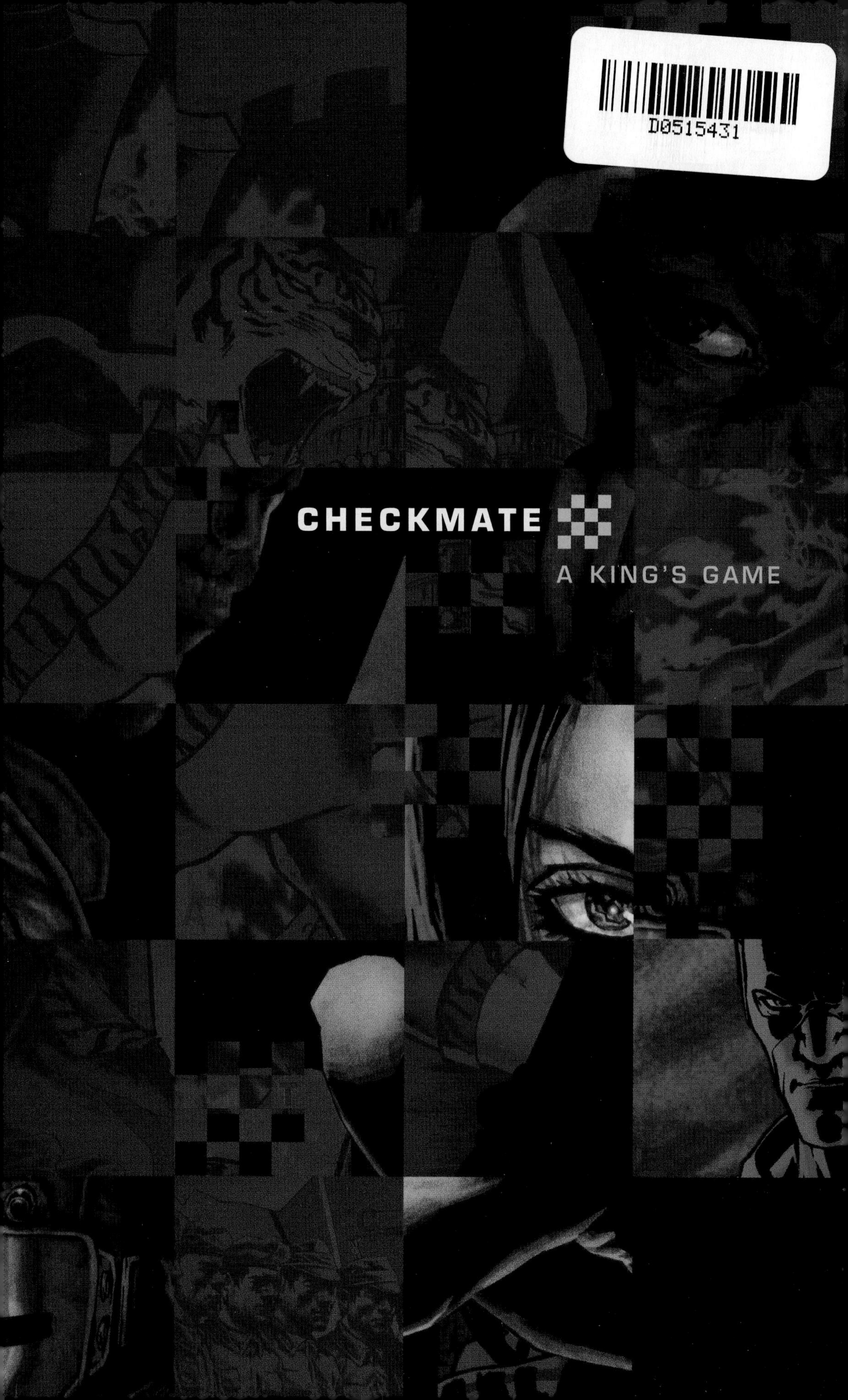
CHECKMATE
A KING'S GAME

Dan DiDio Senior VP-Executive Editor
Joan Hilty Editor-original series
Rachel Gluckstern Associate Editor-original series
Bob Harras Editor-collected edition
Robbin Brosterman Senior Art Director
Paul Levitz President & Publisher
Georg Brewer VP-Design & DC Direct Creative
Richard Bruning Senior VP-Creative Director
Patrick Caldon Executive VP-Finance & Operations
Chris Caramalis VP-Finance
John Cunningham VP-Marketing
Terri Cunningham VP-Managing Editor
Stephanie Fierman Senior VP-Sales & Marketing
Alison Gill VP-Manufacturing
Hank Kanalz VP-General Manager, WildStorm
Jim Lee Editorial Director-WildStorm
Paula Lowitt Senior VP-Business & Legal Affairs
MaryEllen McLaughlin VP-Advertising & Custom Publishing
John Nee VP-Business Development
Gregory Noveck Senior VP-Creative Affairs
Cheryl Rubin Senior VP-Brand Management
Jeff Trojan VP-Business Development, DC Direct
Bob Wayne VP-Sales

Cover illustration by Lee Bermejo & Patricia Mulvihill
Logo design by John J. Hill
Publication design by Amelia Grohman

CHECKMATE: A KING'S GAME
Published by DC Comics. Cover, introduction and compilation
copyright © 2007 DC Comics. All Rights Reserved. Originally
published in single magazine form in CHECKMATE 1-7.
Copyright © 2006 DC Comics. All Rights Reserved.
All characters, their distinctive likenesses and related
elements featured in this publication are trademarks of
DC Comics. The stories, characters and incidents featured
in this publication are entirely fictional. DC Comics does
not read or accept unsolicited submissions of ideas,
stories or artwork.

DC Comics, 1700 Broadway, New York, NY 10019
A Warner Bros. Entertainment Company
Printed in Canada. First Printing.
ISBN: 1-4012-1220-4
ISBN 13: 978-1-4012-1220-9

WRITERS

GREG RUCKA
chapter 1-5

**GREG RUCKA
NUNZIO DeFILIPPIS
CHRISTINA WEIR**
chapter 6-7

ARTIST

JESUS SAIZ

chapters 1-2, 4-5

PENCILLER

CLIFF RICHARDS

chapters 3, 6 & 7

INKERS

BOB WIACEK
and **STEVE BIRD**
chapter 3

FERNANDO BLANCO
chapter 5

DAN GREEN
chapters 6 & 7

BOB WIACEK
chapter 7

A KING'S GAME

LETTERER

TRAVIS LANHAM

COLORISTS

**TANYA & RICHARD HORIE
SANTIAGO ARCAS**

CHECKMATE
created by
PAUL KUPPERBERG
and **STEVE ERWIN**

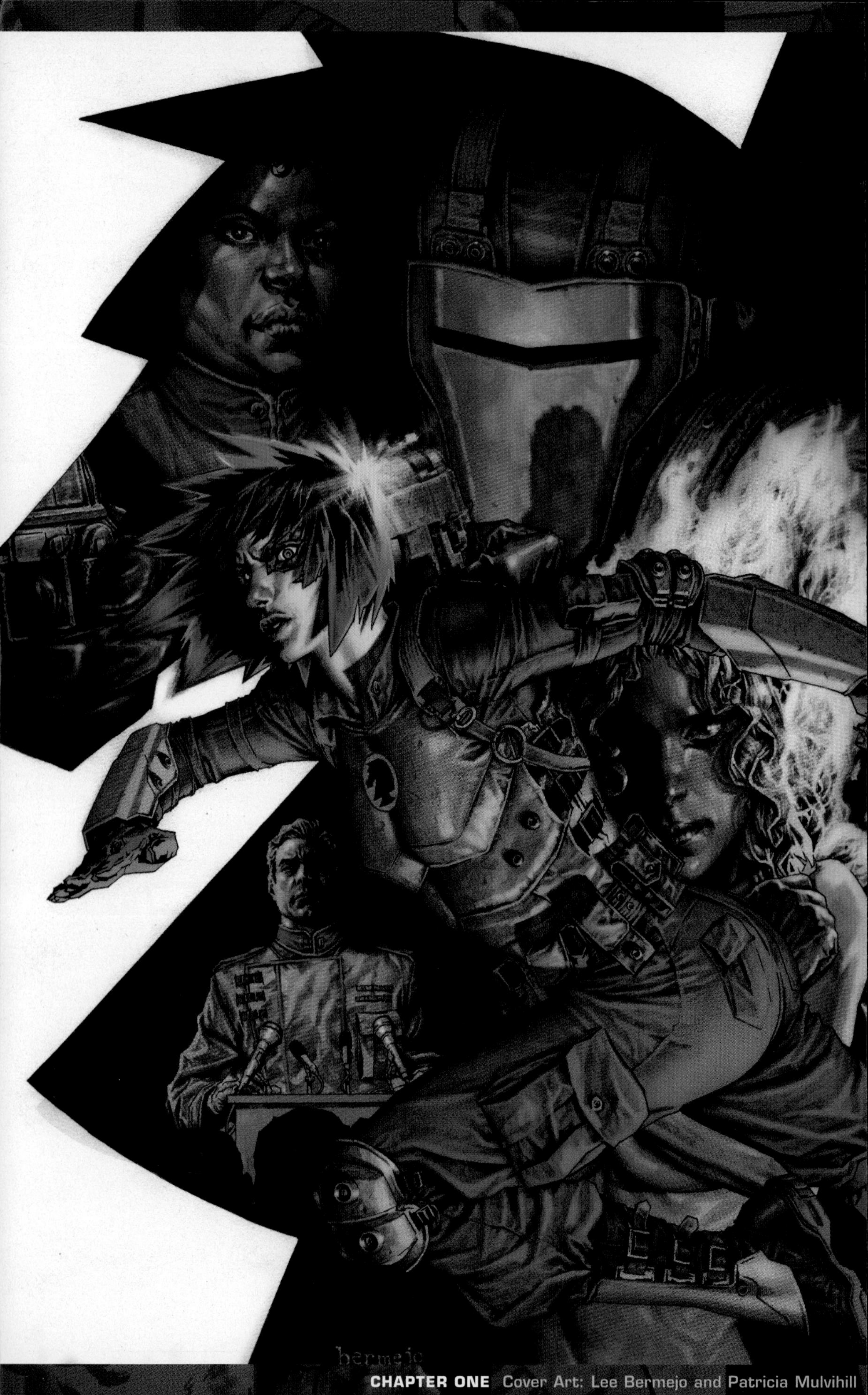
bermejo

CHAPTER ONE Cover Art: Lee Bermejo and Patricia Mulvihill

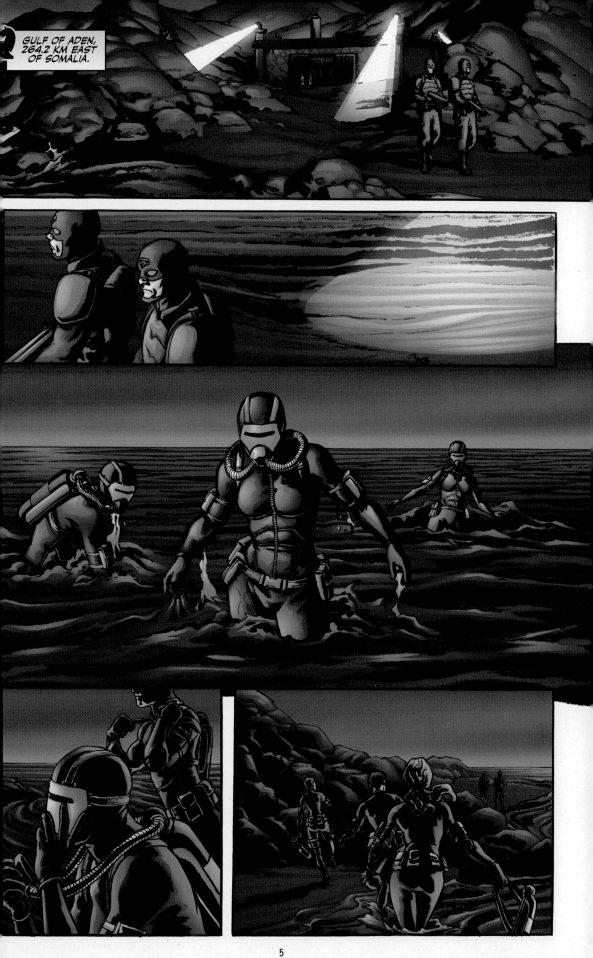

GULF OF ADEN, 264.2 KM EAST OF SOMALIA.

5

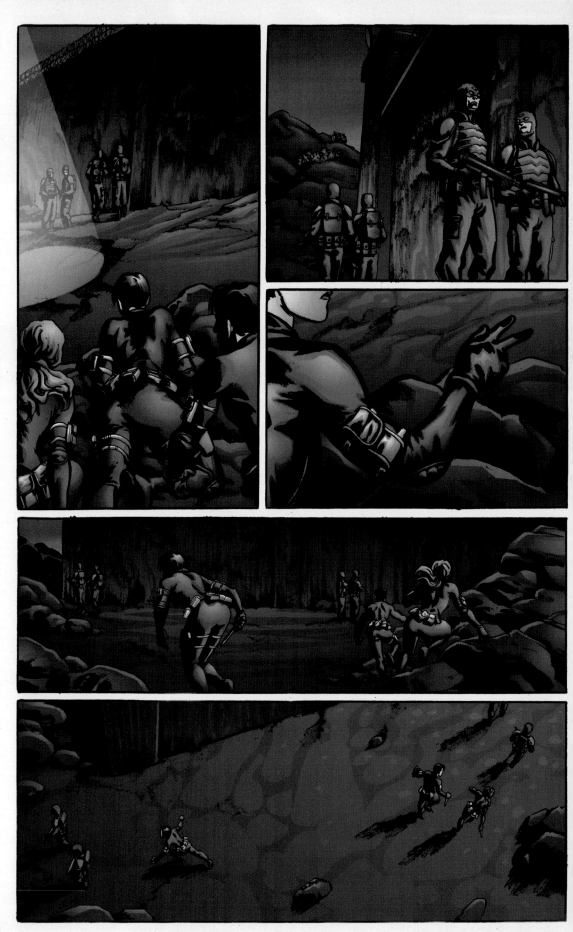

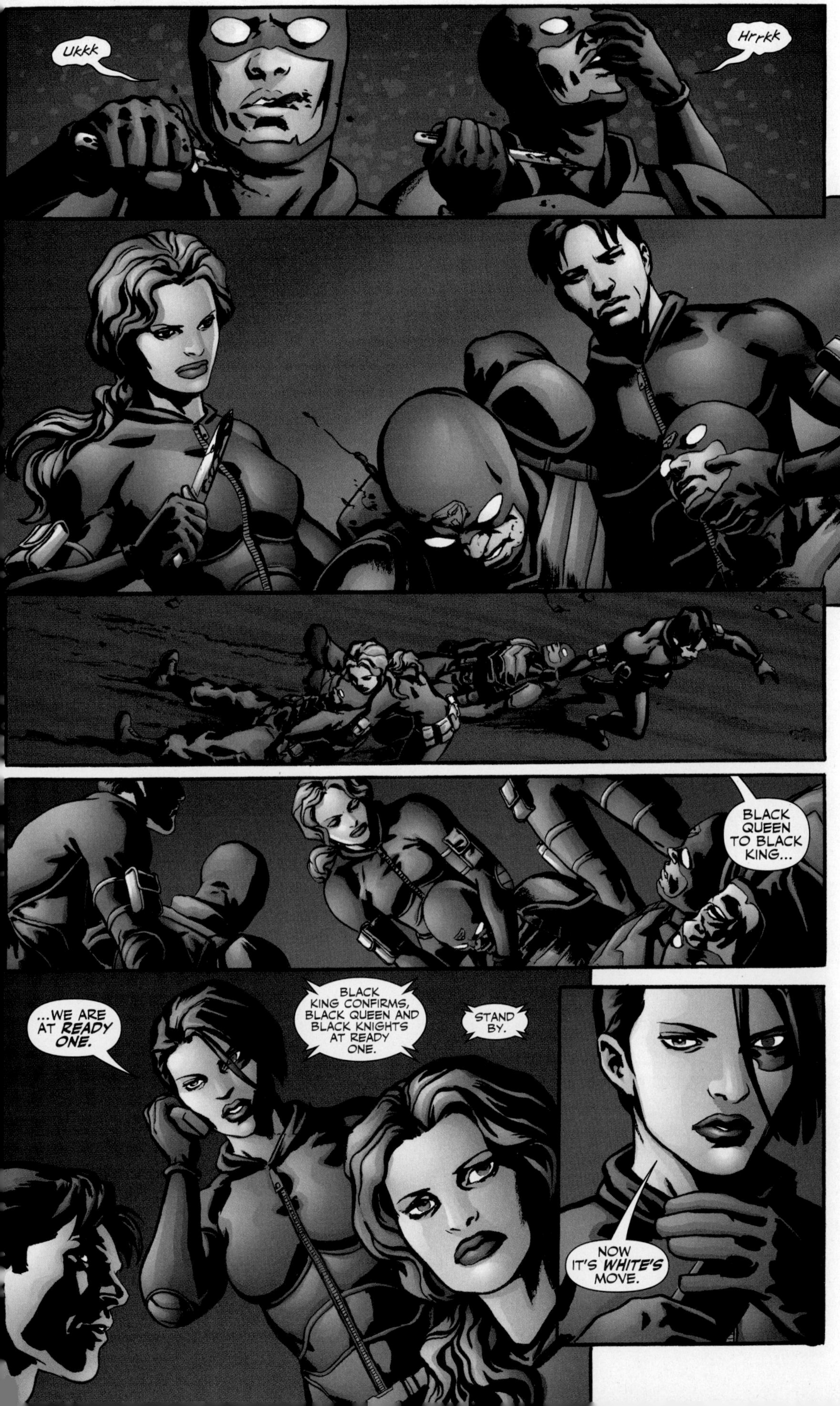
Ukkk
Hrrkk
BLACK QUEEN TO BLACK KING...
...WE ARE AT READY ONE.
BLACK KING CONFIRMS, BLACK QUEEN AND BLACK KNIGHTS AT READY ONE.
STAND BY.
NOW IT'S WHITE'S MOVE.

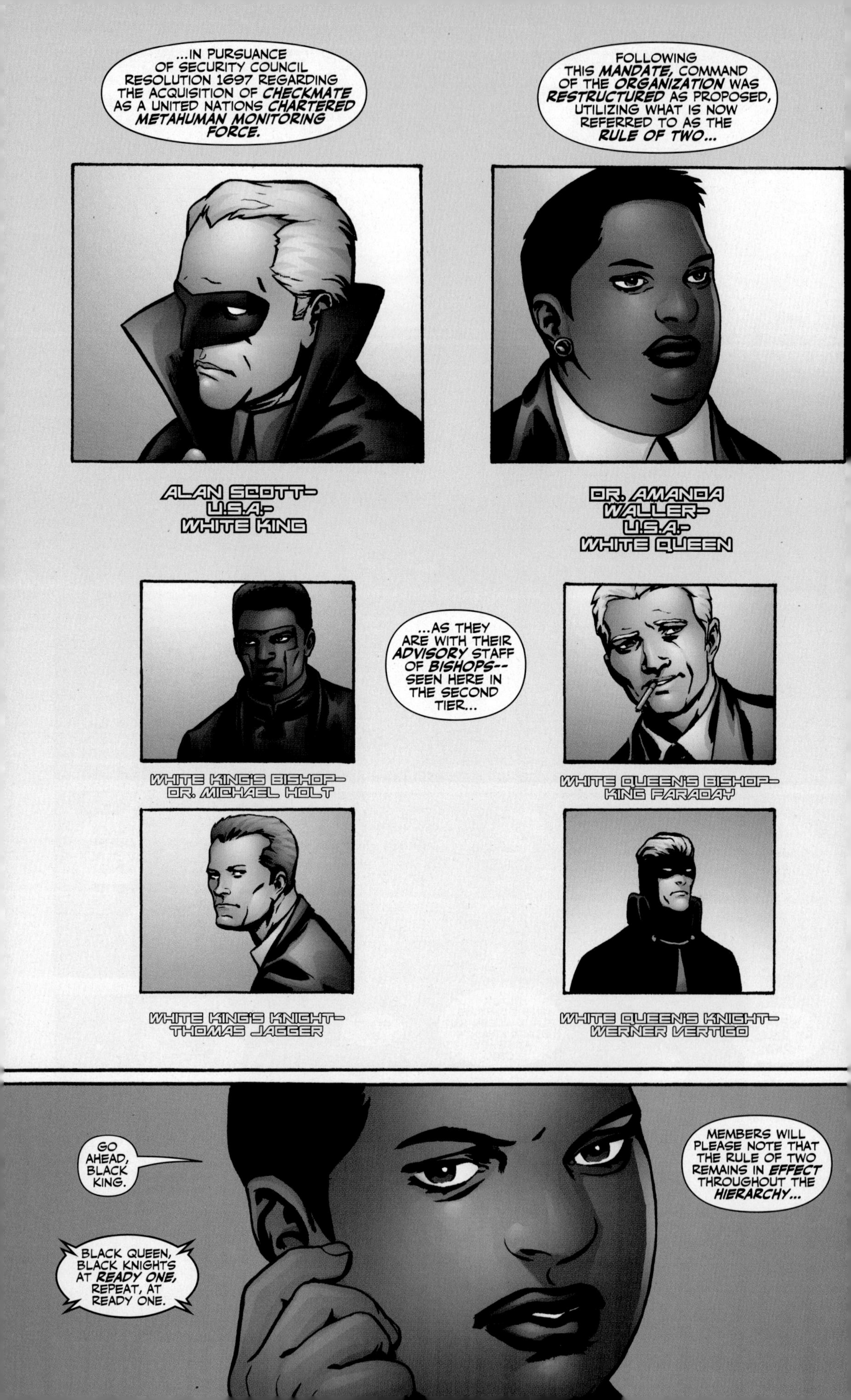
...IN PURSUANCE OF SECURITY COUNCIL RESOLUTION 1697 REGARDING THE ACQUISITION OF CHECKMATE AS A UNITED NATIONS CHARTERED METAHUMAN MONITORING FORCE.
FOLLOWING THIS MANDATE, COMMAND OF THE ORGANIZATION WAS RESTRUCTURED AS PROPOSED, UTILIZING WHAT IS NOW REFERRED TO AS THE RULE OF TWO...
ALAN SCOTT- U.S.A.- WHITE KING
DR. AMANDA WALLER- U.S.A.- WHITE QUEEN
...AS THEY ARE WITH THEIR ADVISORY STAFF OF BISHOPS-- SEEN HERE IN THE SECOND TIER...
WHITE KING'S BISHOP- DR. MICHAEL HOLT
WHITE QUEEN'S BISHOP- KING FARADAY
WHITE KING'S KNIGHT- THOMAS JAGGER
WHITE QUEEN'S KNIGHT- WERNER VERTIGO
MEMBERS WILL PLEASE NOTE THAT THE RULE OF TWO REMAINS IN EFFECT THROUGHOUT THE HIERARCHY...
GO AHEAD, BLACK KING.
BLACK QUEEN, BLACK KNIGHTS AT READY ONE, REPEAT, AT READY ONE.

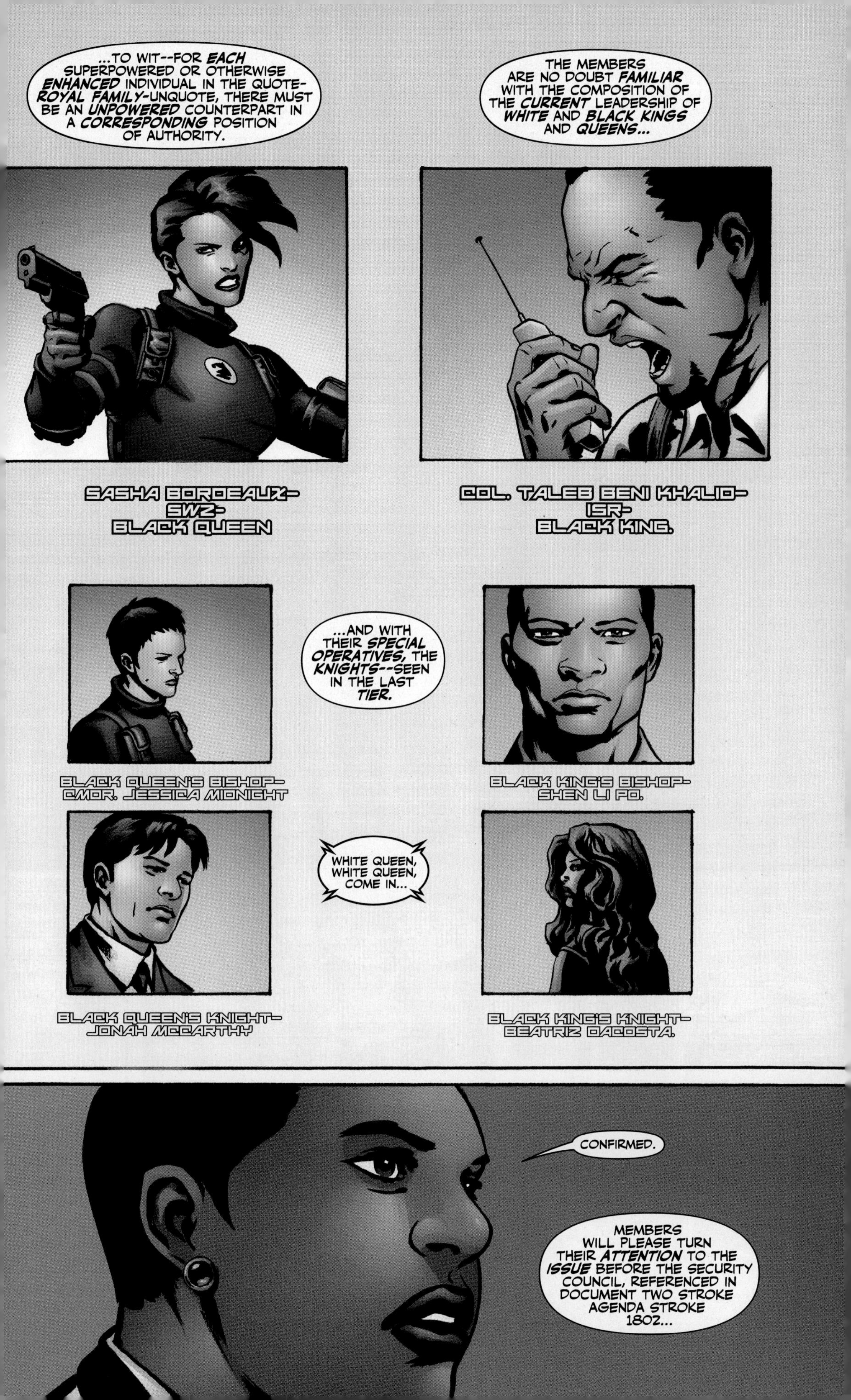
...TO WIT--FOR EACH SUPERPOWERED OR OTHERWISE ENHANCED INDIVIDUAL IN THE QUOTE-ROYAL FAMILY-UNQUOTE, THERE MUST BE AN UNPOWERED COUNTERPART IN A CORRESPONDING POSITION OF AUTHORITY.
THE MEMBERS ARE NO DOUBT FAMILIAR WITH THE COMPOSITION OF THE CURRENT LEADERSHIP OF WHITE AND BLACK KINGS AND QUEENS...
SASHA BORDEAUX- SWZ- BLACK QUEEN
COL. TALEB BENI KHALID- ISR- BLACK KING.
...AND WITH THEIR SPECIAL OPERATIVES, THE KNIGHTS--SEEN IN THE LAST TIER.
BLACK QUEEN'S BISHOP- CMDR. JESSICA MIDNIGHT
BLACK KING'S BISHOP- SHEN LI PO.
WHITE QUEEN, WHITE QUEEN, COME IN...
BLACK QUEEN'S KNIGHT- JONAH MCCARTHY
BLACK KING'S KNIGHT- BEATRIZ DACOSTA.
CONFIRMED.
MEMBERS WILL PLEASE TURN THEIR ATTENTION TO THE ISSUE BEFORE THE SECURITY COUNCIL, REFERENCED IN DOCUMENT TWO STROKE AGENDA STROKE 1802...

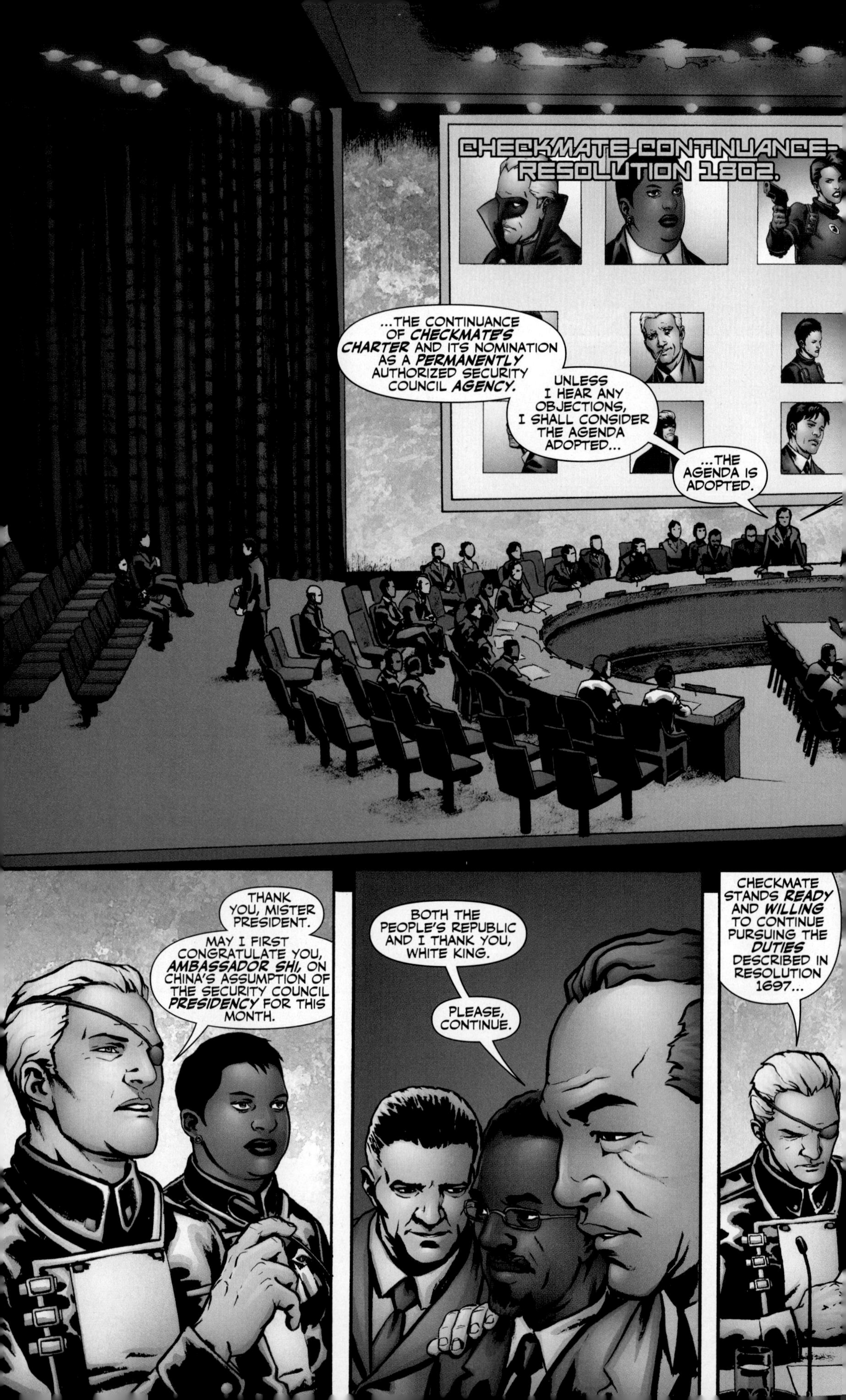

CHECKMATE CONTINUANCE--RESOLUTION 1802.
...THE CONTINUANCE OF CHECKMATE'S CHARTER AND ITS NOMINATION AS A PERMANENTLY AUTHORIZED SECURITY COUNCIL AGENCY.
UNLESS I HEAR ANY OBJECTIONS, I SHALL CONSIDER THE AGENDA ADOPTED...
...THE AGENDA IS ADOPTED.
THANK YOU, MISTER PRESIDENT.
MAY I FIRST CONGRATULATE YOU, AMBASSADOR SHI, ON CHINA'S ASSUMPTION OF THE SECURITY COUNCIL PRESIDENCY FOR THIS MONTH.
BOTH THE PEOPLE'S REPUBLIC AND I THANK YOU, WHITE KING.
PLEASE, CONTINUE.
CHECKMATE STANDS READY AND WILLING TO CONTINUE PURSUING THE DUTIES DESCRIBED IN RESOLUTION 1697...

IN ACCORDANCE WITH THE COUNCIL'S PRIOR CONSULTATION, THE SECURITY COUNCIL *EXTENDS* AN *INVITATION* UNDER RULE 39 TO *ALAN SCOTT*, WHITE *KING*, AND *DOCTOR AMANDA WALLER*, WHITE *QUEEN*...

...TO BRIEF THE COUNCIL ON CHECKMATE'S CURRENT *STATUS*. MISTER SCOTT?

...THAT OF *POLICING* AND *MONITORING* GLOBAL METAHUMAN ACTIVITY, WHILE PROVIDING A DIPLOMATIC CONDUIT FOR SUPER-POWERED *CONFLICT RESOLUTION*.

THE LIST OF CHECKMATE *SUCCESSES* SINCE RESTRUCTURE HAS BEEN *IMPRESSIVE*.

BEGINNING WITH THE SITUATION IN *KAHNDAQ* LAST YEAR, FOLLOWED BY THE *MONSTROSITY INCIDENT* IN *BIALYA*...

...AS WELL AS THE DISRUPTION OF *KOBRA'S* PLANNED CYCLOSARIN ATTACK ON *VATICAN CITY*, CHECKMATE HAS APPREHENDED OR OTHERWISE CURTAILED THE--

THANK YOU, MISTER SCOTT...

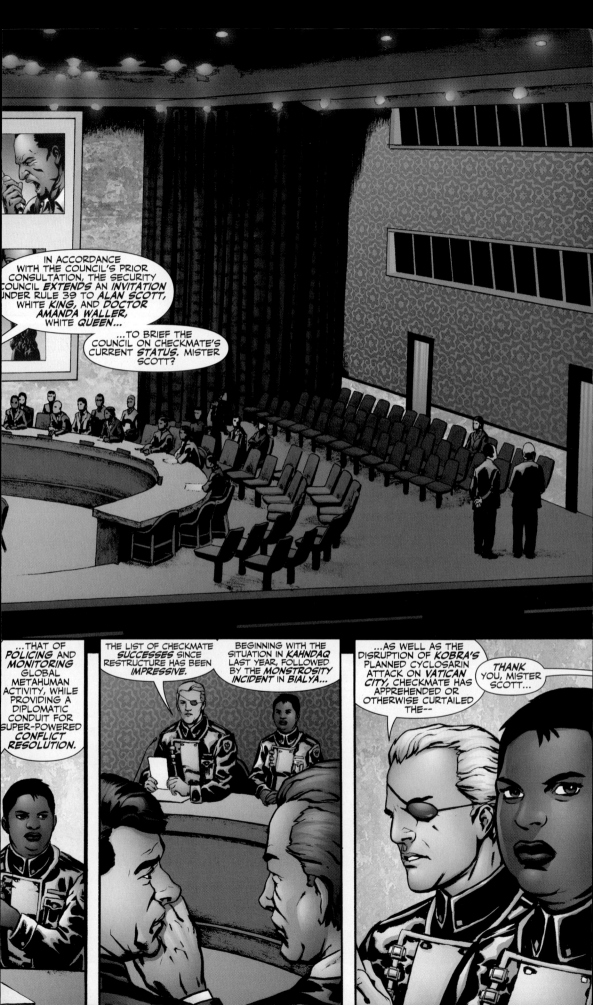

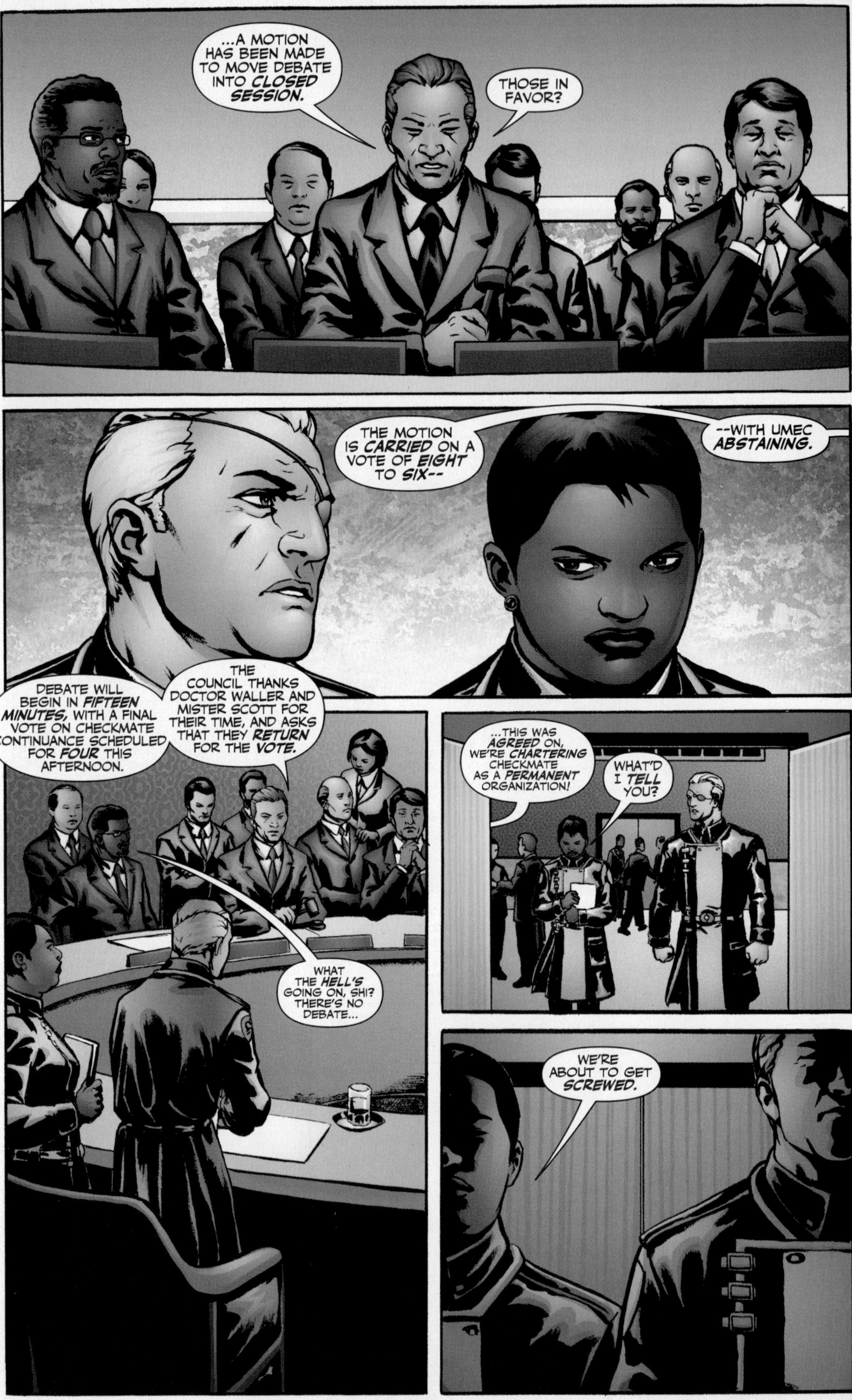
...A MOTION HAS BEEN MADE TO MOVE DEBATE INTO CLOSED SESSION.
THOSE IN FAVOR?
THE MOTION IS CARRIED ON A VOTE OF EIGHT TO SIX--
--WITH UMEC ABSTAINING.
DEBATE WILL BEGIN IN FIFTEEN MINUTES, WITH A FINAL VOTE ON CHECKMATE CONTINUANCE SCHEDULED FOR FOUR THIS AFTERNOON.
THE COUNCIL THANKS DOCTOR WALLER AND MISTER SCOTT FOR THEIR TIME, AND ASKS THAT THEY RETURN FOR THE VOTE.
WHAT THE HELL'S GOING ON, SHI? THERE'S NO DEBATE...
...THIS WAS AGREED ON, WE'RE CHARTERING CHECKMATE AS A PERMANENT ORGANIZATION!
WHAT'D I TELL YOU?
WE'RE ABOUT TO GET SCREWED.

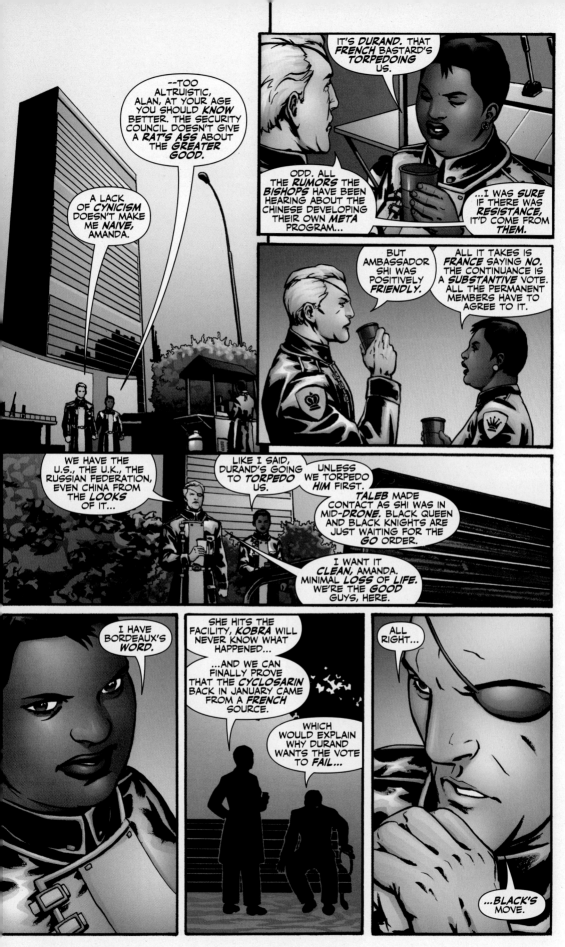

IT'S *DURAND*. THAT *FRENCH BASTARD'S* *TORPEDOING* US.

--TOO *ALTRUISTIC*, ALAN, AT YOUR AGE YOU SHOULD *KNOW* BETTER. THE SECURITY COUNCIL DOESN'T GIVE A *RAT'S ASS* ABOUT THE *GREATER GOOD*.

ODD. ALL THE *RUMORS* THE *BISHOPS* HAVE BEEN HEARING ABOUT THE CHINESE DEVELOPING THEIR OWN *META* PROGRAM...

...I WAS *SURE* IF THERE WAS *RESISTANCE*, IT'D COME FROM *THEM*.

A LACK OF *CYNICISM* DOESN'T MAKE ME *NAIVE*, AMANDA.

BUT AMBASSADOR *SHI* WAS POSITIVELY *FRIENDLY*.

ALL IT TAKES IS *FRANCE* SAYING *NO*. THE CONTINUANCE IS A *SUBSTANTIVE* VOTE. ALL THE PERMANENT MEMBERS HAVE TO AGREE TO IT.

WE HAVE THE U.S., THE U.K., THE RUSSIAN FEDERATION, EVEN CHINA FROM THE *LOOKS* OF IT...

LIKE I SAID, DURAND'S GOING TO *TORPEDO* US.

UNLESS WE TORPEDO *HIM* FIRST. *TALEB* MADE CONTACT AS SHI WAS IN MID-*DRONE*. BLACK QUEEN AND BLACK KNIGHTS ARE JUST WAITING FOR THE *GO* ORDER.

I WANT IT *CLEAN*, AMANDA. MINIMAL *LOSS OF LIFE*. WE'RE THE *GOOD* GUYS, HERE.

I HAVE BORDEAUX'S *WORD*.

SHE HITS THE FACILITY, *KOBRA* WILL NEVER KNOW WHAT HAPPENED...

...AND WE CAN FINALLY PROVE THAT THE *CYCLOSARIN* BACK IN JANUARY CAME FROM A *FRENCH* SOURCE.

WHICH WOULD EXPLAIN WHY DURAND WANTS THE VOTE TO *FAIL*...

ALL RIGHT...

...*BLACK'S* MOVE.

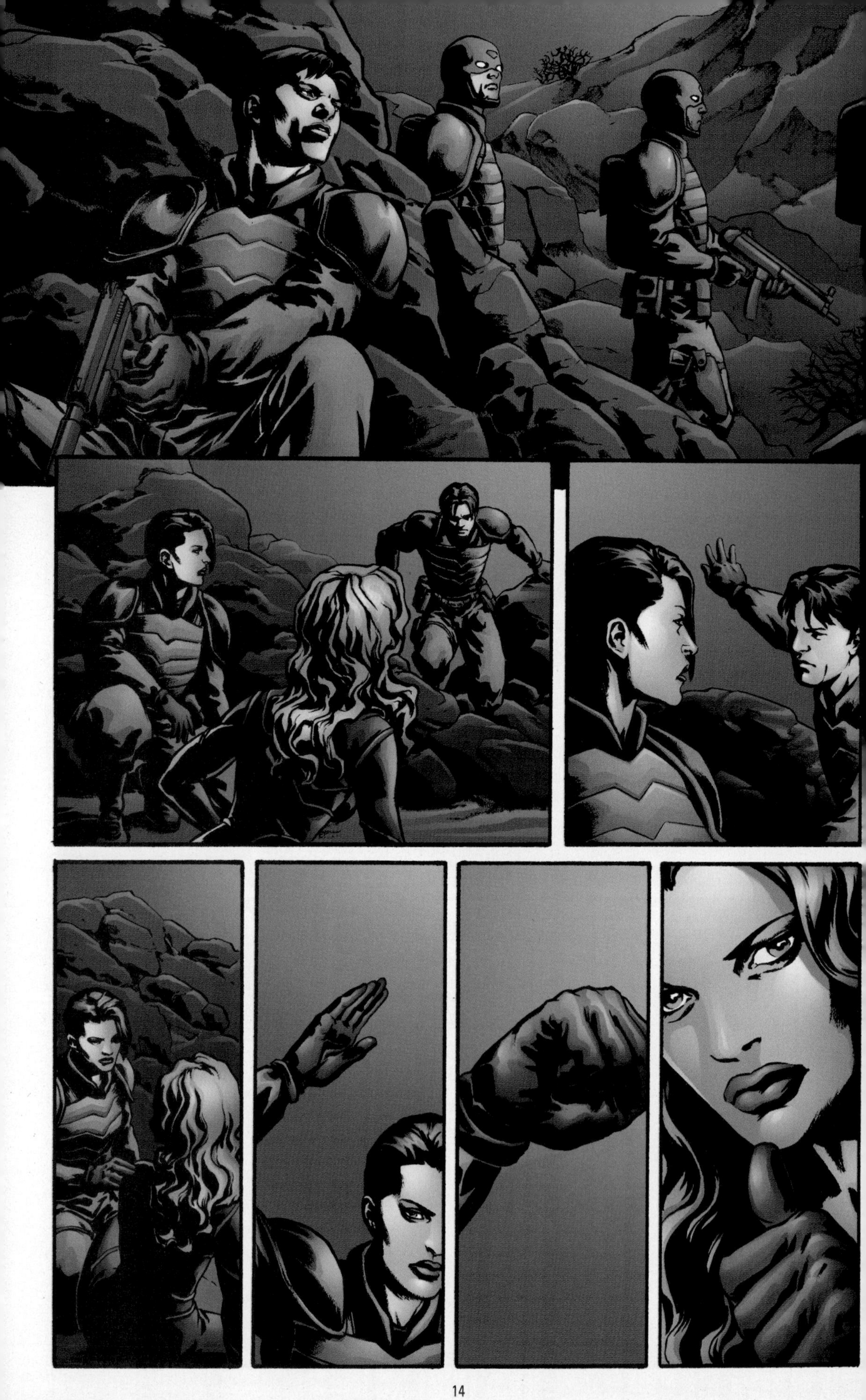

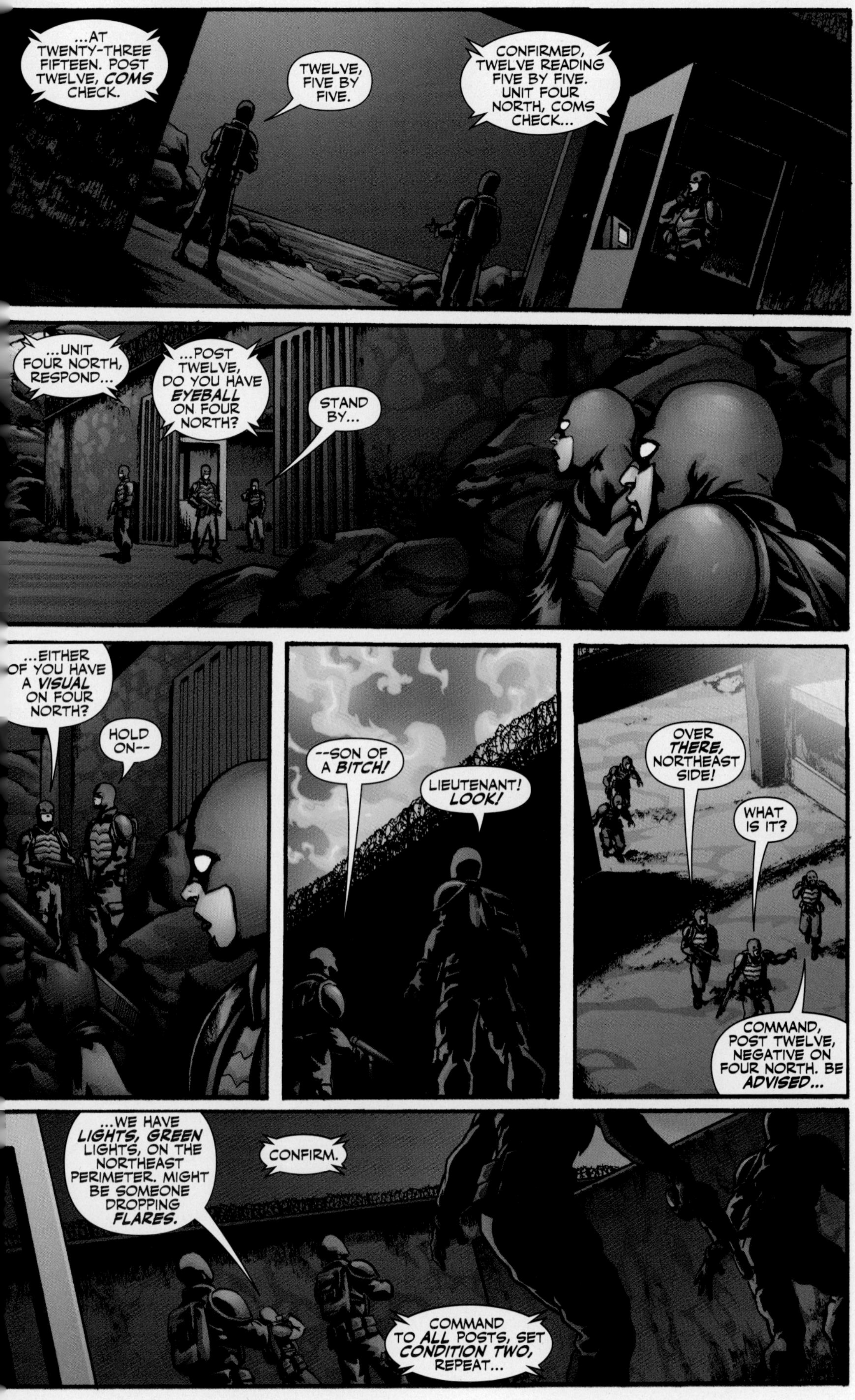
...AT TWENTY-THREE FIFTEEN. POST TWELVE, *COMS* CHECK.
TWELVE, FIVE BY FIVE.
CONFIRMED, TWELVE READING FIVE BY FIVE. UNIT FOUR NORTH, COMS CHECK...
...UNIT FOUR NORTH, RESPOND...
...POST TWELVE, DO YOU HAVE *EYEBALL* ON FOUR NORTH?
STAND BY...
...EITHER OF YOU HAVE A *VISUAL* ON FOUR NORTH?
HOLD ON--
--SON OF A *BITCH!*
LIEUTENANT! *LOOK!*
OVER *THERE,* NORTHEAST SIDE!
WHAT IS IT?
COMMAND, POST TWELVE, NEGATIVE ON FOUR NORTH. BE *ADVISED...*
...WE HAVE *LIGHTS, GREEN* LIGHTS, ON THE NORTHEAST PERIMETER. MIGHT BE SOMEONE DROPPING *FLARES.*
CONFIRM.
COMMAND TO *ALL* POSTS, SET *CONDITION TWO,* REPEAT...

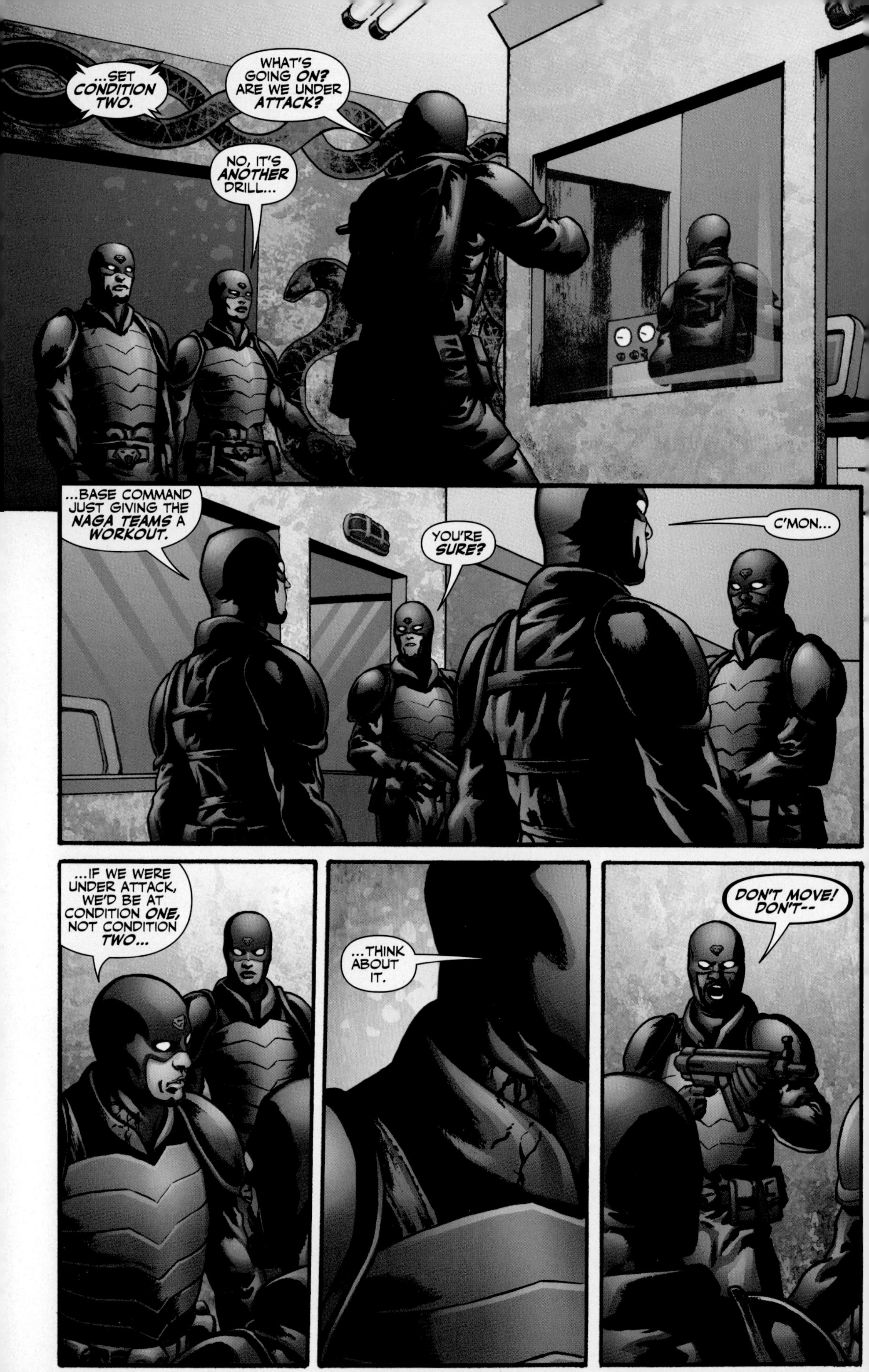
...SET CONDITION TWO.
WHAT'S GOING ON? ARE WE UNDER ATTACK?
NO, IT'S ANOTHER DRILL...
...BASE COMMAND JUST GIVING THE NAGA TEAMS A WORKOUT.
YOU'RE SURE?
C'MON...
...IF WE WERE UNDER ATTACK, WE'D BE AT CONDITION ONE, NOT CONDITION TWO...
...THINK ABOUT IT.
DON'T MOVE! DON'T--

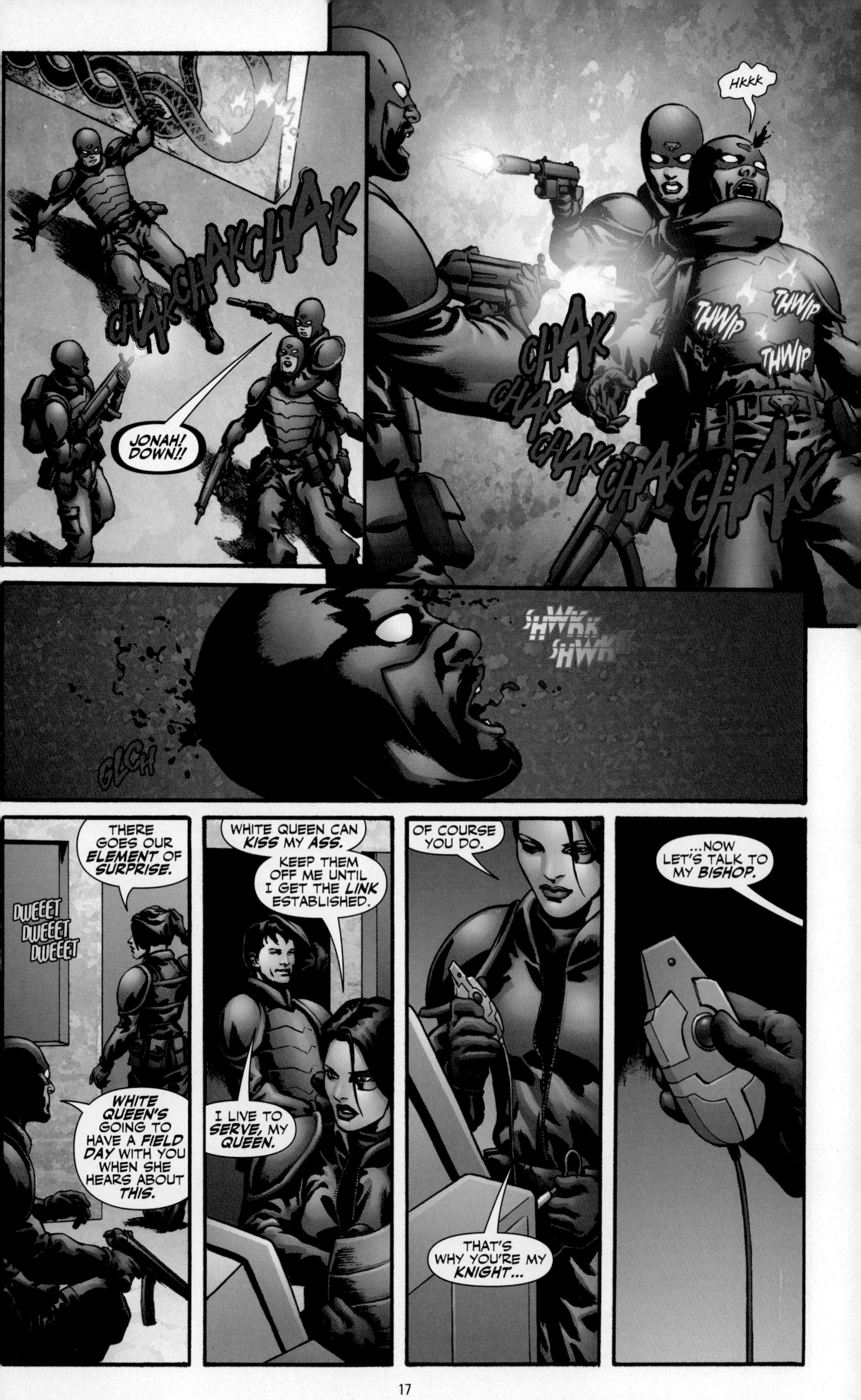
CHAKCHAKCHAK
JONAH! DOWN!!
HKKK
THWIP
THWIP
THWIP
CHAK CHAK CHAK CHAK CHAK
GLCH
THERE GOES OUR ELEMENT OF SURPRISE.
DWEEET DWEEET DWEEET
WHITE QUEEN'S GOING TO HAVE A FIELD DAY WITH YOU WHEN SHE HEARS ABOUT THIS.
WHITE QUEEN CAN KISS MY ASS.
KEEP THEM OFF ME UNTIL I GET THE LINK ESTABLISHED.
I LIVE TO SERVE, MY QUEEN.
OF COURSE YOU DO.
THAT'S WHY YOU'RE MY KNIGHT...
...NOW LET'S TALK TO MY BISHOP.

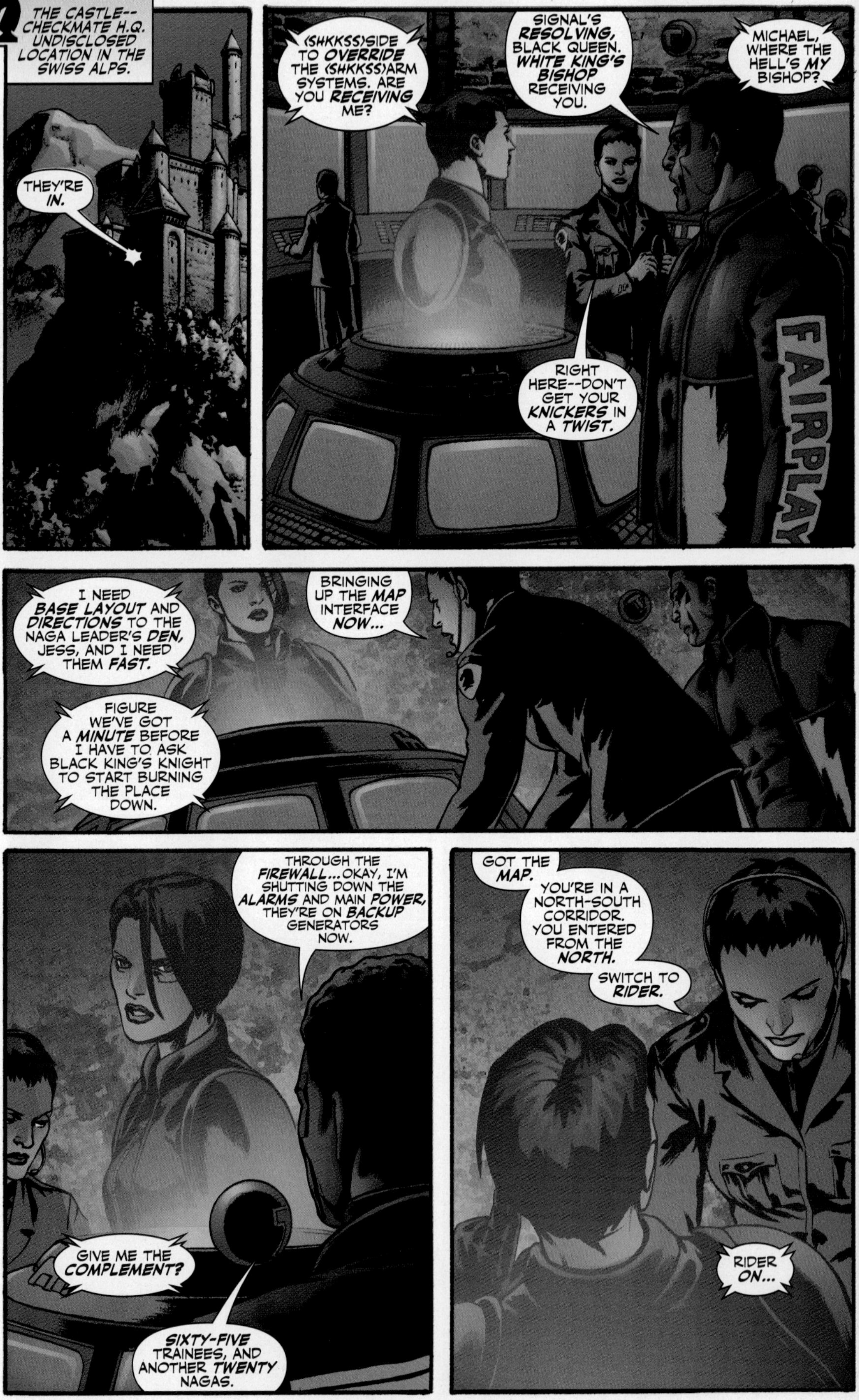
THE CASTLE--CHECKMATE H.Q. UNDISCLOSED LOCATION IN THE SWISS ALPS.
THEY'RE IN.
(SHKKSS)SIDE TO OVERRIDE THE (SHKKSS)ARM SYSTEMS. ARE YOU RECEIVING ME?
SIGNAL'S RESOLVING, BLACK QUEEN. WHITE KING'S BISHOP RECEIVING YOU.
MICHAEL, WHERE THE HELL'S MY BISHOP?
RIGHT HERE--DON'T GET YOUR KNICKERS IN A TWIST.
FAIRPLAY
I NEED BASE LAYOUT AND DIRECTIONS TO THE NAGA LEADER'S DEN, JESS, AND I NEED THEM FAST.
BRINGING UP THE MAP INTERFACE NOW...
FIGURE WE'VE GOT A MINUTE BEFORE I HAVE TO ASK BLACK KING'S KNIGHT TO START BURNING THE PLACE DOWN.
THROUGH THE FIREWALL...OKAY, I'M SHUTTING DOWN THE ALARMS AND MAIN POWER, THEY'RE ON BACKUP GENERATORS NOW.
GIVE ME THE COMPLEMENT?
SIXTY-FIVE TRAINEES, AND ANOTHER TWENTY NAGAS.
GOT THE MAP.
YOU'RE IN A NORTH-SOUTH CORRIDOR. YOU ENTERED FROM THE NORTH.
SWITCH TO RIDER.
RIDER ON...

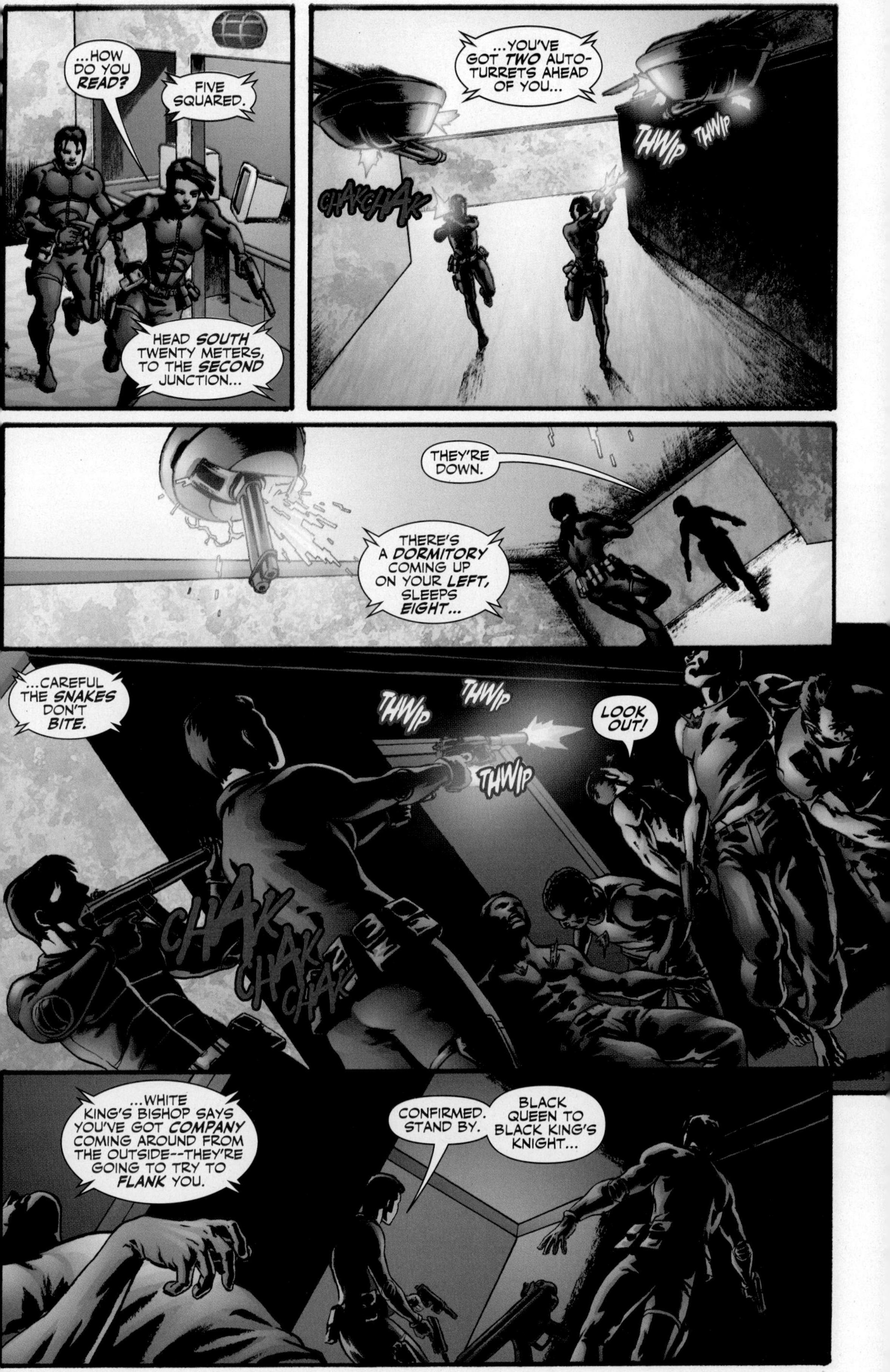
...HOW DO YOU READ?
FIVE SQUARED.
HEAD SOUTH TWENTY METERS, TO THE SECOND JUNCTION...
...YOU'VE GOT TWO AUTO-TURRETS AHEAD OF YOU...
THWIP
THWIP
CHAKCHAK
THEY'RE DOWN.
THERE'S A DORMITORY COMING UP ON YOUR LEFT, SLEEPS EIGHT...
...CAREFUL THE SNAKES DON'T BITE.
THWIP
THWIP
LOOK OUT!
THWIP
CHAK
CHAK
CHAK
CHAK
...WHITE KING'S BISHOP SAYS YOU'VE GOT COMPANY COMING AROUND FROM THE OUTSIDE--THEY'RE GOING TO TRY TO FLANK YOU.
CONFIRMED. STAND BY.
BLACK QUEEN TO BLACK KING'S KNIGHT...

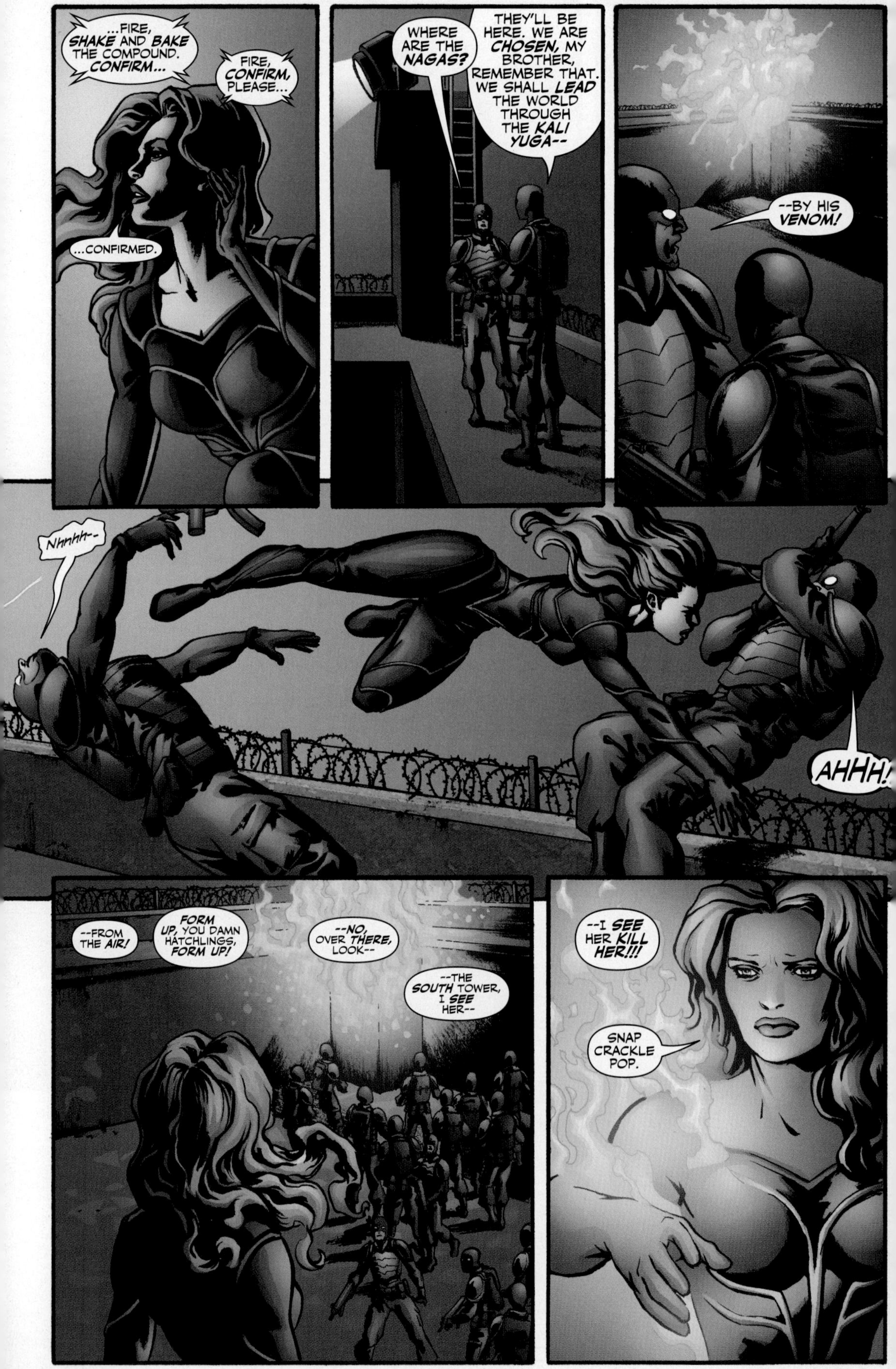
...FIRE, SHAKE AND BAKE THE COMPOUND. CONFIRM...
FIRE, CONFIRM, PLEASE...
...CONFIRMED.
WHERE ARE THE NAGAS?
THEY'LL BE HERE. WE ARE CHOSEN, MY BROTHER, REMEMBER THAT. WE SHALL LEAD THE WORLD THROUGH THE KALI YUGA--
--BY HIS VENOM!
Nhhhh--
AHHH!
--FROM THE AIR!
FORM UP, YOU DAMN HATCHLINGS, FORM UP!
--NO, OVER THERE, LOOK--
--THE SOUTH TOWER, I SEE HER--
--I SEE HER KILL HER!!!
SNAP CRACKLE POP.

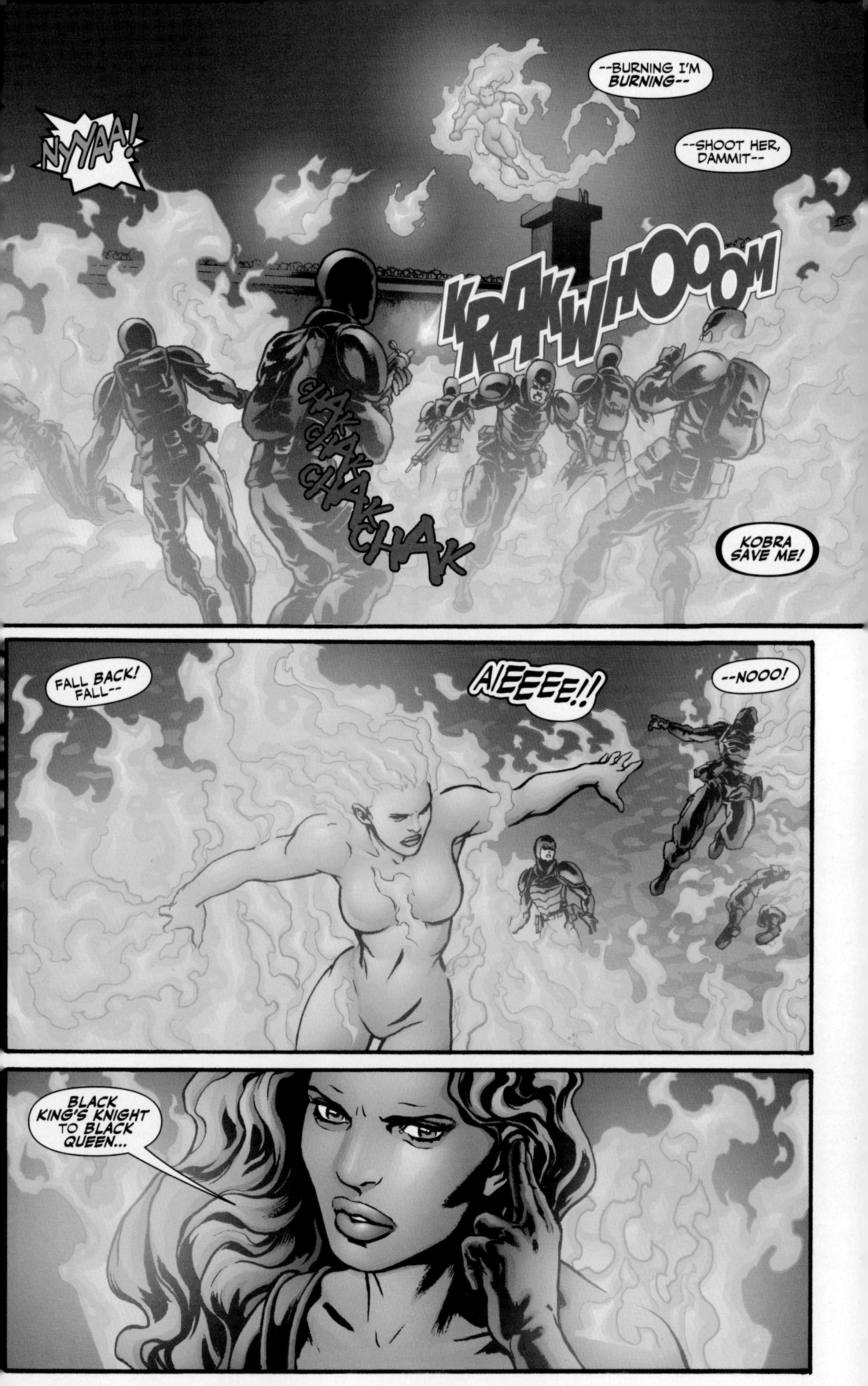
NYYAA!
--BURNING I'M BURNING--
--SHOOT HER, DAMMIT--
KRAKWHOOOM
CHAKCHAKCHAKCHAK
KOBRA SAVE ME!
FALL BACK! FALL--
AIEEEEE!!
--NOOO!
BLACK KING'S KNIGHT TO BLACK QUEEN...

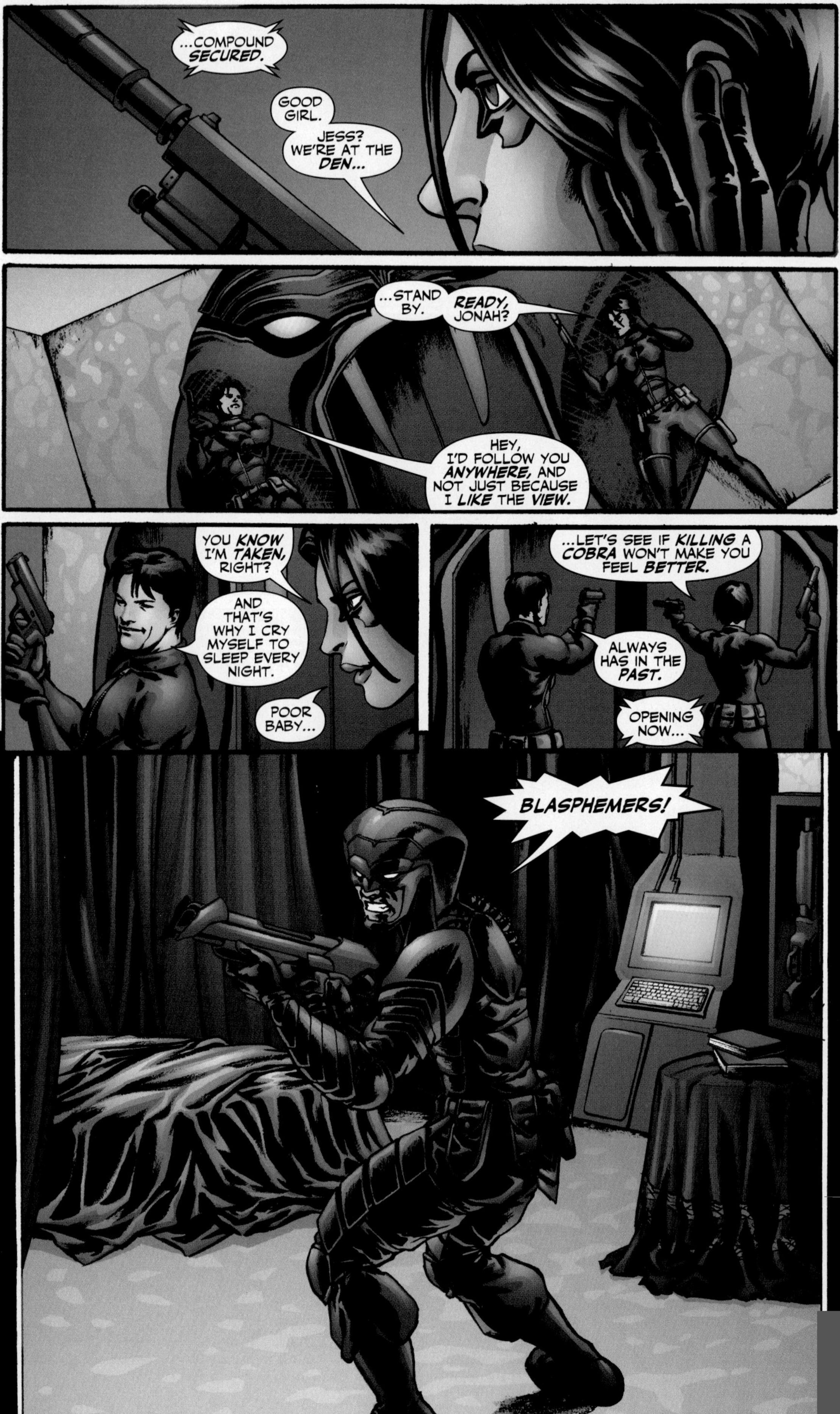
...COMPOUND SECURED.
GOOD GIRL.
JESS? WE'RE AT THE DEN...
...STAND BY.
READY, JONAH?
HEY, I'D FOLLOW YOU ANYWHERE, AND NOT JUST BECAUSE I LIKE THE VIEW.
YOU KNOW I'M TAKEN, RIGHT?
AND THAT'S WHY I CRY MYSELF TO SLEEP EVERY NIGHT.
POOR BABY...
...LET'S SEE IF KILLING A COBRA WON'T MAKE YOU FEEL BETTER.
ALWAYS HAS IN THE PAST.
OPENING NOW...
BLASPHEMERS!

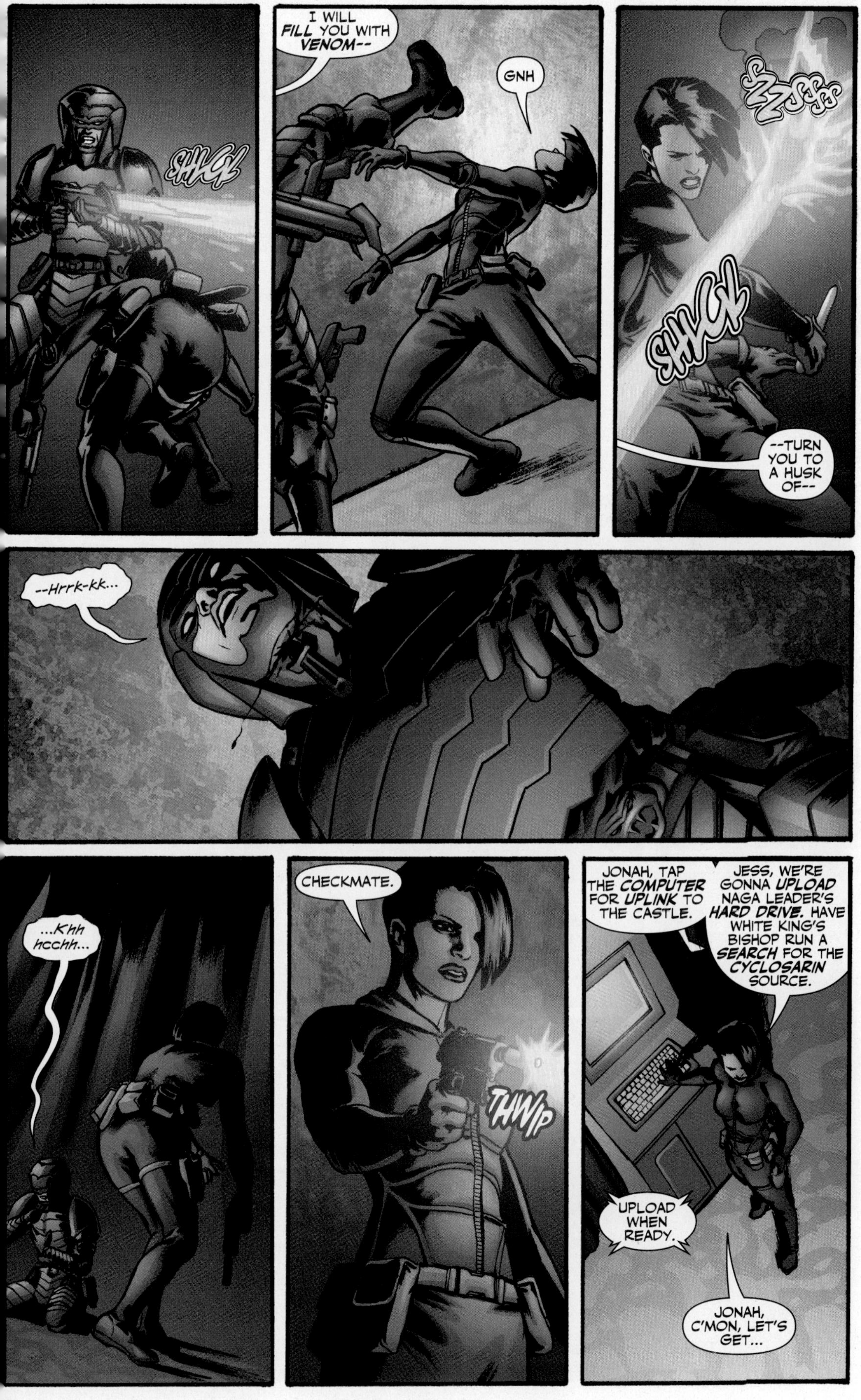
SHLCK
I WILL FILL YOU WITH VENOM--
GNH
SZZSSSS
SHLCK
--TURN YOU TO A HUSK OF--
--Hrrk-kk...
...Khh hcchh...
CHECKMATE.
THWIP
JONAH, TAP THE COMPUTER FOR UPLINK TO THE CASTLE.
JESS, WE'RE GONNA UPLOAD NAGA LEADER'S HARD DRIVE. HAVE WHITE KING'S BISHOP RUN A SEARCH FOR THE CYCLOSARIN SOURCE.
UPLOAD WHEN READY.
JONAH, C'MON, LET'S GET...

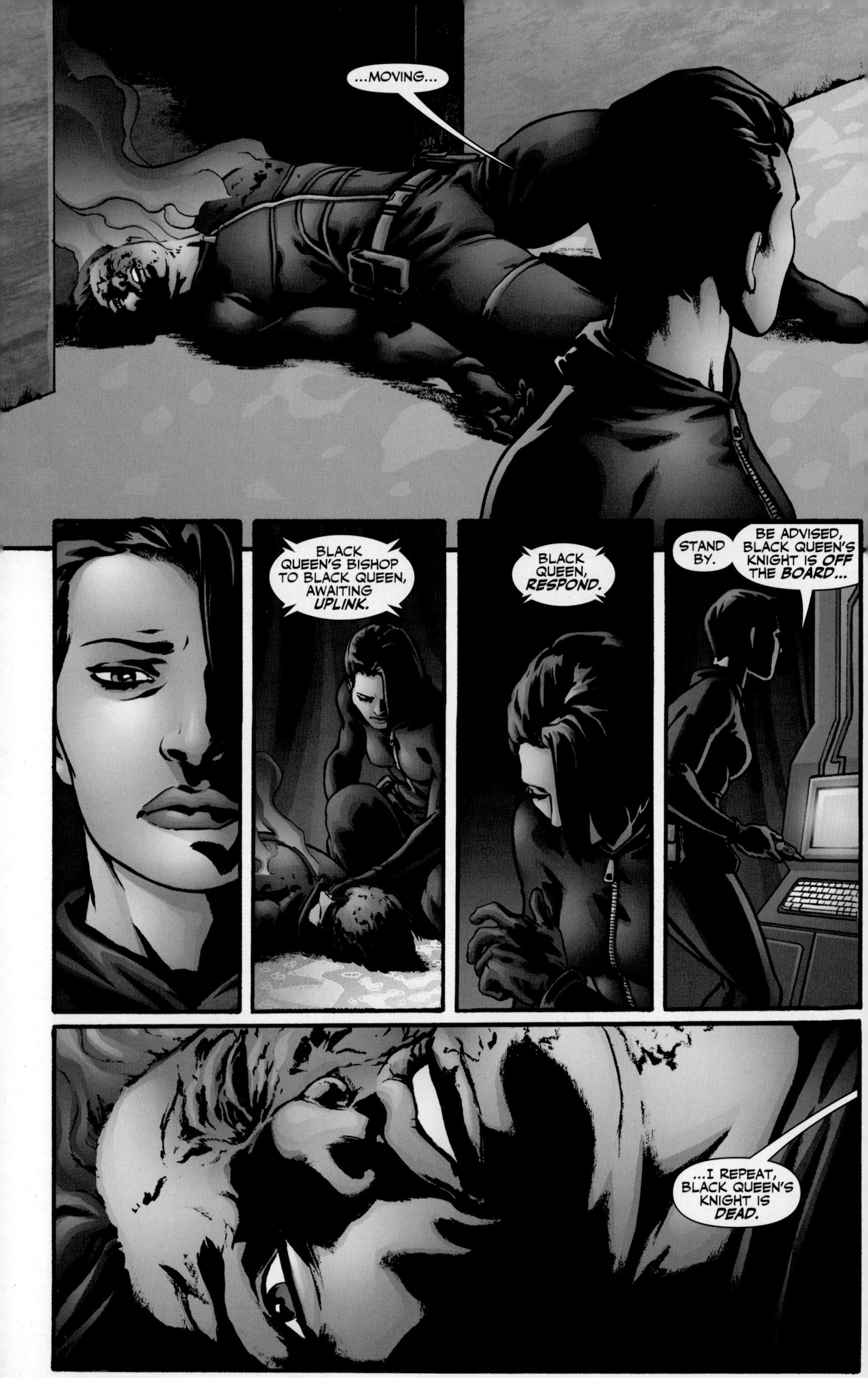
...MOVING...
BLACK QUEEN'S BISHOP TO BLACK QUEEN, AWAITING UPLINK.
BLACK QUEEN, RESPOND.
STAND BY.
BE ADVISED, BLACK QUEEN'S KNIGHT IS OFF THE BOARD...
...I REPEAT, BLACK QUEEN'S KNIGHT IS DEAD.

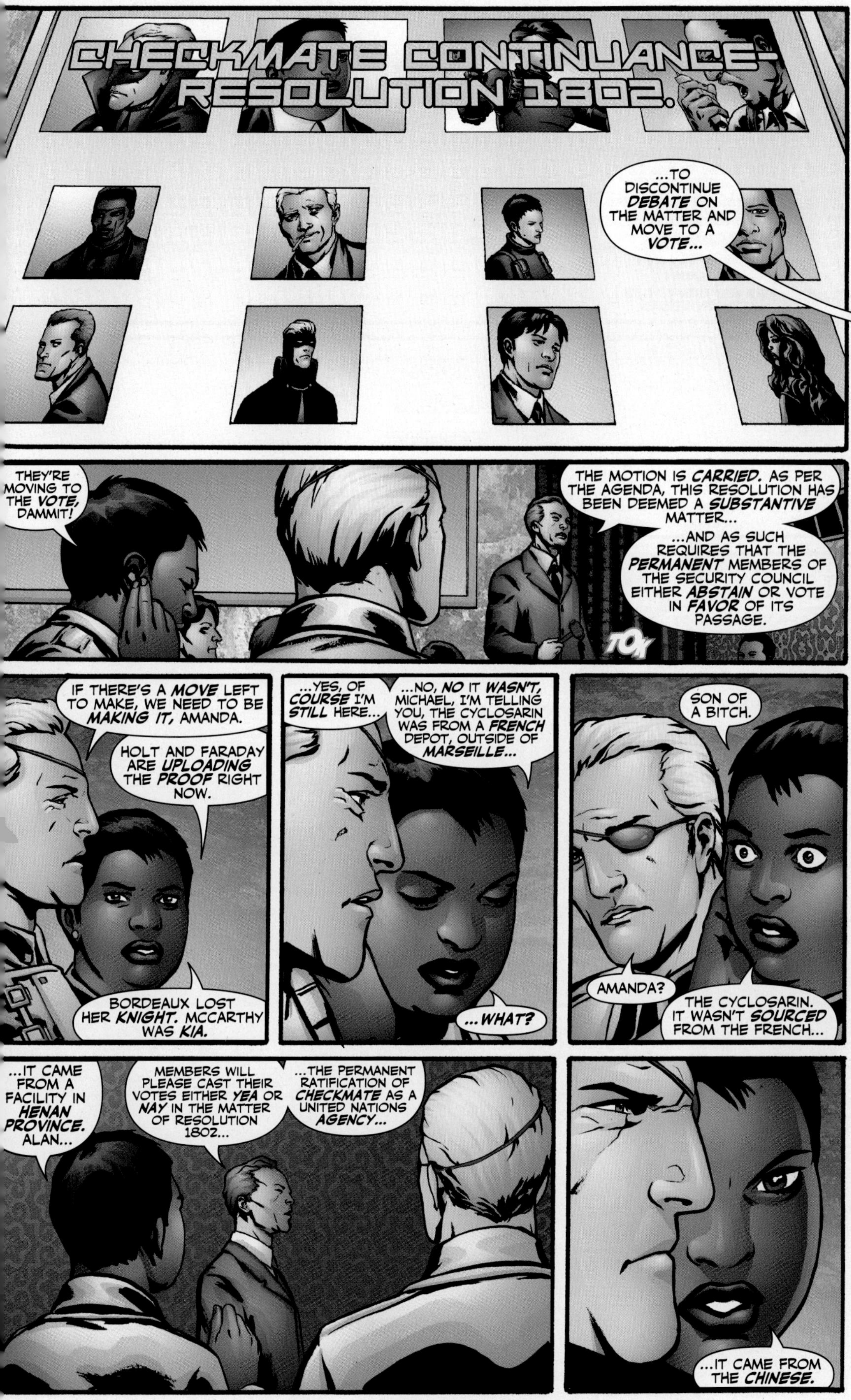
CHECKMATE CONTINUANCE-RESOLUTION 1802.
...TO DISCONTINUE DEBATE ON THE MATTER AND MOVE TO A VOTE...
THEY'RE MOVING TO THE VOTE, DAMMIT!
THE MOTION IS CARRIED. AS PER THE AGENDA, THIS RESOLUTION HAS BEEN DEEMED A SUBSTANTIVE MATTER...
...AND AS SUCH REQUIRES THAT THE PERMANENT MEMBERS OF THE SECURITY COUNCIL EITHER ABSTAIN OR VOTE IN FAVOR OF ITS PASSAGE.
TOK
IF THERE'S A MOVE LEFT TO MAKE, WE NEED TO BE MAKING IT, AMANDA.
HOLT AND FARADAY ARE UPLOADING THE PROOF RIGHT NOW.
BORDEAUX LOST HER KNIGHT. MCCARTHY WAS KIA.
...YES, OF COURSE I'M STILL HERE...
...NO, NO IT WASN'T, MICHAEL, I'M TELLING YOU, THE CYCLOSARIN WAS FROM A FRENCH DEPOT, OUTSIDE OF MARSEILLE...
...WHAT?
SON OF A BITCH.
AMANDA?
THE CYCLOSARIN. IT WASN'T SOURCED FROM THE FRENCH...
...IT CAME FROM A FACILITY IN HENAN PROVINCE. ALAN...
MEMBERS WILL PLEASE CAST THEIR VOTES EITHER YEA OR NAY IN THE MATTER OF RESOLUTION 1802...
...THE PERMANENT RATIFICATION OF CHECKMATE AS A UNITED NATIONS AGENCY...
...IT CAME FROM THE CHINESE.

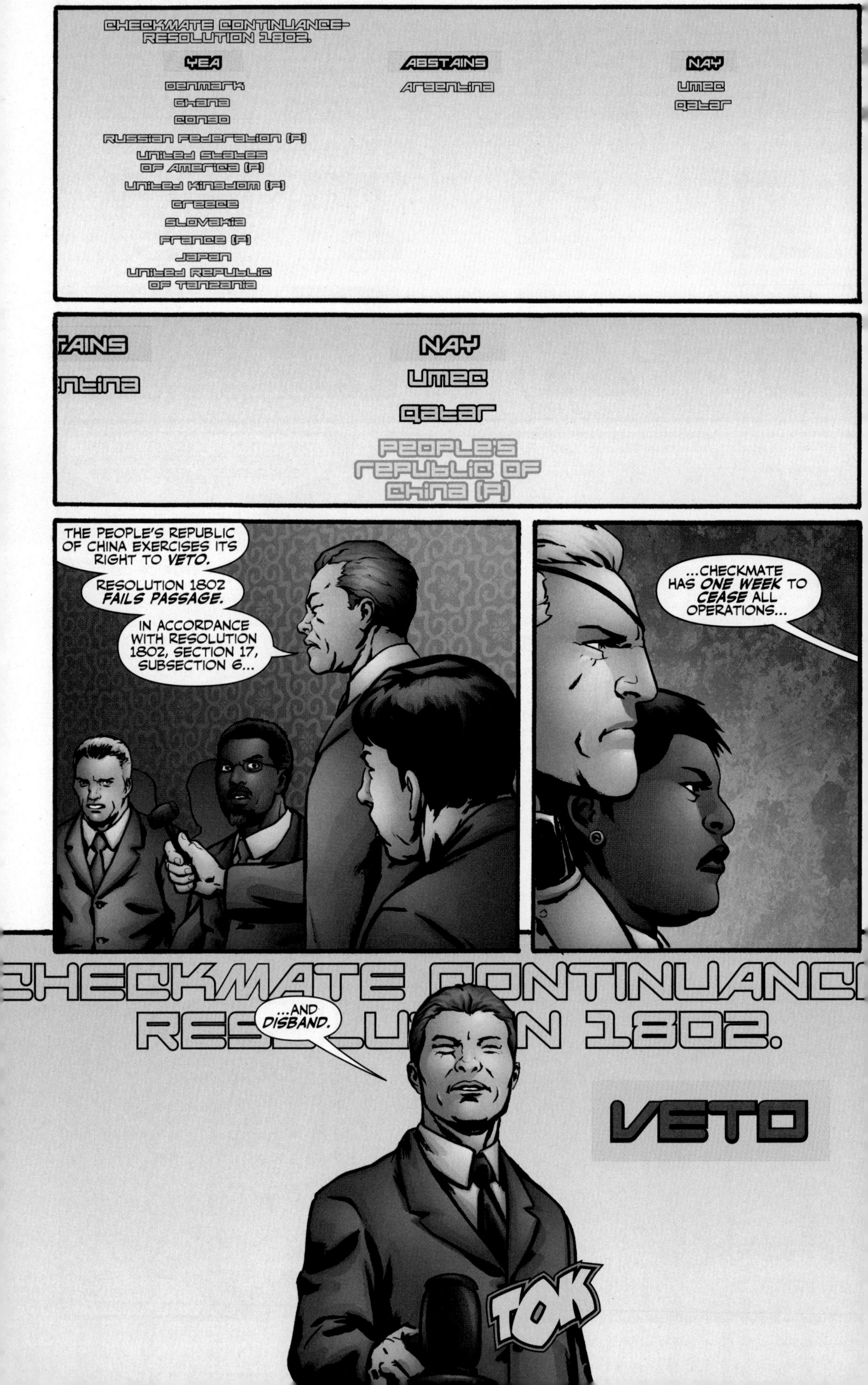
CHECKMATE CONTINUANCE-
RESOLUTION 1802.
YEA
DENMARK
GHANA
CONGO
RUSSIAN FEDERATION (P)
UNITED STATES
OF AMERICA (P)
UNITED KINGDOM (P)
GREECE
SLOVAKIA
FRANCE (P)
JAPAN
UNITED REPUBLIC
OF TANZANIA
ABSTAINS
ARGENTINA
NAY
UMEC
QATAR
NAY
UMEC
QATAR
PEOPLE'S
REPUBLIC OF
CHINA (P)
THE PEOPLE'S REPUBLIC OF CHINA EXERCISES ITS RIGHT TO VETO.
RESOLUTION 1802 FAILS PASSAGE.
IN ACCORDANCE WITH RESOLUTION 1802, SECTION 17, SUBSECTION 6...
...CHECKMATE HAS ONE WEEK TO CEASE ALL OPERATIONS...
...AND DISBAND.
VETO
TOK

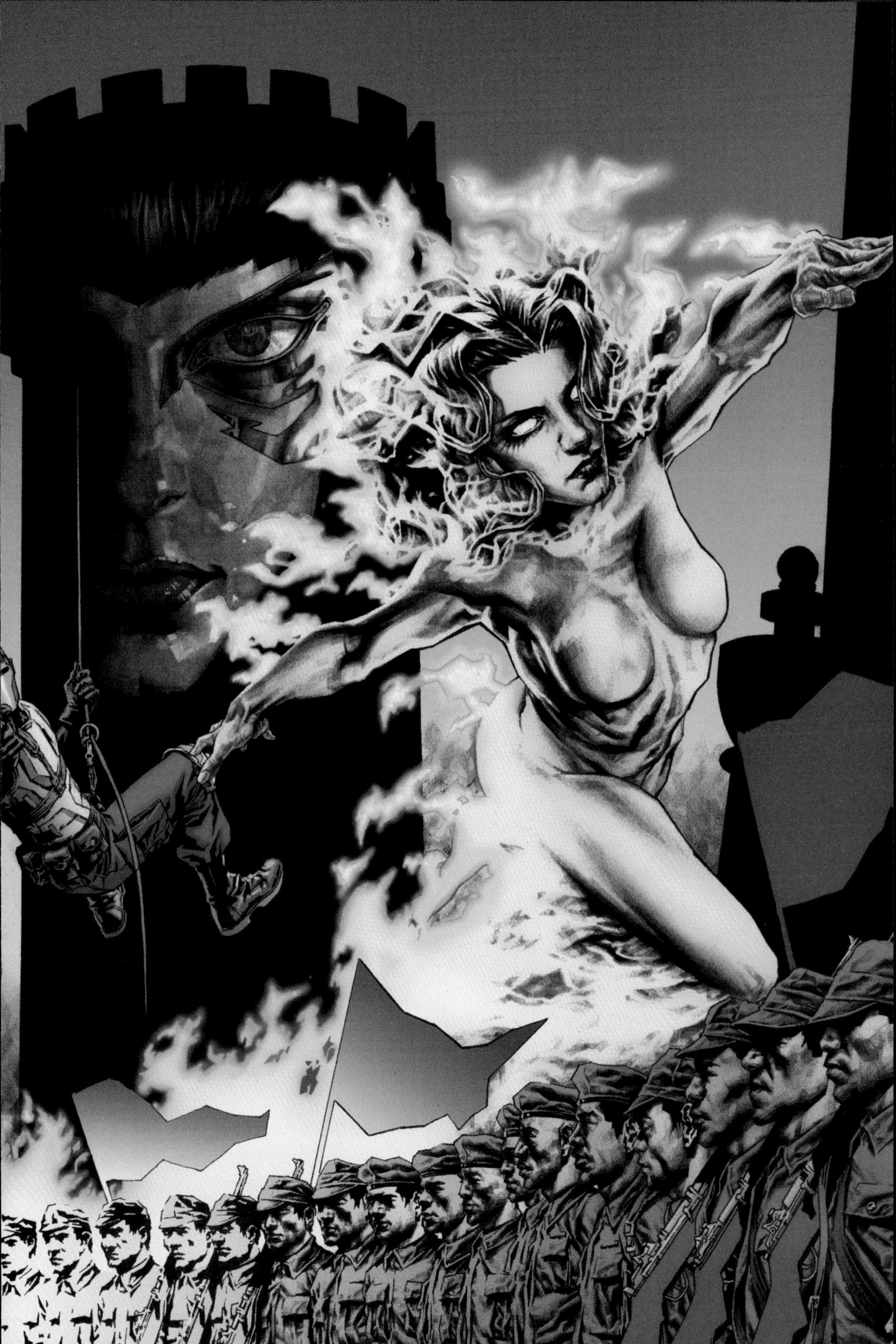

CHAPTER TWO Cover Art: Lee Bermejo and Patricia Mulvihill

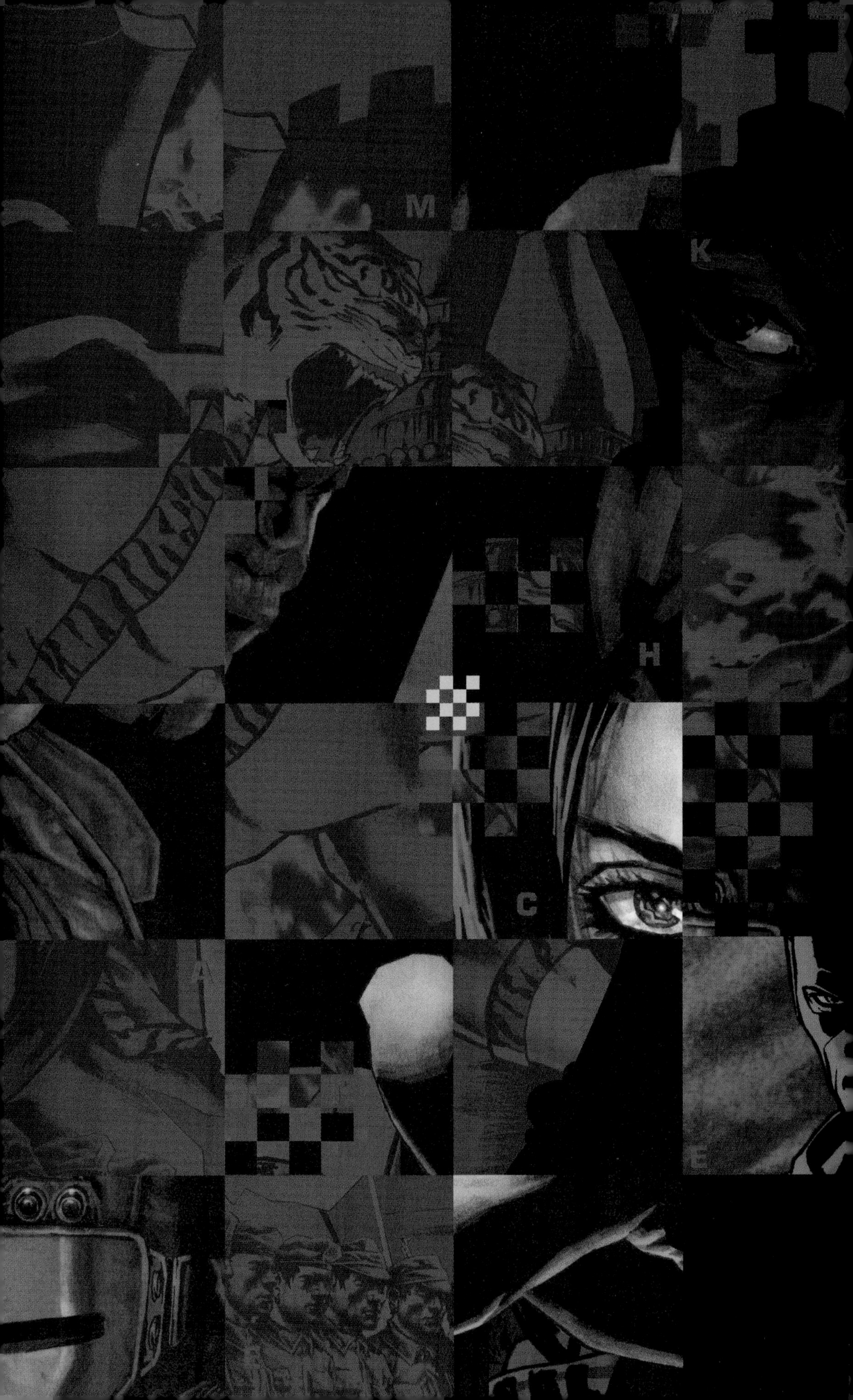
M
K
H
C
A
E

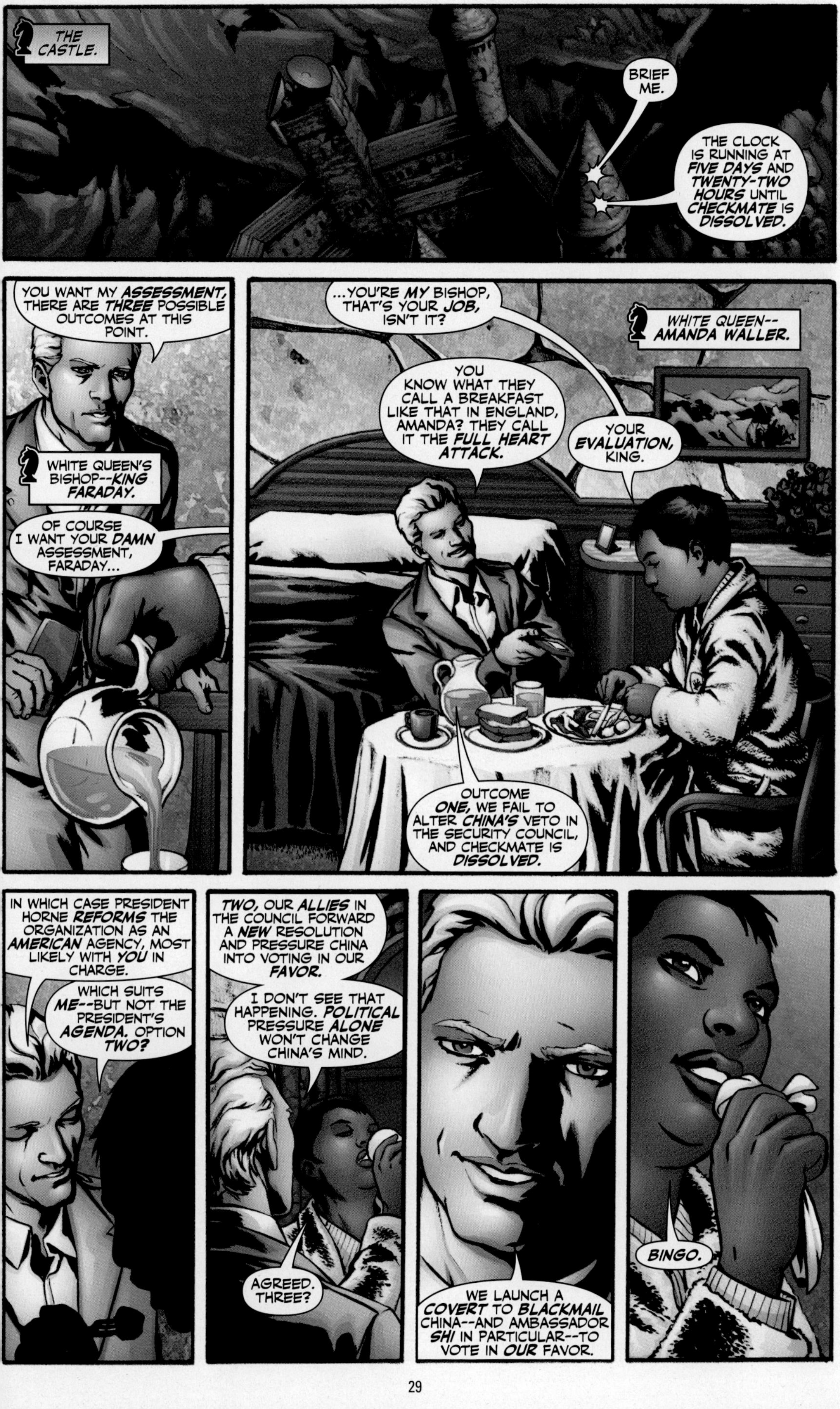
THE CASTLE.
BRIEF ME.
THE CLOCK IS RUNNING AT FIVE DAYS AND TWENTY-TWO HOURS UNTIL CHECKMATE IS DISSOLVED.
YOU WANT MY ASSESSMENT, THERE ARE THREE POSSIBLE OUTCOMES AT THIS POINT.
WHITE QUEEN'S BISHOP--KING FARADAY.
OF COURSE I WANT YOUR DAMN ASSESSMENT, FARADAY...
...YOU'RE MY BISHOP, THAT'S YOUR JOB, ISN'T IT?
WHITE QUEEN--AMANDA WALLER.
YOU KNOW WHAT THEY CALL A BREAKFAST LIKE THAT IN ENGLAND, AMANDA? THEY CALL IT THE FULL HEART ATTACK.
YOUR EVALUATION, KING.
OUTCOME ONE, WE FAIL TO ALTER CHINA'S VETO IN THE SECURITY COUNCIL, AND CHECKMATE IS DISSOLVED.
IN WHICH CASE PRESIDENT HORNE REFORMS THE ORGANIZATION AS AN AMERICAN AGENCY, MOST LIKELY WITH YOU IN CHARGE.
WHICH SUITS ME--BUT NOT THE PRESIDENT'S AGENDA. OPTION TWO?
TWO, OUR ALLIES IN THE COUNCIL FORWARD A NEW RESOLUTION AND PRESSURE CHINA INTO VOTING IN OUR FAVOR.
I DON'T SEE THAT HAPPENING. POLITICAL PRESSURE ALONE WON'T CHANGE CHINA'S MIND.
AGREED. THREE?
WE LAUNCH A COVERT TO BLACKMAIL CHINA--AND AMBASSADOR SHI IN PARTICULAR--TO VOTE IN OUR FAVOR.
BINGO.

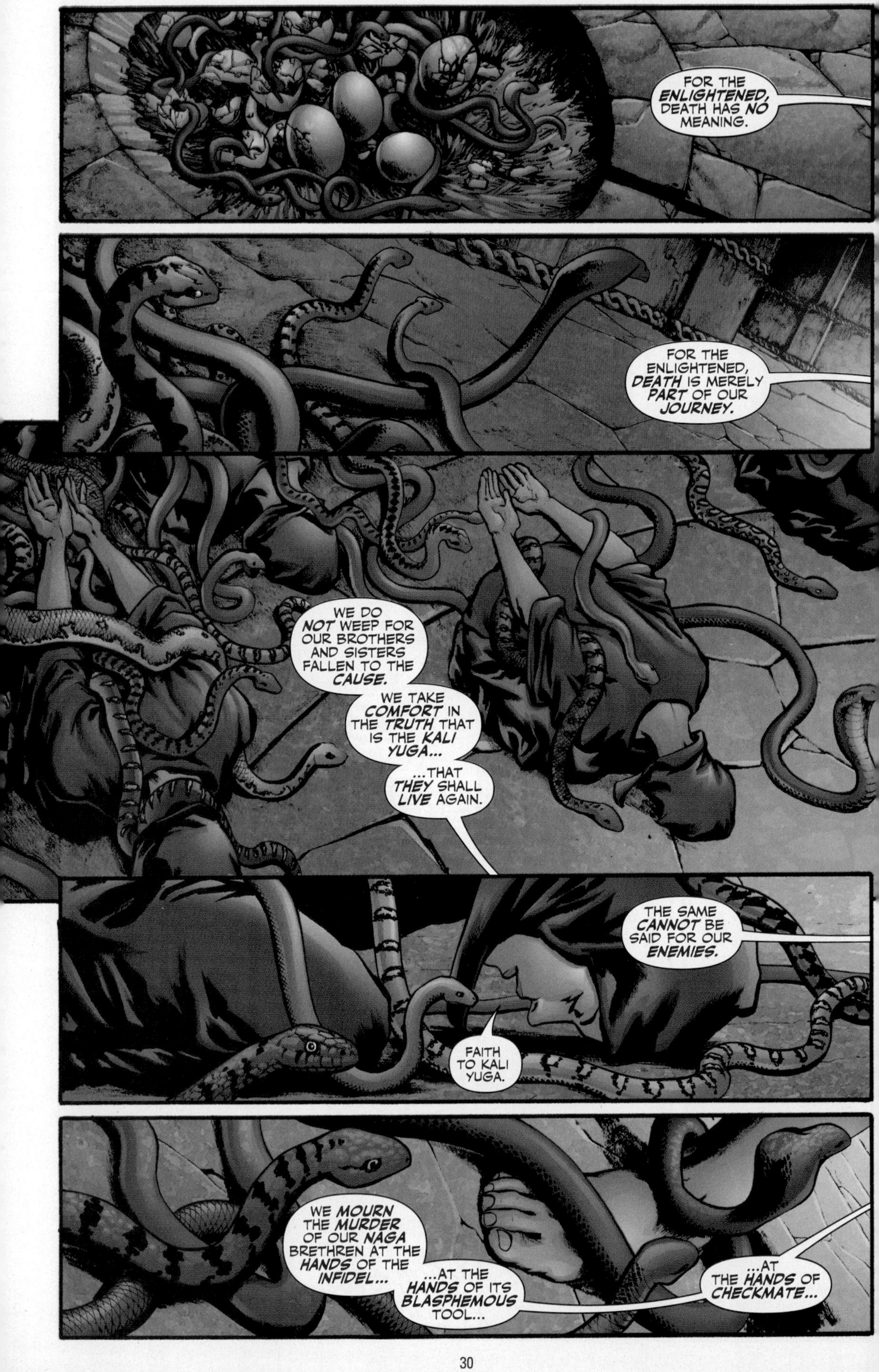
FOR THE ENLIGHTENED, DEATH HAS NO MEANING.
FOR THE ENLIGHTENED, DEATH IS MERELY PART OF OUR JOURNEY.
WE DO NOT WEEP FOR OUR BROTHERS AND SISTERS FALLEN TO THE CAUSE.
WE TAKE COMFORT IN THE TRUTH THAT IS THE KALI YUGA...
...THAT THEY SHALL LIVE AGAIN.
THE SAME CANNOT BE SAID FOR OUR ENEMIES.
FAITH TO KALI YUGA.
WE MOURN THE MURDER OF OUR NAGA BRETHREN AT THE HANDS OF THE INFIDEL...
...AT THE HANDS OF ITS BLASPHEMOUS TOOL...
...AT THE HANDS OF CHECKMATE...

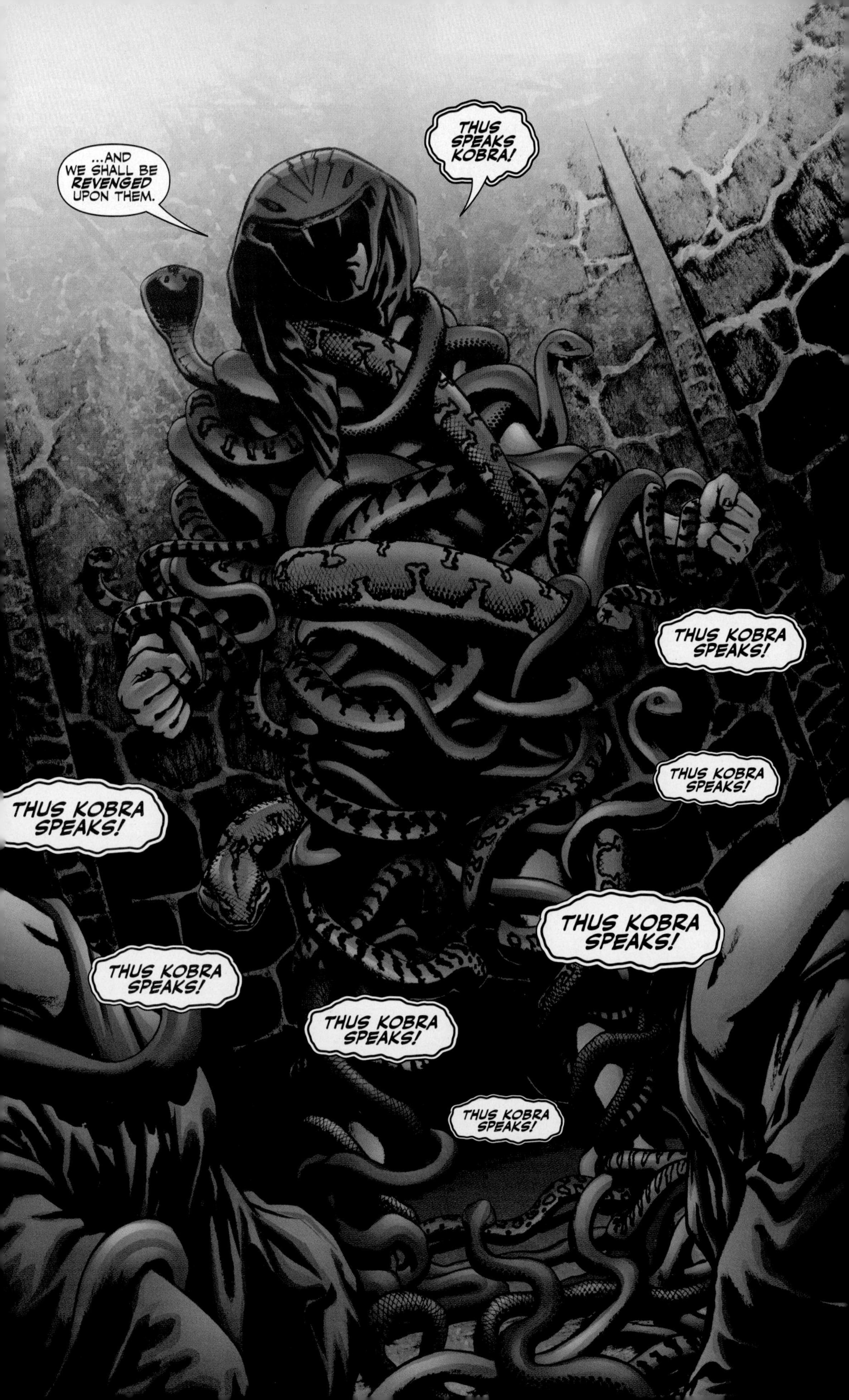
...AND WE SHALL BE *REVENGED* UPON THEM.
THUS SPEAKS KOBRA!
THUS KOBRA SPEAKS!
THUS KOBRA SPEAKS!
THUS KOBRA SPEAKS!
THUS KOBRA SPEAKS!
THUS KOBRA SPEAKS!
THUS KOBRA SPEAKS!
THUS KOBRA SPEAKS!

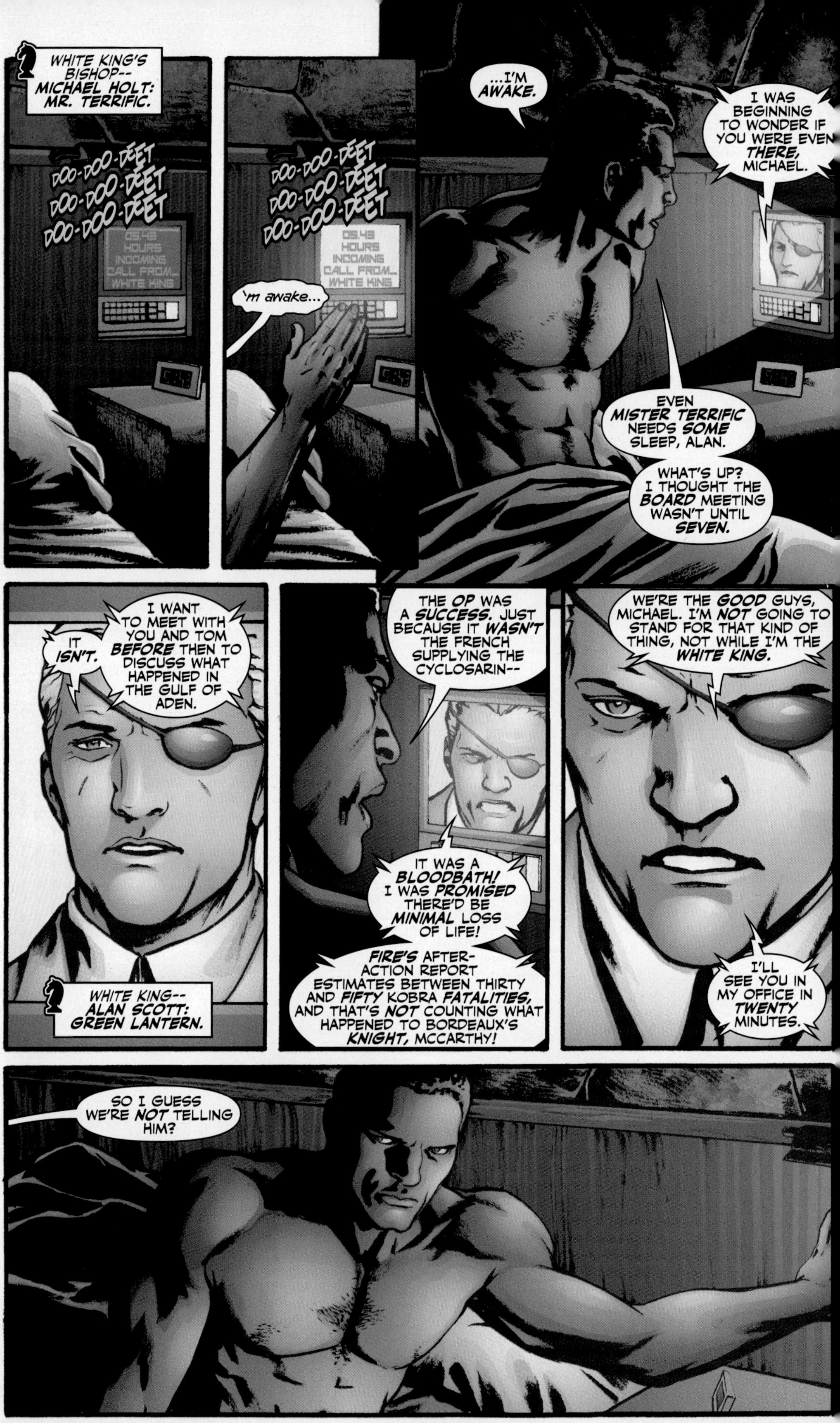

WHITE KING'S BISHOP-- MICHAEL HOLT: MR. TERRIFIC.
DOO-DOO-DEET DOO-DOO-DEET DOO-DOO-DEET
05.43 HOURS INCOMING CALL FROM... WHITE KING
DOO-DOO-DEET DOO-DOO-DEET DOO-DOO-DEET
05.43 HOURS INCOMING CALL FROM... WHITE KING
'm awake...
...I'M AWAKE.
I WAS BEGINNING TO WONDER IF YOU WERE EVEN THERE, MICHAEL.
EVEN MISTER TERRIFIC NEEDS SOME SLEEP, ALAN.
WHAT'S UP? I THOUGHT THE BOARD MEETING WASN'T UNTIL SEVEN.
IT ISN'T.
I WANT TO MEET WITH YOU AND TOM BEFORE THEN TO DISCUSS WHAT HAPPENED IN THE GULF OF ADEN.
WHITE KING-- ALAN SCOTT: GREEN LANTERN.
THE OP WAS A SUCCESS. JUST BECAUSE IT WASN'T THE FRENCH SUPPLYING THE CYCLOSARIN--
IT WAS A BLOODBATH! I WAS PROMISED THERE'D BE MINIMAL LOSS OF LIFE!
FIRE'S AFTER-ACTION REPORT ESTIMATES BETWEEN THIRTY AND FIFTY KOBRA FATALITIES, AND THAT'S NOT COUNTING WHAT HAPPENED TO BORDEAUX'S KNIGHT, MCCARTHY!
WE'RE THE GOOD GUYS, MICHAEL. I'M NOT GOING TO STAND FOR THAT KIND OF THING, NOT WHILE I'M THE WHITE KING.
I'LL SEE YOU IN MY OFFICE IN TWENTY MINUTES.
SO I GUESS WE'RE NOT TELLING HIM?

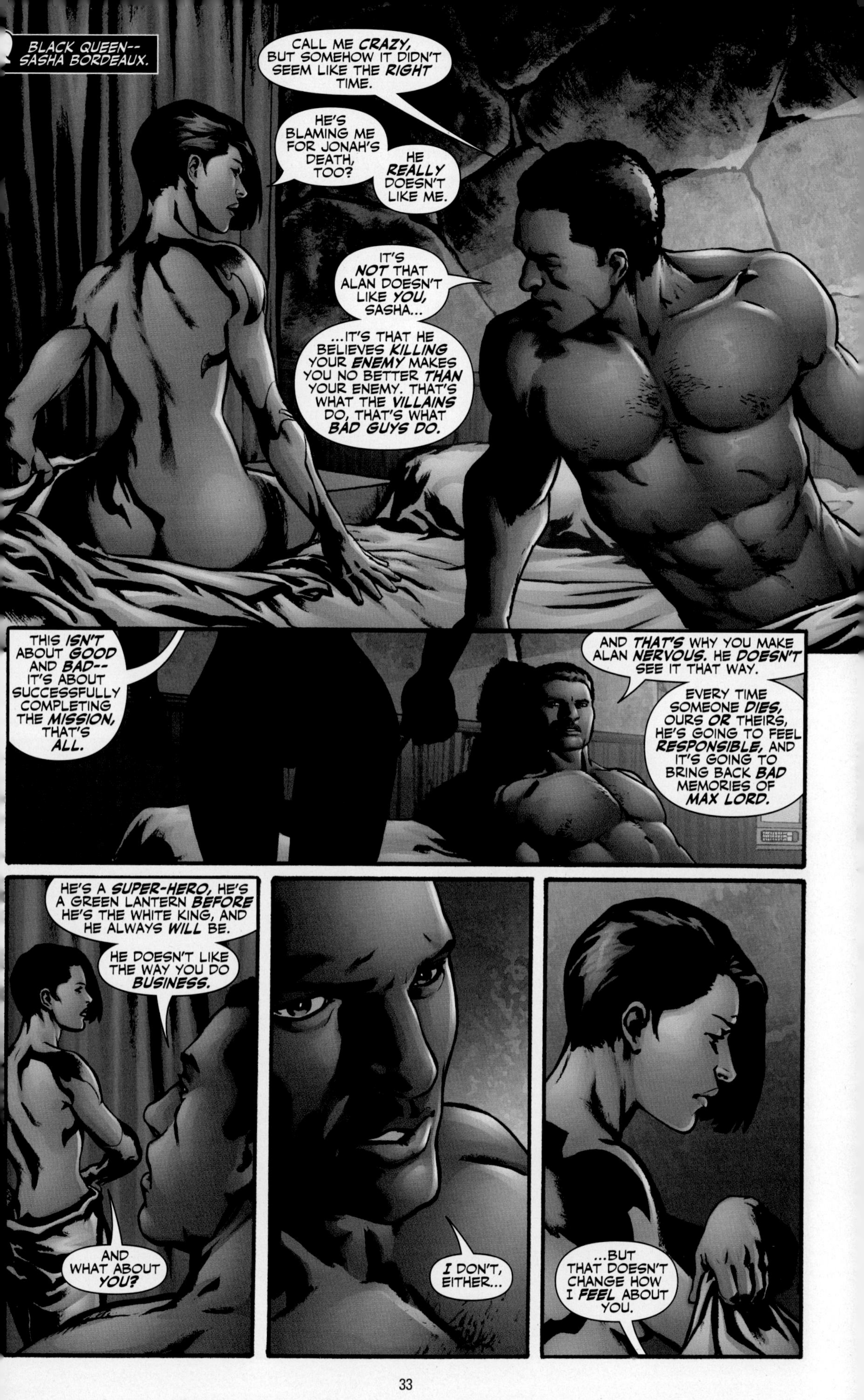
BLACK QUEEN-- SASHA BORDEAUX.
CALL ME CRAZY, BUT SOMEHOW IT DIDN'T SEEM LIKE THE RIGHT TIME.
HE'S BLAMING ME FOR JONAH'S DEATH, TOO?
HE REALLY DOESN'T LIKE ME.
IT'S NOT THAT ALAN DOESN'T LIKE YOU, SASHA...
...IT'S THAT HE BELIEVES KILLING YOUR ENEMY MAKES YOU NO BETTER THAN YOUR ENEMY. THAT'S WHAT THE VILLAINS DO, THAT'S WHAT BAD GUYS DO.
THIS ISN'T ABOUT GOOD AND BAD-- IT'S ABOUT SUCCESSFULLY COMPLETING THE MISSION, THAT'S ALL.
AND THAT'S WHY YOU MAKE ALAN NERVOUS. HE DOESN'T SEE IT THAT WAY.
EVERY TIME SOMEONE DIES, OURS OR THEIRS, HE'S GOING TO FEEL RESPONSIBLE, AND IT'S GOING TO BRING BACK BAD MEMORIES OF MAX LORD.
HE'S A SUPER-HERO, HE'S A GREEN LANTERN BEFORE HE'S THE WHITE KING, AND HE ALWAYS WILL BE.
HE DOESN'T LIKE THE WAY YOU DO BUSINESS.
AND WHAT ABOUT YOU?
I DON'T, EITHER...
...BUT THAT DOESN'T CHANGE HOW I FEEL ABOUT YOU.

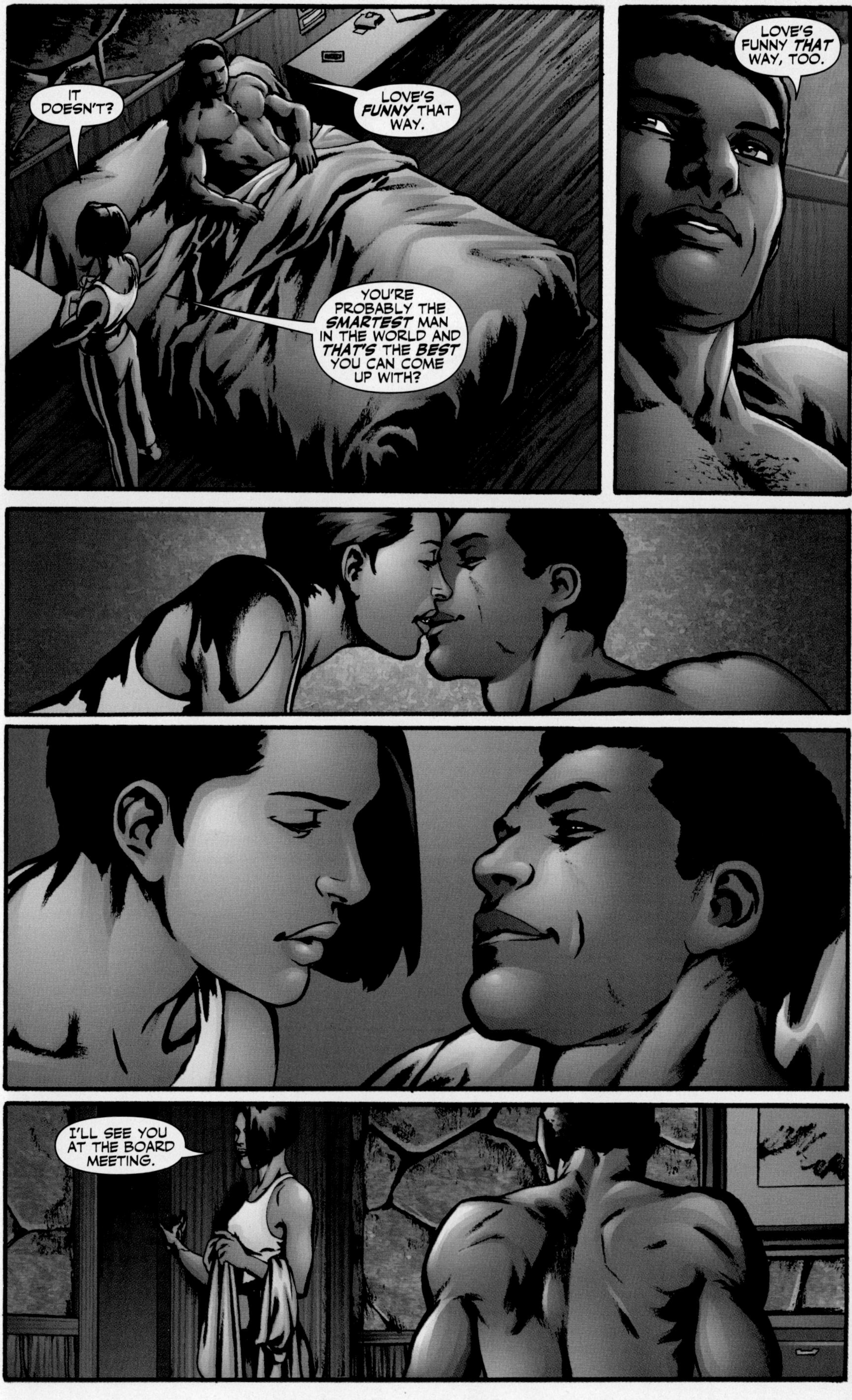
IT DOESN'T?
LOVE'S FUNNY THAT WAY.
YOU'RE PROBABLY THE SMARTEST MAN IN THE WORLD AND THAT'S THE BEST YOU CAN COME UP WITH?
LOVE'S FUNNY THAT WAY, TOO.
I'LL SEE YOU AT THE BOARD MEETING.

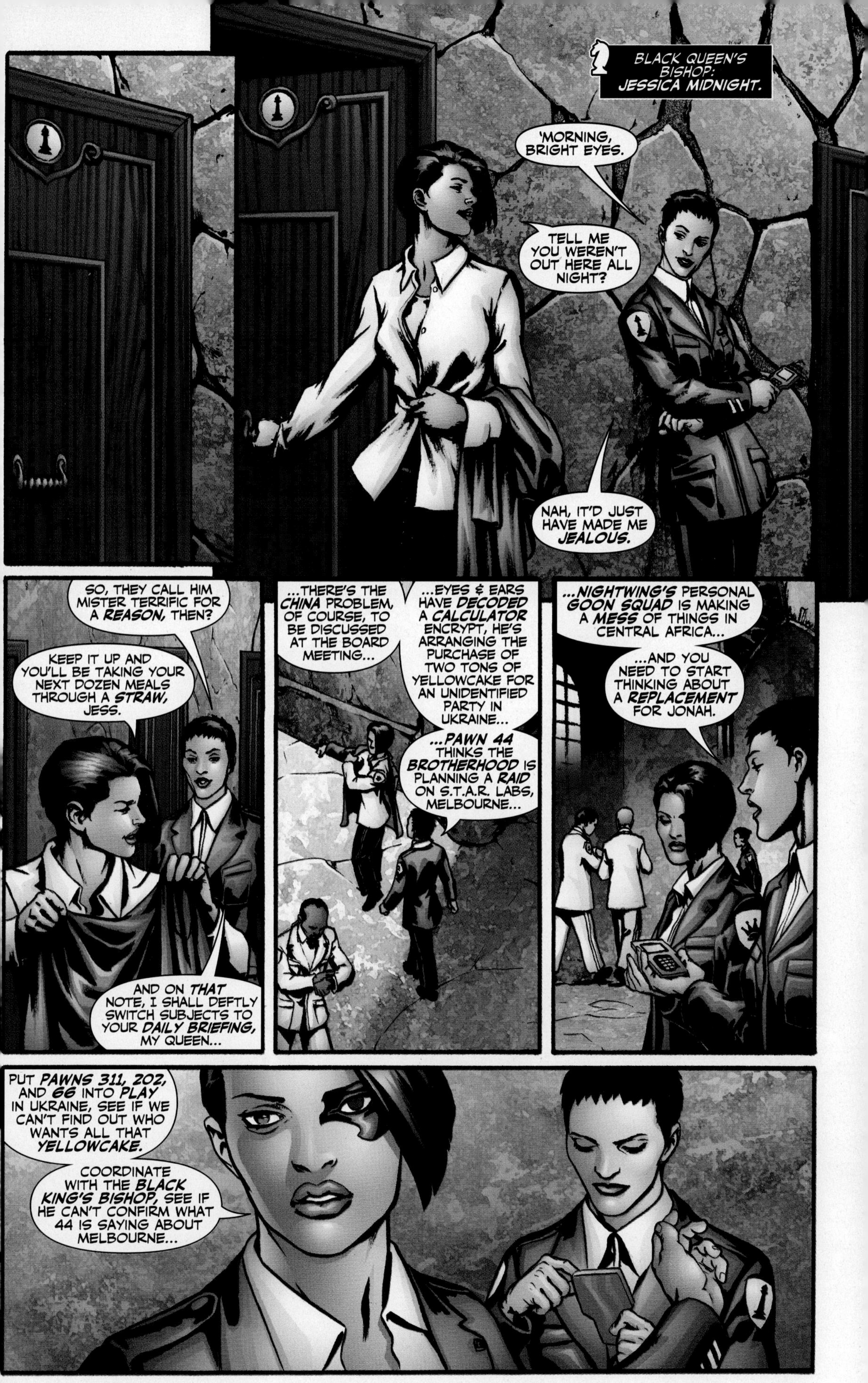
BLACK QUEEN'S BISHOP: JESSICA MIDNIGHT.
'MORNING, BRIGHT EYES.
TELL ME YOU WEREN'T OUT HERE ALL NIGHT?
NAH, IT'D JUST HAVE MADE ME JEALOUS.
SO, THEY CALL HIM MISTER TERRIFIC FOR A REASON, THEN?
KEEP IT UP AND YOU'LL BE TAKING YOUR NEXT DOZEN MEALS THROUGH A STRAW, JESS.
AND ON THAT NOTE, I SHALL DEFTLY SWITCH SUBJECTS TO YOUR DAILY BRIEFING, MY QUEEN...
...THERE'S THE CHINA PROBLEM, OF COURSE, TO BE DISCUSSED AT THE BOARD MEETING...
...EYES & EARS HAVE DECODED A CALCULATOR ENCRYPT, HE'S ARRANGING THE PURCHASE OF TWO TONS OF YELLOWCAKE FOR AN UNIDENTIFIED PARTY IN UKRAINE...
...PAWN 44 THINKS THE BROTHERHOOD IS PLANNING A RAID ON S.T.A.R. LABS, MELBOURNE...
...NIGHTWING'S PERSONAL GOON SQUAD IS MAKING A MESS OF THINGS IN CENTRAL AFRICA...
...AND YOU NEED TO START THINKING ABOUT A REPLACEMENT FOR JONAH.
PUT PAWNS 311, 202, AND 66 INTO PLAY IN UKRAINE, SEE IF WE CAN'T FIND OUT WHO WANTS ALL THAT YELLOWCAKE.
COORDINATE WITH THE BLACK KING'S BISHOP, SEE IF HE CAN'T CONFIRM WHAT 44 IS SAYING ABOUT MELBOURNE...

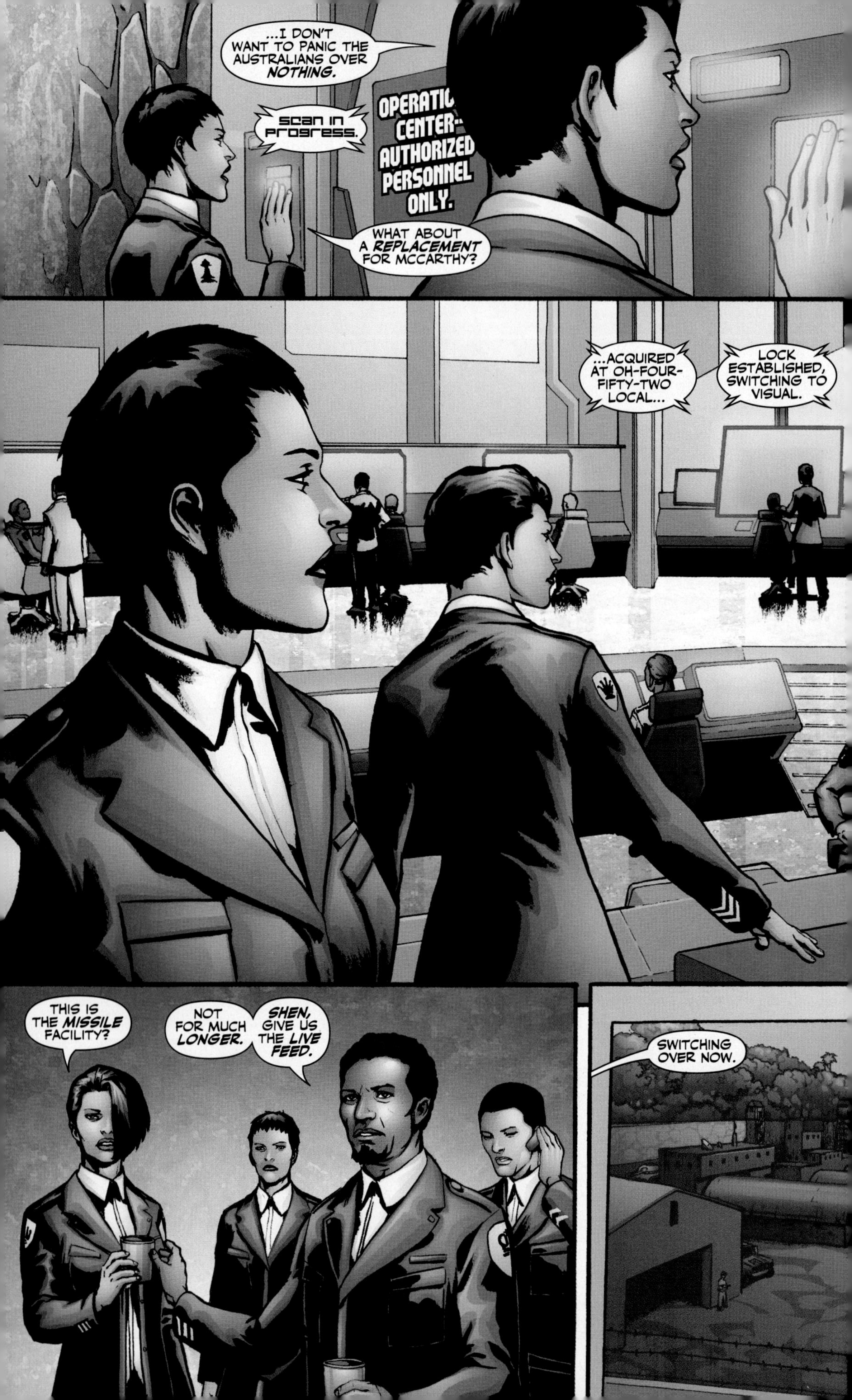

...I DON'T WANT TO PANIC THE AUSTRALIANS OVER NOTHING.
SCAN IN PROGRESS.
OPERATIO CENTER-AUTHORIZED PERSONNEL ONLY.
WHAT ABOUT A REPLACEMENT FOR MCCARTHY?
...ACQUIRED AT OH-FOUR-FIFTY-TWO LOCAL...
LOCK ESTABLISHED, SWITCHING TO VISUAL.
THIS IS THE MISSILE FACILITY?
NOT FOR MUCH LONGER.
SHEN, GIVE US THE LIVE FEED.
SWITCHING OVER NOW.

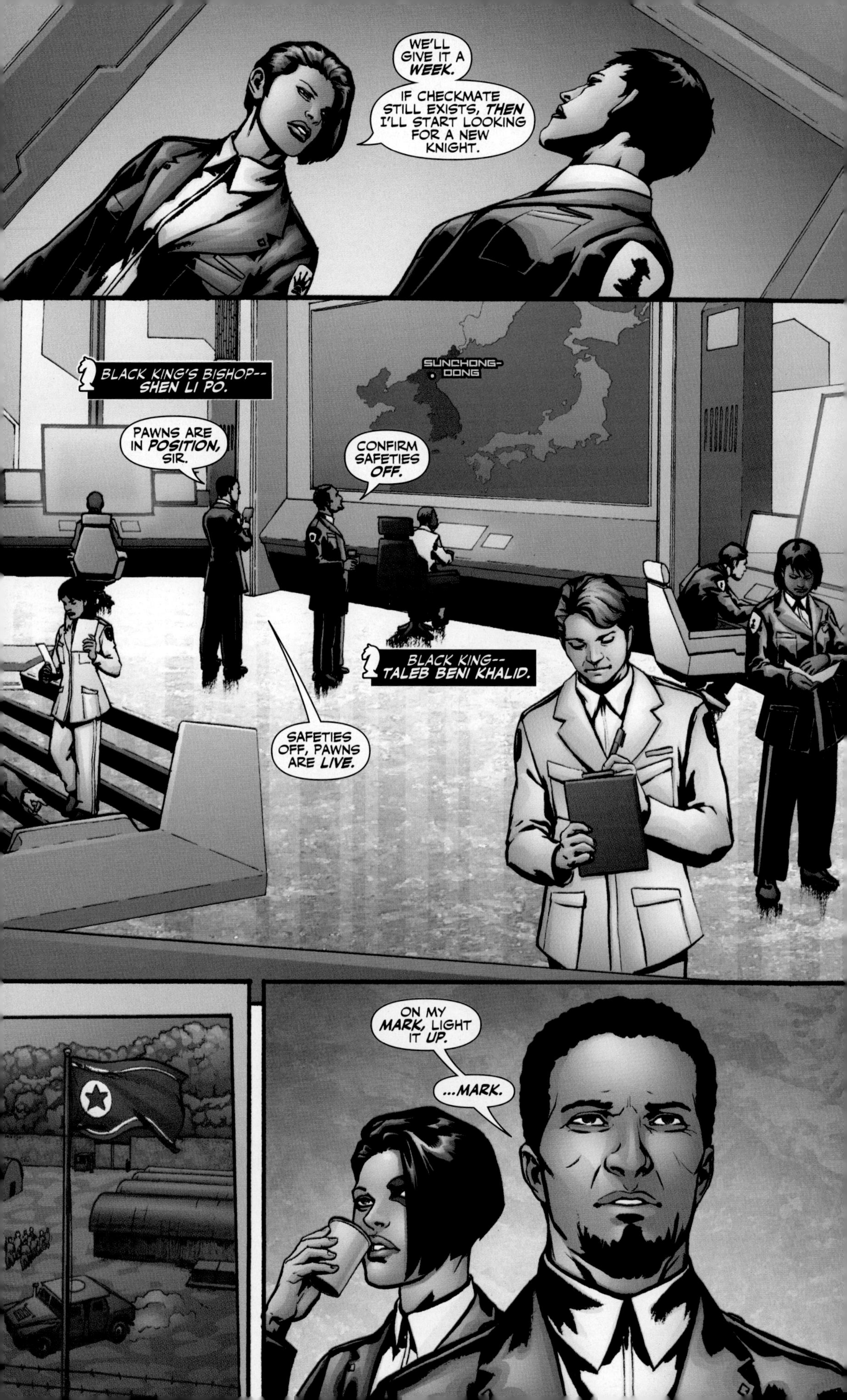

WE'LL GIVE IT A WEEK.
IF CHECKMATE STILL EXISTS, THEN I'LL START LOOKING FOR A NEW KNIGHT.
SUNCHONG-DONG
BLACK KING'S BISHOP-- SHEN LI PO.
PAWNS ARE IN POSITION, SIR.
CONFIRM SAFETIES OFF.
BLACK KING-- TALEB BENI KHALID.
SAFETIES OFF, PAWNS ARE LIVE.
ON MY MARK, LIGHT IT UP.
...MARK.

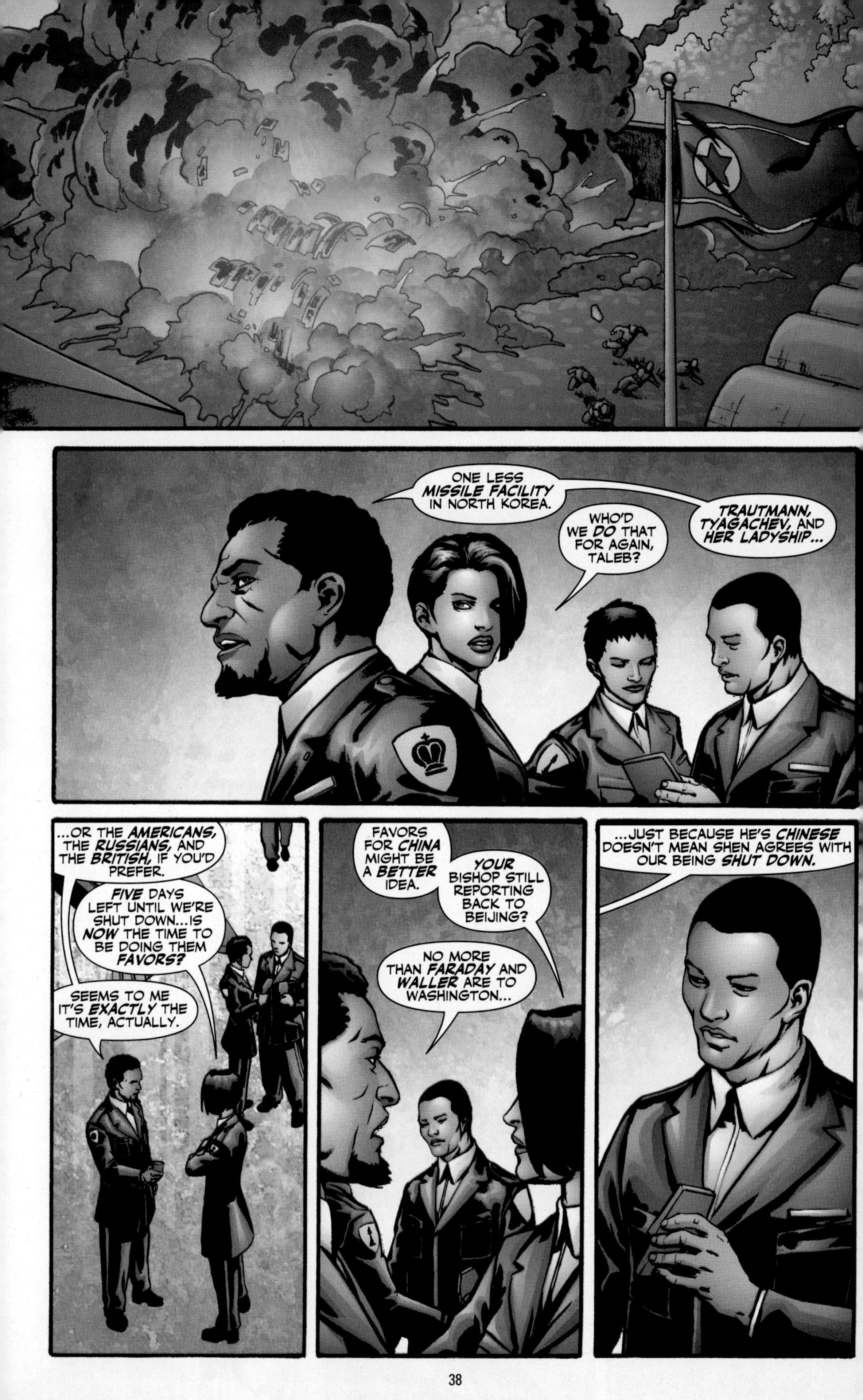
ONE LESS MISSILE FACILITY IN NORTH KOREA.
WHO'D WE DO THAT FOR AGAIN, TALEB?
TRAUTMANN, TYAGACHEV, AND HER LADYSHIP...
...OR THE AMERICANS, THE RUSSIANS, AND THE BRITISH, IF YOU'D PREFER.
FIVE DAYS LEFT UNTIL WE'RE SHUT DOWN...IS NOW THE TIME TO BE DOING THEM FAVORS?
SEEMS TO ME IT'S EXACTLY THE TIME, ACTUALLY.
FAVORS FOR CHINA MIGHT BE A BETTER IDEA.
YOUR BISHOP STILL REPORTING BACK TO BEIJING?
NO MORE THAN FARADAY AND WALLER ARE TO WASHINGTON...
...JUST BECAUSE HE'S CHINESE DOESN'T MEAN SHEN AGREES WITH OUR BEING SHUT DOWN.

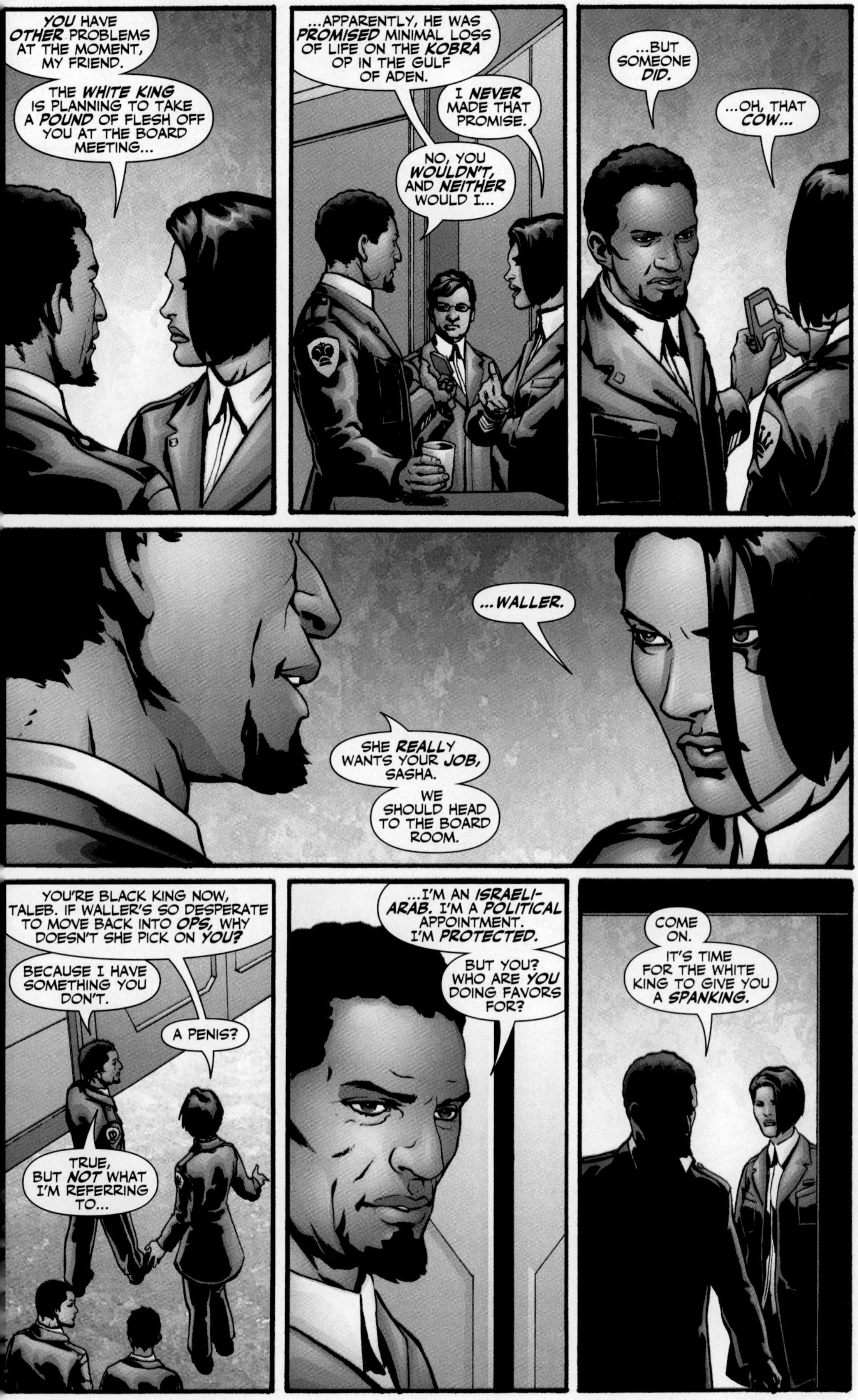
YOU HAVE OTHER PROBLEMS AT THE MOMENT, MY FRIEND.
THE WHITE KING IS PLANNING TO TAKE A POUND OF FLESH OFF YOU AT THE BOARD MEETING...
...APPARENTLY, HE WAS PROMISED MINIMAL LOSS OF LIFE ON THE KOBRA OP IN THE GULF OF ADEN.
I NEVER MADE THAT PROMISE.
NO, YOU WOULDN'T, AND NEITHER WOULD I...
...BUT SOMEONE DID.
...OH, THAT COW...
...WALLER.
SHE REALLY WANTS YOUR JOB, SASHA.
WE SHOULD HEAD TO THE BOARD ROOM.
YOU'RE BLACK KING NOW, TALEB. IF WALLER'S SO DESPERATE TO MOVE BACK INTO OPS, WHY DOESN'T SHE PICK ON YOU?
BECAUSE I HAVE SOMETHING YOU DON'T.
A PENIS?
TRUE, BUT NOT WHAT I'M REFERRING TO...
...I'M AN ISRAELI-ARAB. I'M A POLITICAL APPOINTMENT. I'M PROTECTED.
BUT YOU? WHO ARE YOU DOING FAVORS FOR?
COME ON.
IT'S TIME FOR THE WHITE KING TO GIVE YOU A SPANKING.

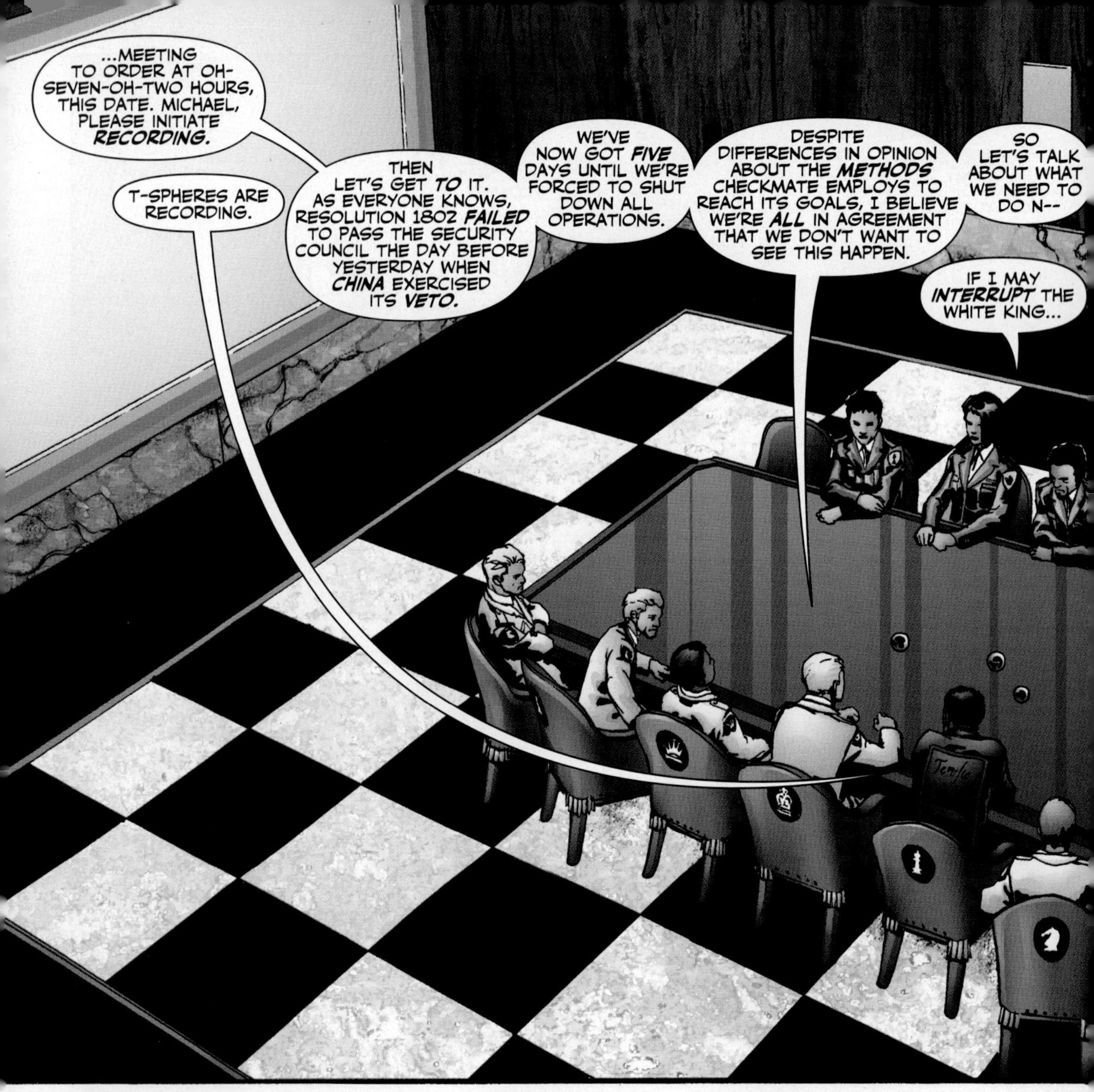
...MEETING TO ORDER AT OH-SEVEN-OH-TWO HOURS, THIS DATE. MICHAEL, PLEASE INITIATE RECORDING.
T-SPHERES ARE RECORDING.
THEN LET'S GET TO IT. AS EVERYONE KNOWS, RESOLUTION 1802 FAILED TO PASS THE SECURITY COUNCIL THE DAY BEFORE YESTERDAY WHEN CHINA EXERCISED ITS VETO.
WE'VE NOW GOT FIVE DAYS UNTIL WE'RE FORCED TO SHUT DOWN ALL OPERATIONS.
DESPITE DIFFERENCES IN OPINION ABOUT THE METHODS CHECKMATE EMPLOYS TO REACH ITS GOALS, I BELIEVE WE'RE ALL IN AGREEMENT THAT WE DON'T WANT TO SEE THIS HAPPEN.
SO LET'S TALK ABOUT WHAT WE NEED TO DO N--
IF I MAY INTERRUPT THE WHITE KING...

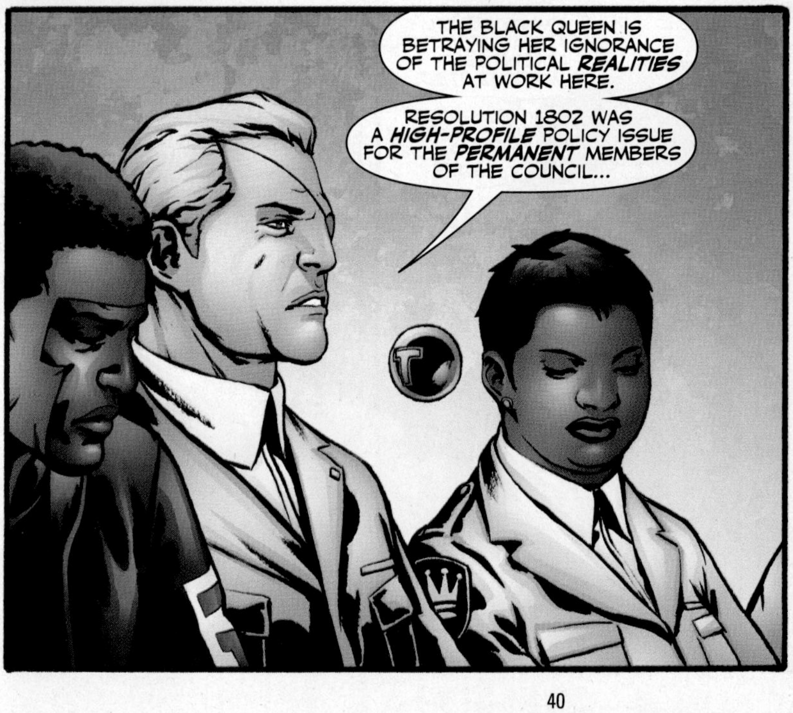
THE BLACK QUEEN IS BETRAYING HER IGNORANCE OF THE POLITICAL REALITIES AT WORK HERE.
RESOLUTION 1802 WAS A HIGH-PROFILE POLICY ISSUE FOR THE PERMANENT MEMBERS OF THE COUNCIL...

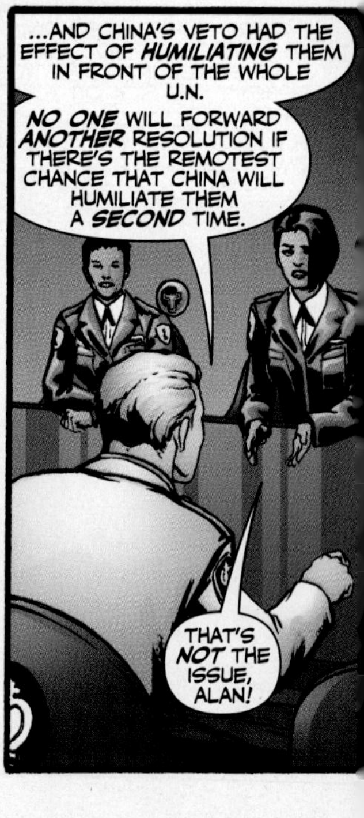
...AND CHINA'S VETO HAD THE EFFECT OF HUMILIATING THEM IN FRONT OF THE WHOLE U.N.
NO ONE WILL FORWARD ANOTHER RESOLUTION IF THERE'S THE REMOTEST CHANCE THAT CHINA WILL HUMILIATE THEM A SECOND TIME.
THAT'S NOT THE ISSUE, ALAN!

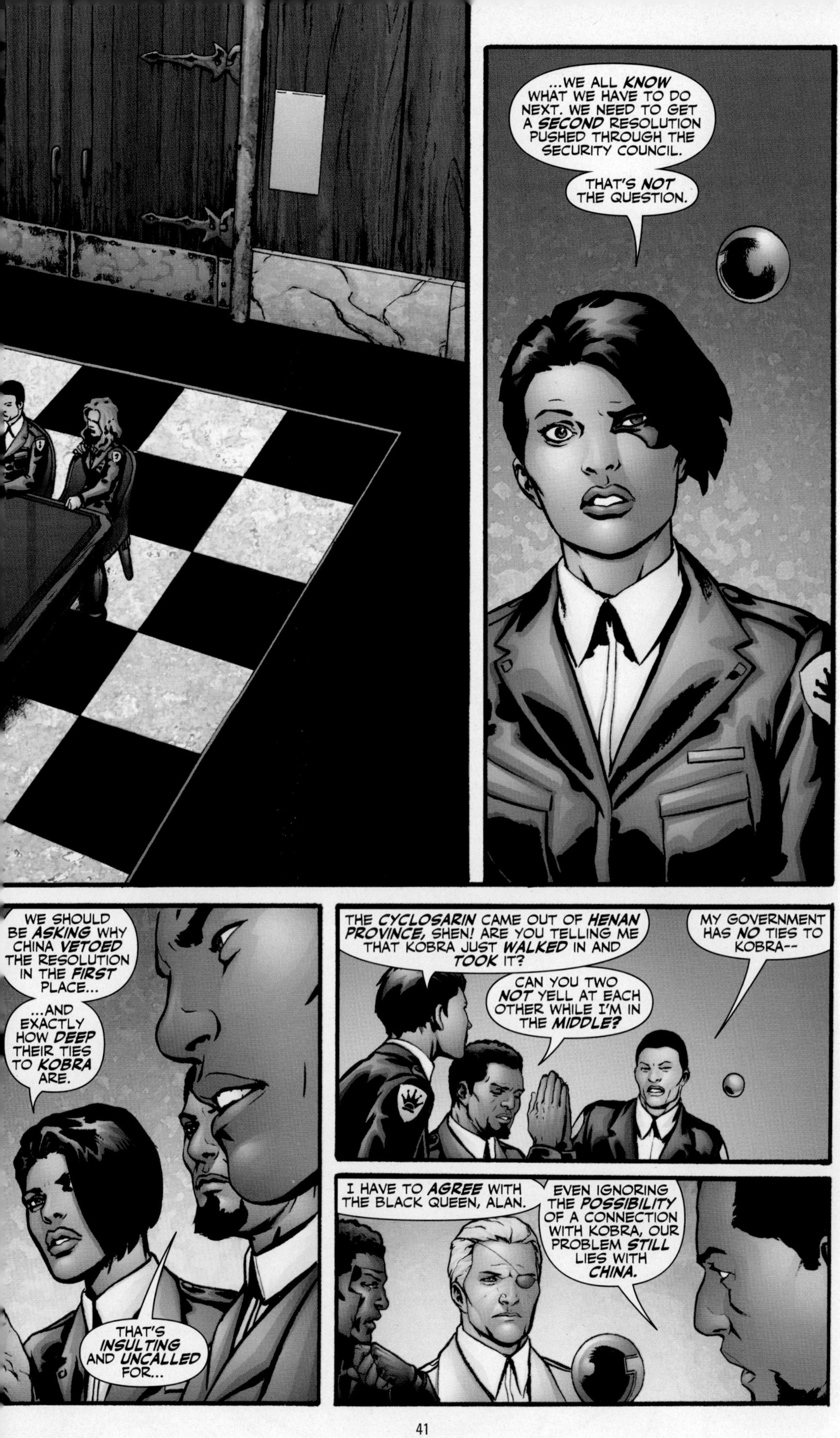
...WE ALL KNOW WHAT WE HAVE TO DO NEXT. WE NEED TO GET A SECOND RESOLUTION PUSHED THROUGH THE SECURITY COUNCIL.
THAT'S NOT THE QUESTION.
WE SHOULD BE ASKING WHY CHINA VETOED THE RESOLUTION IN THE FIRST PLACE...
...AND EXACTLY HOW DEEP THEIR TIES TO KOBRA ARE.
THAT'S INSULTING AND UNCALLED FOR...
THE CYCLOSARIN CAME OUT OF HENAN PROVINCE, SHEN! ARE YOU TELLING ME THAT KOBRA JUST WALKED IN AND TOOK IT?
CAN YOU TWO NOT YELL AT EACH OTHER WHILE I'M IN THE MIDDLE?
MY GOVERNMENT HAS NO TIES TO KOBRA--
I HAVE TO AGREE WITH THE BLACK QUEEN, ALAN.
EVEN IGNORING THE POSSIBILITY OF A CONNECTION WITH KOBRA, OUR PROBLEM STILL LIES WITH CHINA.

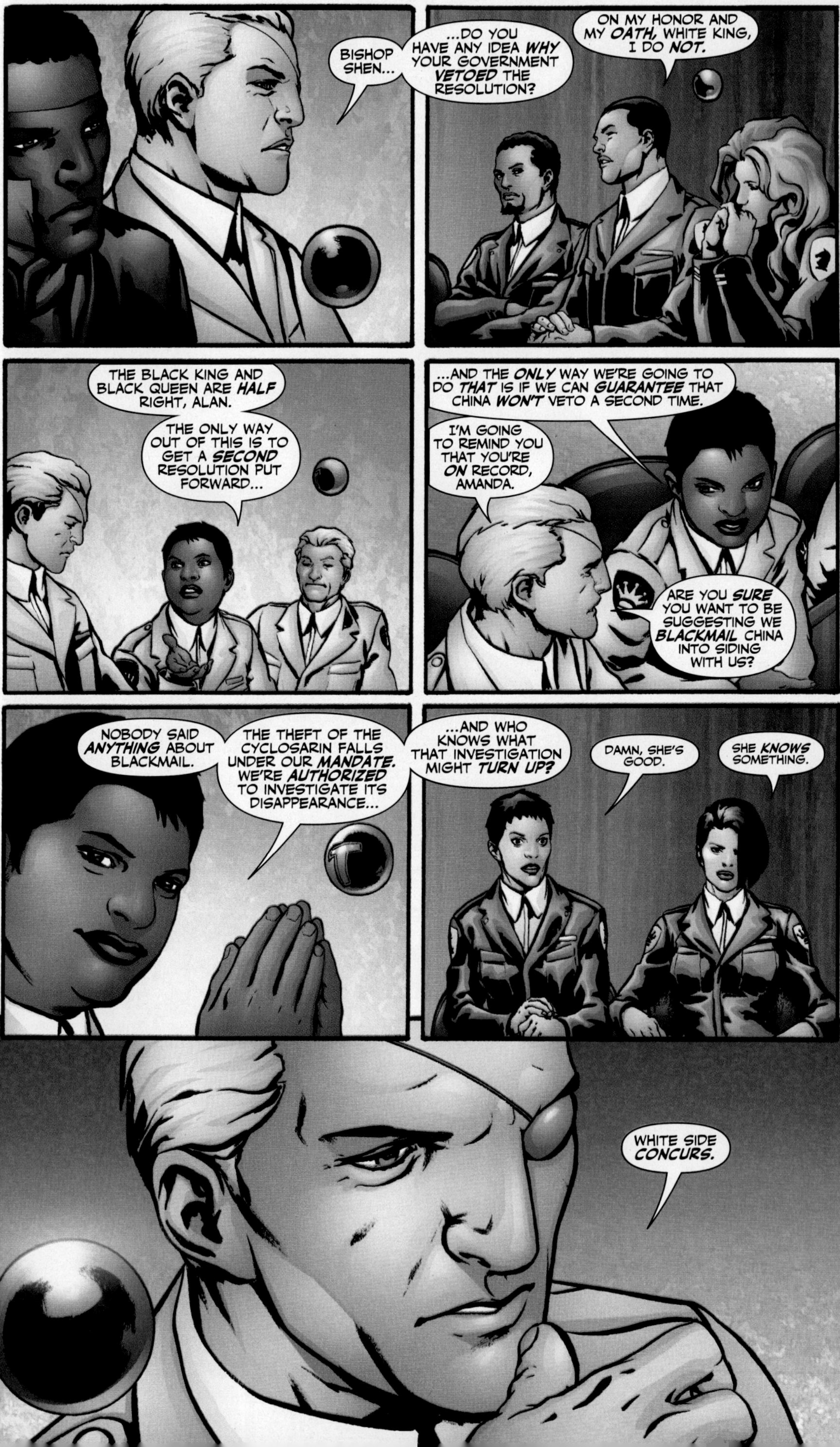
BISHOP SHEN...
...DO YOU HAVE ANY IDEA WHY YOUR GOVERNMENT VETOED THE RESOLUTION?
ON MY HONOR AND MY OATH, WHITE KING, I DO NOT.
THE BLACK KING AND BLACK QUEEN ARE HALF RIGHT, ALAN.
THE ONLY WAY OUT OF THIS IS TO GET A SECOND RESOLUTION PUT FORWARD...
...AND THE ONLY WAY WE'RE GOING TO DO THAT IS IF WE CAN GUARANTEE THAT CHINA WON'T VETO A SECOND TIME.
I'M GOING TO REMIND YOU THAT YOU'RE ON RECORD, AMANDA.
ARE YOU SURE YOU WANT TO BE SUGGESTING WE BLACKMAIL CHINA INTO SIDING WITH US?
NOBODY SAID ANYTHING ABOUT BLACKMAIL.
THE THEFT OF THE CYCLOSARIN FALLS UNDER OUR MANDATE. WE'RE AUTHORIZED TO INVESTIGATE ITS DISAPPEARANCE...
...AND WHO KNOWS WHAT THAT INVESTIGATION MIGHT TURN UP?
DAMN, SHE'S GOOD.
SHE KNOWS SOMETHING.
WHITE SIDE CONCURS.

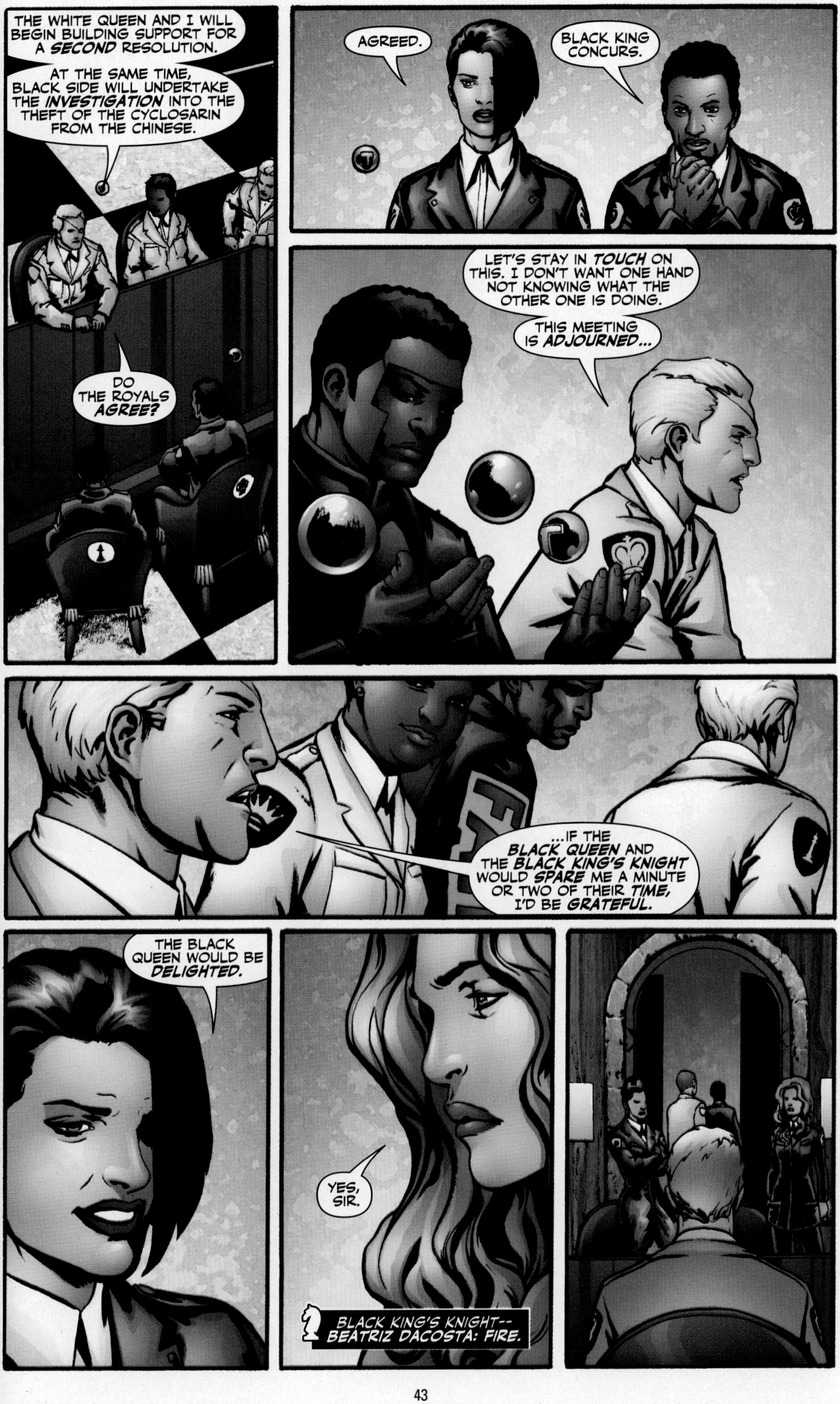
THE WHITE QUEEN AND I WILL BEGIN BUILDING SUPPORT FOR A SECOND RESOLUTION.
AT THE SAME TIME, BLACK SIDE WILL UNDERTAKE THE INVESTIGATION INTO THE THEFT OF THE CYCLOSARIN FROM THE CHINESE.
DO THE ROYALS AGREE?
AGREED.
BLACK KING CONCURS.
LET'S STAY IN TOUCH ON THIS. I DON'T WANT ONE HAND NOT KNOWING WHAT THE OTHER ONE IS DOING.
THIS MEETING IS ADJOURNED...
...IF THE BLACK QUEEN AND THE BLACK KING'S KNIGHT WOULD SPARE ME A MINUTE OR TWO OF THEIR TIME, I'D BE GRATEFUL.
THE BLACK QUEEN WOULD BE DELIGHTED.
YES, SIR.
BLACK KING'S KNIGHT-- BEATRIZ DACOSTA: FIRE.

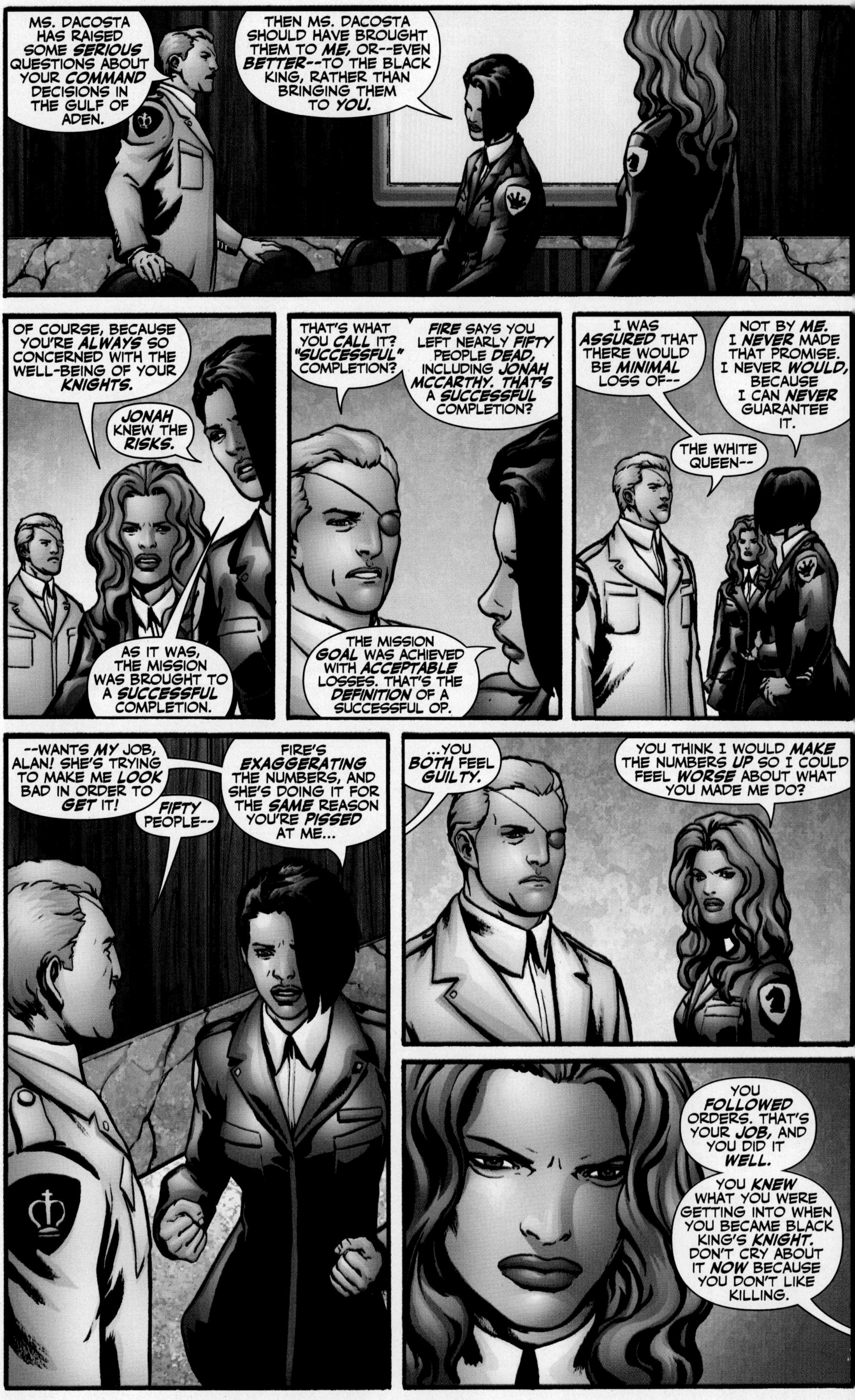

MS. DACOSTA HAS RAISED SOME SERIOUS QUESTIONS ABOUT YOUR COMMAND DECISIONS IN THE GULF OF ADEN.
THEN MS. DACOSTA SHOULD HAVE BROUGHT THEM TO ME, OR--EVEN BETTER--TO THE BLACK KING, RATHER THAN BRINGING THEM TO YOU.
OF COURSE, BECAUSE YOU'RE ALWAYS SO CONCERNED WITH THE WELL-BEING OF YOUR KNIGHTS.
JONAH KNEW THE RISKS.
AS IT WAS, THE MISSION WAS BROUGHT TO A SUCCESSFUL COMPLETION.
THAT'S WHAT YOU CALL IT? "SUCCESSFUL" COMPLETION?
FIRE SAYS YOU LEFT NEARLY FIFTY PEOPLE DEAD, INCLUDING JONAH MCCARTHY. THAT'S A SUCCESSFUL COMPLETION?
THE MISSION GOAL WAS ACHIEVED WITH ACCEPTABLE LOSSES. THAT'S THE DEFINITION OF A SUCCESSFUL OP.
I WAS ASSURED THAT THERE WOULD BE MINIMAL LOSS OF--
NOT BY ME. I NEVER MADE THAT PROMISE. I NEVER WOULD, BECAUSE I CAN NEVER GUARANTEE IT.
THE WHITE QUEEN--
--WANTS MY JOB, ALAN! SHE'S TRYING TO MAKE ME LOOK BAD IN ORDER TO GET IT!
FIFTY PEOPLE--
FIRE'S EXAGGERATING THE NUMBERS, AND SHE'S DOING IT FOR THE SAME REASON YOU'RE PISSED AT ME...
...YOU BOTH FEEL GUILTY.
YOU THINK I WOULD MAKE THE NUMBERS UP SO I COULD FEEL WORSE ABOUT WHAT YOU MADE ME DO?
YOU FOLLOWED ORDERS. THAT'S YOUR JOB, AND YOU DID IT WELL.
YOU KNEW WHAT YOU WERE GETTING INTO WHEN YOU BECAME BLACK KING'S KNIGHT. DON'T CRY ABOUT IT NOW BECAUSE YOU DON'T LIKE KILLING.

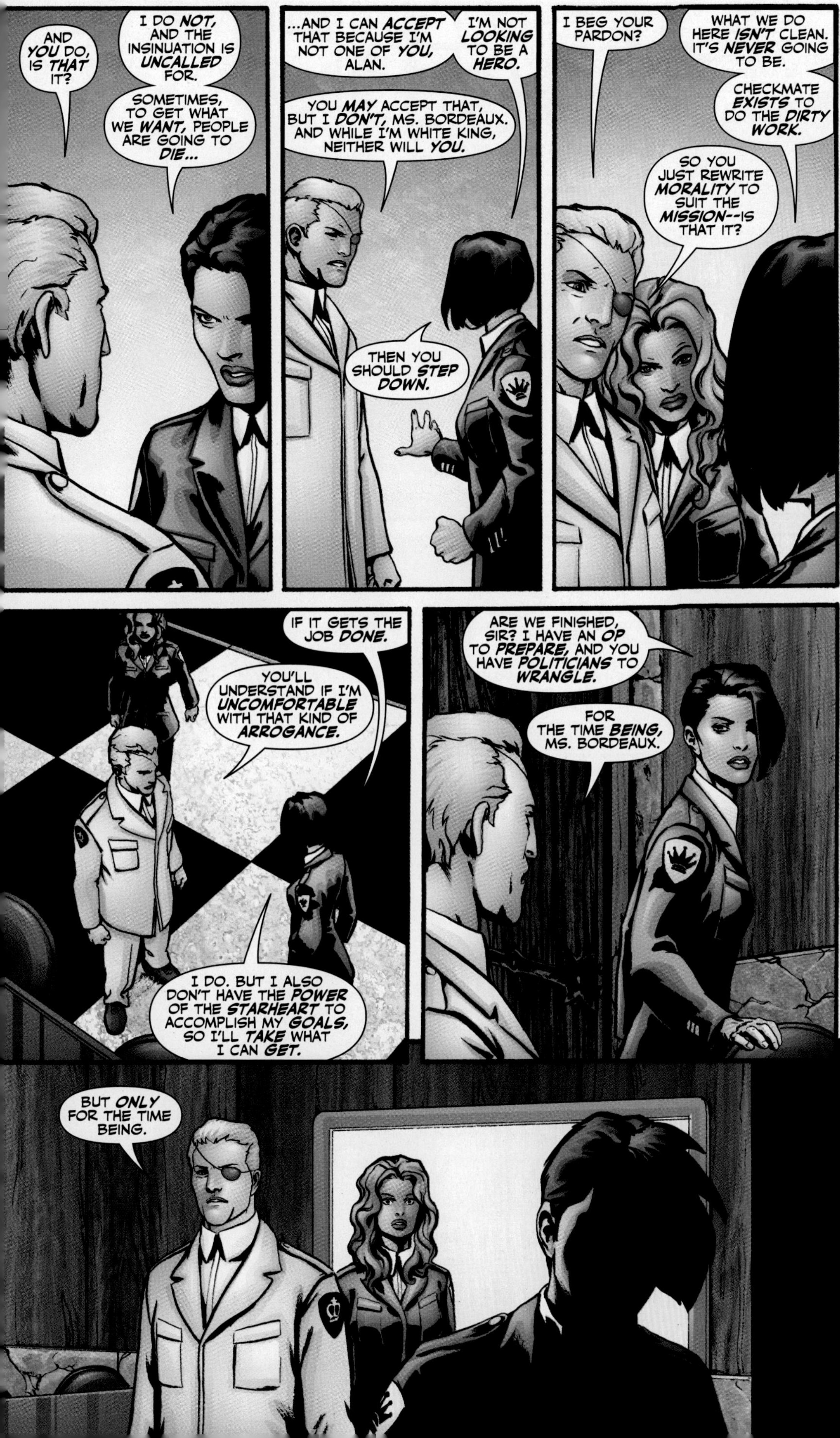
AND YOU DO, IS THAT IT?
I DO NOT, AND THE INSINUATION IS UNCALLED FOR.
SOMETIMES, TO GET WHAT WE WANT, PEOPLE ARE GOING TO DIE...
...AND I CAN ACCEPT THAT BECAUSE I'M NOT ONE OF YOU, ALAN.
I'M NOT LOOKING TO BE A HERO.
YOU MAY ACCEPT THAT, BUT I DON'T, MS. BORDEAUX. AND WHILE I'M WHITE KING, NEITHER WILL YOU.
THEN YOU SHOULD STEP DOWN.
I BEG YOUR PARDON?
WHAT WE DO HERE ISN'T CLEAN. IT'S NEVER GOING TO BE.
CHECKMATE EXISTS TO DO THE DIRTY WORK.
SO YOU JUST REWRITE MORALITY TO SUIT THE MISSION--IS THAT IT?
IF IT GETS THE JOB DONE.
YOU'LL UNDERSTAND IF I'M UNCOMFORTABLE WITH THAT KIND OF ARROGANCE.
I DO. BUT I ALSO DON'T HAVE THE POWER OF THE STARHEART TO ACCOMPLISH MY GOALS, SO I'LL TAKE WHAT I CAN GET.
ARE WE FINISHED, SIR? I HAVE AN OP TO PREPARE, AND YOU HAVE POLITICIANS TO WRANGLE.
FOR THE TIME BEING, MS. BORDEAUX.
BUT ONLY FOR THE TIME BEING.

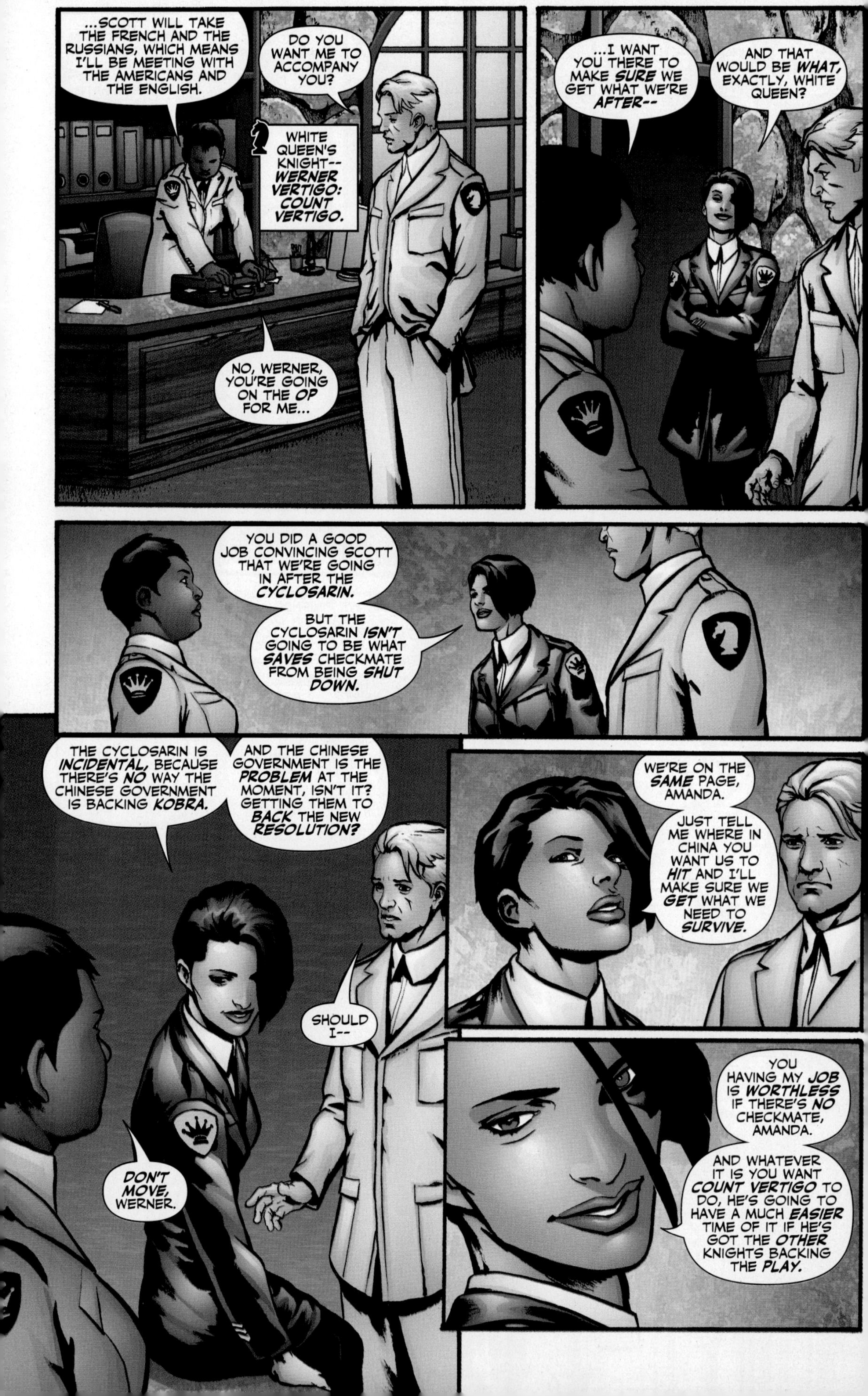
...SCOTT WILL TAKE THE FRENCH AND THE RUSSIANS, WHICH MEANS I'LL BE MEETING WITH THE AMERICANS AND THE ENGLISH.
DO YOU WANT ME TO ACCOMPANY YOU?
WHITE QUEEN'S KNIGHT-- WERNER VERTIGO: COUNT VERTIGO.
NO, WERNER, YOU'RE GOING ON THE OP FOR ME...
...I WANT YOU THERE TO MAKE SURE WE GET WHAT WE'RE AFTER--
AND THAT WOULD BE WHAT, EXACTLY, WHITE QUEEN?
YOU DID A GOOD JOB CONVINCING SCOTT THAT WE'RE GOING IN AFTER THE CYCLOSARIN.
BUT THE CYCLOSARIN ISN'T GOING TO BE WHAT SAVES CHECKMATE FROM BEING SHUT DOWN.
THE CYCLOSARIN IS INCIDENTAL, BECAUSE THERE'S NO WAY THE CHINESE GOVERNMENT IS BACKING KOBRA.
AND THE CHINESE GOVERNMENT IS THE PROBLEM AT THE MOMENT, ISN'T IT? GETTING THEM TO BACK THE NEW RESOLUTION?
SHOULD I--
DON'T MOVE, WERNER.
WE'RE ON THE SAME PAGE, AMANDA.
JUST TELL ME WHERE IN CHINA YOU WANT US TO HIT AND I'LL MAKE SURE WE GET WHAT WE NEED TO SURVIVE.
YOU HAVING MY JOB IS WORTHLESS IF THERE'S NO CHECKMATE, AMANDA.
AND WHATEVER IT IS YOU WANT COUNT VERTIGO TO DO, HE'S GOING TO HAVE A MUCH EASIER TIME OF IT IF HE'S GOT THE OTHER KNIGHTS BACKING THE PLAY.

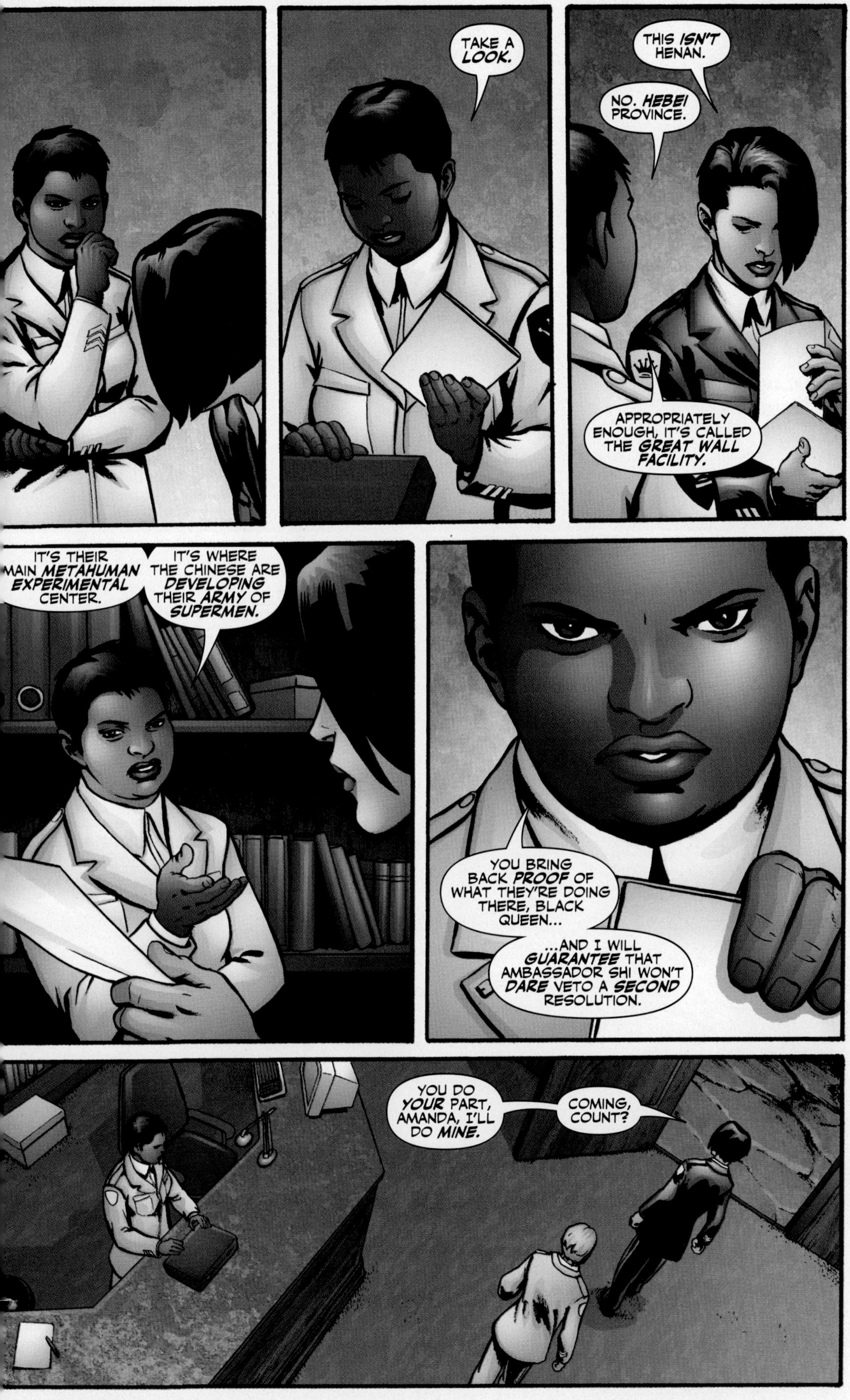
TAKE A LOOK.
THIS ISN'T HENAN.
NO. HEBEI PROVINCE.
APPROPRIATELY ENOUGH, IT'S CALLED THE GREAT WALL FACILITY.
IT'S THEIR MAIN METAHUMAN EXPERIMENTAL CENTER.
IT'S WHERE THE CHINESE ARE DEVELOPING THEIR ARMY OF SUPERMEN.
YOU BRING BACK PROOF OF WHAT THEY'RE DOING THERE, BLACK QUEEN...
...AND I WILL GUARANTEE THAT AMBASSADOR SHI WON'T DARE VETO A SECOND RESOLUTION.
YOU DO YOUR PART, AMANDA, I'LL DO MINE.
COMING, COUNT?

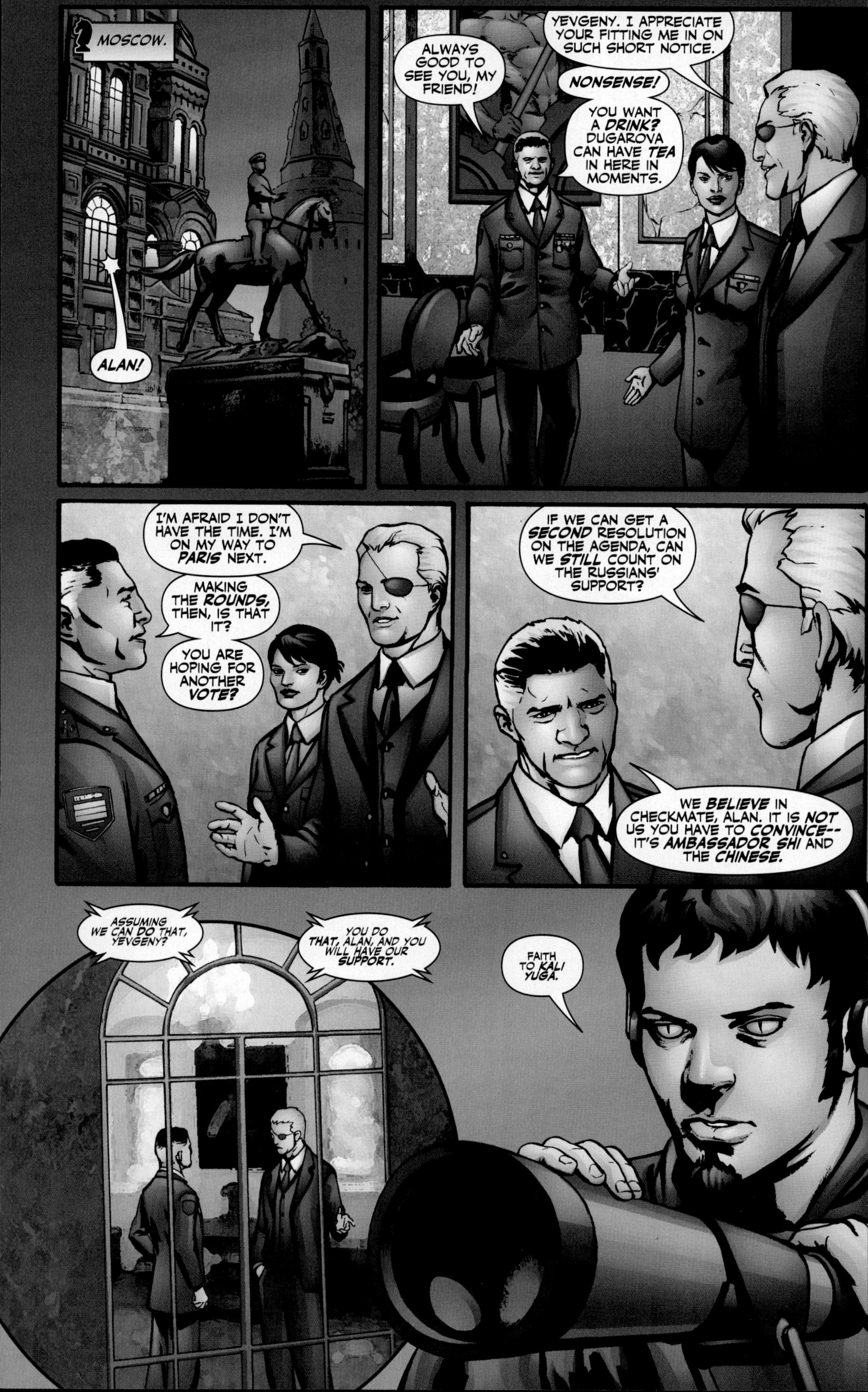
MOSCOW.
ALAN!
ALWAYS GOOD TO SEE YOU, MY FRIEND!
YEVGENY. I APPRECIATE YOUR FITTING ME IN ON SUCH SHORT NOTICE.
NONSENSE!
YOU WANT A DRINK? DUGAROVA CAN HAVE TEA IN HERE IN MOMENTS.
I'M AFRAID I DON'T HAVE THE TIME. I'M ON MY WAY TO PARIS NEXT.
MAKING THE ROUNDS, THEN, IS THAT IT?
YOU ARE HOPING FOR ANOTHER VOTE?
IF WE CAN GET A SECOND RESOLUTION ON THE AGENDA, CAN WE STILL COUNT ON THE RUSSIANS' SUPPORT?
WE BELIEVE IN CHECKMATE, ALAN. IT IS NOT US YOU HAVE TO CONVINCE-- IT'S AMBASSADOR SHI AND THE CHINESE.
ASSUMING WE CAN DO THAT, YEVGENY?
YOU DO THAT, ALAN, AND YOU WILL HAVE OUR SUPPORT.
FAITH TO KALI YUGA.

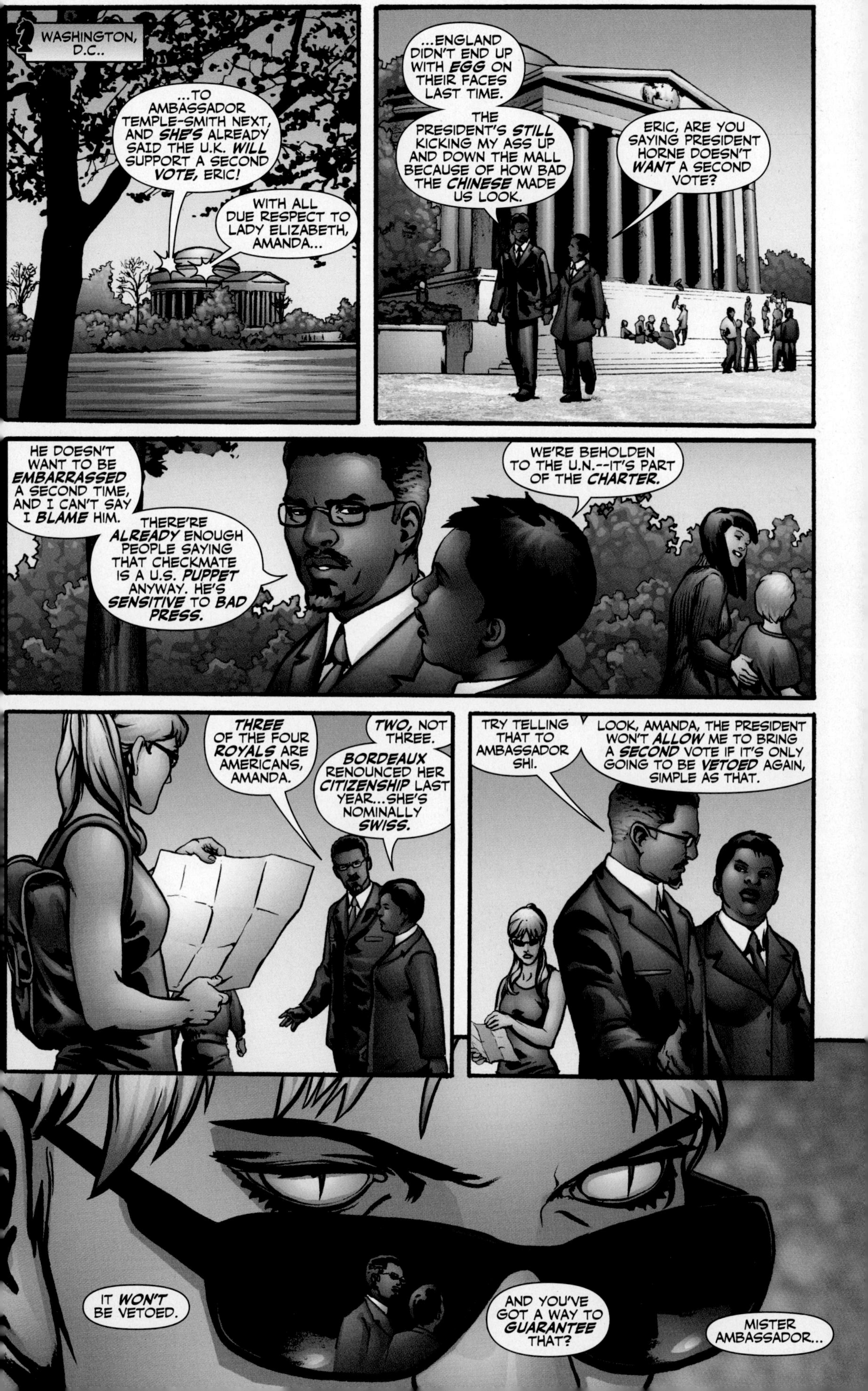
WASHINGTON, D.C..
...TO AMBASSADOR TEMPLE-SMITH NEXT, AND SHE'S ALREADY SAID THE U.K. WILL SUPPORT A SECOND VOTE, ERIC!
WITH ALL DUE RESPECT TO LADY ELIZABETH, AMANDA...
...ENGLAND DIDN'T END UP WITH EGG ON THEIR FACES LAST TIME.
THE PRESIDENT'S STILL KICKING MY ASS UP AND DOWN THE MALL BECAUSE OF HOW BAD THE CHINESE MADE US LOOK.
ERIC, ARE YOU SAYING PRESIDENT HORNE DOESN'T WANT A SECOND VOTE?
HE DOESN'T WANT TO BE EMBARRASSED A SECOND TIME, AND I CAN'T SAY I BLAME HIM.
THERE'RE ALREADY ENOUGH PEOPLE SAYING THAT CHECKMATE IS A U.S. PUPPET ANYWAY. HE'S SENSITIVE TO BAD PRESS.
WE'RE BEHOLDEN TO THE U.N.--IT'S PART OF THE CHARTER.
THREE OF THE FOUR ROYALS ARE AMERICANS, AMANDA.
TWO, NOT THREE.
BORDEAUX RENOUNCED HER CITIZENSHIP LAST YEAR...SHE'S NOMINALLY SWISS.
TRY TELLING THAT TO AMBASSADOR SHI.
LOOK, AMANDA, THE PRESIDENT WON'T ALLOW ME TO BRING A SECOND VOTE IF IT'S ONLY GOING TO BE VETOED AGAIN, SIMPLE AS THAT.
IT WON'T BE VETOED.
AND YOU'VE GOT A WAY TO GUARANTEE THAT?
MISTER AMBASSADOR...

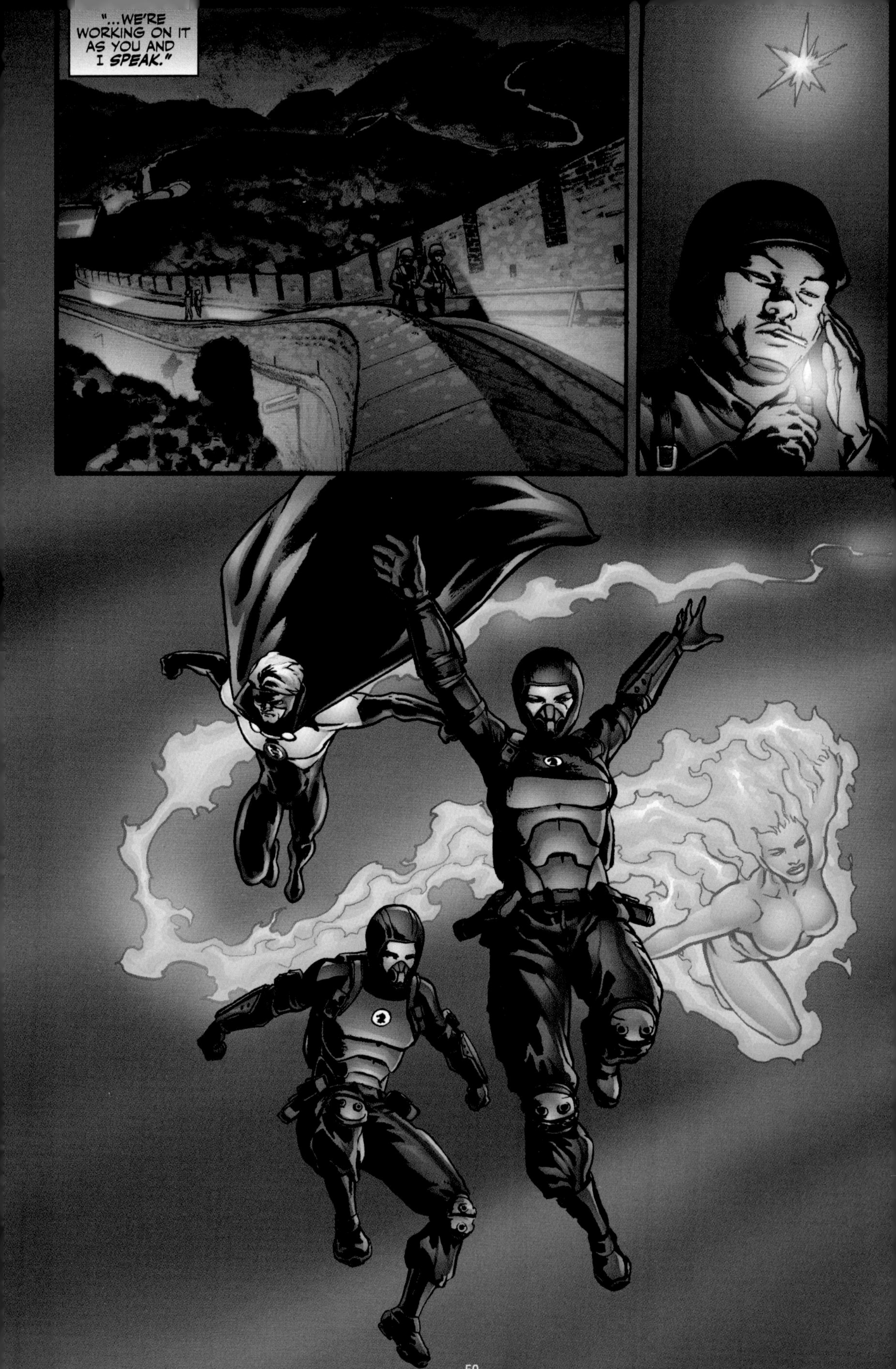
"...WE'RE WORKING ON IT AS YOU AND I SPEAK."

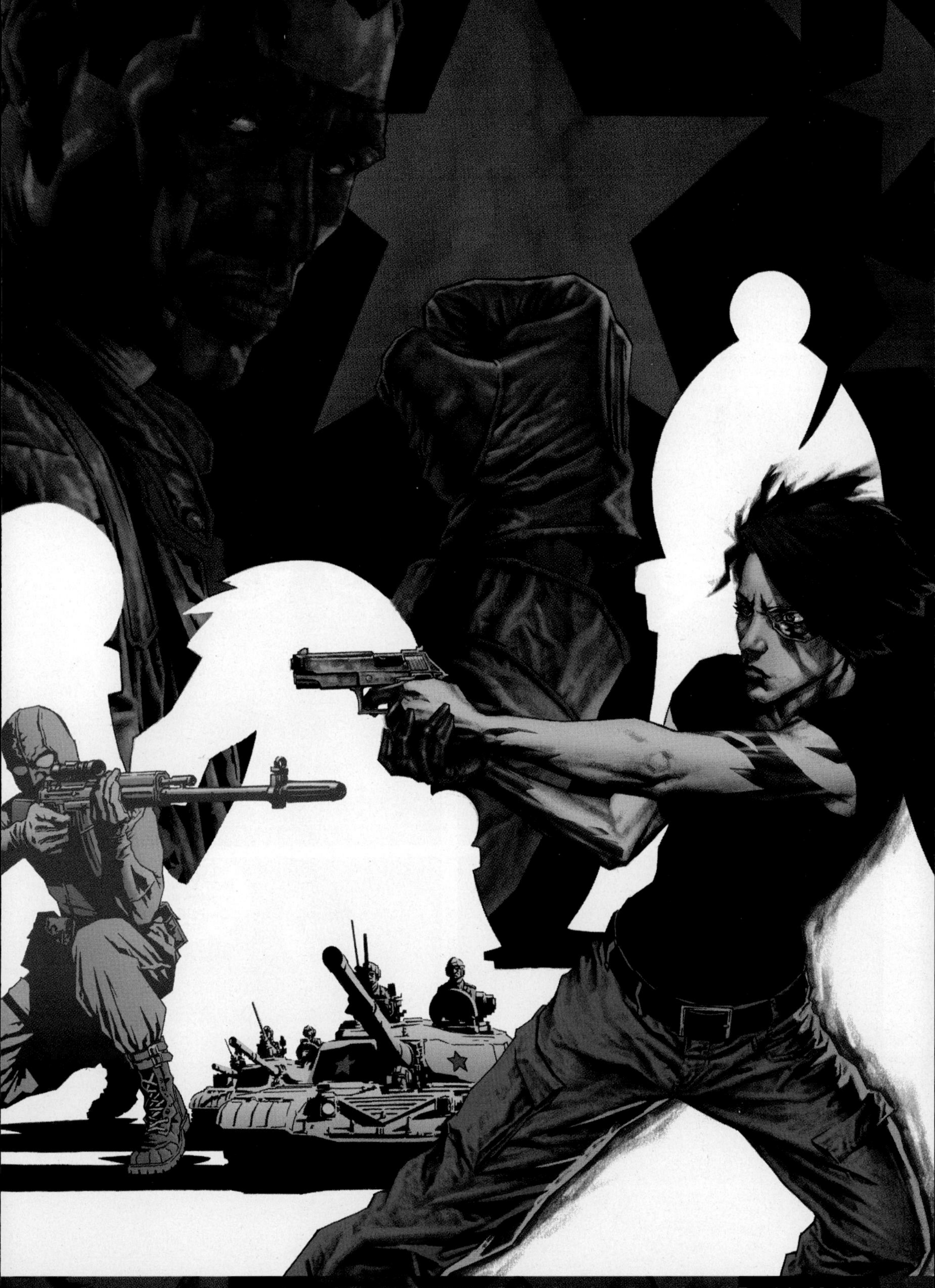

CHAPTER THREE Cover Art: Lee Bermejo and Patricia Mulvihill

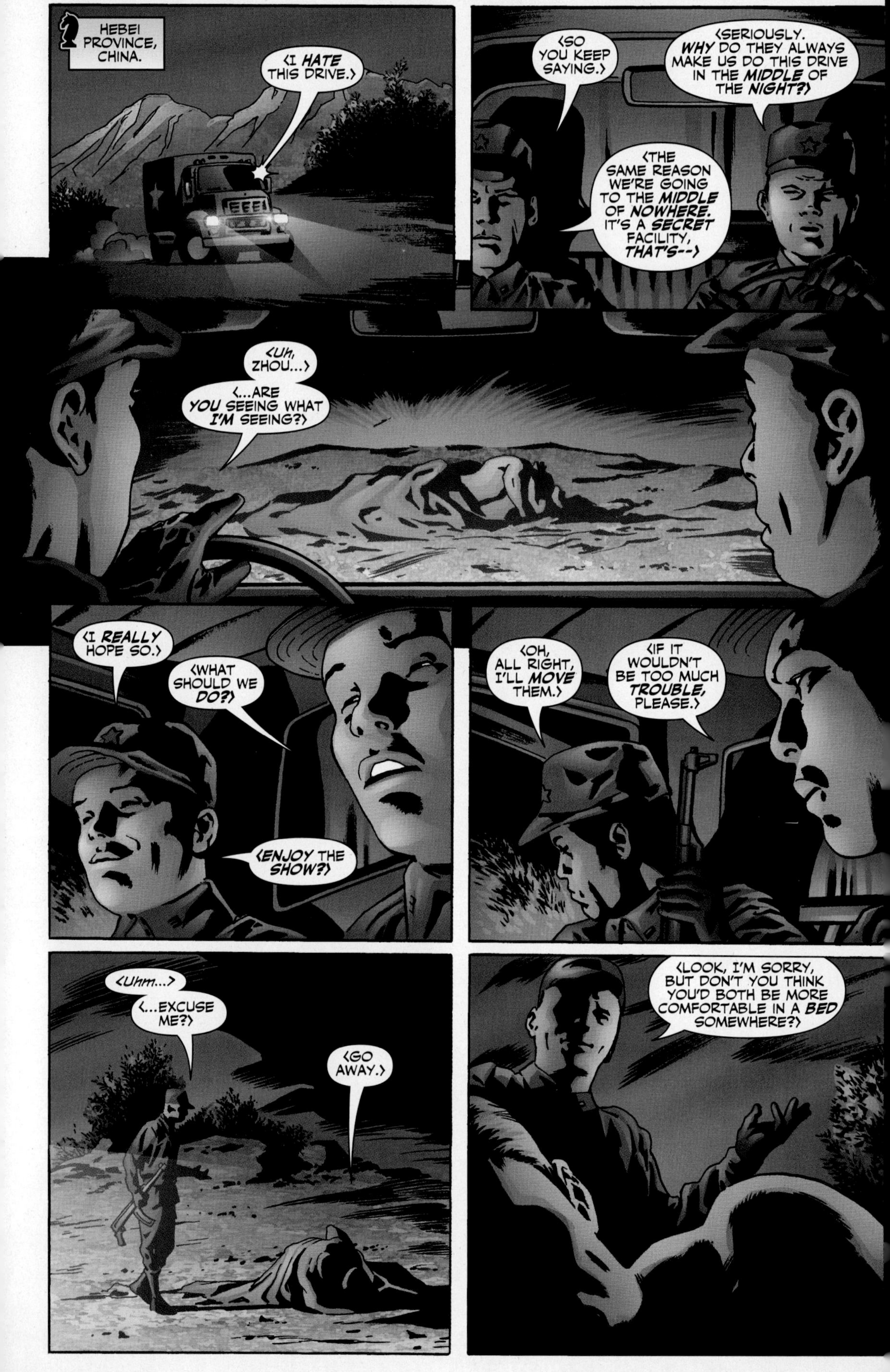
HEBEI PROVINCE, CHINA.
‹I HATE THIS DRIVE.›
‹SERIOUSLY. WHY DO THEY ALWAYS MAKE US DO THIS DRIVE IN THE MIDDLE OF THE NIGHT?›
‹SO YOU KEEP SAYING.›
‹THE SAME REASON WE'RE GOING TO THE MIDDLE OF NOWHERE. IT'S A SECRET FACILITY, THAT'S--›
‹Uh, ZHOU...›
‹...ARE YOU SEEING WHAT I'M SEEING?›
‹I REALLY HOPE SO.›
‹WHAT SHOULD WE DO?›
‹ENJOY THE SHOW?›
‹OH, ALL RIGHT, I'LL MOVE THEM.›
‹IF IT WOULDN'T BE TOO MUCH TROUBLE, PLEASE.›
‹Uhm...›
‹...EXCUSE ME?›
‹GO AWAY.›
‹LOOK, I'M SORRY, BUT DON'T YOU THINK YOU'D BOTH BE MORE COMFORTABLE IN A BED SOMEWHERE?›

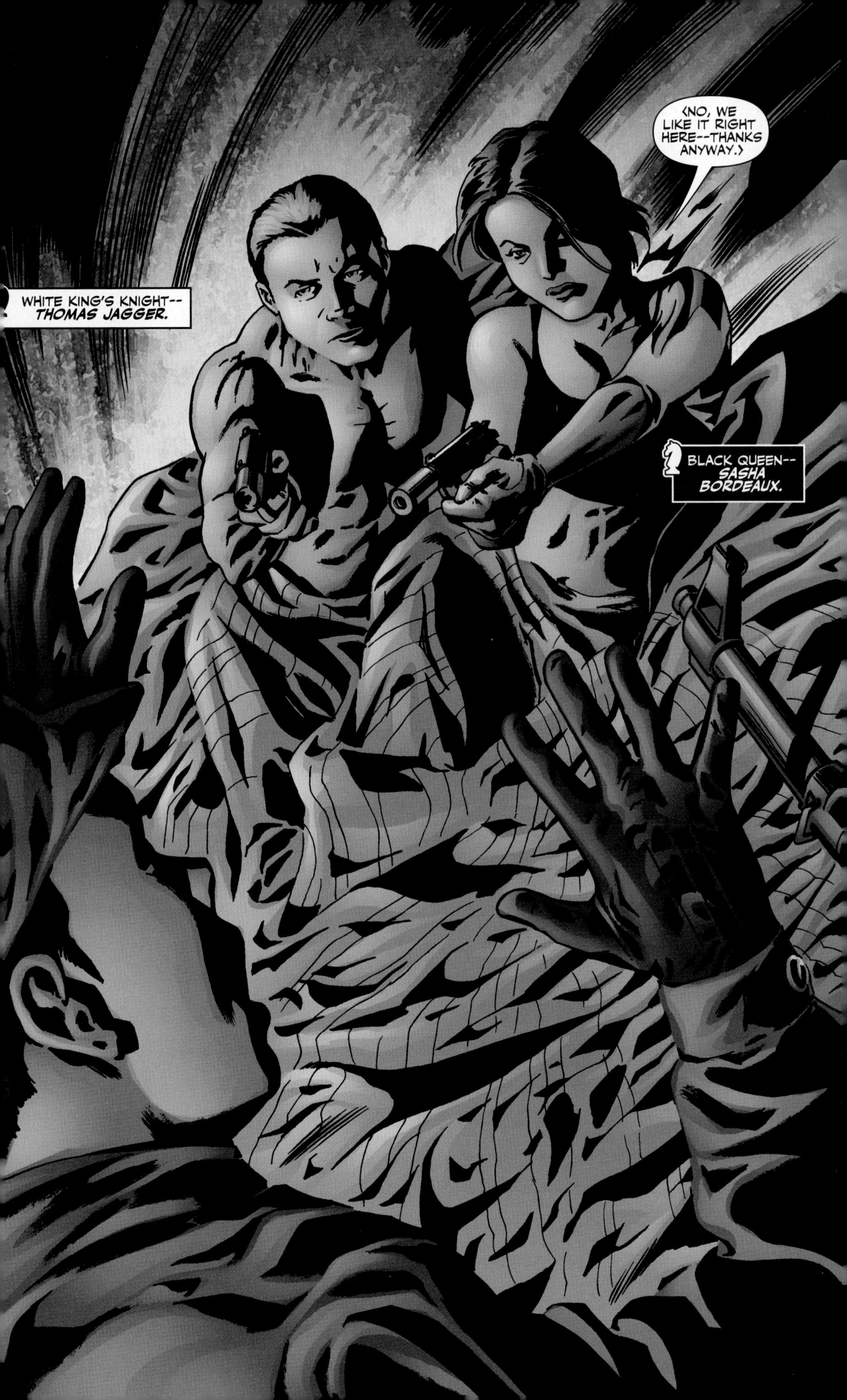

WHITE KING'S KNIGHT-- THOMAS JAGGER.
‹NO, WE LIKE IT RIGHT HERE--THANKS ANYWAY.›
BLACK QUEEN-- SASHA BORDEAUX.

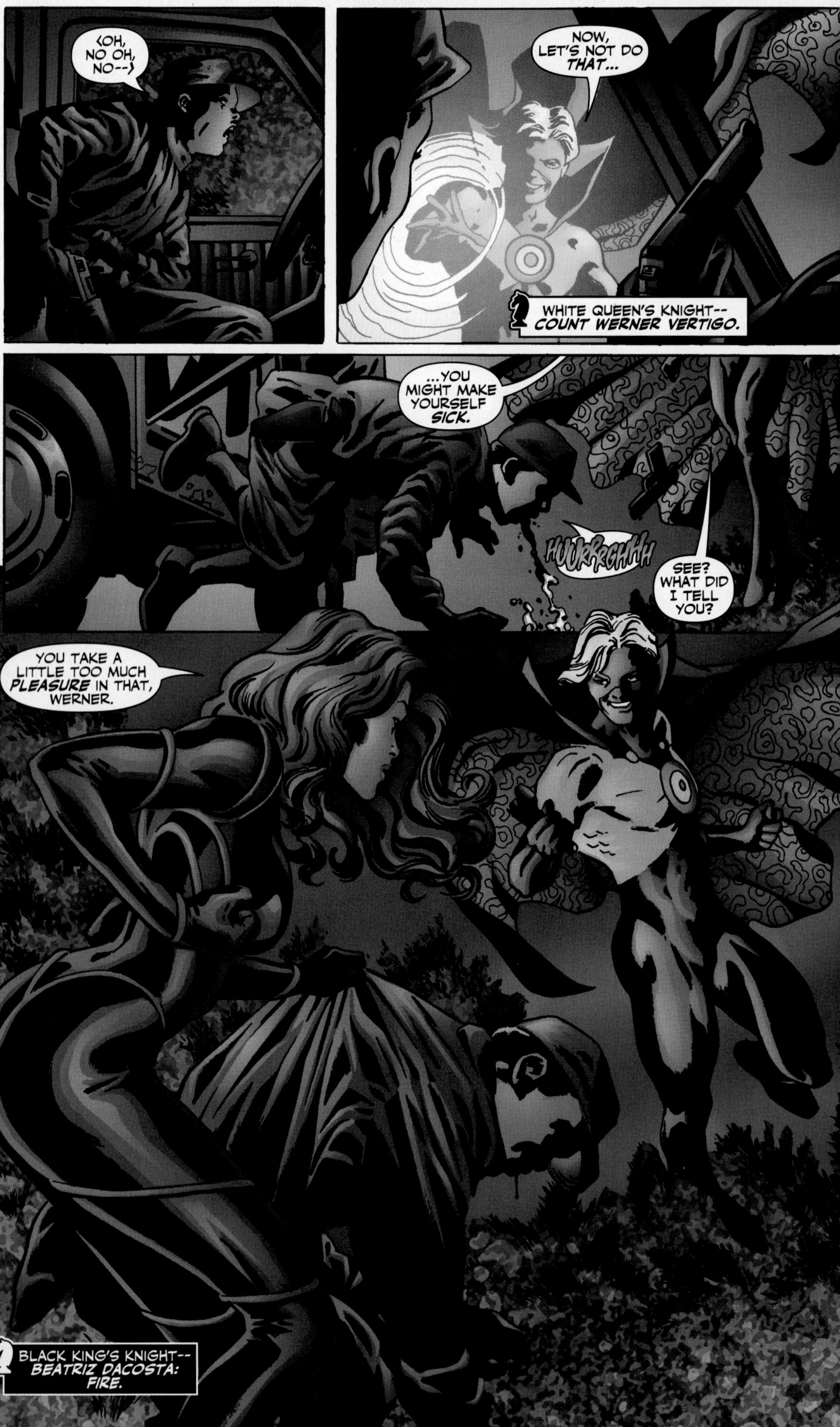

<OH, NO OH, NO-->
NOW, LET'S NOT DO *THAT*...
WHITE QUEEN'S KNIGHT-- *COUNT WERNER VERTIGO.*
...YOU MIGHT MAKE YOURSELF *SICK.*
HUURRGHHH
SEE? WHAT DID I TELL YOU?
YOU TAKE A LITTLE TOO MUCH *PLEASURE* IN THAT, WERNER.
BLACK KING'S KNIGHT-- *BEATRIZ DACOSTA: FIRE.*

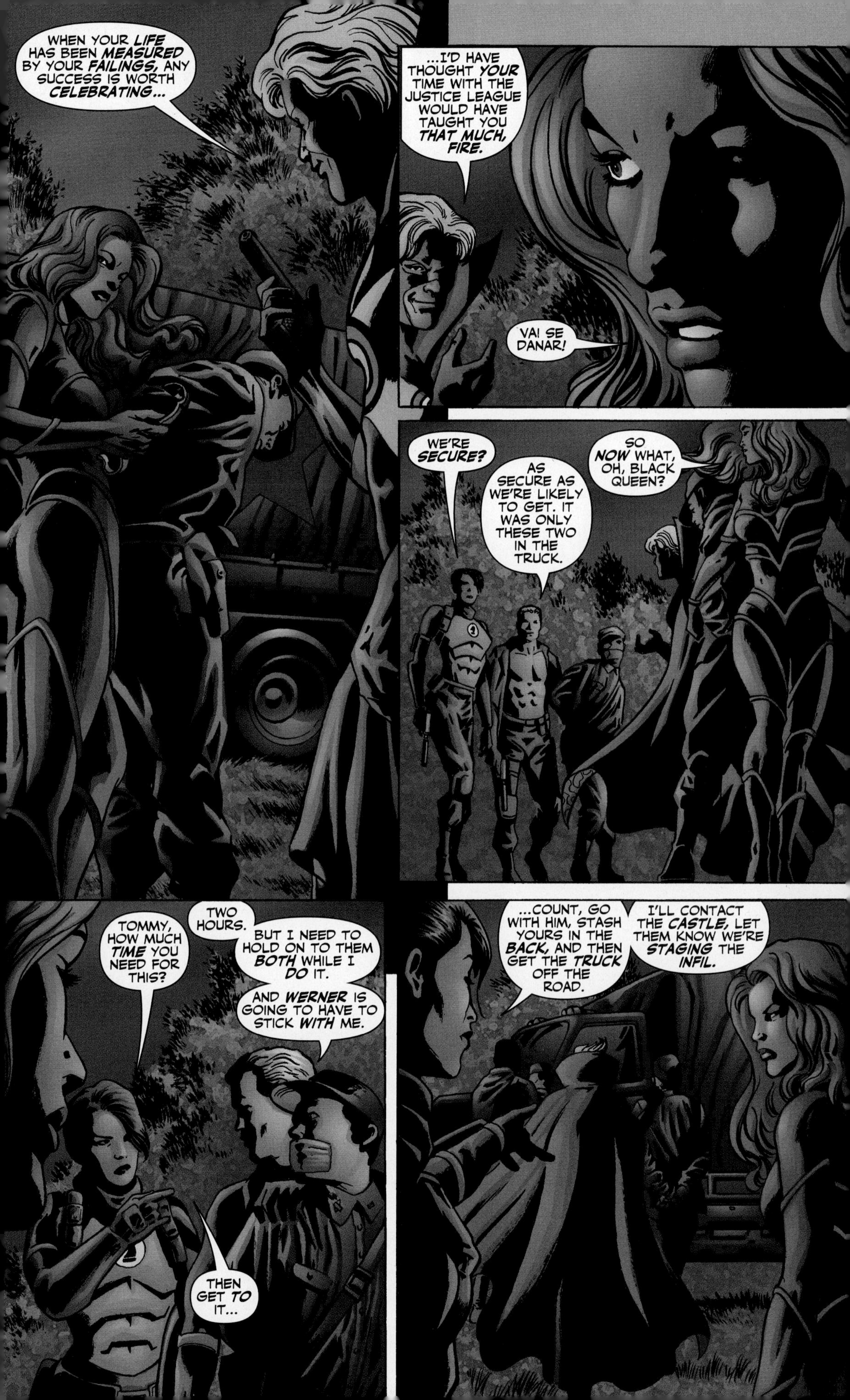
WHEN YOUR LIFE HAS BEEN MEASURED BY YOUR FAILINGS, ANY SUCCESS IS WORTH CELEBRATING...
...I'D HAVE THOUGHT YOUR TIME WITH THE JUSTICE LEAGUE WOULD HAVE TAUGHT YOU THAT MUCH, FIRE.
VAI SE DANAR!
WE'RE SECURE?
AS SECURE AS WE'RE LIKELY TO GET. IT WAS ONLY THESE TWO IN THE TRUCK.
SO NOW WHAT, OH, BLACK QUEEN?
TOMMY, HOW MUCH TIME YOU NEED FOR THIS?
TWO HOURS.
BUT I NEED TO HOLD ON TO THEM BOTH WHILE I DO IT.
AND WERNER IS GOING TO HAVE TO STICK WITH ME.
THEN GET TO IT...
...COUNT, GO WITH HIM, STASH YOURS IN THE BACK, AND THEN GET THE TRUCK OFF THE ROAD.
I'LL CONTACT THE CASTLE, LET THEM KNOW WE'RE STAGING THE INFIL.

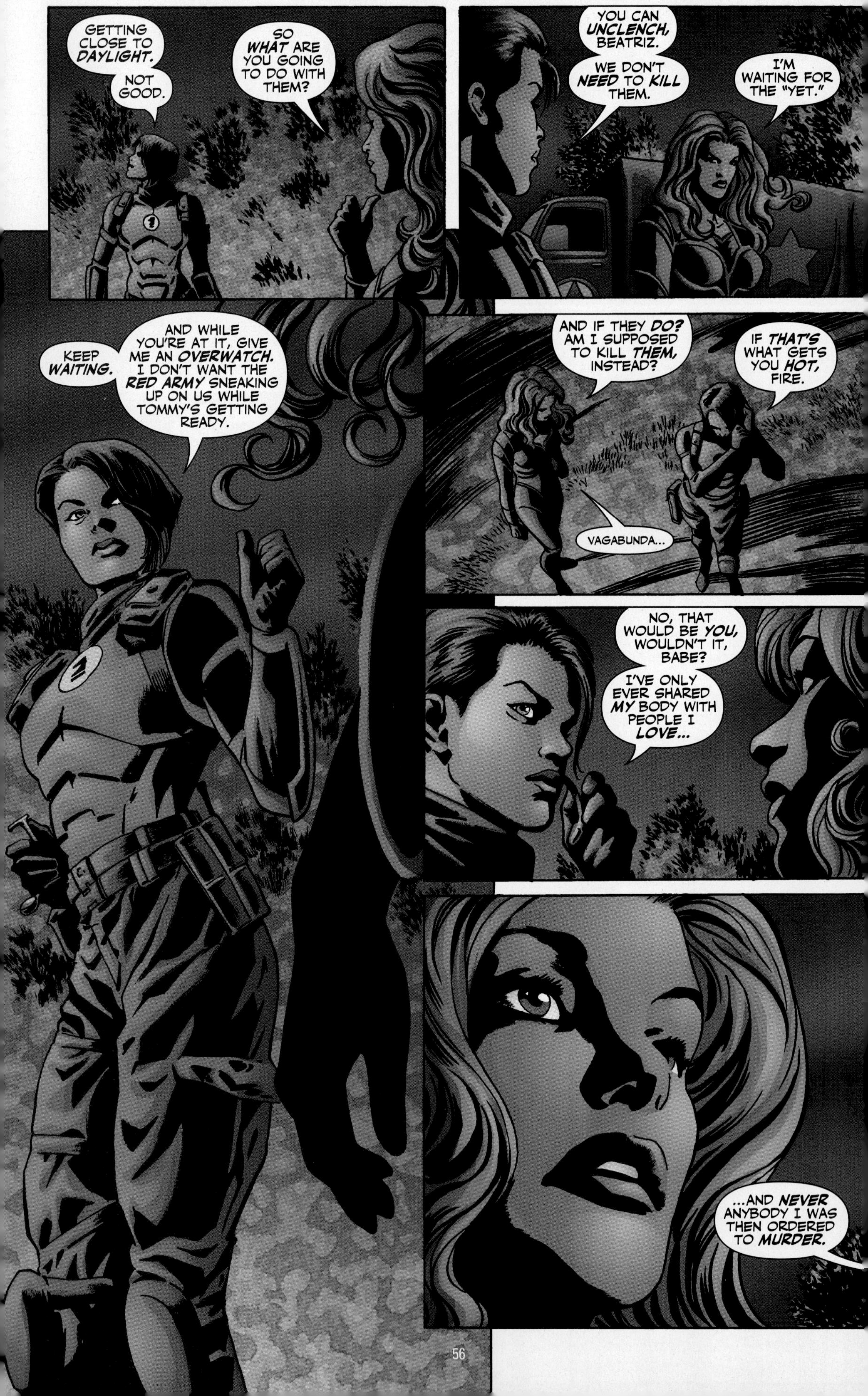
GETTING CLOSE TO DAYLIGHT.
NOT GOOD.
SO WHAT ARE YOU GOING TO DO WITH THEM?
YOU CAN UNCLENCH, BEATRIZ.
WE DON'T NEED TO KILL THEM.
I'M WAITING FOR THE "YET."
KEEP WAITING.
AND WHILE YOU'RE AT IT, GIVE ME AN OVERWATCH. I DON'T WANT THE RED ARMY SNEAKING UP ON US WHILE TOMMY'S GETTING READY.
AND IF THEY DO? AM I SUPPOSED TO KILL THEM, INSTEAD?
IF THAT'S WHAT GETS YOU HOT, FIRE.
VAGABUNDA...
NO, THAT WOULD BE YOU, WOULDN'T IT, BABE?
I'VE ONLY EVER SHARED MY BODY WITH PEOPLE I LOVE...
...AND NEVER ANYBODY I WAS THEN ORDERED TO MURDER.

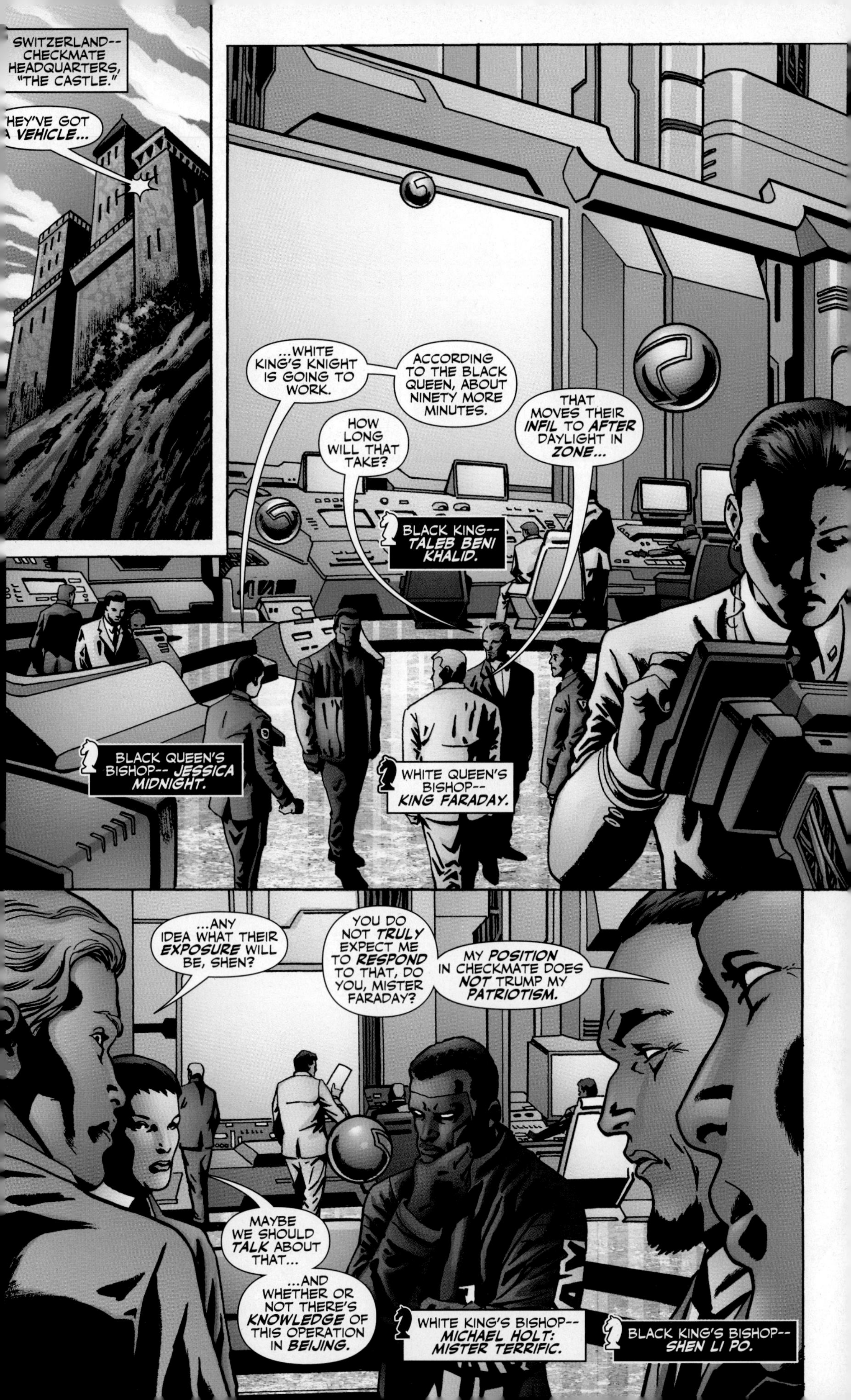

SWITZERLAND-- CHECKMATE HEADQUARTERS, "THE CASTLE."
HEY'VE GOT A VEHICLE...
...WHITE KING'S KNIGHT IS GOING TO WORK.
HOW LONG WILL THAT TAKE?
ACCORDING TO THE BLACK QUEEN, ABOUT NINETY MORE MINUTES.
THAT MOVES THEIR INFIL TO AFTER DAYLIGHT IN ZONE...
BLACK KING-- TALEB BENI KHALID.
BLACK QUEEN'S BISHOP-- JESSICA MIDNIGHT.
WHITE QUEEN'S BISHOP-- KING FARADAY.
...ANY IDEA WHAT THEIR EXPOSURE WILL BE, SHEN?
YOU DO NOT TRULY EXPECT ME TO RESPOND TO THAT, DO YOU, MISTER FARADAY?
MY POSITION IN CHECKMATE DOES NOT TRUMP MY PATRIOTISM.
MAYBE WE SHOULD TALK ABOUT THAT...
...AND WHETHER OR NOT THERE'S KNOWLEDGE OF THIS OPERATION IN BEIJING.
WHITE KING'S BISHOP-- MICHAEL HOLT: MISTER TERRIFIC.
BLACK KING'S BISHOP-- SHEN LI PO.

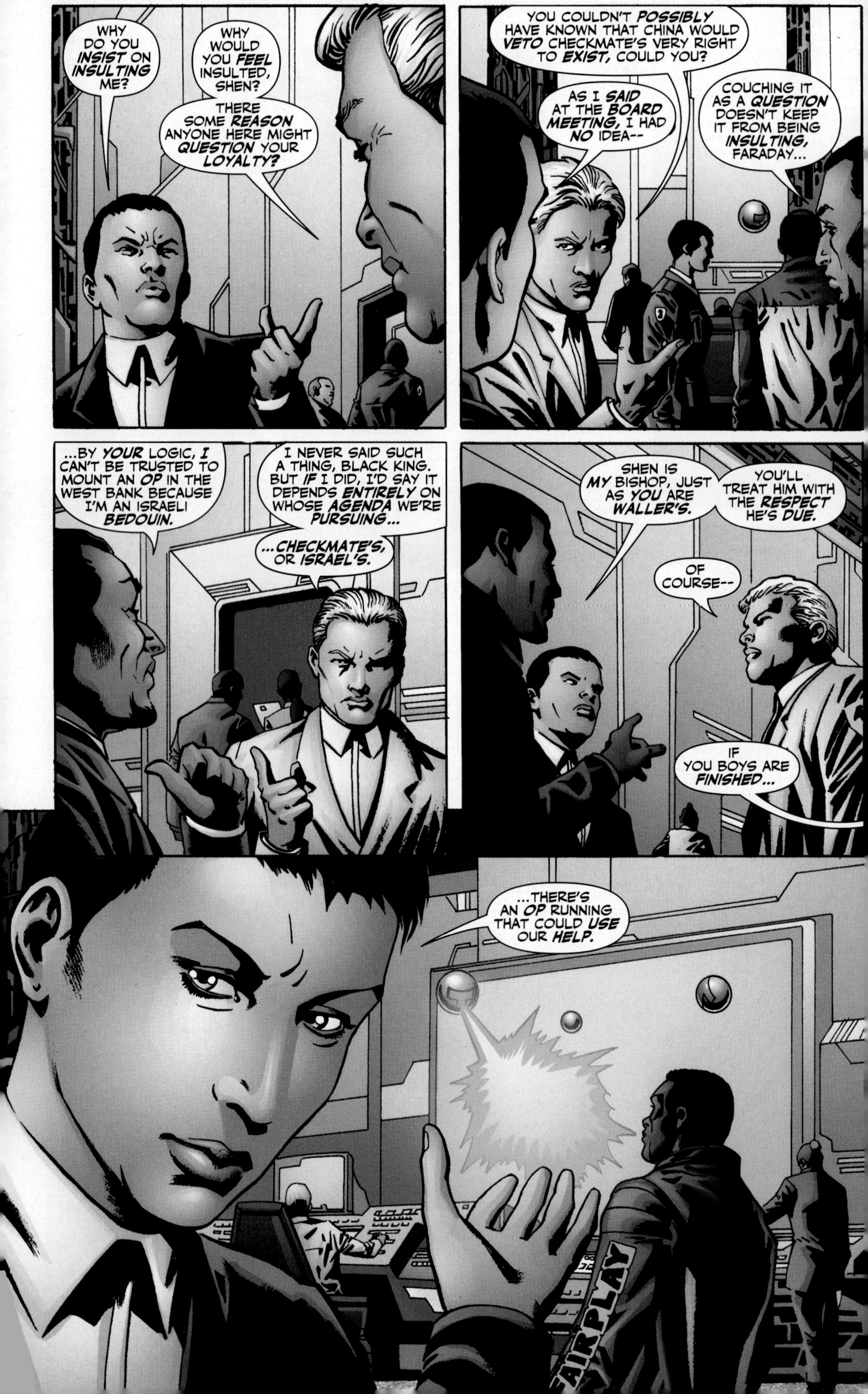
WHY DO YOU INSIST ON INSULTING ME?
WHY WOULD YOU FEEL INSULTED, SHEN?
THERE SOME REASON ANYONE HERE MIGHT QUESTION YOUR LOYALTY?
YOU COULDN'T POSSIBLY HAVE KNOWN THAT CHINA WOULD VETO CHECKMATE'S VERY RIGHT TO EXIST, COULD YOU?
AS I SAID AT THE BOARD MEETING, I HAD NO IDEA--
COUCHING IT AS A QUESTION DOESN'T KEEP IT FROM BEING INSULTING, FARADAY...
...BY YOUR LOGIC, I CAN'T BE TRUSTED TO MOUNT AN OP IN THE WEST BANK BECAUSE I'M AN ISRAELI BEDOUIN.
I NEVER SAID SUCH A THING, BLACK KING. BUT IF I DID, I'D SAY IT DEPENDS ENTIRELY ON WHOSE AGENDA WE'RE PURSUING...
...CHECKMATE'S, OR ISRAEL'S.
SHEN IS MY BISHOP, JUST AS YOU ARE WALLER'S.
YOU'LL TREAT HIM WITH THE RESPECT HE'S DUE.
OF COURSE--
IF YOU BOYS ARE FINISHED...
...THERE'S AN OP RUNNING THAT COULD USE OUR HELP.
FAIRPLAY

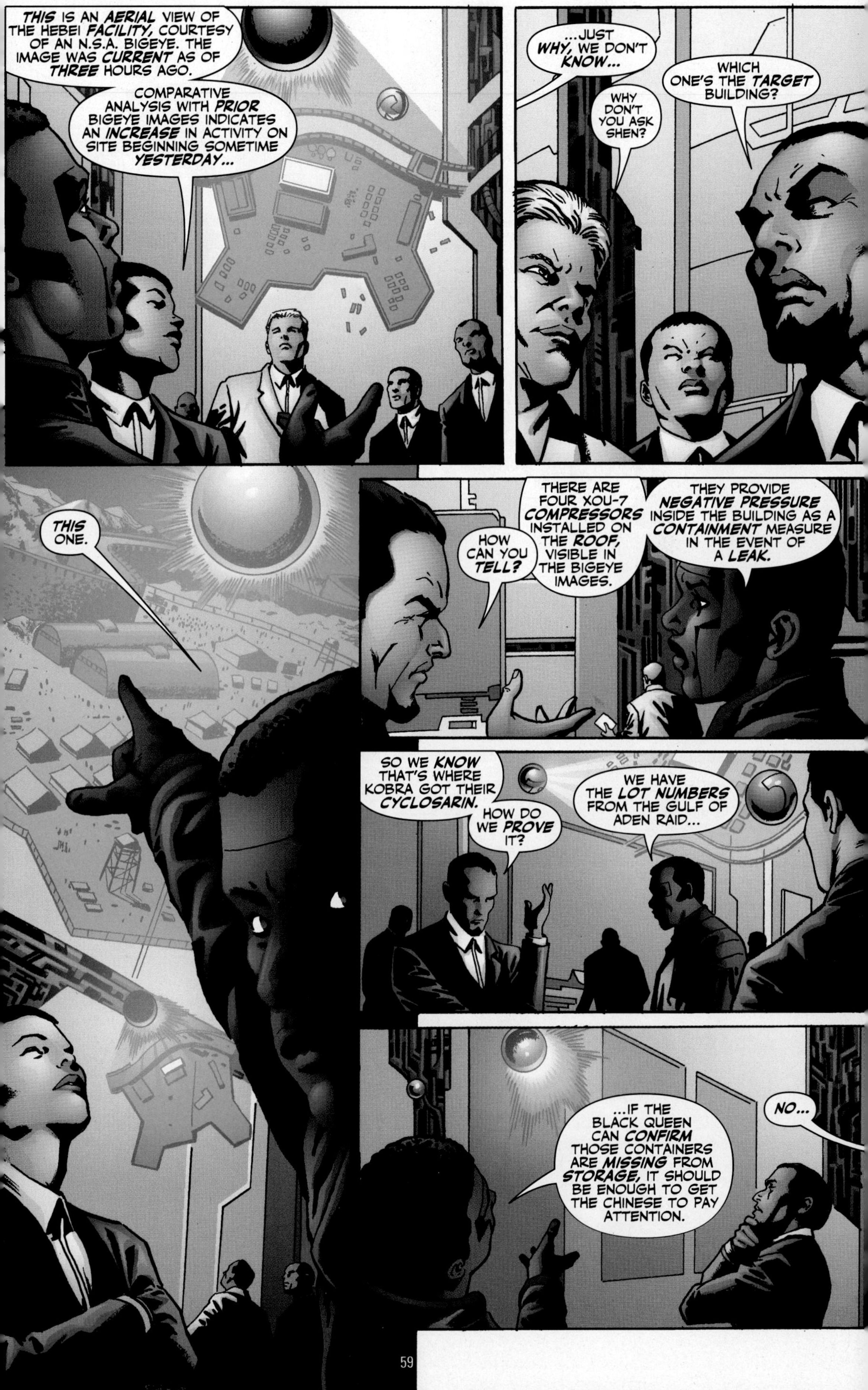
THIS IS AN AERIAL VIEW OF THE HEBEI FACILITY, COURTESY OF AN N.S.A. BIGEYE. THE IMAGE WAS CURRENT AS OF THREE HOURS AGO.
COMPARATIVE ANALYSIS WITH PRIOR BIGEYE IMAGES INDICATES AN INCREASE IN ACTIVITY ON SITE BEGINNING SOMETIME YESTERDAY...
...JUST WHY, WE DON'T KNOW...
WHY DON'T YOU ASK SHEN?
WHICH ONE'S THE TARGET BUILDING?
THIS ONE.
HOW CAN YOU TELL?
THERE ARE FOUR XOU-7 COMPRESSORS INSTALLED ON THE ROOF, VISIBLE IN THE BIGEYE IMAGES.
THEY PROVIDE NEGATIVE PRESSURE INSIDE THE BUILDING AS A CONTAINMENT MEASURE IN THE EVENT OF A LEAK.
SO WE KNOW THAT'S WHERE KOBRA GOT THEIR CYCLOSARIN.
HOW DO WE PROVE IT?
WE HAVE THE LOT NUMBERS FROM THE GULF OF ADEN RAID...
...IF THE BLACK QUEEN CAN CONFIRM THOSE CONTAINERS ARE MISSING FROM STORAGE, IT SHOULD BE ENOUGH TO GET THE CHINESE TO PAY ATTENTION.
NO...

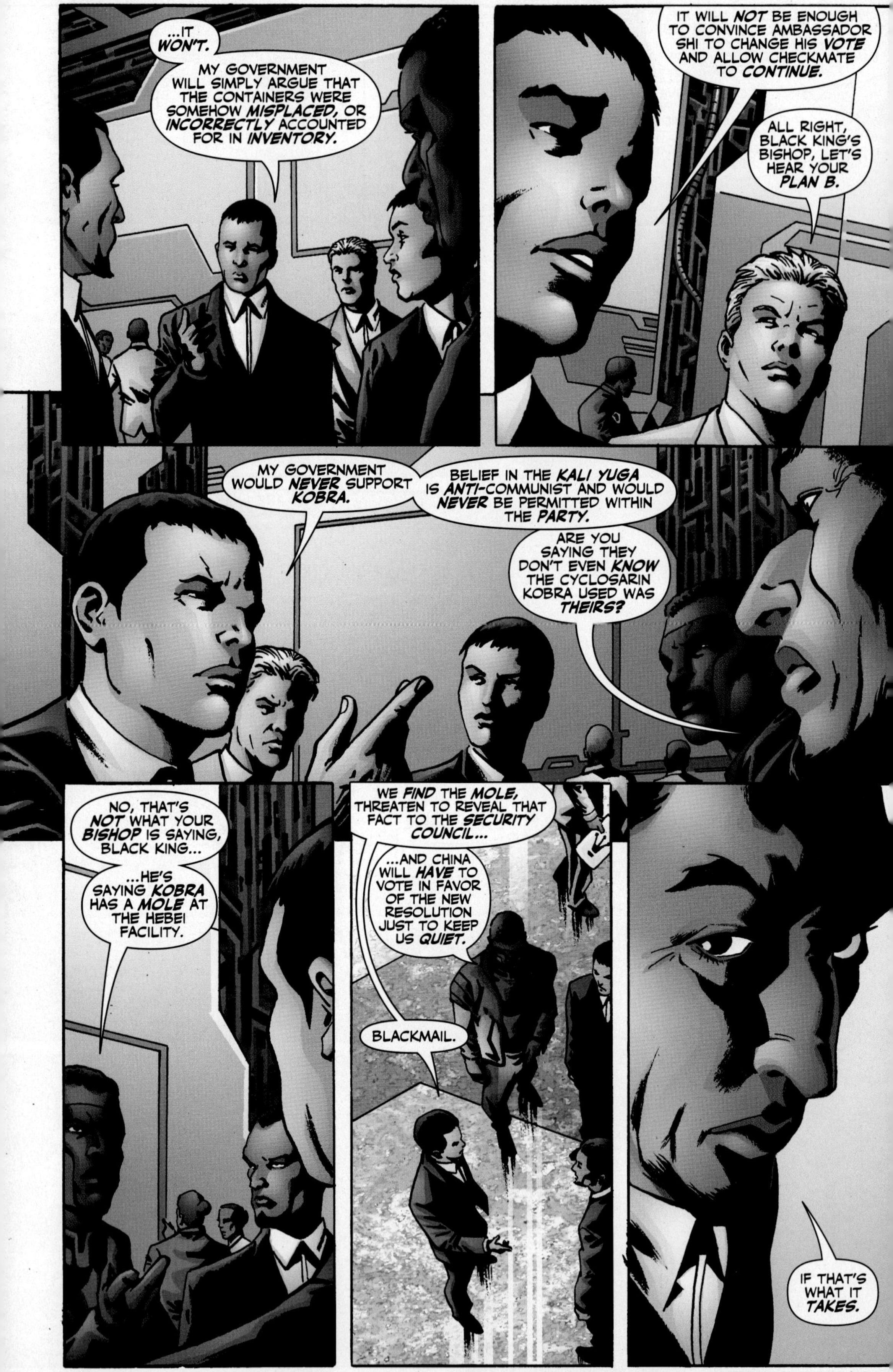
...IT WON'T.
MY GOVERNMENT WILL SIMPLY ARGUE THAT THE CONTAINERS WERE SOMEHOW MISPLACED, OR INCORRECTLY ACCOUNTED FOR IN INVENTORY.
IT WILL NOT BE ENOUGH TO CONVINCE AMBASSADOR SHI TO CHANGE HIS VOTE AND ALLOW CHECKMATE TO CONTINUE.
ALL RIGHT, BLACK KING'S BISHOP, LET'S HEAR YOUR PLAN B.
MY GOVERNMENT WOULD NEVER SUPPORT KOBRA.
BELIEF IN THE KALI YUGA IS ANTI-COMMUNIST AND WOULD NEVER BE PERMITTED WITHIN THE PARTY.
ARE YOU SAYING THEY DON'T EVEN KNOW THE CYCLOSARIN KOBRA USED WAS THEIRS?
NO, THAT'S NOT WHAT YOUR BISHOP IS SAYING, BLACK KING...
...HE'S SAYING KOBRA HAS A MOLE AT THE HEBEI FACILITY.
WE FIND THE MOLE, THREATEN TO REVEAL THAT FACT TO THE SECURITY COUNCIL...
...AND CHINA WILL HAVE TO VOTE IN FAVOR OF THE NEW RESOLUTION JUST TO KEEP US QUIET.
BLACKMAIL.
IF THAT'S WHAT IT TAKES.

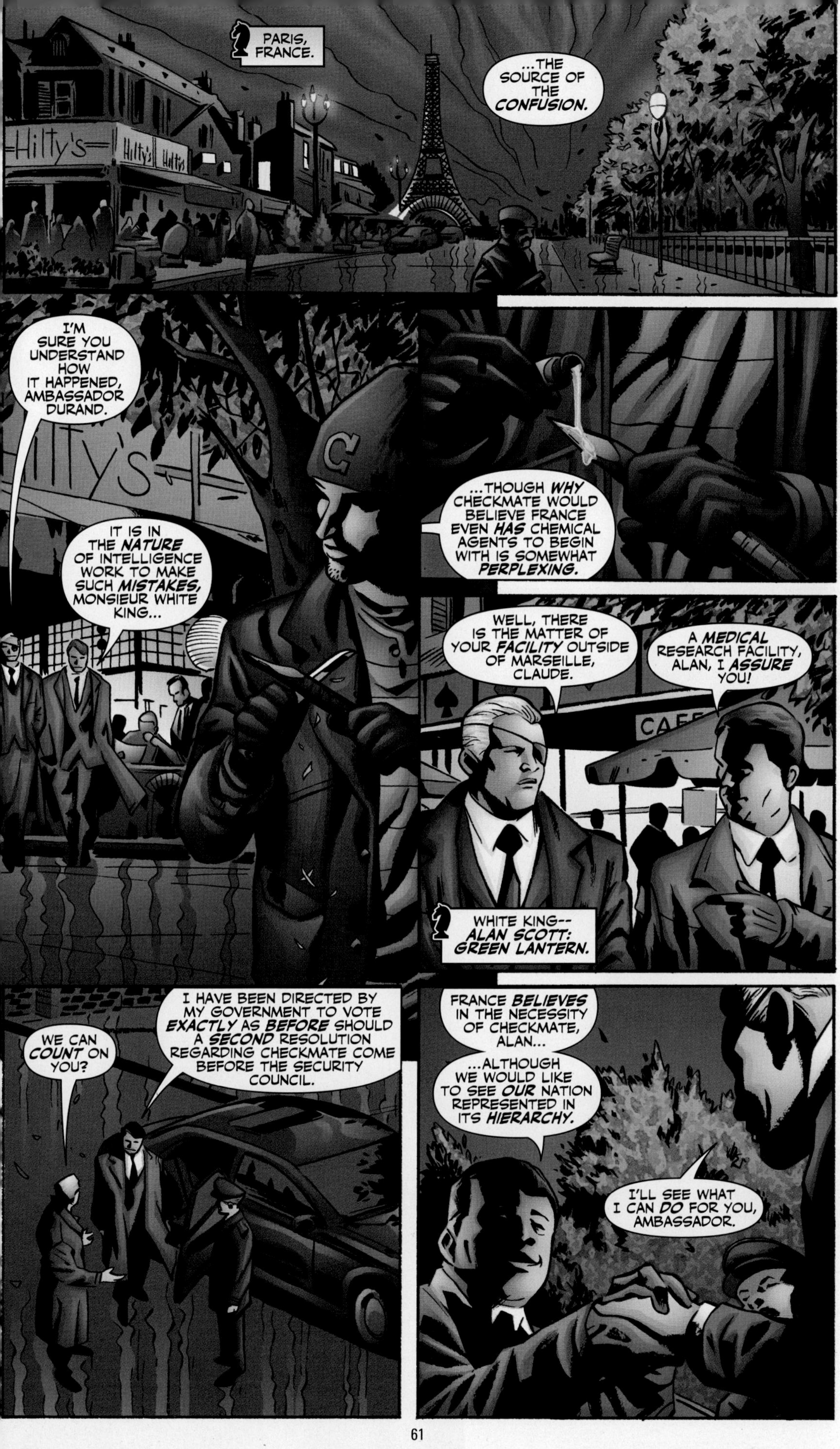
PARIS, FRANCE.
...THE SOURCE OF THE CONFUSION.
Hilty's
I'M SURE YOU UNDERSTAND HOW IT HAPPENED, AMBASSADOR DURAND.
...THOUGH WHY CHECKMATE WOULD BELIEVE FRANCE EVEN HAS CHEMICAL AGENTS TO BEGIN WITH IS SOMEWHAT PERPLEXING.
IT IS IN THE NATURE OF INTELLIGENCE WORK TO MAKE SUCH MISTAKES, MONSIEUR WHITE KING...
WELL, THERE IS THE MATTER OF YOUR FACILITY OUTSIDE OF MARSEILLE, CLAUDE.
A MEDICAL RESEARCH FACILITY, ALAN, I ASSURE YOU!
WHITE KING-- ALAN SCOTT: GREEN LANTERN.
WE CAN COUNT ON YOU?
I HAVE BEEN DIRECTED BY MY GOVERNMENT TO VOTE EXACTLY AS BEFORE SHOULD A SECOND RESOLUTION REGARDING CHECKMATE COME BEFORE THE SECURITY COUNCIL.
FRANCE BELIEVES IN THE NECESSITY OF CHECKMATE, ALAN...
...ALTHOUGH WE WOULD LIKE TO SEE OUR NATION REPRESENTED IN ITS HIERARCHY.
I'LL SEE WHAT I CAN DO FOR YOU, AMBASSADOR.

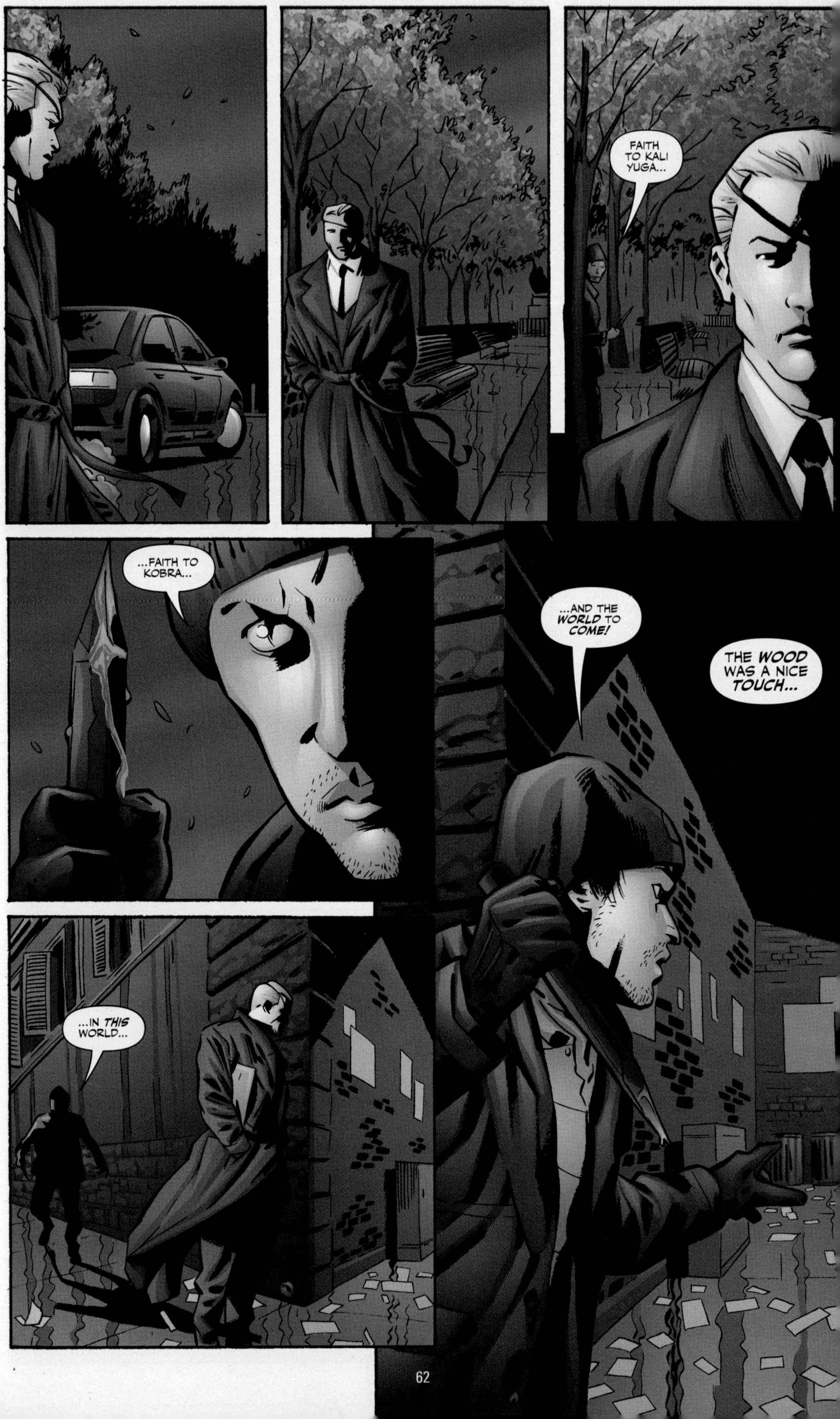
FAITH TO KALI YUGA...
...FAITH TO KOBRA...
...AND THE WORLD TO COME!
THE WOOD WAS A NICE TOUCH...
...IN THIS WORLD...

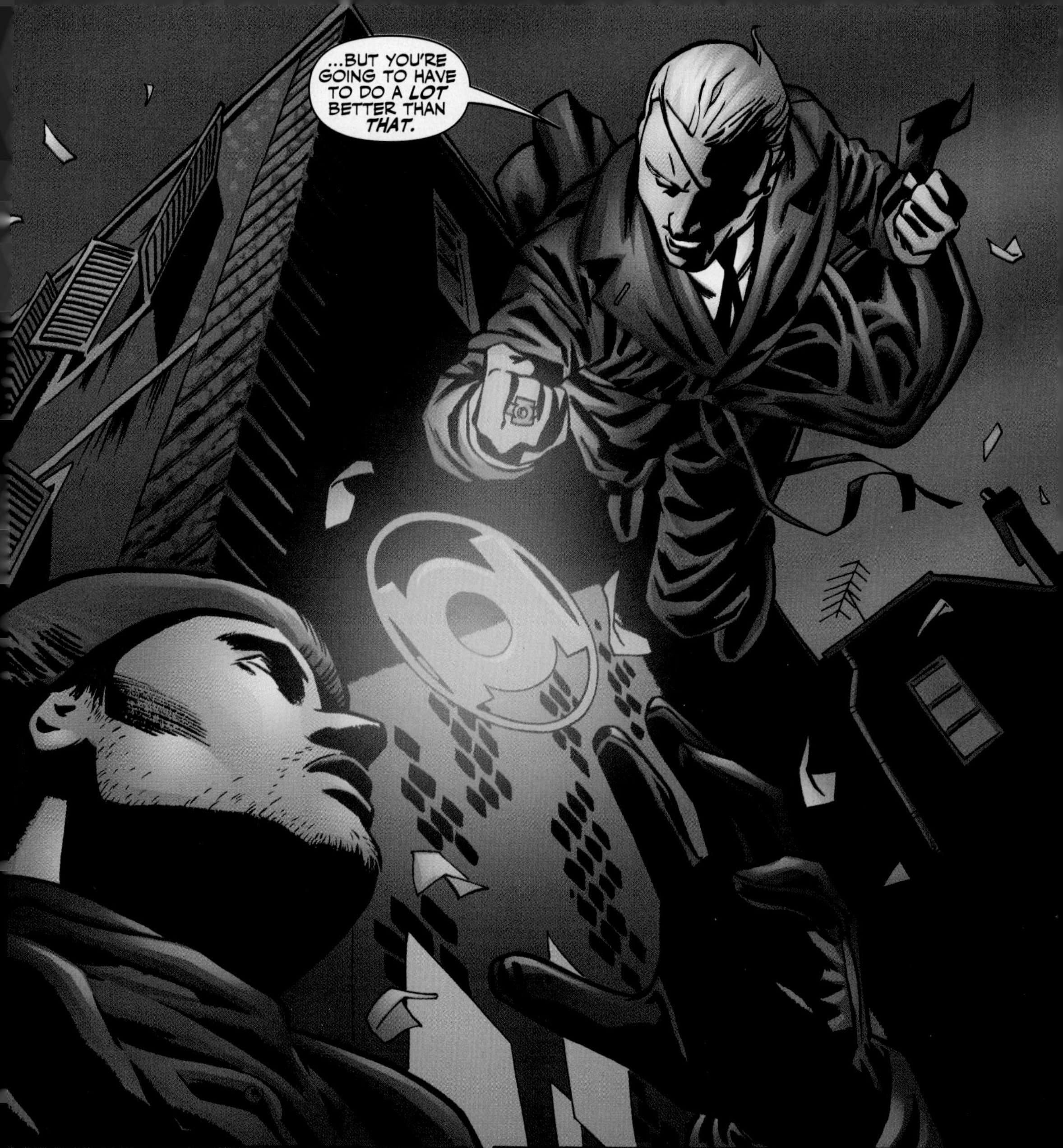
...BUT YOU'RE GOING TO HAVE TO DO A LOT BETTER THAN THAT.

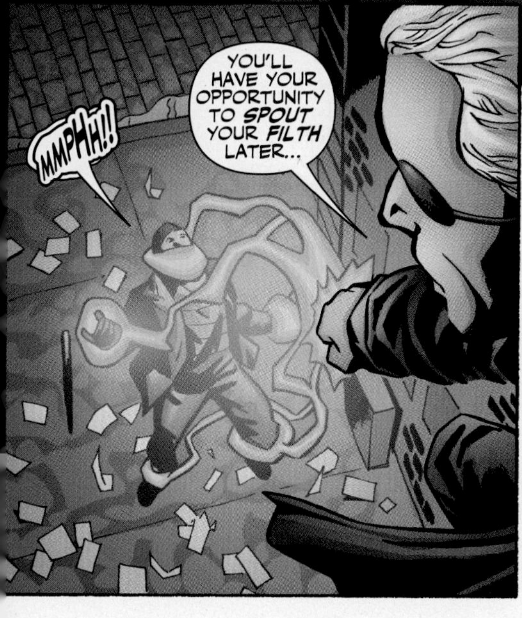
MMPHH!!
YOU'LL HAVE YOUR OPPORTUNITY TO SPOUT YOUR FILTH LATER...

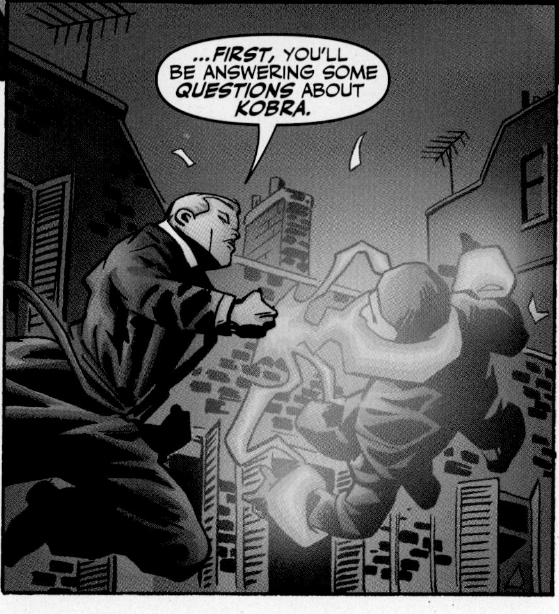
...FIRST, YOU'LL BE ANSWERING SOME QUESTIONS ABOUT KOBRA.

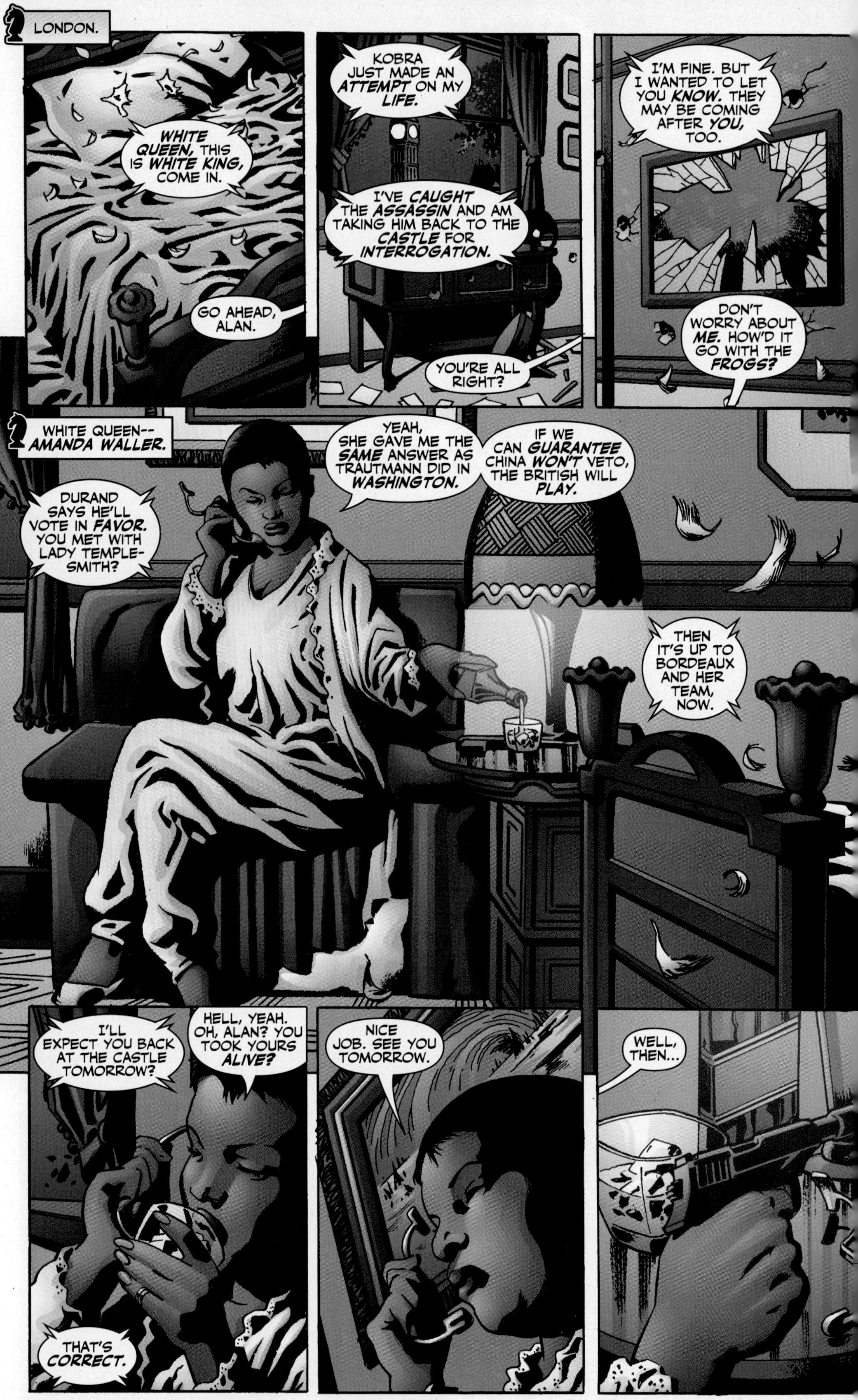
LONDON.
WHITE QUEEN, THIS IS WHITE KING, COME IN.
GO AHEAD, ALAN.
KOBRA JUST MADE AN ATTEMPT ON MY LIFE.
I'VE CAUGHT THE ASSASSIN AND AM TAKING HIM BACK TO THE CASTLE FOR INTERROGATION.
YOU'RE ALL RIGHT?
I'M FINE. BUT I WANTED TO LET YOU KNOW. THEY MAY BE COMING AFTER YOU, TOO.
DON'T WORRY ABOUT ME. HOW'D IT GO WITH THE FROGS?
WHITE QUEEN-- AMANDA WALLER.
DURAND SAYS HE'LL VOTE IN FAVOR. YOU MET WITH LADY TEMPLE-SMITH?
YEAH, SHE GAVE ME THE SAME ANSWER AS TRAUTMANN DID IN WASHINGTON.
IF WE CAN GUARANTEE CHINA WON'T VETO, THE BRITISH WILL PLAY.
THEN IT'S UP TO BORDEAUX AND HER TEAM, NOW.
I'LL EXPECT YOU BACK AT THE CASTLE TOMORROW?
THAT'S CORRECT.
HELL, YEAH. OH, ALAN? YOU TOOK YOURS ALIVE?
NICE JOB. SEE YOU TOMORROW.
WELL, THEN...

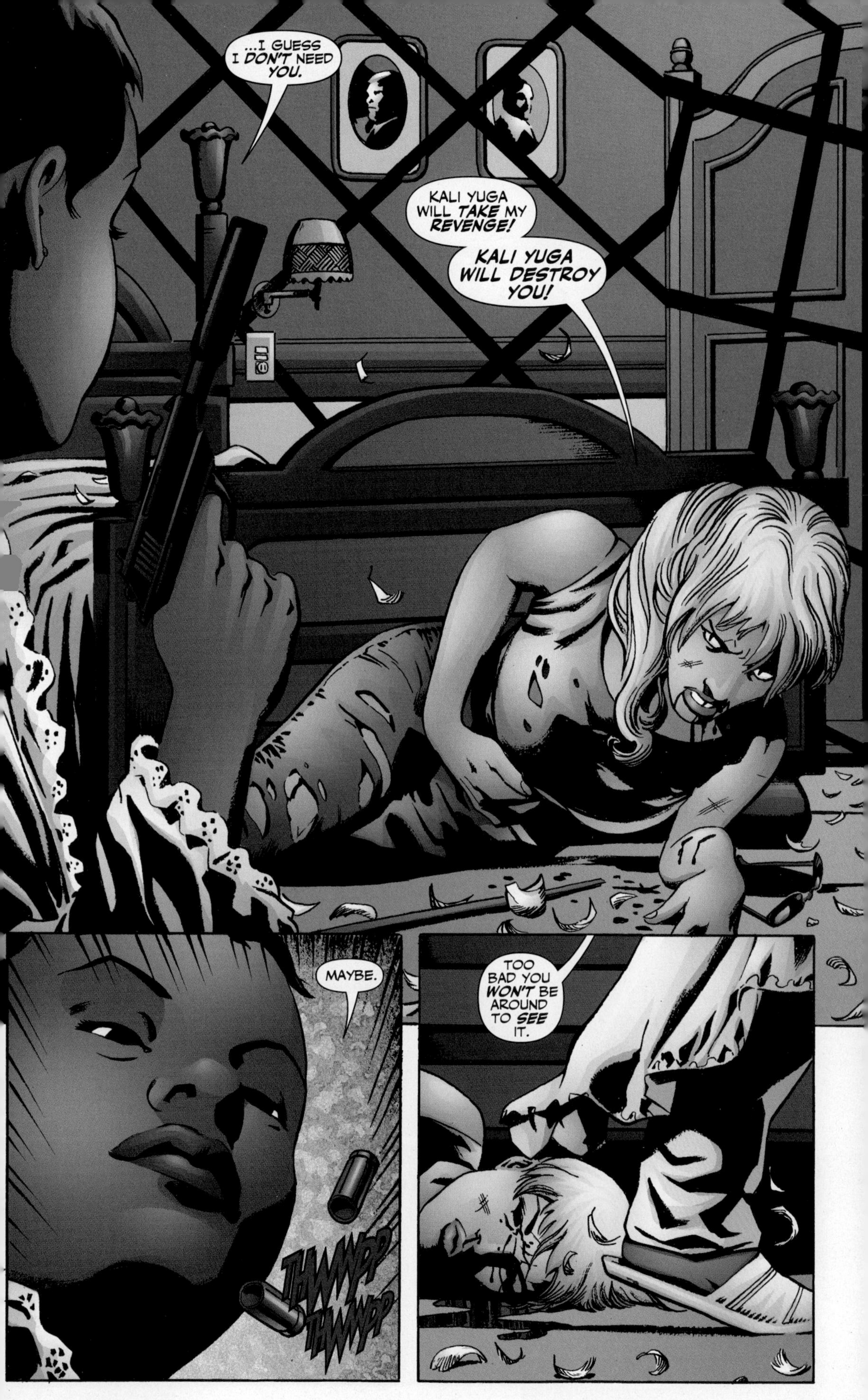
...I GUESS I DON'T NEED YOU.
KALI YUGA WILL TAKE MY REVENGE!
KALI YUGA WILL DESTROY YOU!
MAYBE.
THWIPP THWIPP
TOO BAD YOU WON'T BE AROUND TO SEE IT.

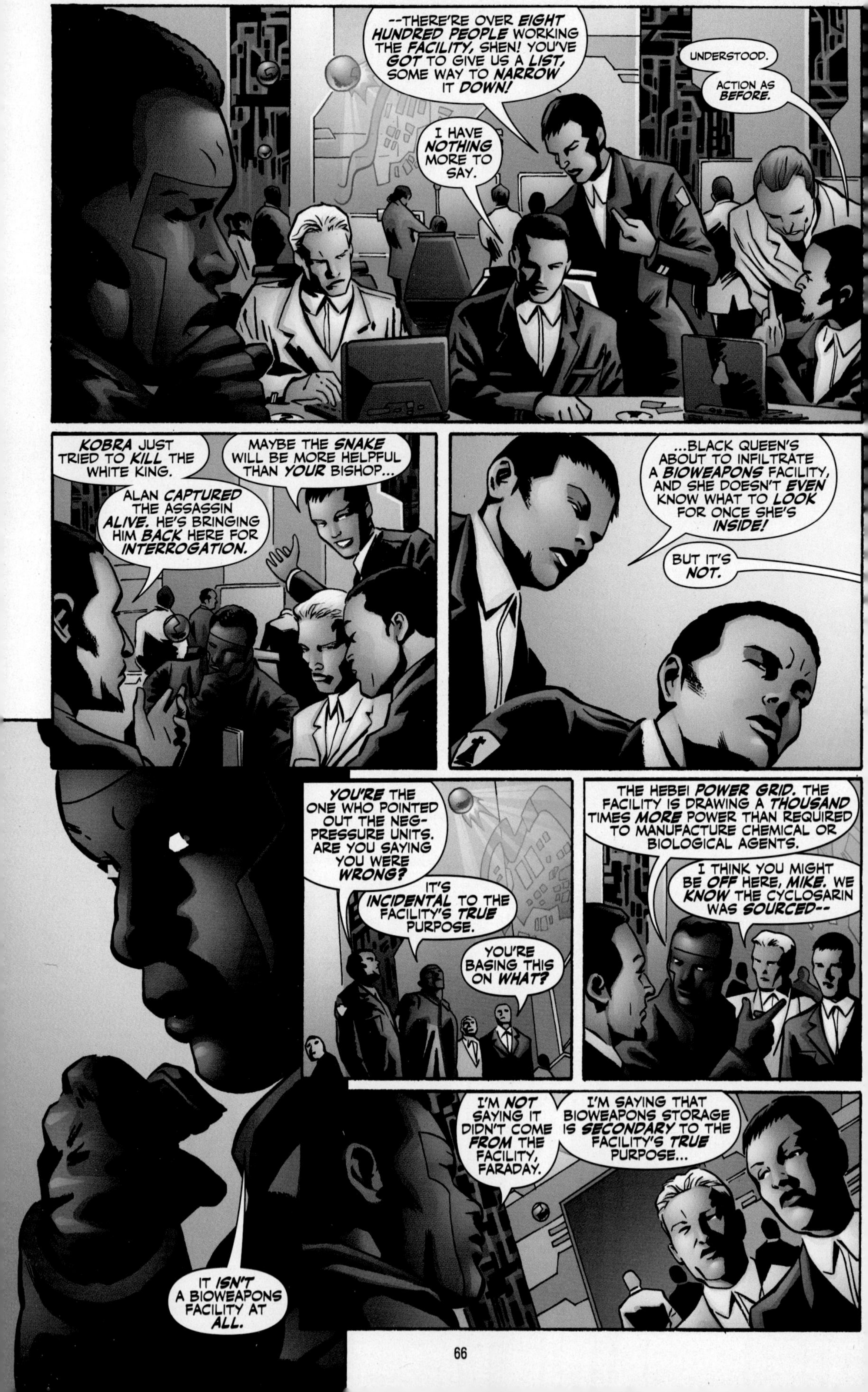
--THERE'RE OVER EIGHT HUNDRED PEOPLE WORKING THE FACILITY, SHEN! YOU'VE GOT TO GIVE US A LIST, SOME WAY TO NARROW IT DOWN!
I HAVE NOTHING MORE TO SAY.
UNDERSTOOD.
ACTION AS BEFORE.
KOBRA JUST TRIED TO KILL THE WHITE KING.
MAYBE THE SNAKE WILL BE MORE HELPFUL THAN YOUR BISHOP...
ALAN CAPTURED THE ASSASSIN ALIVE. HE'S BRINGING HIM BACK HERE FOR INTERROGATION.
...BLACK QUEEN'S ABOUT TO INFILTRATE A BIOWEAPONS FACILITY, AND SHE DOESN'T EVEN KNOW WHAT TO LOOK FOR ONCE SHE'S INSIDE!
BUT IT'S NOT.
YOU'RE THE ONE WHO POINTED OUT THE NEG-PRESSURE UNITS. ARE YOU SAYING YOU WERE WRONG?
IT'S INCIDENTAL TO THE FACILITY'S TRUE PURPOSE.
YOU'RE BASING THIS ON WHAT?
THE HEBEI POWER GRID. THE FACILITY IS DRAWING A THOUSAND TIMES MORE POWER THAN REQUIRED TO MANUFACTURE CHEMICAL OR BIOLOGICAL AGENTS.
I THINK YOU MIGHT BE OFF HERE, MIKE. WE KNOW THE CYCLOSARIN WAS SOURCED--
I'M NOT SAYING IT DIDN'T COME FROM THE FACILITY, FARADAY.
I'M SAYING THAT BIOWEAPONS STORAGE IS SECONDARY TO THE FACILITY'S TRUE PURPOSE...
IT ISN'T A BIOWEAPONS FACILITY AT ALL.

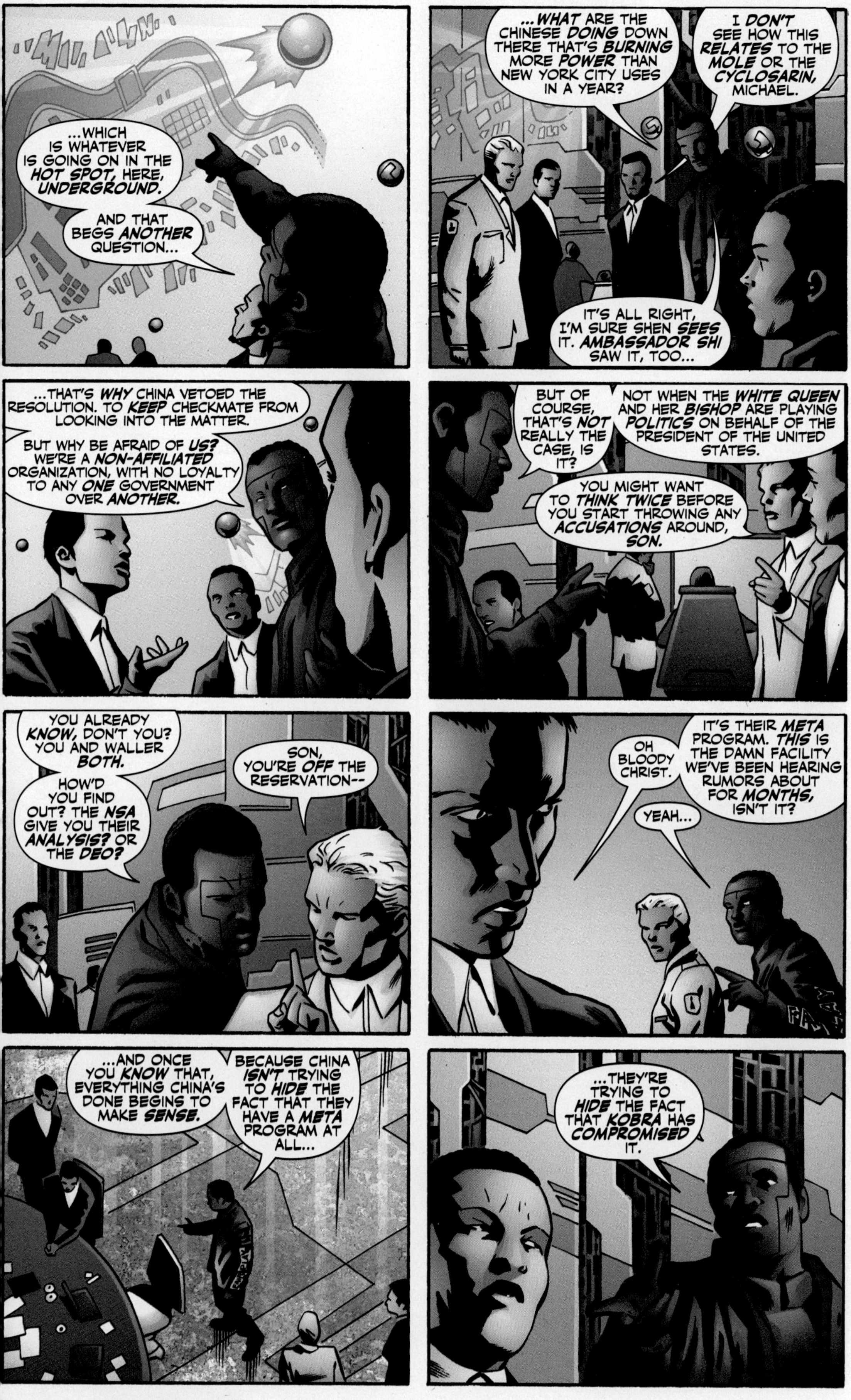

...WHICH IS WHATEVER IS GOING ON IN THE HOT SPOT, HERE, UNDERGROUND.
AND THAT BEGS ANOTHER QUESTION...
...WHAT ARE THE CHINESE DOING DOWN THERE THAT'S BURNING MORE POWER THAN NEW YORK CITY USES IN A YEAR?
I DON'T SEE HOW THIS RELATES TO THE MOLE OR THE CYCLOSARIN, MICHAEL.
IT'S ALL RIGHT, I'M SURE SHEN SEES IT. AMBASSADOR SHI SAW IT, TOO...
...THAT'S WHY CHINA VETOED THE RESOLUTION. TO KEEP CHECKMATE FROM LOOKING INTO THE MATTER.
BUT WHY BE AFRAID OF US? WE'RE A NON-AFFILIATED ORGANIZATION, WITH NO LOYALTY TO ANY ONE GOVERNMENT OVER ANOTHER.
BUT OF COURSE, THAT'S NOT REALLY THE CASE, IS IT?
NOT WHEN THE WHITE QUEEN AND HER BISHOP ARE PLAYING POLITICS ON BEHALF OF THE PRESIDENT OF THE UNITED STATES.
YOU MIGHT WANT TO THINK TWICE BEFORE YOU START THROWING ANY ACCUSATIONS AROUND, SON.
YOU ALREADY KNOW, DON'T YOU? YOU AND WALLER BOTH.
HOW'D YOU FIND OUT? THE NSA GIVE YOU THEIR ANALYSIS? OR THE DEO?
SON, YOU'RE OFF THE RESERVATION--
OH BLOODY CHRIST.
IT'S THEIR META PROGRAM. THIS IS THE DAMN FACILITY WE'VE BEEN HEARING RUMORS ABOUT FOR MONTHS, ISN'T IT?
YEAH...
...AND ONCE YOU KNOW THAT, EVERYTHING CHINA'S DONE BEGINS TO MAKE SENSE.
BECAUSE CHINA ISN'T TRYING TO HIDE THE FACT THAT THEY HAVE A META PROGRAM AT ALL...
...THEY'RE TRYING TO HIDE THE FACT THAT KOBRA HAS COMPROMISED IT.

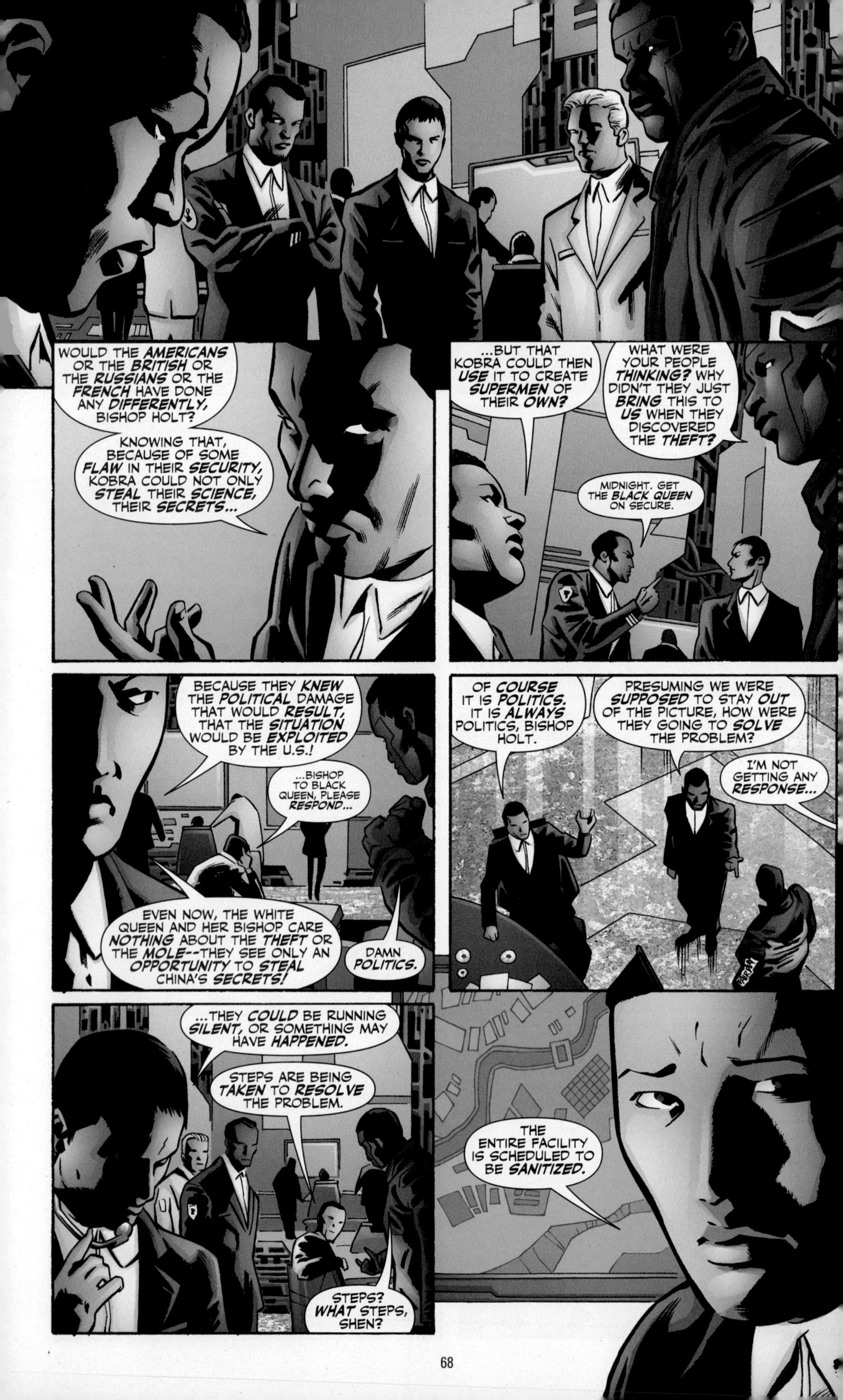

WOULD THE AMERICANS OR THE BRITISH OR THE RUSSIANS OR THE FRENCH HAVE DONE ANY DIFFERENTLY, BISHOP HOLT?
KNOWING THAT, BECAUSE OF SOME FLAW IN THEIR SECURITY, KOBRA COULD NOT ONLY STEAL THEIR SCIENCE, THEIR SECRETS...
...BUT THAT KOBRA COULD THEN USE IT TO CREATE SUPERMEN OF THEIR OWN?
WHAT WERE YOUR PEOPLE THINKING? WHY DIDN'T THEY JUST BRING THIS TO US WHEN THEY DISCOVERED THE THEFT?
MIDNIGHT. GET THE BLACK QUEEN ON SECURE.
BECAUSE THEY KNEW THE POLITICAL DAMAGE THAT WOULD RESULT, THAT THE SITUATION WOULD BE EXPLOITED BY THE U.S.!
...BISHOP TO BLACK QUEEN, PLEASE RESPOND...
EVEN NOW, THE WHITE QUEEN AND HER BISHOP CARE NOTHING ABOUT THE THEFT OR THE MOLE--THEY SEE ONLY AN OPPORTUNITY TO STEAL CHINA'S SECRETS!
DAMN POLITICS.
OF COURSE IT IS POLITICS. IT IS ALWAYS POLITICS, BISHOP HOLT.
PRESUMING WE WERE SUPPOSED TO STAY OUT OF THE PICTURE, HOW WERE THEY GOING TO SOLVE THE PROBLEM?
I'M NOT GETTING ANY RESPONSE...
...THEY COULD BE RUNNING SILENT, OR SOMETHING MAY HAVE HAPPENED.
STEPS ARE BEING TAKEN TO RESOLVE THE PROBLEM.
STEPS? WHAT STEPS, SHEN?
THE ENTIRE FACILITY IS SCHEDULED TO BE SANITIZED.

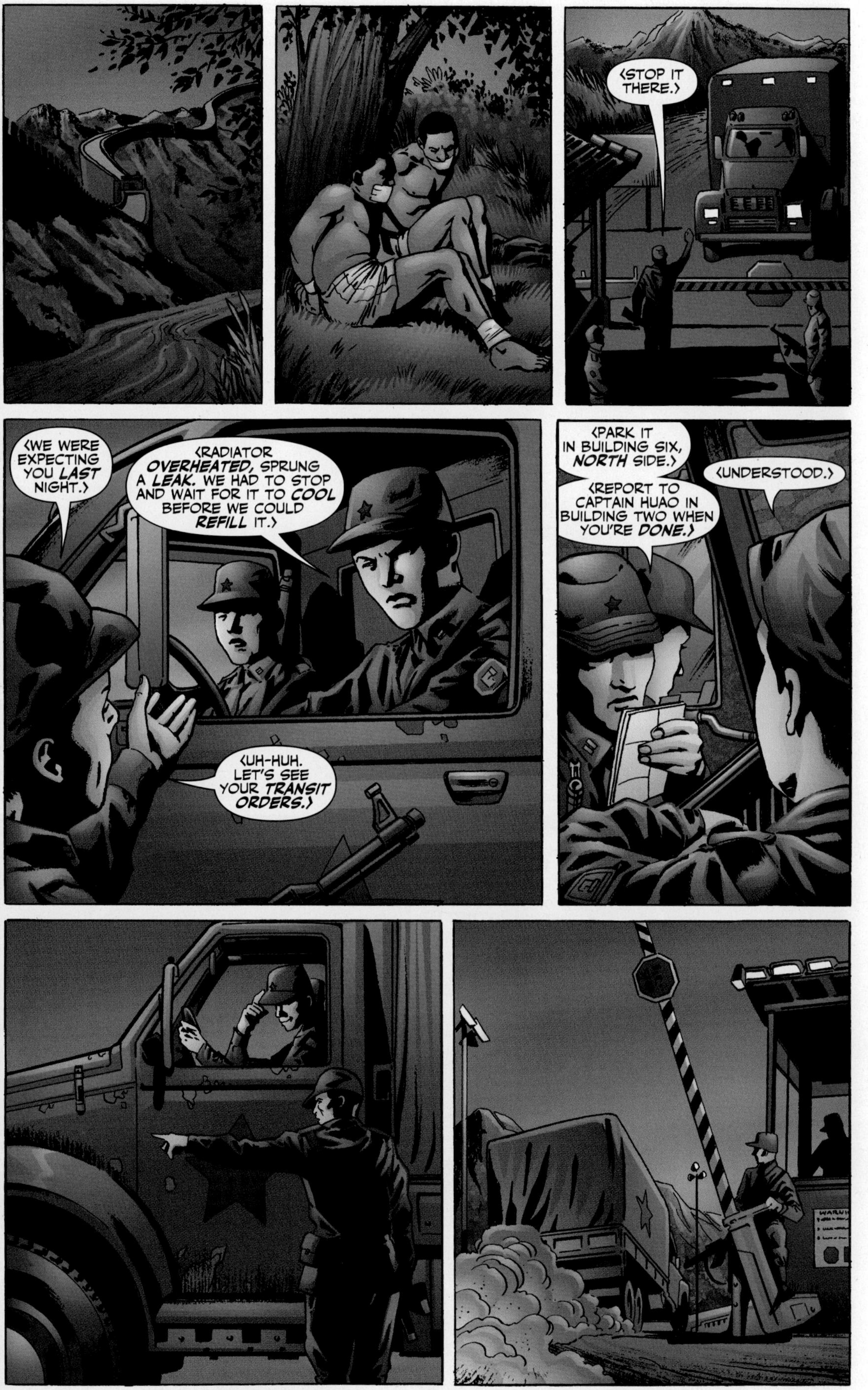

<STOP IT THERE.>
<WE WERE EXPECTING YOU *LAST* NIGHT.>
<RADIATOR *OVERHEATED,* SPRUNG A *LEAK.* WE HAD TO STOP AND WAIT FOR IT TO *COOL* BEFORE WE COULD *REFILL* IT.>
<UH-HUH. LET'S SEE YOUR *TRANSIT ORDERS.*>
<PARK IT IN BUILDING SIX, *NORTH* SIDE.>
<REPORT TO CAPTAIN HUAO IN BUILDING TWO WHEN YOU'RE *DONE.*>
<UNDERSTOOD.>

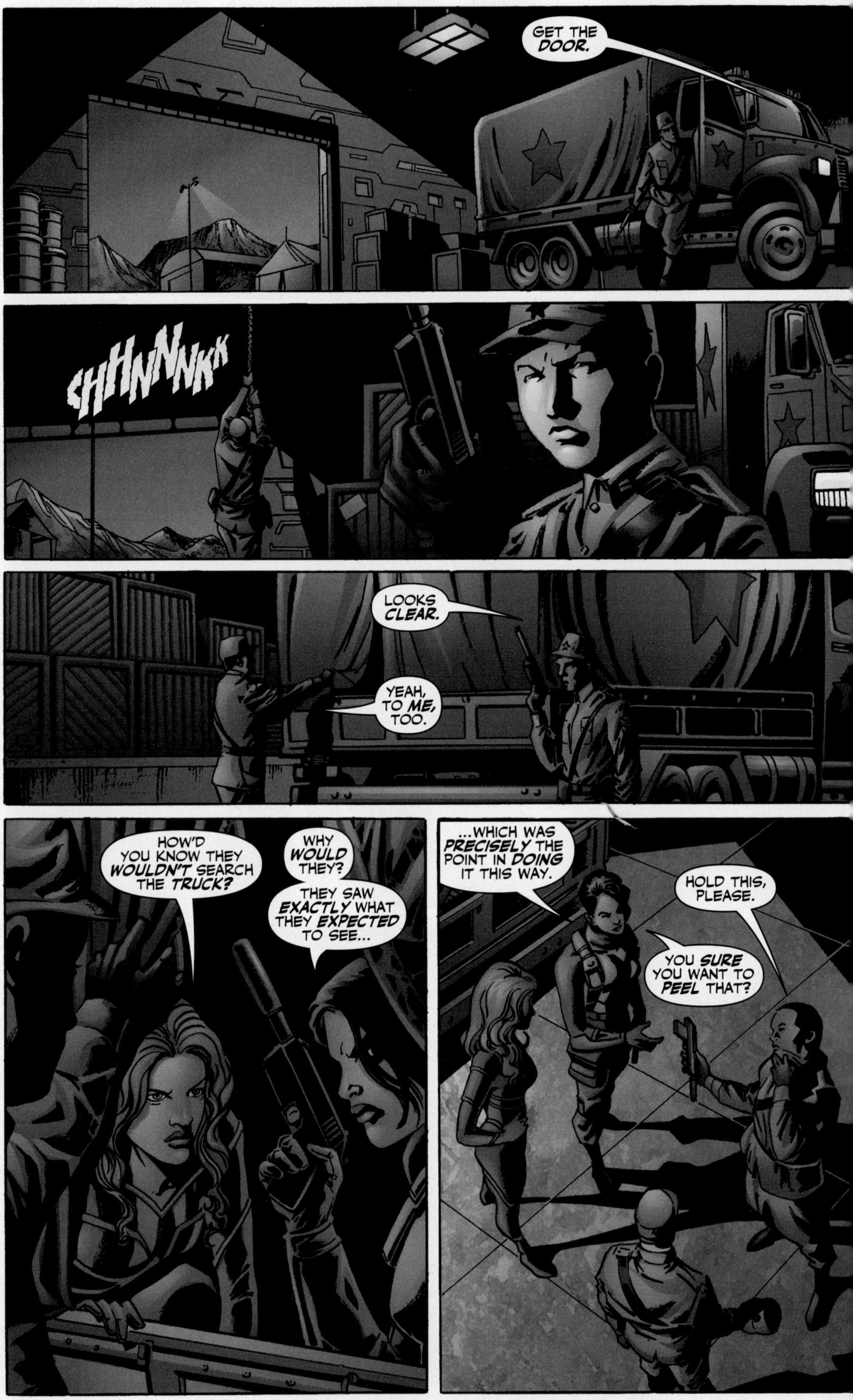

GET THE DOOR.
CHHNNNKK
LOOKS CLEAR.
YEAH, TO ME, TOO.
HOW'D YOU KNOW THEY WOULDN'T SEARCH THE TRUCK?
WHY WOULD THEY?
THEY SAW EXACTLY WHAT THEY EXPECTED TO SEE...
...WHICH WAS PRECISELY THE POINT IN DOING IT THIS WAY.
HOLD THIS, PLEASE.
YOU SURE YOU WANT TO PEEL THAT?

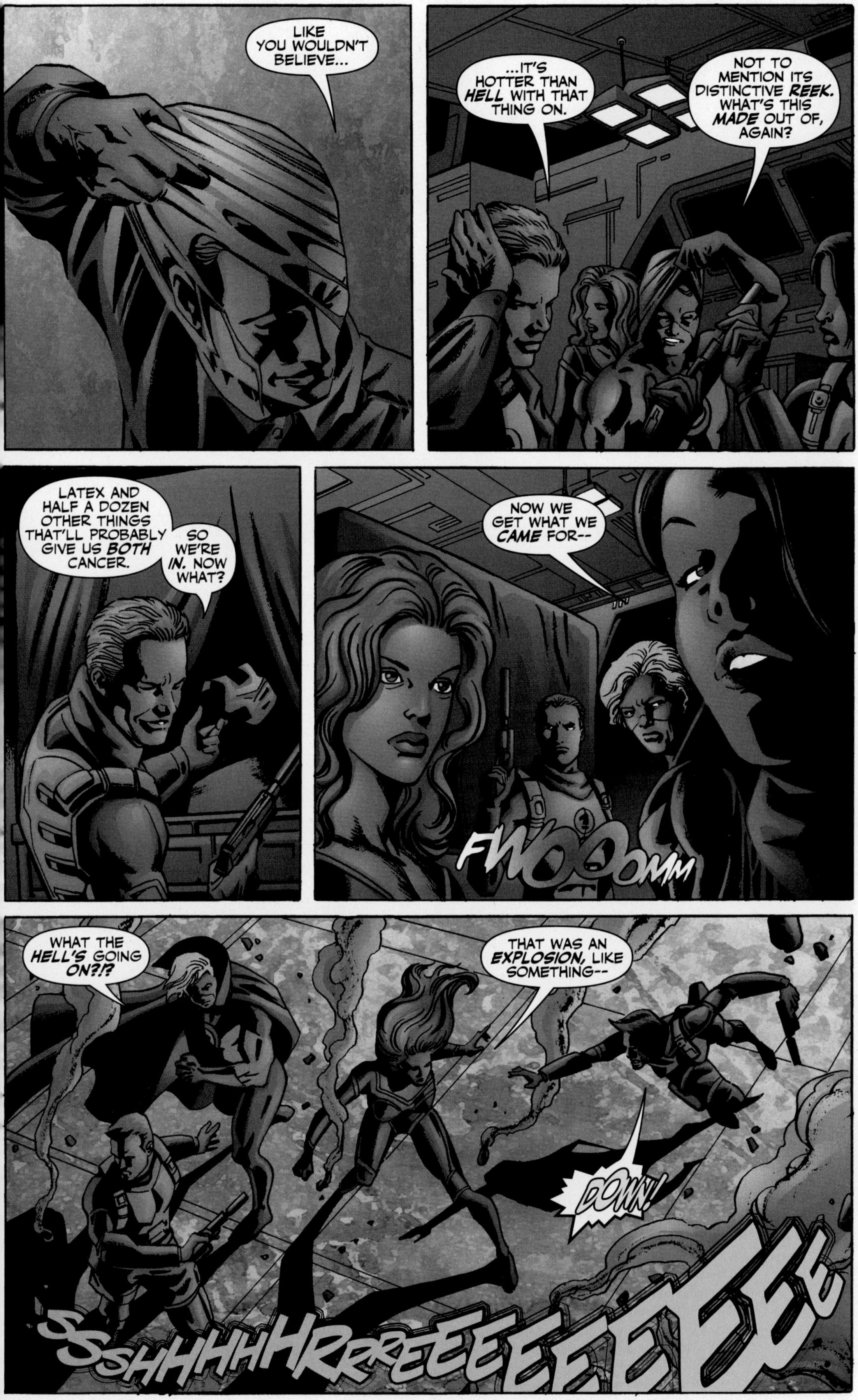
LIKE YOU WOULDN'T BELIEVE...
...IT'S HOTTER THAN HELL WITH THAT THING ON.
NOT TO MENTION ITS DISTINCTIVE REEK. WHAT'S THIS MADE OUT OF, AGAIN?
LATEX AND HALF A DOZEN OTHER THINGS THAT'LL PROBABLY GIVE US BOTH CANCER.
SO WE'RE IN. NOW WHAT?
NOW WE GET WHAT WE CAME FOR--
FWOOOOMM
WHAT THE HELL'S GOING ON?!?
THAT WAS AN EXPLOSION, LIKE SOMETHING--
DOWN!
SSSHHHHHRRRREEEEEEEEEEEE

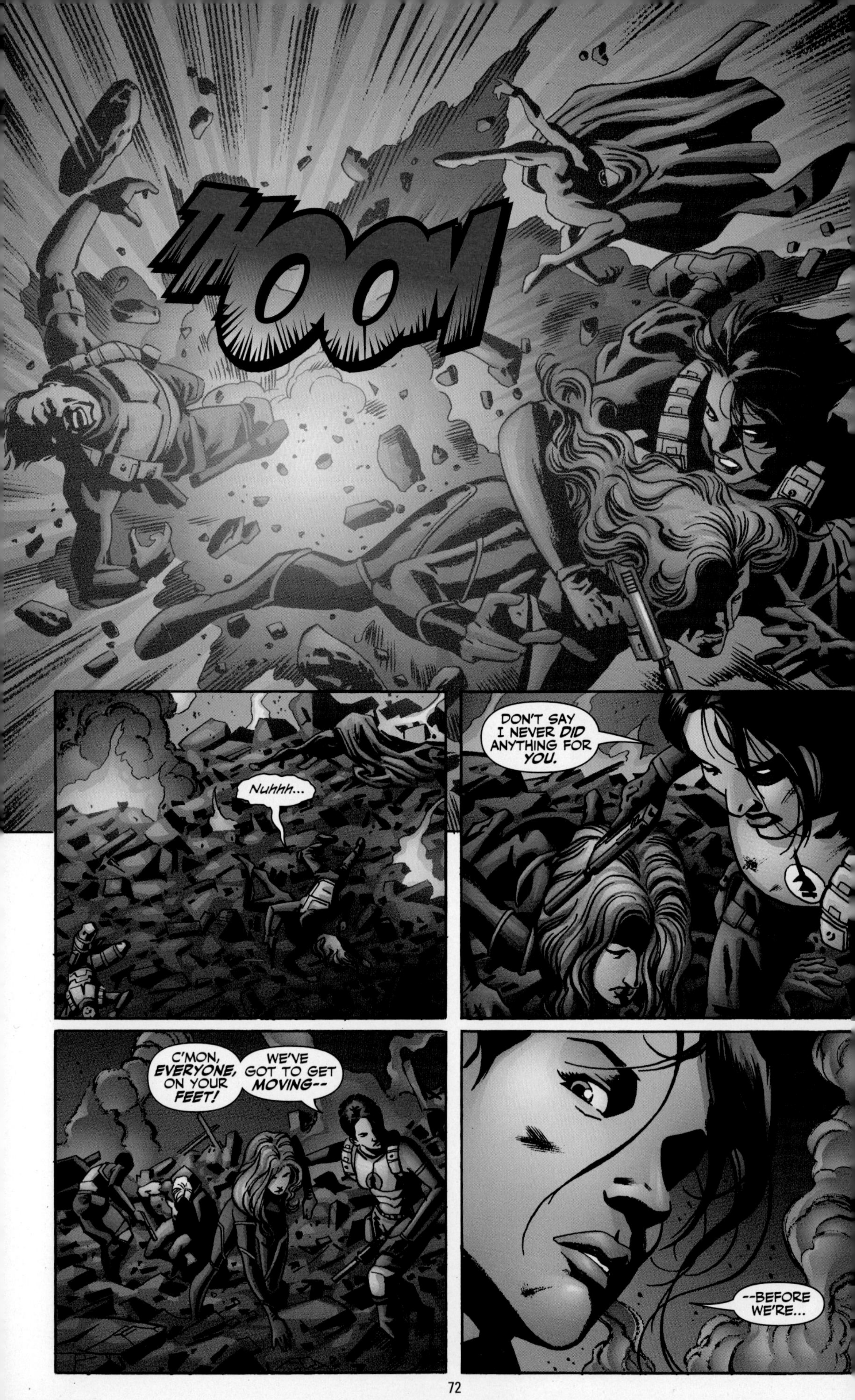
THOOM
Nuhhh...
DON'T SAY I NEVER DID ANYTHING FOR YOU.
C'MON, EVERYONE, ON YOUR FEET!
WE'VE GOT TO GET MOVING--
--BEFORE WE'RE...

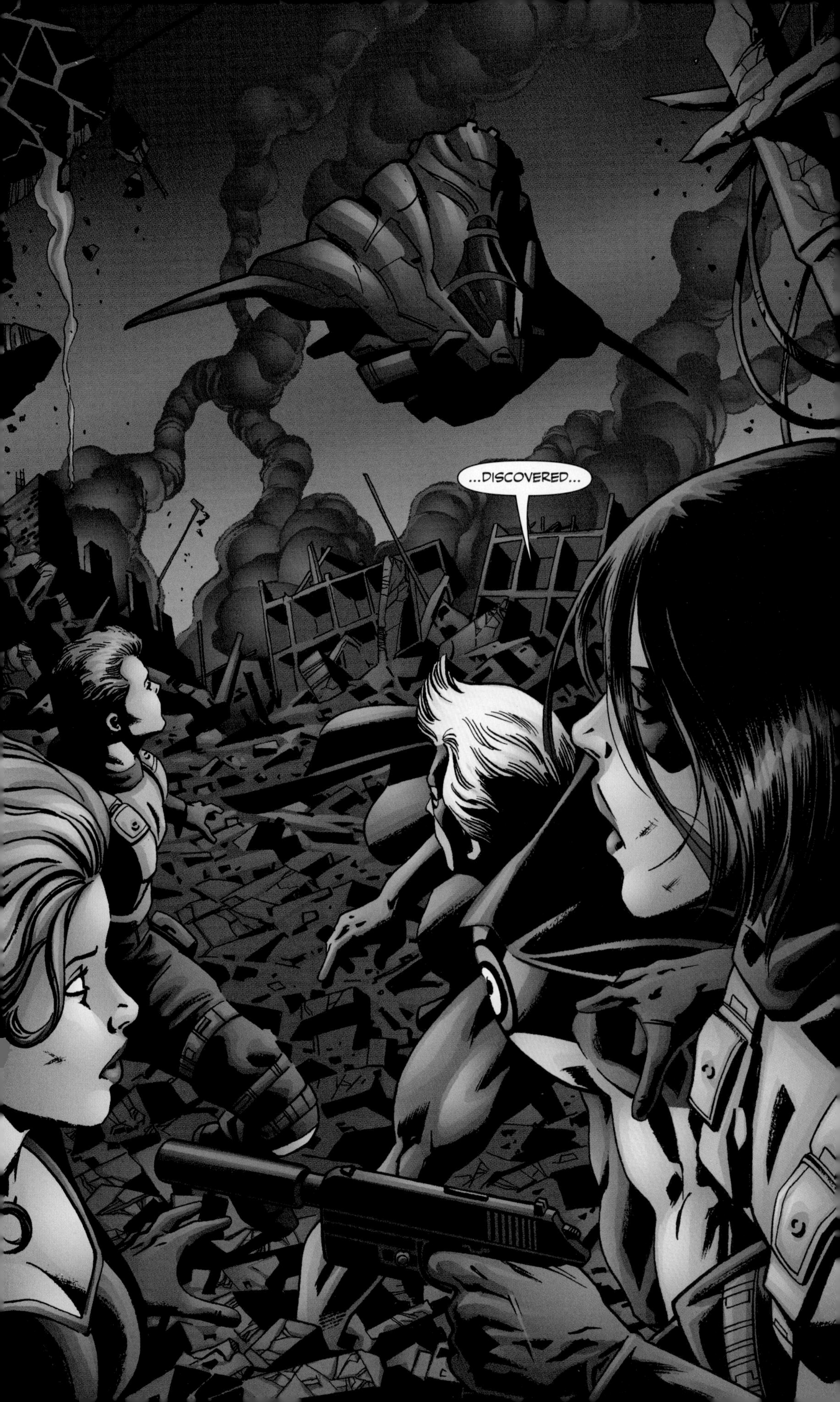
...DISCOVERED...

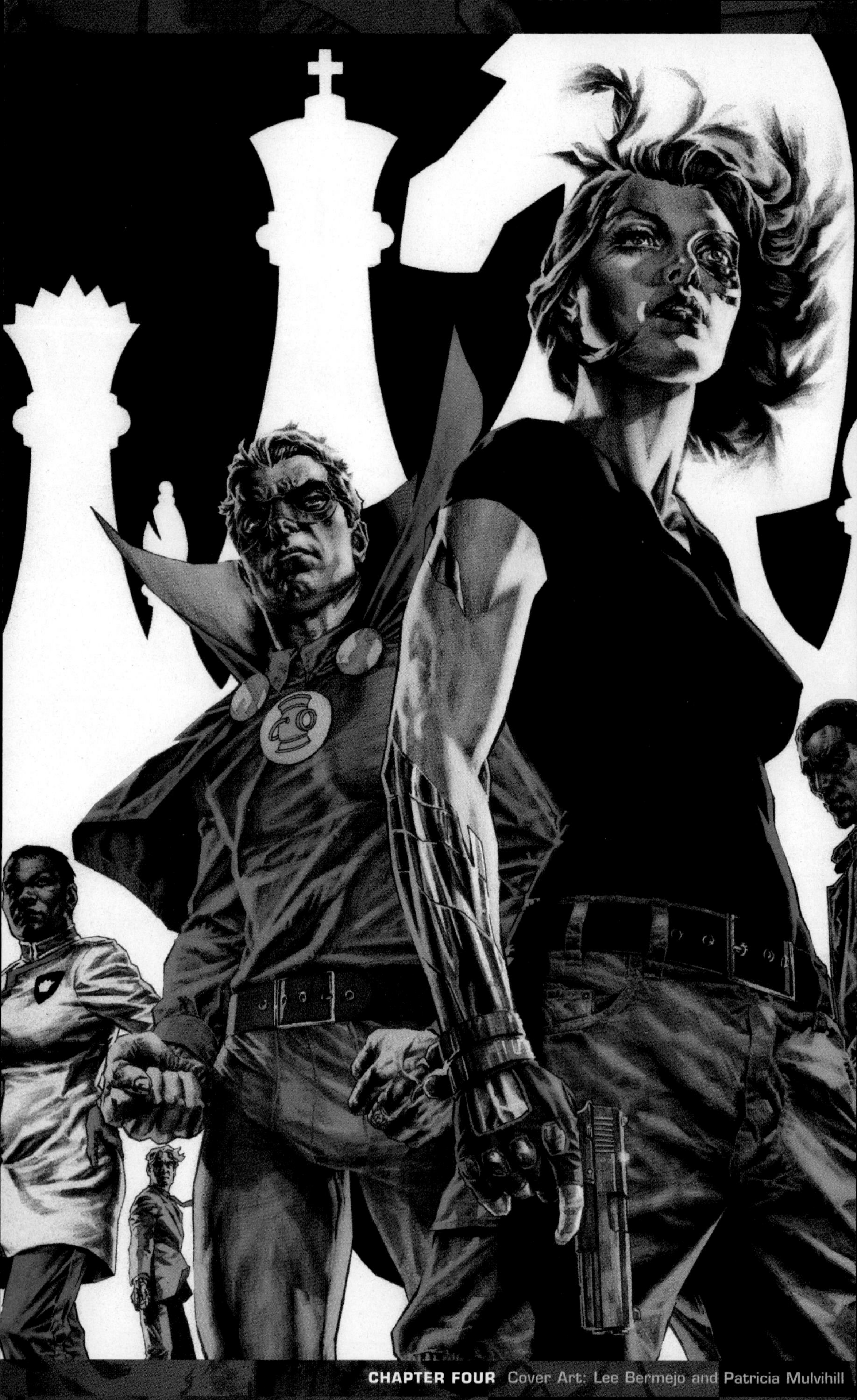

CHAPTER FOUR Cover Art: Lee Bermejo and Patricia Mulvihill

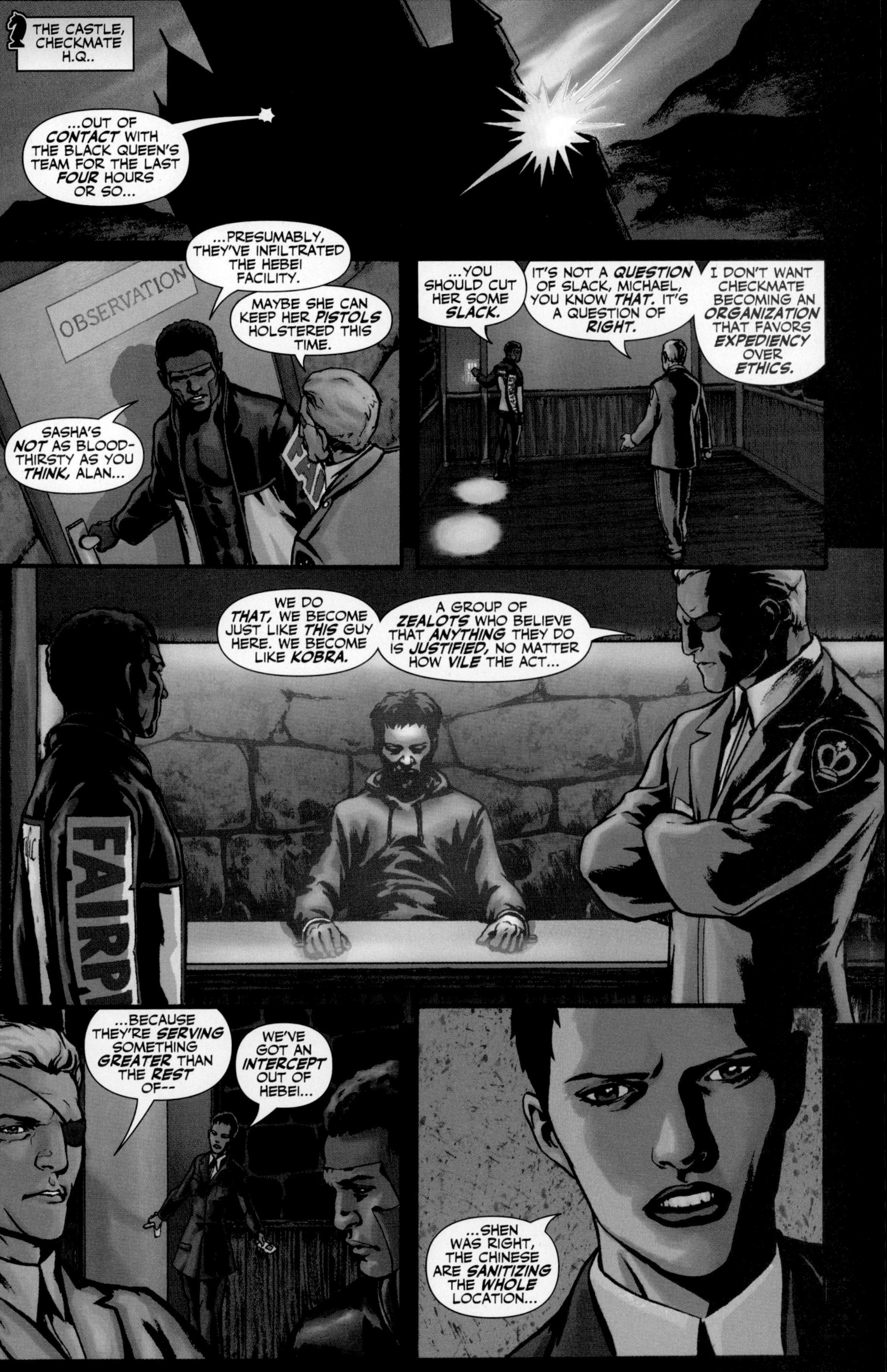
THE CASTLE, CHECKMATE H.Q..
...OUT OF CONTACT WITH THE BLACK QUEEN'S TEAM FOR THE LAST FOUR HOURS OR SO...
...PRESUMABLY, THEY'VE INFILTRATED THE HEBEI FACILITY.
MAYBE SHE CAN KEEP HER PISTOLS HOLSTERED THIS TIME.
OBSERVATION
SASHA'S NOT AS BLOOD-THIRSTY AS YOU THINK, ALAN...
...YOU SHOULD CUT HER SOME SLACK.
IT'S NOT A QUESTION OF SLACK, MICHAEL, YOU KNOW THAT. IT'S A QUESTION OF RIGHT.
I DON'T WANT CHECKMATE BECOMING AN ORGANIZATION THAT FAVORS EXPEDIENCY OVER ETHICS.
WE DO THAT, WE BECOME JUST LIKE THIS GUY HERE. WE BECOME LIKE KOBRA.
A GROUP OF ZEALOTS WHO BELIEVE THAT ANYTHING THEY DO IS JUSTIFIED, NO MATTER HOW VILE THE ACT...
...BECAUSE THEY'RE SERVING SOMETHING GREATER THAN THE REST OF--
WE'VE GOT AN INTERCEPT OUT OF HEBEI...
...SHEN WAS RIGHT, THE CHINESE ARE SANITIZING THE WHOLE LOCATION...

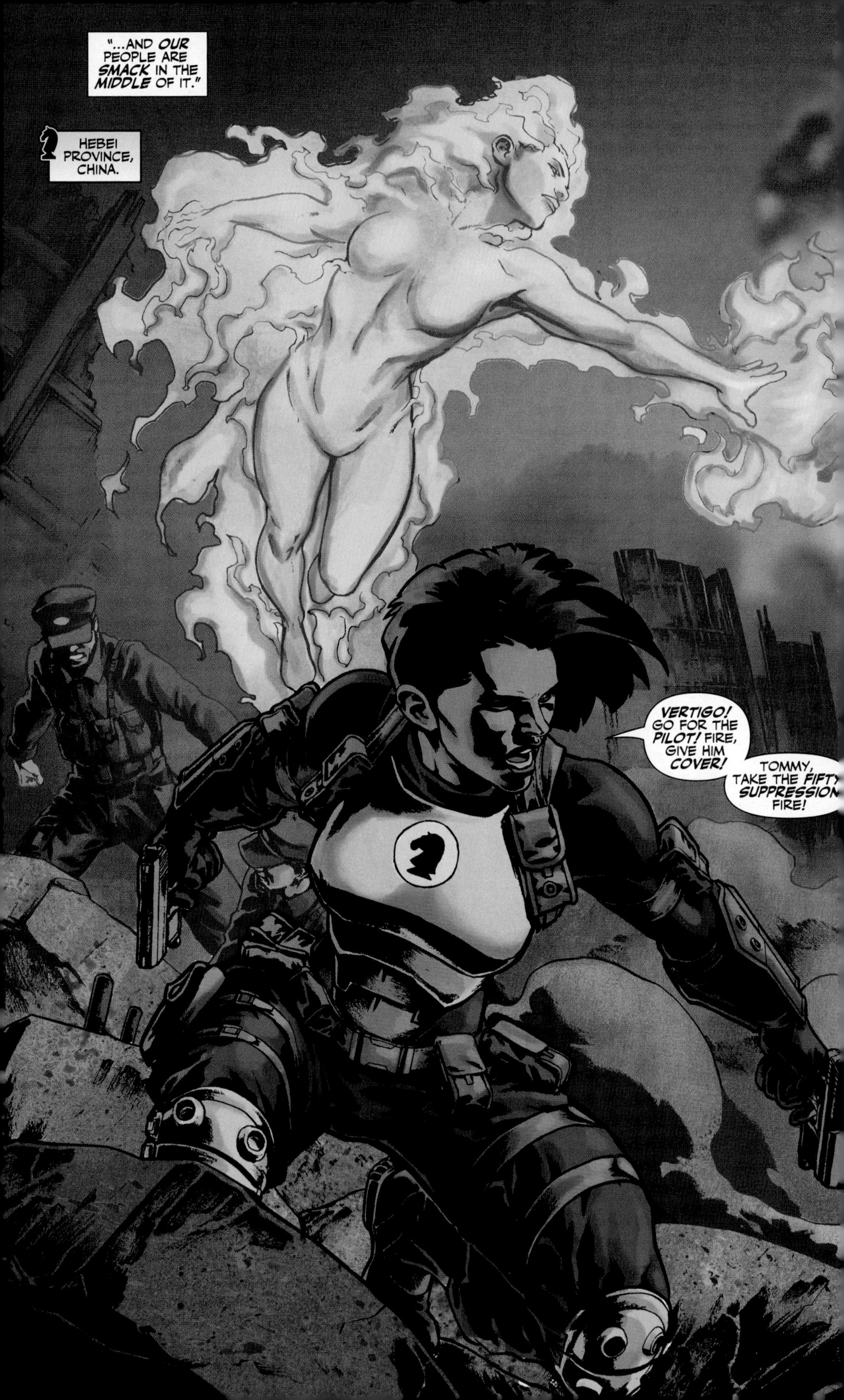
"...AND OUR PEOPLE ARE SMACK IN THE MIDDLE OF IT."
HEBEI PROVINCE, CHINA.
VERTIGO! GO FOR THE PILOT! FIRE, GIVE HIM COVER!
TOMMY, TAKE THE FIFTY SUPPRESSION FIRE!

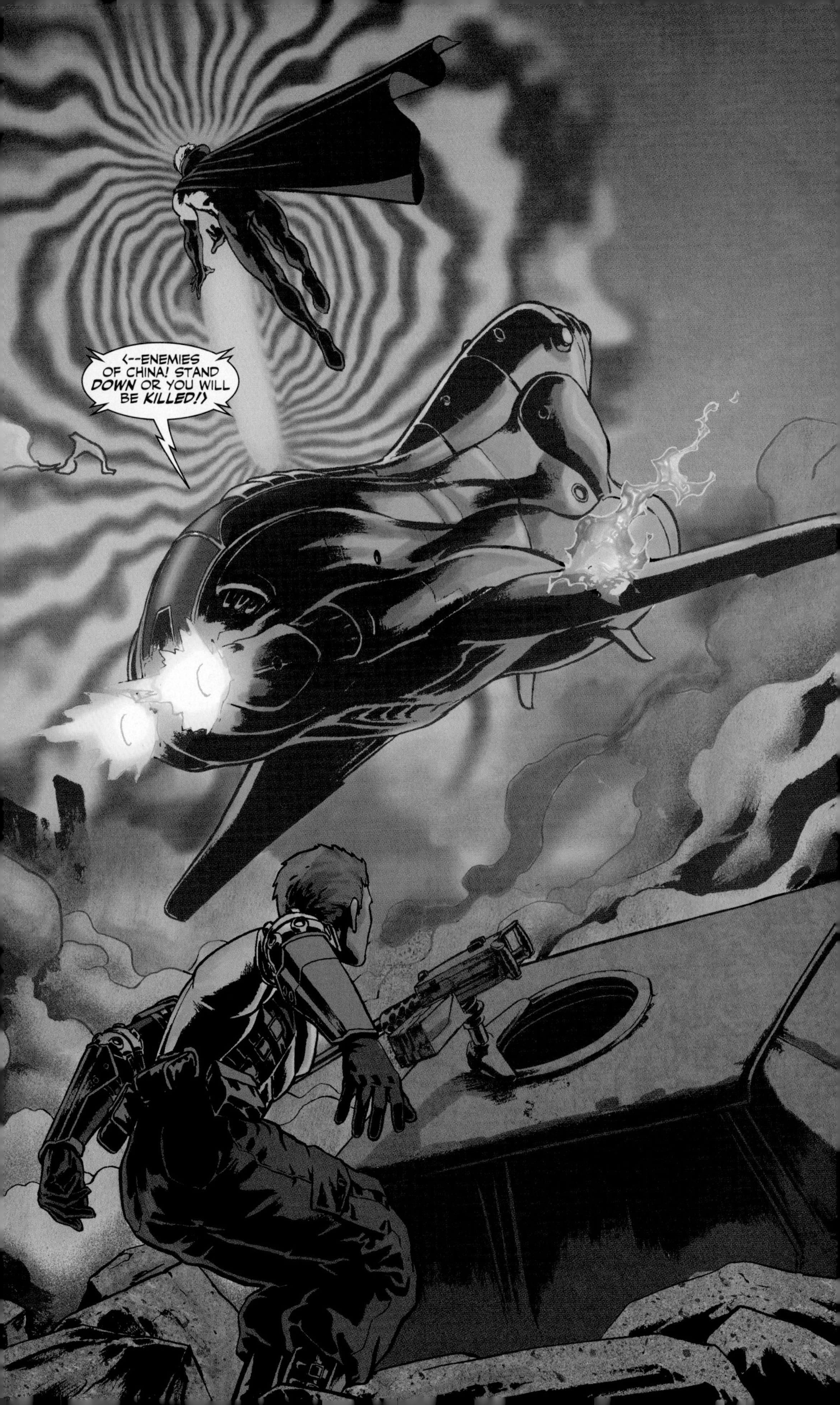

<--ENEMIES OF CHINA! STAND DOWN OR YOU WILL BE KILLED!>

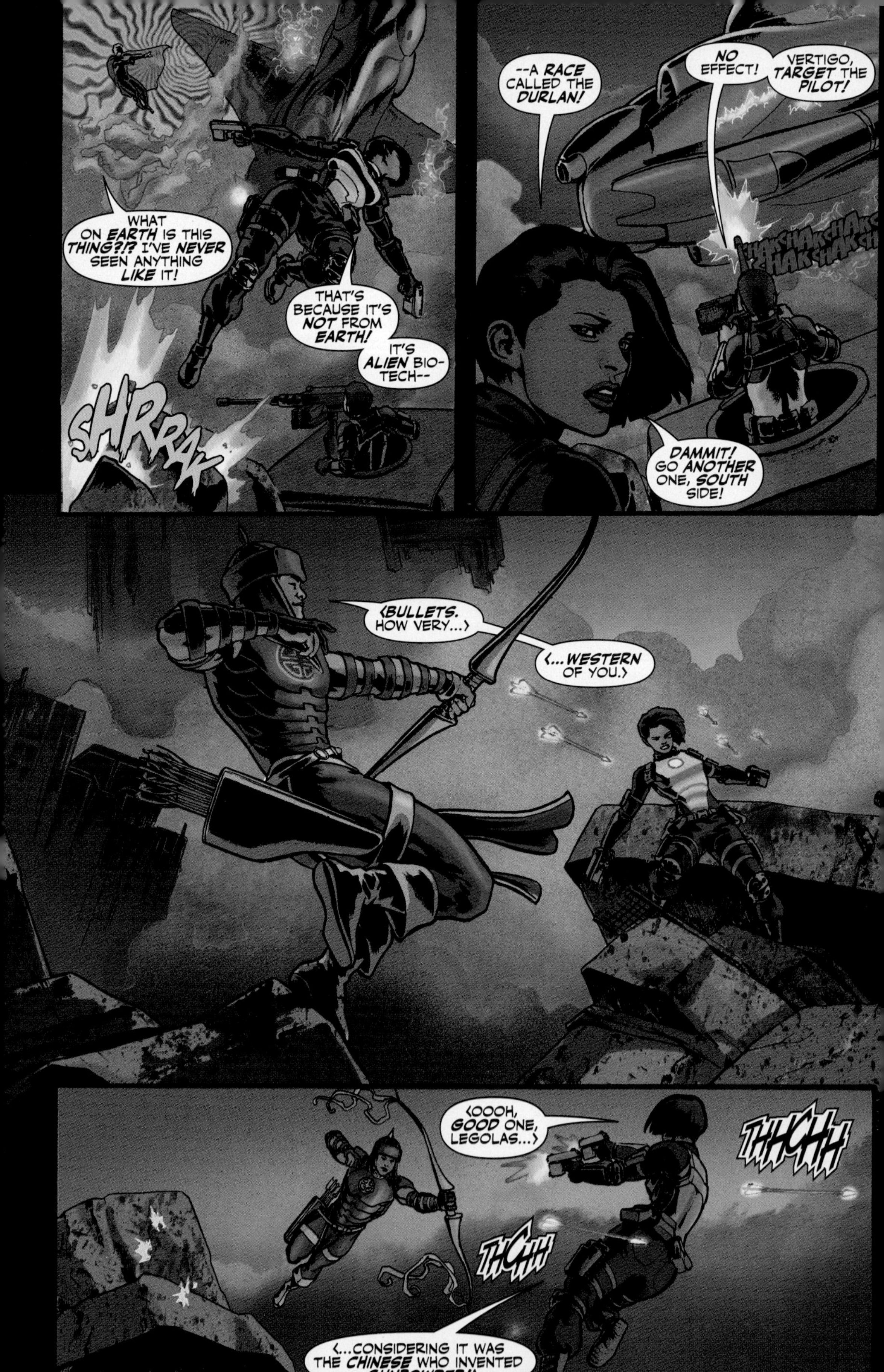
WHAT ON EARTH IS THIS THING?!? I'VE NEVER SEEN ANYTHING LIKE IT!
THAT'S BECAUSE IT'S NOT FROM EARTH!
IT'S ALIEN BIO-TECH--
SHRRAK
--A RACE CALLED THE DURLAN!
NO EFFECT!
VERTIGO, TARGET THE PILOT!
DAMMIT! GO ANOTHER ONE, SOUTH SIDE!
‹BULLETS. HOW VERY...›
‹...WESTERN OF YOU.›
‹OOOH, GOOD ONE, LEGOLAS...›
THHCHH
THCHH
‹...CONSIDERING IT WAS THE CHINESE WHO INVENTED GUNPOWDER!›

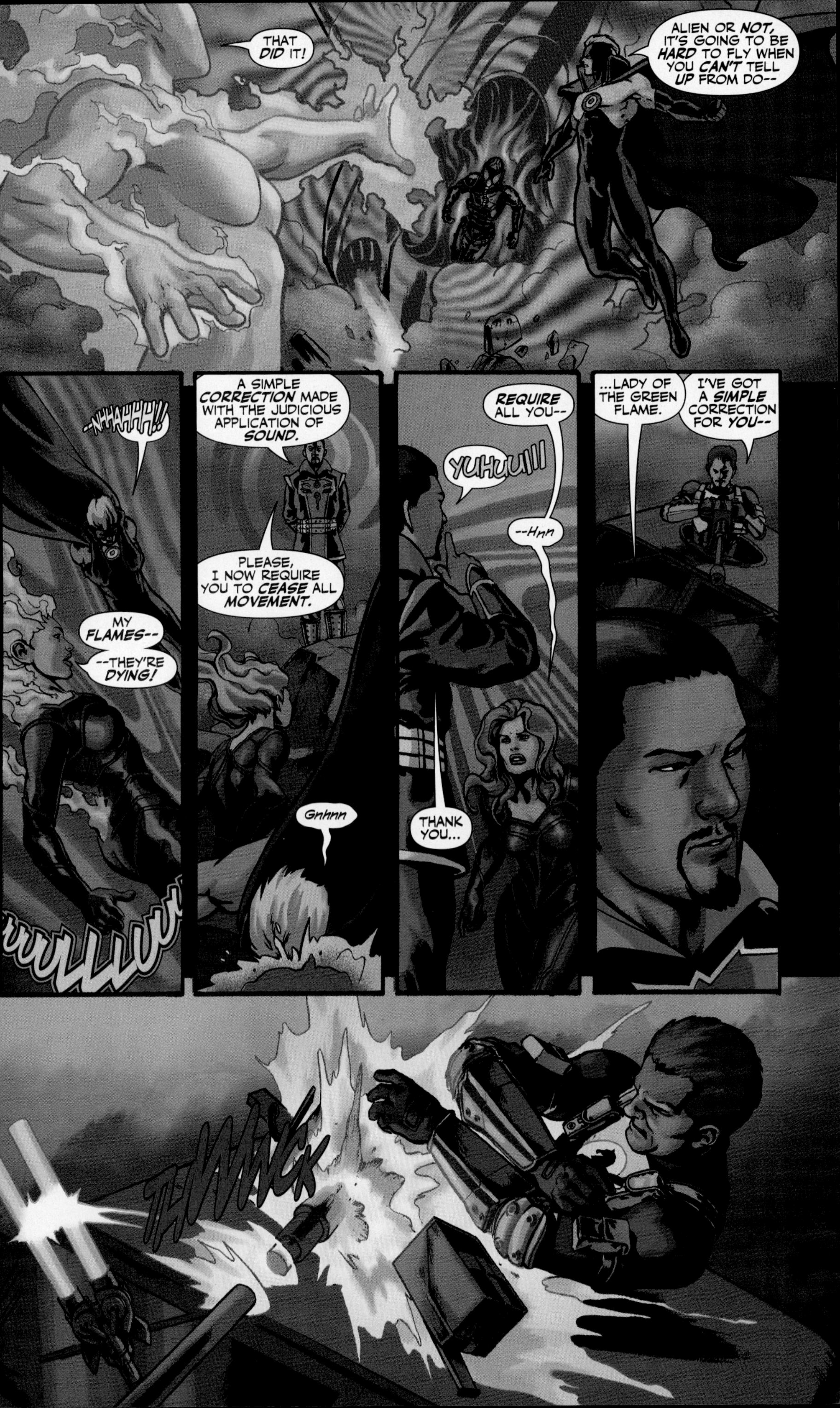
THAT DID IT!
ALIEN OR NOT, IT'S GOING TO BE HARD TO FLY WHEN YOU CAN'T TELL UP FROM DO--
--NHAAHHH!!
MY FLAMES--
--THEY'RE DYING!
A SIMPLE CORRECTION MADE WITH THE JUDICIOUS APPLICATION OF SOUND.
PLEASE, I NOW REQUIRE YOU TO CEASE ALL MOVEMENT.
Gnhnn
REQUIRE ALL YOU--
YUHUUII!
--Hnn
THANK YOU...
...LADY OF THE GREEN FLAME.
I'VE GOT A SIMPLE CORRECTION FOR YOU--

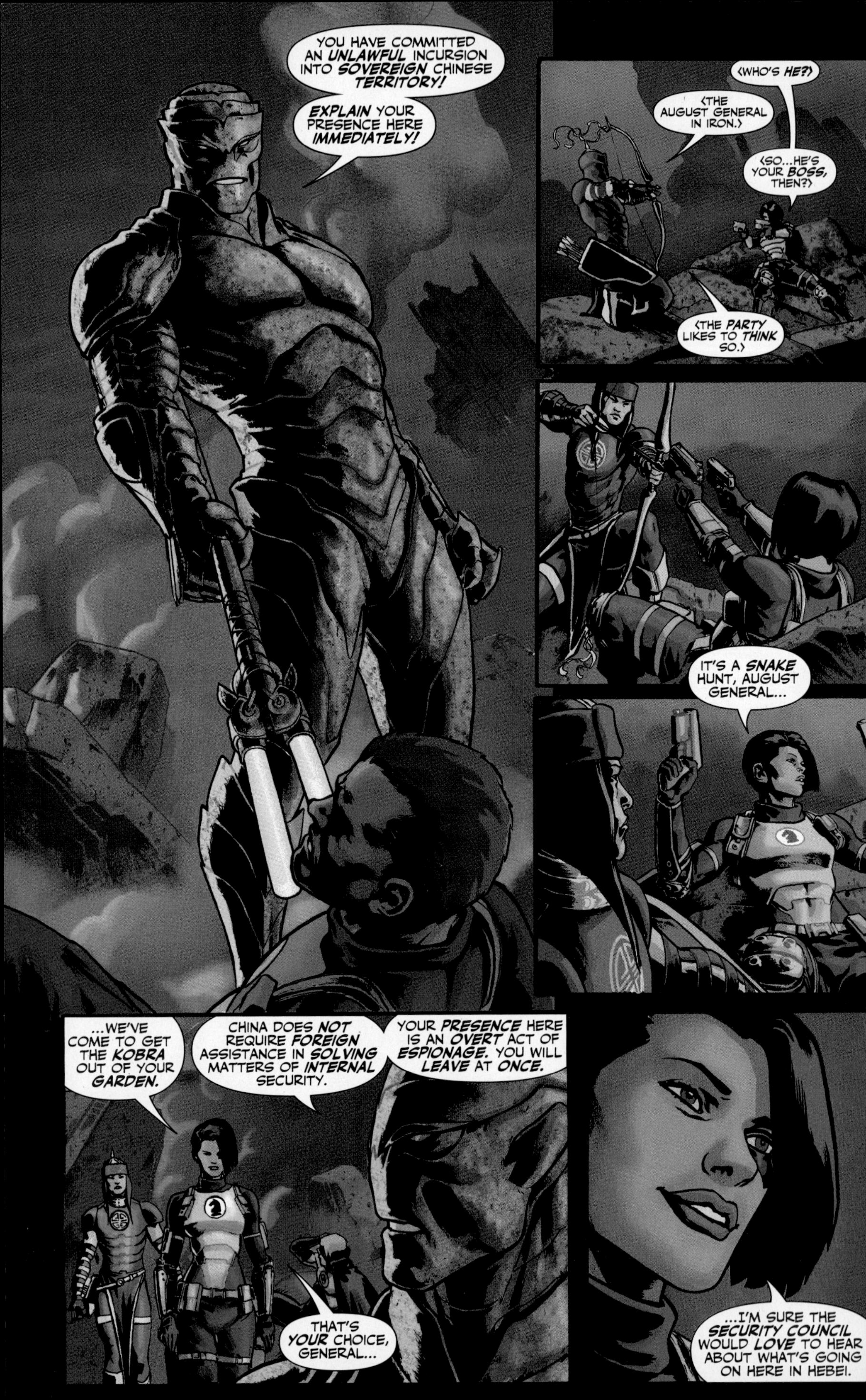
YOU HAVE COMMITTED AN UNLAWFUL INCURSION INTO SOVEREIGN CHINESE TERRITORY!
EXPLAIN YOUR PRESENCE HERE IMMEDIATELY!
‹WHO'S HE?›
‹THE AUGUST GENERAL IN IRON.›
‹SO...HE'S YOUR BOSS, THEN?›
‹THE PARTY LIKES TO THINK SO.›
IT'S A SNAKE HUNT, AUGUST GENERAL...
...WE'VE COME TO GET THE KOBRA OUT OF YOUR GARDEN.
CHINA DOES NOT REQUIRE FOREIGN ASSISTANCE IN SOLVING MATTERS OF INTERNAL SECURITY.
YOUR PRESENCE HERE IS AN OVERT ACT OF ESPIONAGE. YOU WILL LEAVE AT ONCE.
THAT'S YOUR CHOICE, GENERAL...
...I'M SURE THE SECURITY COUNCIL WOULD LOVE TO HEAR ABOUT WHAT'S GOING ON HERE IN HEBEI.

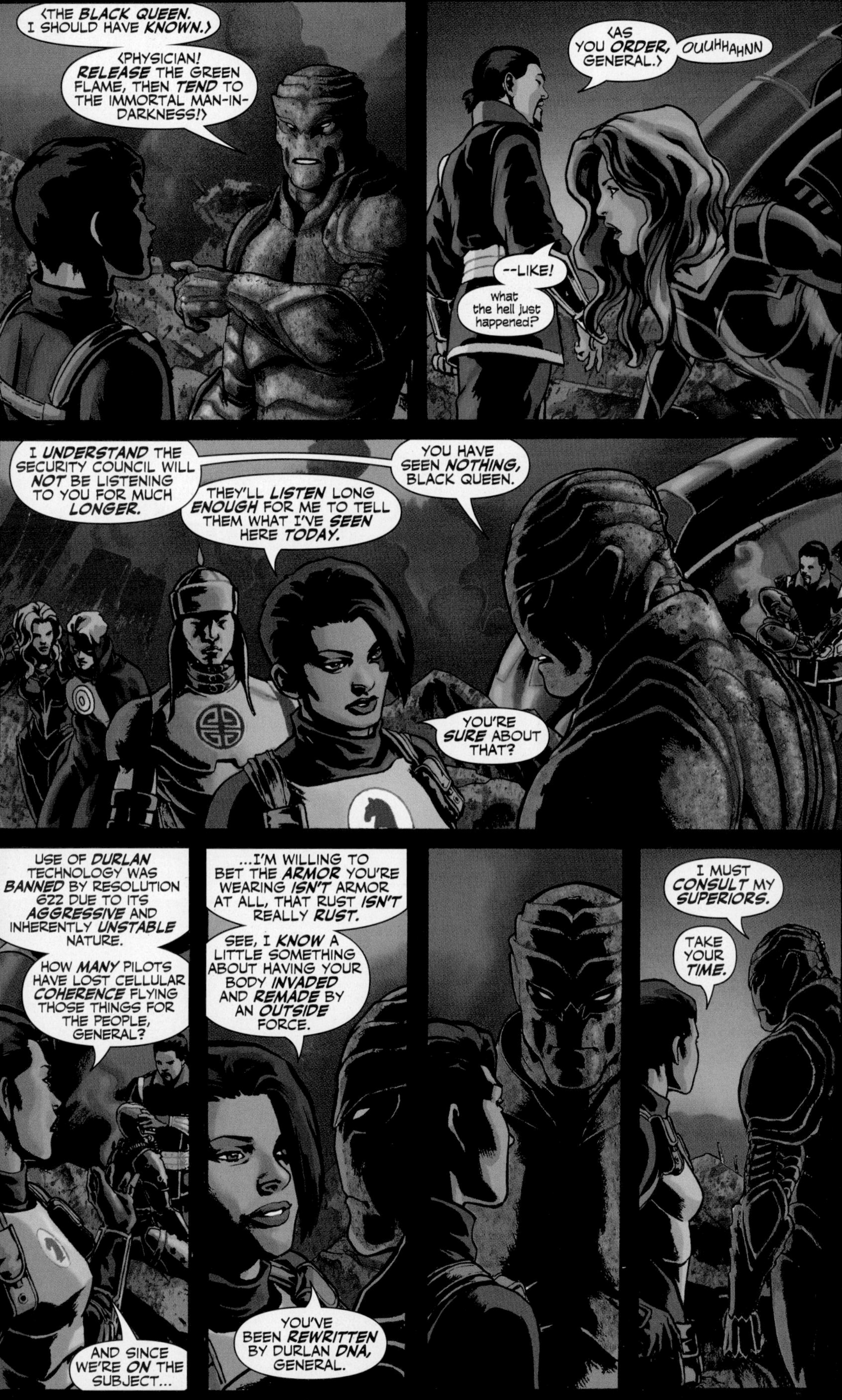
‹THE BLACK QUEEN. I SHOULD HAVE KNOWN.›
‹PHYSICIAN! RELEASE THE GREEN FLAME, THEN TEND TO THE IMMORTAL MAN-IN-DARKNESS!›
‹AS YOU ORDER, GENERAL.›
OUUHHAHNN
--LIKE!
what the hell just happened?
I UNDERSTAND THE SECURITY COUNCIL WILL NOT BE LISTENING TO YOU FOR MUCH LONGER.
YOU HAVE SEEN NOTHING, BLACK QUEEN.
THEY'LL LISTEN LONG ENOUGH FOR ME TO TELL THEM WHAT I'VE SEEN HERE TODAY.
YOU'RE SURE ABOUT THAT?
USE OF DURLAN TECHNOLOGY WAS BANNED BY RESOLUTION 622 DUE TO ITS AGGRESSIVE AND INHERENTLY UNSTABLE NATURE.
HOW MANY PILOTS HAVE LOST CELLULAR COHERENCE FLYING THOSE THINGS FOR THE PEOPLE, GENERAL?
AND SINCE WE'RE ON THE SUBJECT...
...I'M WILLING TO BET THE ARMOR YOU'RE WEARING ISN'T ARMOR AT ALL, THAT RUST ISN'T REALLY RUST.
SEE, I KNOW A LITTLE SOMETHING ABOUT HAVING YOUR BODY INVADED AND REMADE BY AN OUTSIDE FORCE.
YOU'VE BEEN REWRITTEN BY DURLAN DNA, GENERAL.
I MUST CONSULT MY SUPERIORS.
TAKE YOUR TIME.

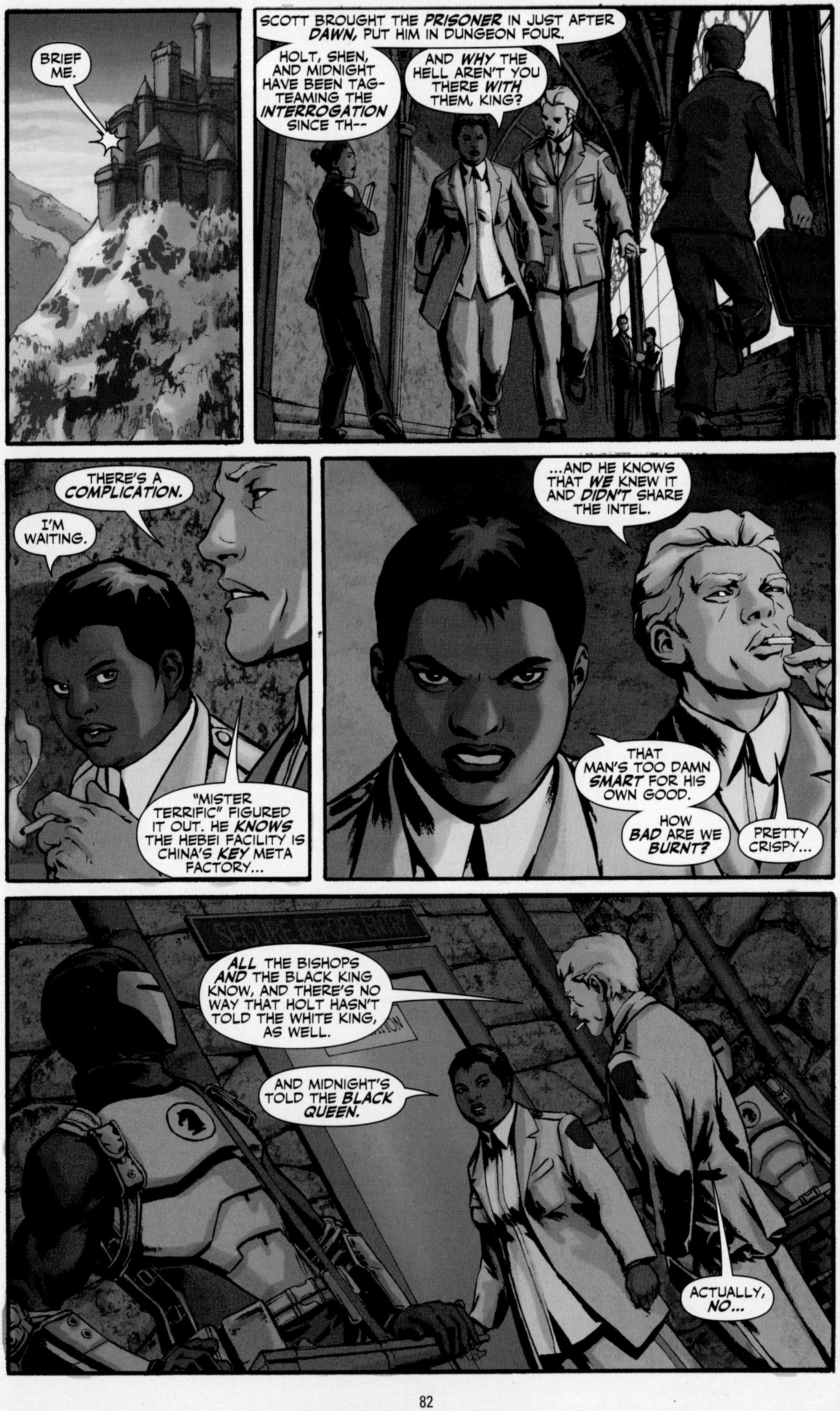
BRIEF ME.
SCOTT BROUGHT THE PRISONER IN JUST AFTER DAWN, PUT HIM IN DUNGEON FOUR.
HOLT, SHEN, AND MIDNIGHT HAVE BEEN TAG-TEAMING THE INTERROGATION SINCE TH--
AND WHY THE HELL AREN'T YOU THERE WITH THEM, KING?
THERE'S A COMPLICATION.
I'M WAITING.
"MISTER TERRIFIC" FIGURED IT OUT. HE KNOWS THE HEBEI FACILITY IS CHINA'S KEY META FACTORY...
...AND HE KNOWS THAT WE KNEW IT AND DIDN'T SHARE THE INTEL.
THAT MAN'S TOO DAMN SMART FOR HIS OWN GOOD.
HOW BAD ARE WE BURNT?
PRETTY CRISPY...
ALL THE BISHOPS AND THE BLACK KING KNOW, AND THERE'S NO WAY THAT HOLT HASN'T TOLD THE WHITE KING, AS WELL.
AND MIDNIGHT'S TOLD THE BLACK QUEEN.
ACTUALLY, NO...

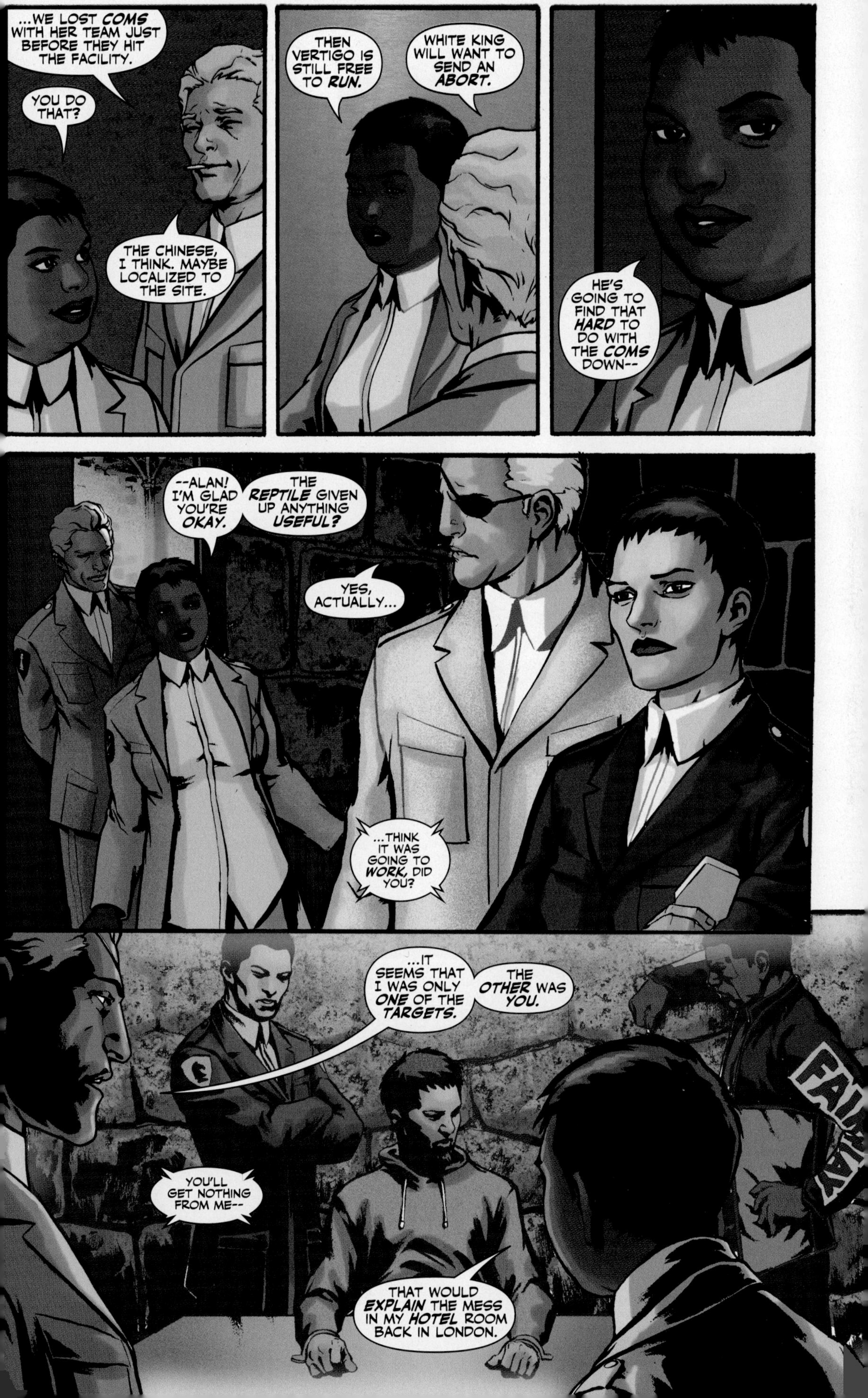
...WE LOST COMS WITH HER TEAM JUST BEFORE THEY HIT THE FACILITY.
YOU DO THAT?
THE CHINESE, I THINK. MAYBE LOCALIZED TO THE SITE.
THEN VERTIGO IS STILL FREE TO RUN.
WHITE KING WILL WANT TO SEND AN ABORT.
HE'S GOING TO FIND THAT HARD TO DO WITH THE COMS DOWN--
--ALAN! I'M GLAD YOU'RE OKAY.
THE REPTILE GIVEN UP ANYTHING USEFUL?
YES, ACTUALLY...
...THINK IT WAS GOING TO WORK, DID YOU?
...IT SEEMS THAT I WAS ONLY ONE OF THE TARGETS.
THE OTHER WAS YOU.
YOU'LL GET NOTHING FROM ME--
THAT WOULD EXPLAIN THE MESS IN MY HOTEL ROOM BACK IN LONDON.

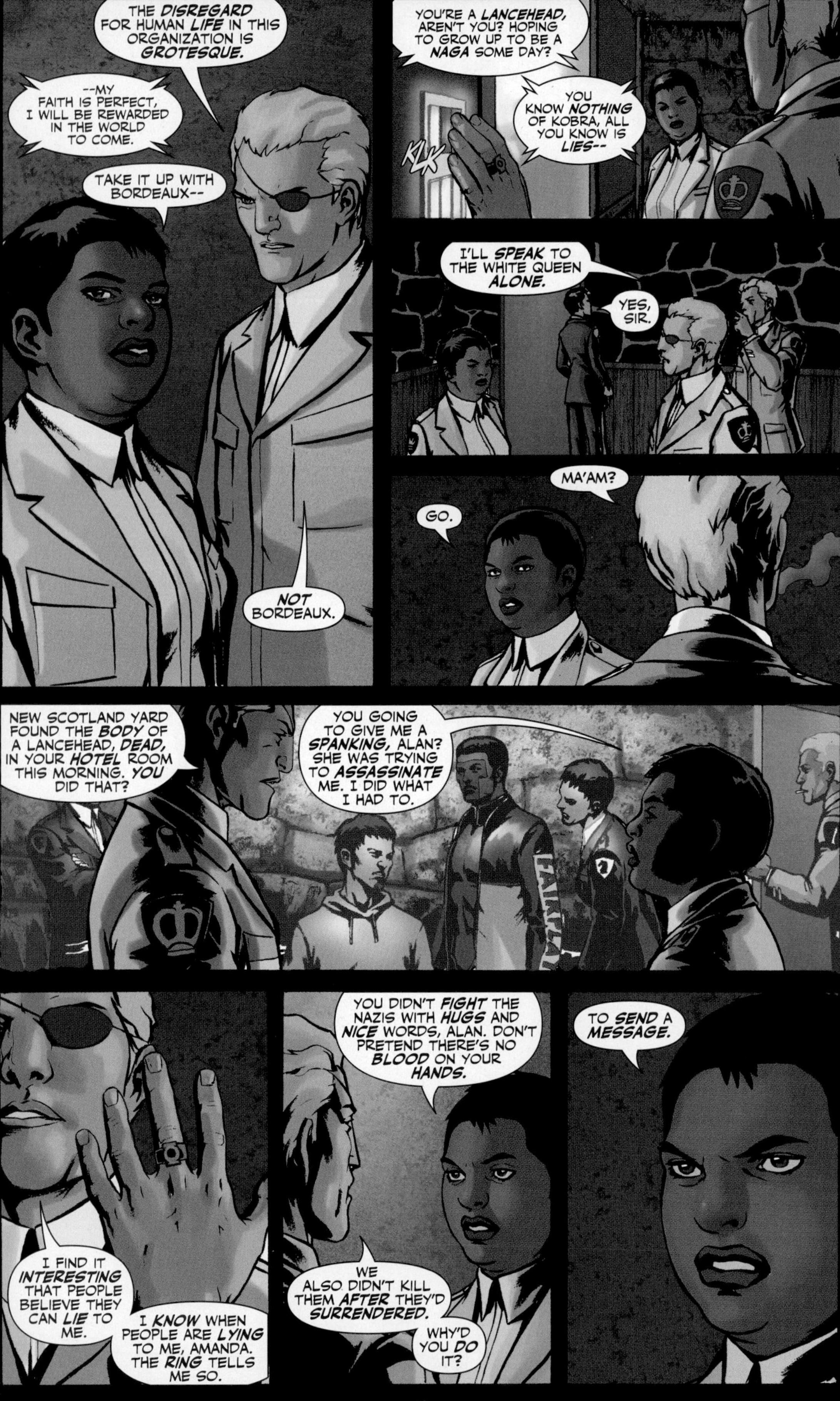

THE DISREGARD FOR HUMAN LIFE IN THIS ORGANIZATION IS GROTESQUE.
--MY FAITH IS PERFECT, I WILL BE REWARDED IN THE WORLD TO COME.
TAKE IT UP WITH BORDEAUX--
NOT BORDEAUX.
YOU'RE A LANCEHEAD, AREN'T YOU? HOPING TO GROW UP TO BE A NAGA SOME DAY?
KLK
YOU KNOW NOTHING OF KOBRA, ALL YOU KNOW IS LIES--
I'LL SPEAK TO THE WHITE QUEEN ALONE.
YES, SIR.
MA'AM?
GO.
NEW SCOTLAND YARD FOUND THE BODY OF A LANCEHEAD, DEAD, IN YOUR HOTEL ROOM THIS MORNING. YOU DID THAT?
YOU GOING TO GIVE ME A SPANKING, ALAN? SHE WAS TRYING TO ASSASSINATE ME. I DID WHAT I HAD TO.
I FIND IT INTERESTING THAT PEOPLE BELIEVE THEY CAN LIE TO ME.
I KNOW WHEN PEOPLE ARE LYING TO ME, AMANDA. THE RING TELLS ME SO.
YOU DIDN'T FIGHT THE NAZIS WITH HUGS AND NICE WORDS, ALAN. DON'T PRETEND THERE'S NO BLOOD ON YOUR HANDS.
WE ALSO DIDN'T KILL THEM AFTER THEY'D SURRENDERED.
WHY'D YOU DO IT?
TO SEND A MESSAGE.

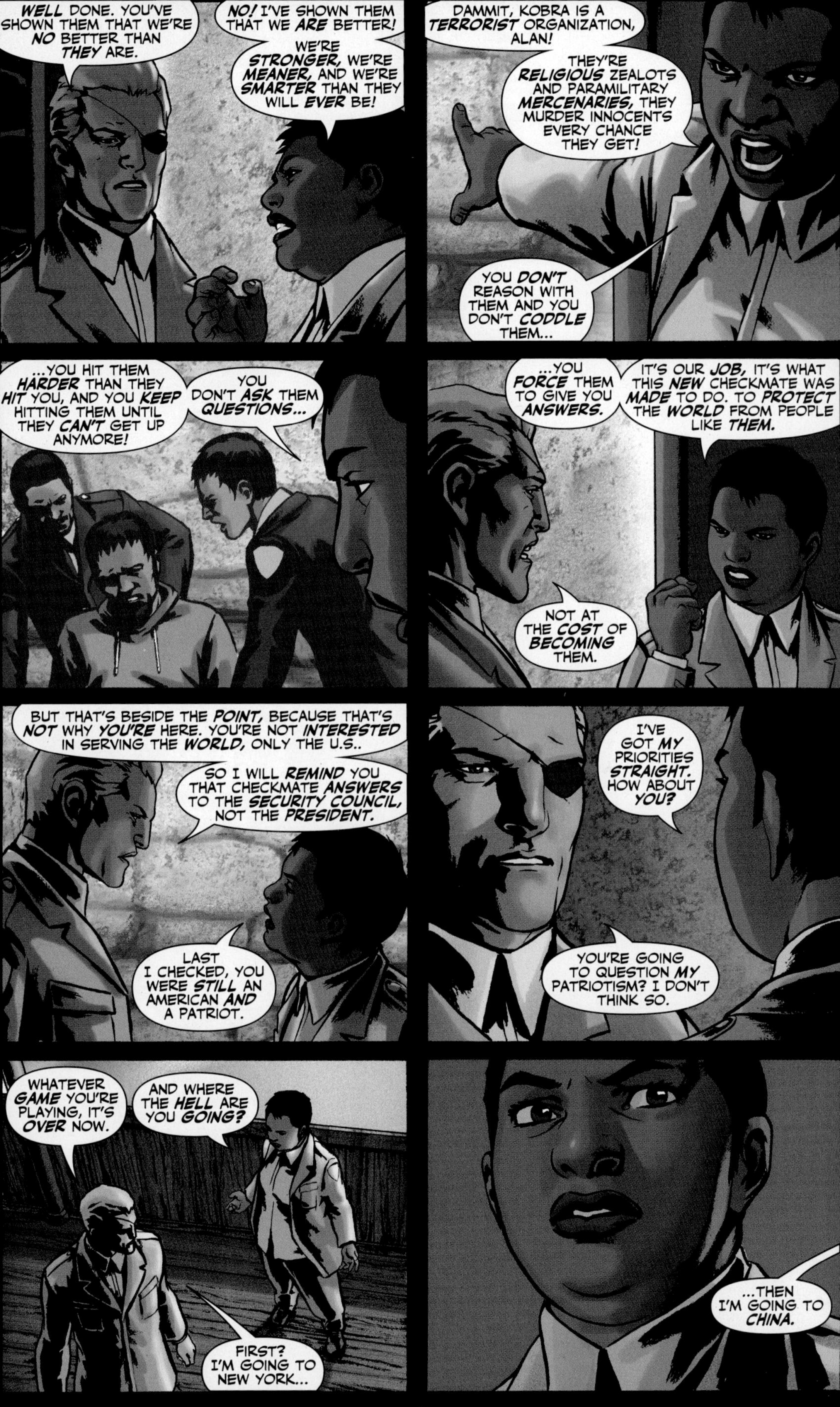
WELL DONE. YOU'VE SHOWN THEM THAT WE'RE NO BETTER THAN THEY ARE.
NO! I'VE SHOWN THEM THAT WE ARE BETTER!
WE'RE STRONGER, WE'RE MEANER, AND WE'RE SMARTER THAN THEY WILL EVER BE!
DAMMIT, KOBRA IS A TERRORIST ORGANIZATION, ALAN!
THEY'RE RELIGIOUS ZEALOTS AND PARAMILITARY MERCENARIES, THEY MURDER INNOCENTS EVERY CHANCE THEY GET!
YOU DON'T REASON WITH THEM AND YOU DON'T CODDLE THEM...
...YOU HIT THEM HARDER THAN THEY HIT YOU, AND YOU KEEP HITTING THEM UNTIL THEY CAN'T GET UP ANYMORE!
YOU DON'T ASK THEM QUESTIONS...
...YOU FORCE THEM TO GIVE YOU ANSWERS.
IT'S OUR JOB, IT'S WHAT THIS NEW CHECKMATE WAS MADE TO DO. TO PROTECT THE WORLD FROM PEOPLE LIKE THEM.
NOT AT THE COST OF BECOMING THEM.
BUT THAT'S BESIDE THE POINT, BECAUSE THAT'S NOT WHY YOU'RE HERE. YOU'RE NOT INTERESTED IN SERVING THE WORLD, ONLY THE U.S..
SO I WILL REMIND YOU THAT CHECKMATE ANSWERS TO THE SECURITY COUNCIL, NOT THE PRESIDENT.
LAST I CHECKED, YOU WERE STILL AN AMERICAN AND A PATRIOT.
I'VE GOT MY PRIORITIES STRAIGHT. HOW ABOUT YOU?
YOU'RE GOING TO QUESTION MY PATRIOTISM? I DON'T THINK SO.
WHATEVER GAME YOU'RE PLAYING, IT'S OVER NOW.
AND WHERE THE HELL ARE YOU GOING?
FIRST? I'M GOING TO NEW YORK...
...THEN I'M GOING TO CHINA.

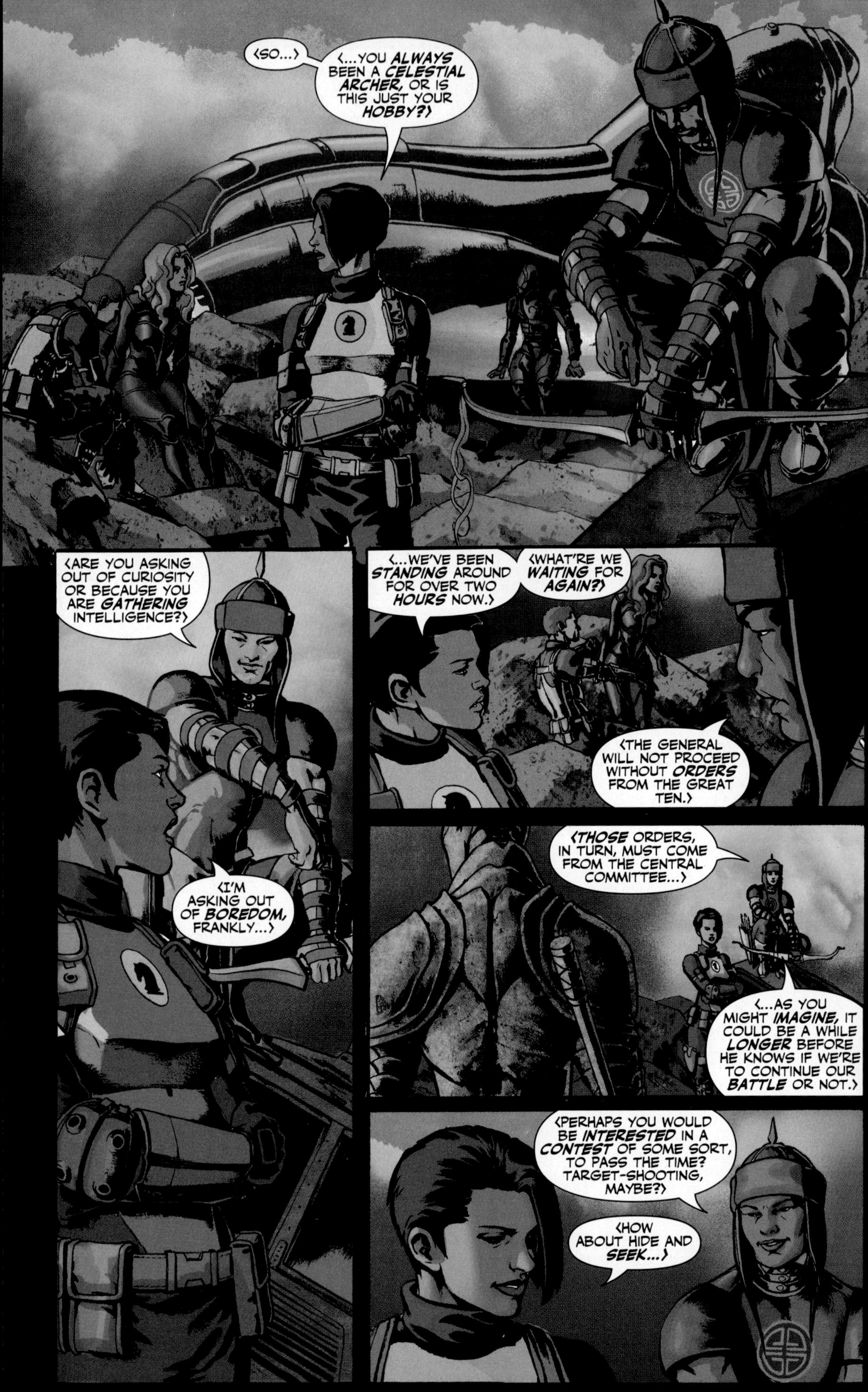
‹SO...›
‹...YOU ALWAYS BEEN A CELESTIAL ARCHER, OR IS THIS JUST YOUR HOBBY?›
‹ARE YOU ASKING OUT OF CURIOSITY OR BECAUSE YOU ARE GATHERING INTELLIGENCE?›
‹I'M ASKING OUT OF BOREDOM, FRANKLY...›
‹...WE'VE BEEN STANDING AROUND FOR OVER TWO HOURS NOW.›
‹WHAT'RE WE WAITING FOR AGAIN?›
‹THE GENERAL WILL NOT PROCEED WITHOUT ORDERS FROM THE GREAT TEN.›
‹THOSE ORDERS, IN TURN, MUST COME FROM THE CENTRAL COMMITTEE...›
‹...AS YOU MIGHT IMAGINE, IT COULD BE A WHILE LONGER BEFORE HE KNOWS IF WE'RE TO CONTINUE OUR BATTLE OR NOT.›
‹PERHAPS YOU WOULD BE INTERESTED IN A CONTEST OF SOME SORT, TO PASS THE TIME? TARGET-SHOOTING, MAYBE?›
‹HOW ABOUT HIDE AND SEEK...›

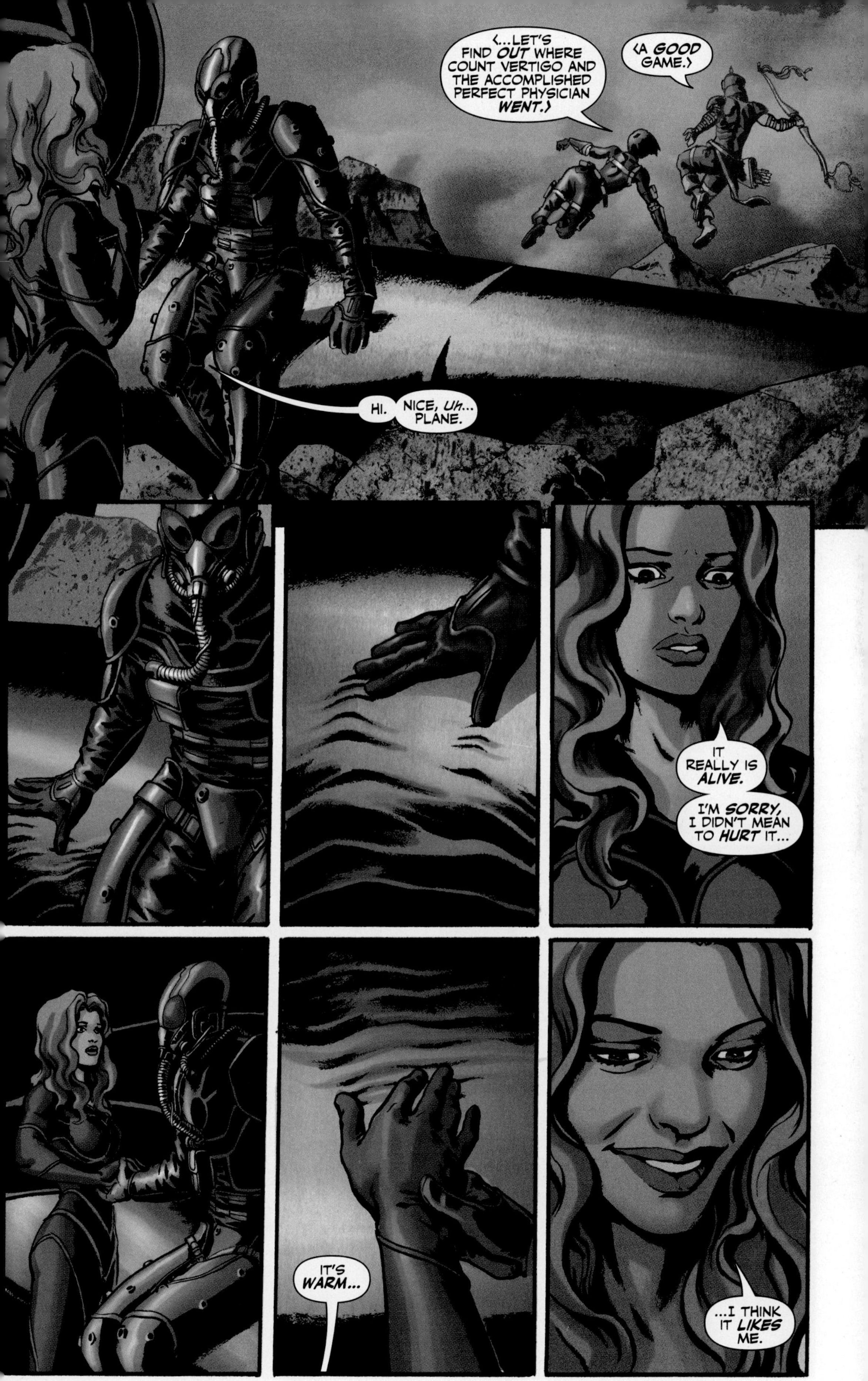
‹...LET'S FIND OUT WHERE COUNT VERTIGO AND THE ACCOMPLISHED PERFECT PHYSICIAN WENT.›
‹A GOOD GAME.›
HI.
NICE, UH... PLANE.
IT REALLY IS ALIVE.
I'M SORRY, I DIDN'T MEAN TO HURT IT...
IT'S WARM...
...I THINK IT LIKES ME.

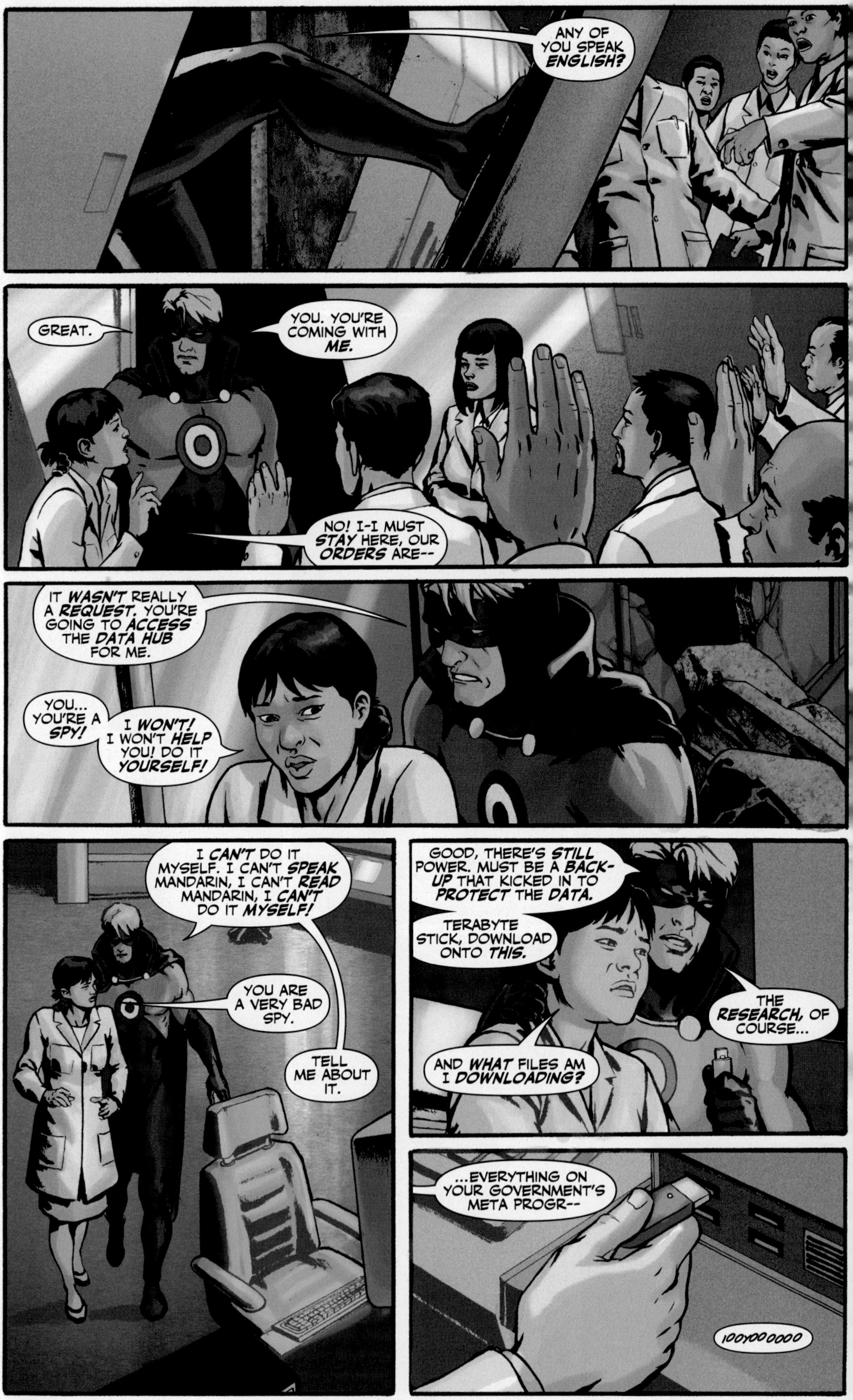
ANY OF YOU SPEAK ENGLISH?
GREAT.
YOU. YOU'RE COMING WITH ME.
NO! I-I MUST STAY HERE, OUR ORDERS ARE--
IT WASN'T REALLY A REQUEST. YOU'RE GOING TO ACCESS THE DATA HUB FOR ME.
YOU... YOU'RE A SPY!
I WON'T! I WON'T HELP YOU! DO IT YOURSELF!
I CAN'T DO IT MYSELF. I CAN'T SPEAK MANDARIN, I CAN'T READ MANDARIN, I CAN'T DO IT MYSELF!
YOU ARE A VERY BAD SPY.
TELL ME ABOUT IT.
GOOD, THERE'S STILL POWER. MUST BE A BACK-UP THAT KICKED IN TO PROTECT THE DATA.
TERABYTE STICK, DOWNLOAD ONTO THIS.
AND WHAT FILES AM I DOWNLOADING?
THE RESEARCH, OF COURSE...
...EVERYTHING ON YOUR GOVERNMENT'S META PROGR--
100Y00000

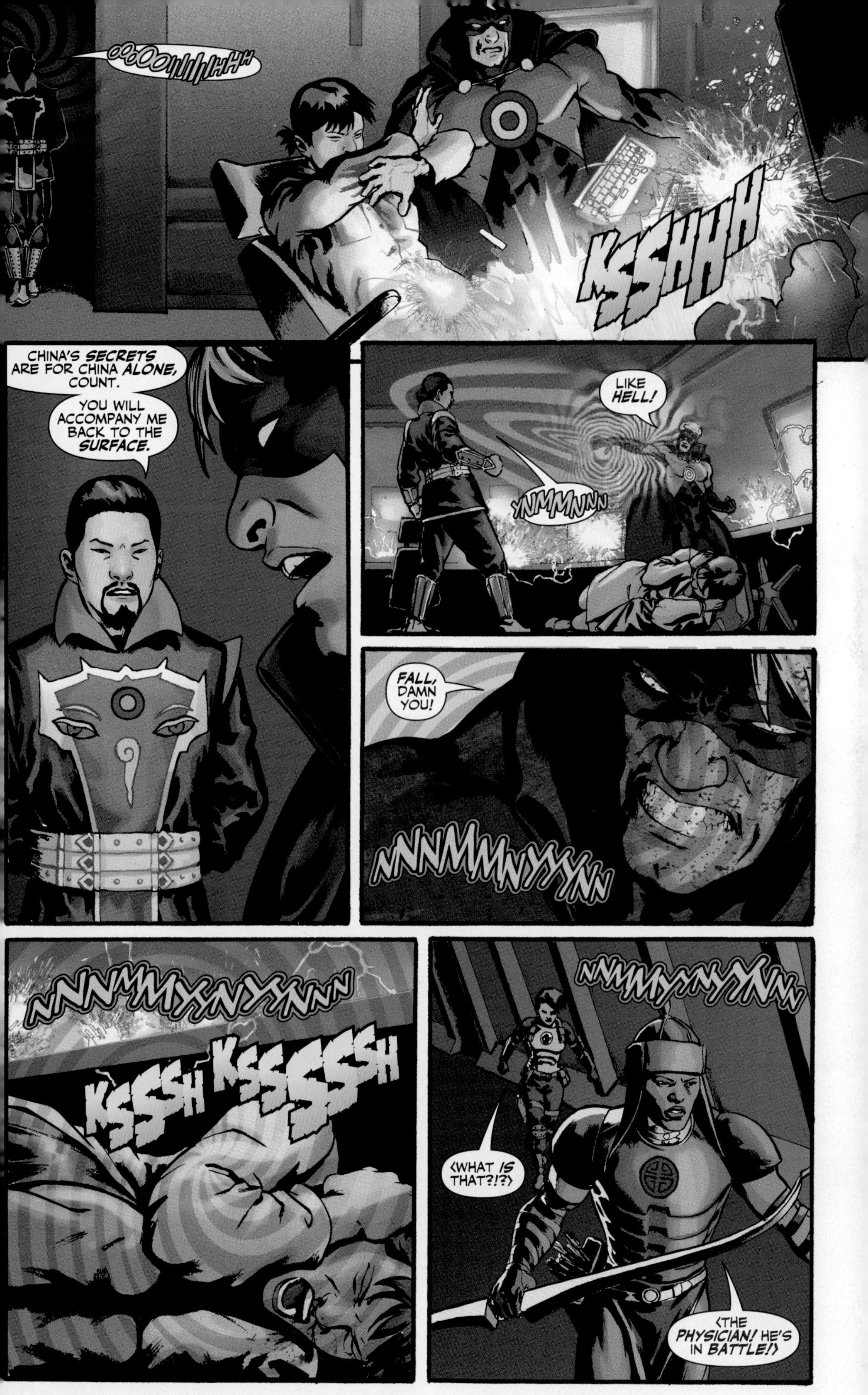

oooOOHHHHHHHH
KSSHHH
CHINA'S SECRETS ARE FOR CHINA ALONE, COUNT.
YOU WILL ACCOMPANY ME BACK TO THE SURFACE.
LIKE HELL!
YNMMNNN
FALL, DAMN YOU!
NNNMMNYYYNN
NNNMMYNYNNNN
KSSSH KSSSSSH
NNMMYNYNNN
<WHAT IS THAT?!?>
<THE PHYSICIAN! HE'S IN BATTLE!>

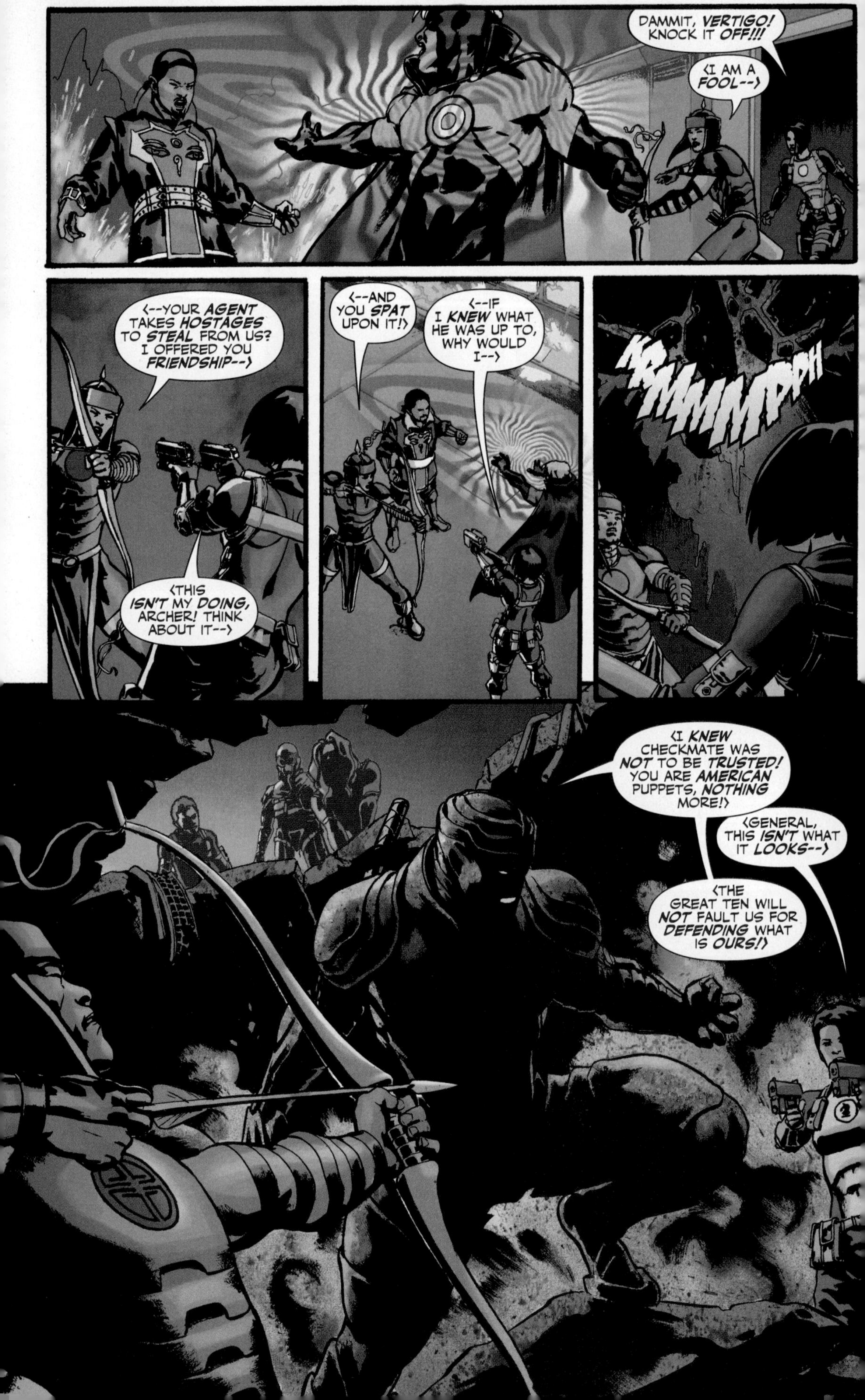
DAMMIT, VERTIGO! KNOCK IT OFF!!!
<I AM A FOOL-->
<--YOUR AGENT TAKES HOSTAGES TO STEAL FROM US? I OFFERED YOU FRIENDSHIP-->
<THIS ISN'T MY DOING, ARCHER! THINK ABOUT IT-->
<--AND YOU SPAT UPON IT!>
<--IF I KNEW WHAT HE WAS UP TO, WHY WOULD I-->
<I KNEW CHECKMATE WAS NOT TO BE TRUSTED! YOU ARE AMERICAN PUPPETS, NOTHING MORE!>
<GENERAL, THIS ISN'T WHAT IT LOOKS-->
<THE GREAT TEN WILL NOT FAULT US FOR DEFENDING WHAT IS OURS!>

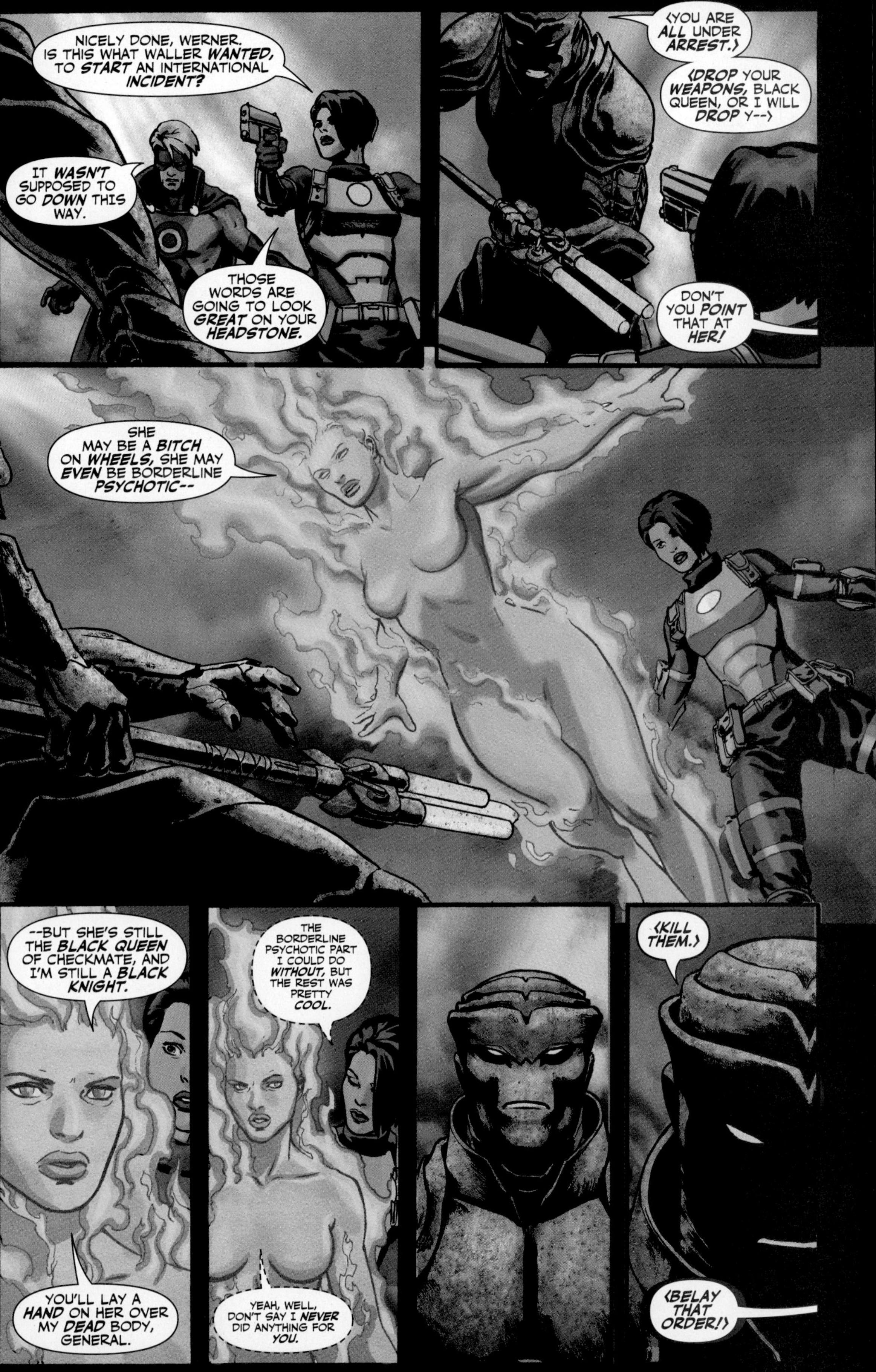
NICELY DONE, WERNER. IS THIS WHAT WALLER WANTED, TO START AN INTERNATIONAL INCIDENT?
IT WASN'T SUPPOSED TO GO DOWN THIS WAY.
THOSE WORDS ARE GOING TO LOOK GREAT ON YOUR HEADSTONE.
<YOU ARE ALL UNDER ARREST.>
<DROP YOUR WEAPONS, BLACK QUEEN, OR I WILL DROP Y-->
DON'T YOU POINT THAT AT HER!
SHE MAY BE A BITCH ON WHEELS, SHE MAY EVEN BE BORDERLINE PSYCHOTIC--
--BUT SHE'S STILL THE BLACK QUEEN OF CHECKMATE, AND I'M STILL A BLACK KNIGHT.
YOU'LL LAY A HAND ON HER OVER MY DEAD BODY, GENERAL.
THE BORDERLINE PSYCHOTIC PART I COULD DO WITHOUT, BUT THE REST WAS PRETTY COOL.
YEAH, WELL, DON'T SAY I NEVER DID ANYTHING FOR YOU.
<KILL THEM.>
<BELAY THAT ORDER!>

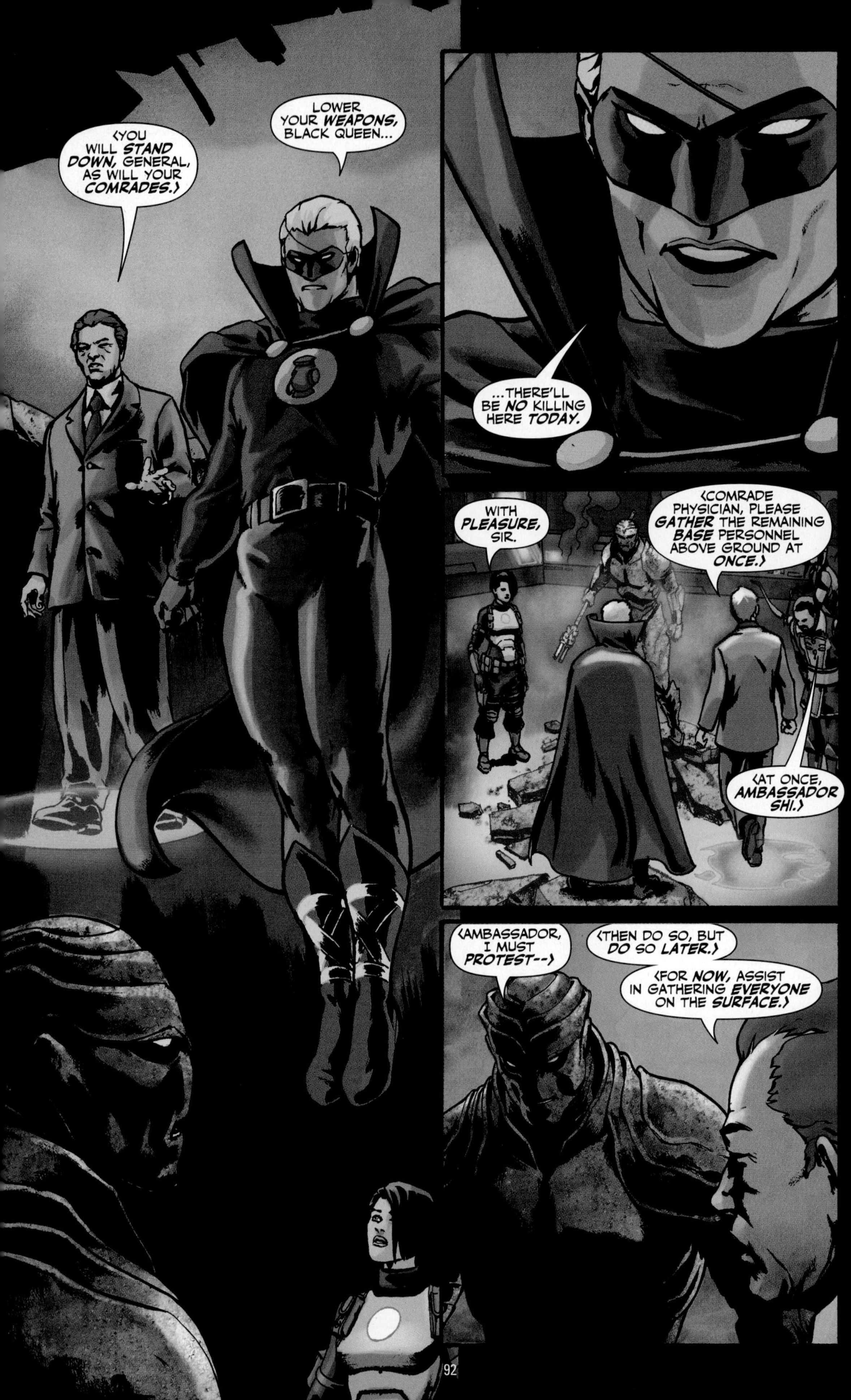
⟨YOU WILL STAND DOWN, GENERAL, AS WILL YOUR COMRADES.⟩
LOWER YOUR WEAPONS, BLACK QUEEN...
...THERE'LL BE NO KILLING HERE TODAY.
⟨COMRADE PHYSICIAN, PLEASE GATHER THE REMAINING BASE PERSONNEL ABOVE GROUND AT ONCE.⟩
WITH PLEASURE, SIR.
⟨AT ONCE, AMBASSADOR SHI.⟩
⟨AMBASSADOR, I MUST PROTEST--⟩
⟨THEN DO SO, BUT DO SO LATER.⟩
⟨FOR NOW, ASSIST IN GATHERING EVERYONE ON THE SURFACE.⟩

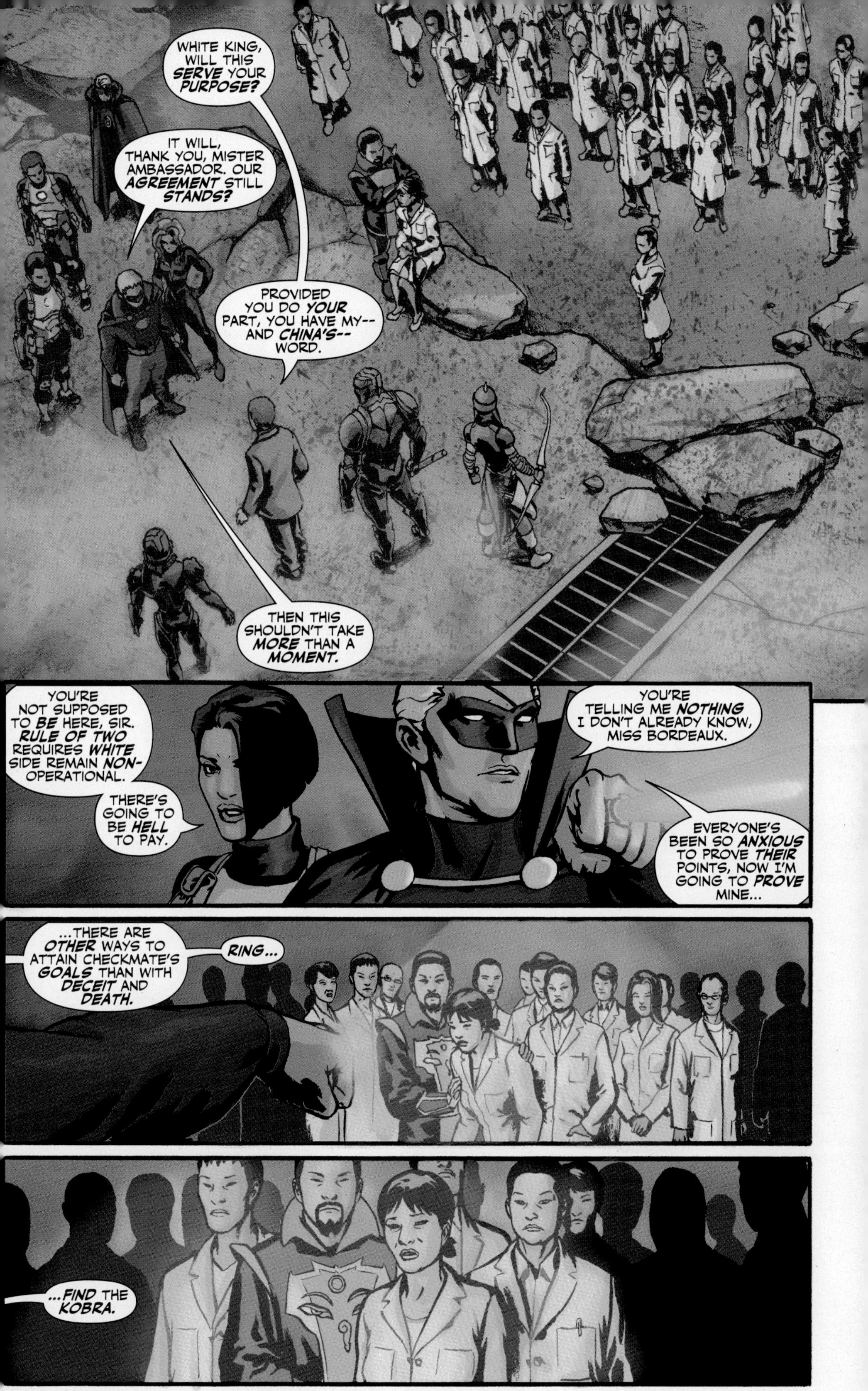
WHITE KING, WILL THIS SERVE YOUR PURPOSE?
IT WILL, THANK YOU, MISTER AMBASSADOR. OUR AGREEMENT STILL STANDS?
PROVIDED YOU DO YOUR PART, YOU HAVE MY-- AND CHINA'S-- WORD.
THEN THIS SHOULDN'T TAKE MORE THAN A MOMENT.
YOU'RE NOT SUPPOSED TO BE HERE, SIR. RULE OF TWO REQUIRES WHITE SIDE REMAIN NON-OPERATIONAL.
THERE'S GOING TO BE HELL TO PAY.
YOU'RE TELLING ME NOTHING I DON'T ALREADY KNOW, MISS BORDEAUX.
EVERYONE'S BEEN SO ANXIOUS TO PROVE THEIR POINTS, NOW I'M GOING TO PROVE MINE...
...THERE ARE OTHER WAYS TO ATTAIN CHECKMATE'S GOALS THAN WITH DECEIT AND DEATH.
RING...
...FIND THE KOBRA.

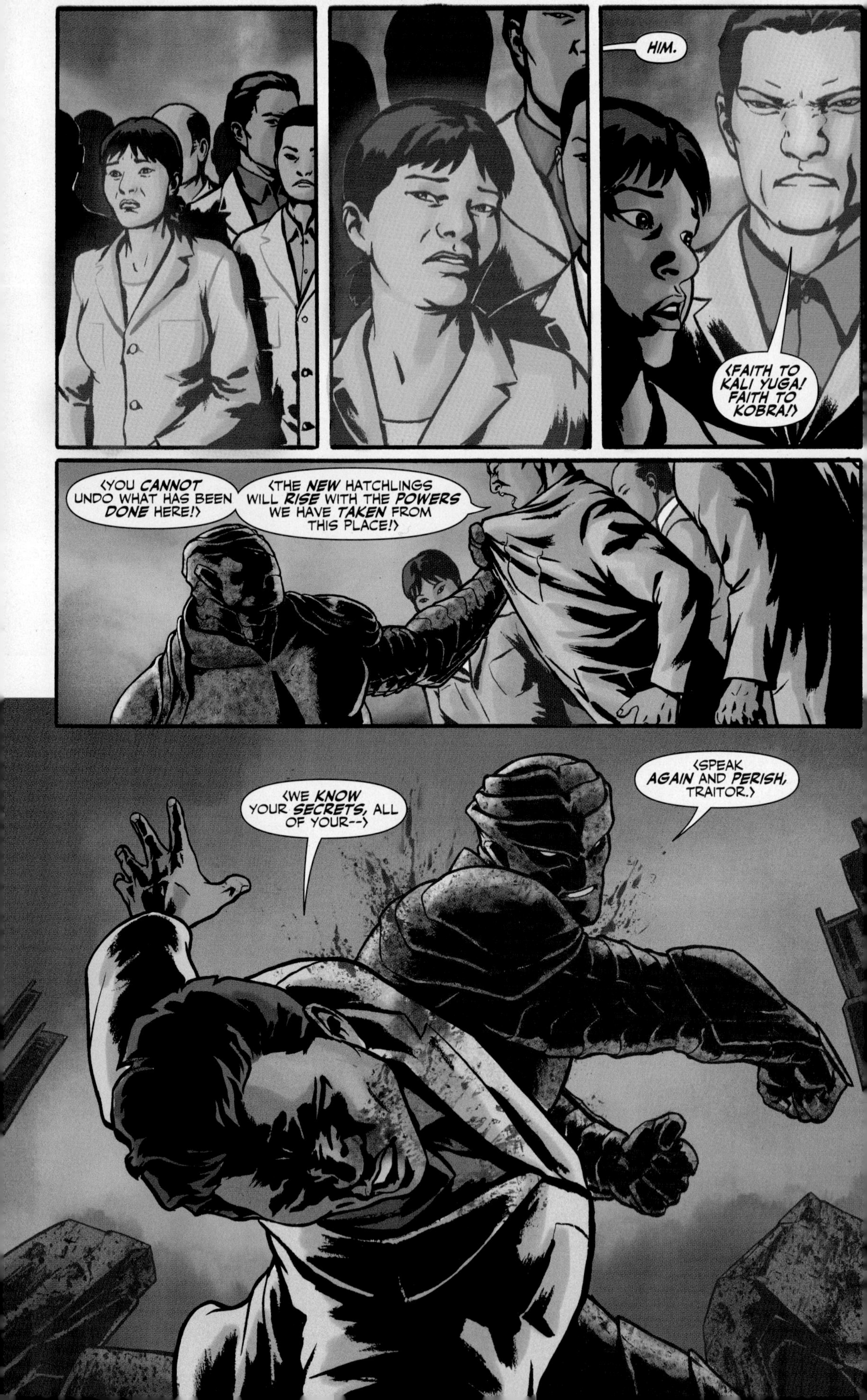
HIM.
‹FAITH TO KALI YUGA! FAITH TO KOBRA!›
‹YOU CANNOT UNDO WHAT HAS BEEN DONE HERE!›
‹THE NEW HATCHLINGS WILL RISE WITH THE POWERS WE HAVE TAKEN FROM THIS PLACE!›
‹WE KNOW YOUR SECRETS, ALL OF YOUR--›
‹SPEAK AGAIN AND PERISH, TRAITOR.›

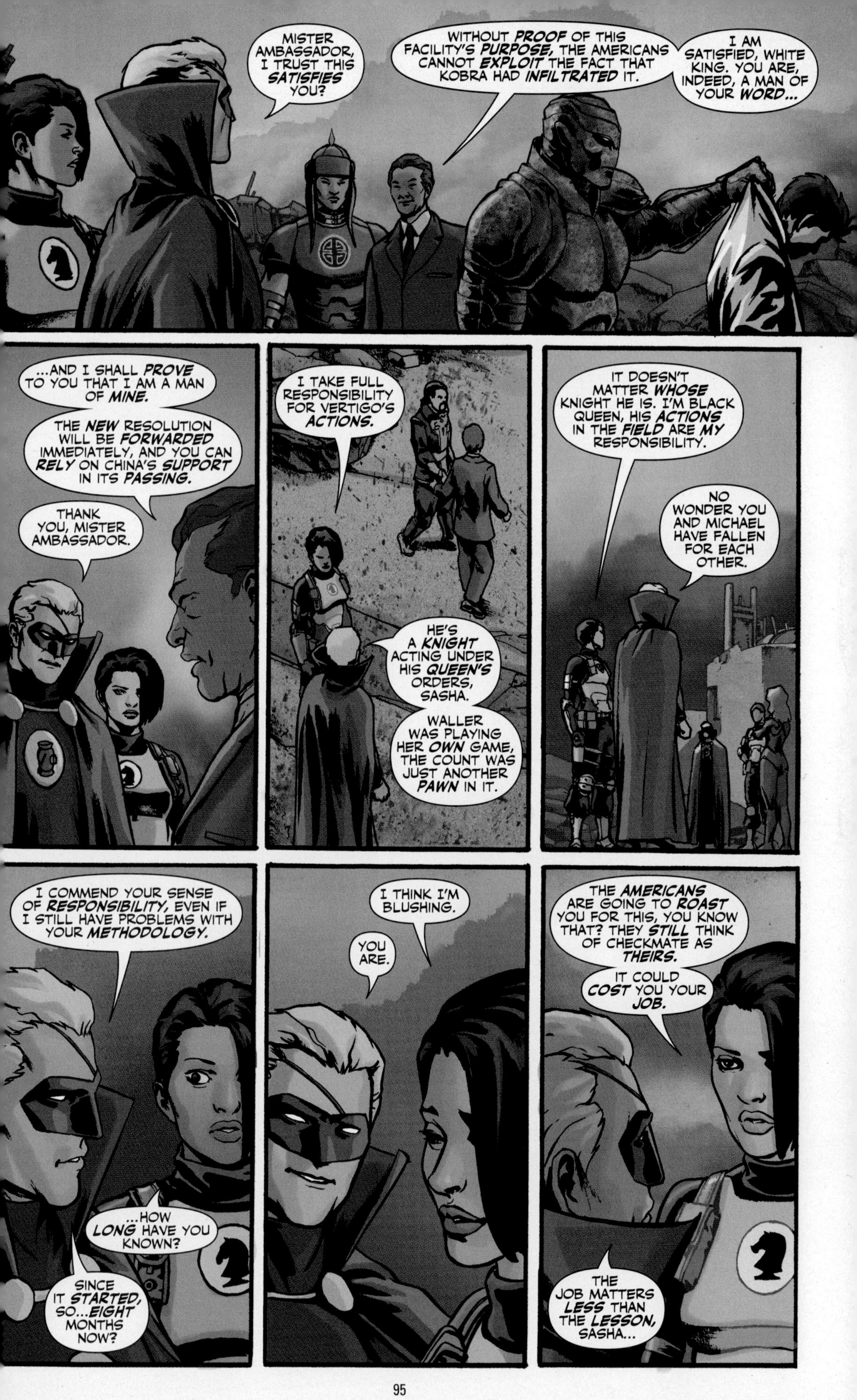
MISTER AMBASSADOR, I TRUST THIS SATISFIES YOU?
WITHOUT PROOF OF THIS FACILITY'S PURPOSE, THE AMERICANS CANNOT EXPLOIT THE FACT THAT KOBRA HAD INFILTRATED IT.
I AM SATISFIED, WHITE KING. YOU ARE, INDEED, A MAN OF YOUR WORD...
...AND I SHALL PROVE TO YOU THAT I AM A MAN OF MINE.
THE NEW RESOLUTION WILL BE FORWARDED IMMEDIATELY, AND YOU CAN RELY ON CHINA'S SUPPORT IN ITS PASSING.
THANK YOU, MISTER AMBASSADOR.
I TAKE FULL RESPONSIBILITY FOR VERTIGO'S ACTIONS.
HE'S A KNIGHT ACTING UNDER HIS QUEEN'S ORDERS, SASHA.
WALLER WAS PLAYING HER OWN GAME, THE COUNT WAS JUST ANOTHER PAWN IN IT.
IT DOESN'T MATTER WHOSE KNIGHT HE IS. I'M BLACK QUEEN, HIS ACTIONS IN THE FIELD ARE MY RESPONSIBILITY.
NO WONDER YOU AND MICHAEL HAVE FALLEN FOR EACH OTHER.
I COMMEND YOUR SENSE OF RESPONSIBILITY, EVEN IF I STILL HAVE PROBLEMS WITH YOUR METHODOLOGY.
...HOW LONG HAVE YOU KNOWN?
SINCE IT STARTED, SO...EIGHT MONTHS NOW?
I THINK I'M BLUSHING.
YOU ARE.
THE AMERICANS ARE GOING TO ROAST YOU FOR THIS, YOU KNOW THAT? THEY STILL THINK OF CHECKMATE AS THEIRS.
IT COULD COST YOU YOUR JOB.
THE JOB MATTERS LESS THAN THE LESSON, SASHA...

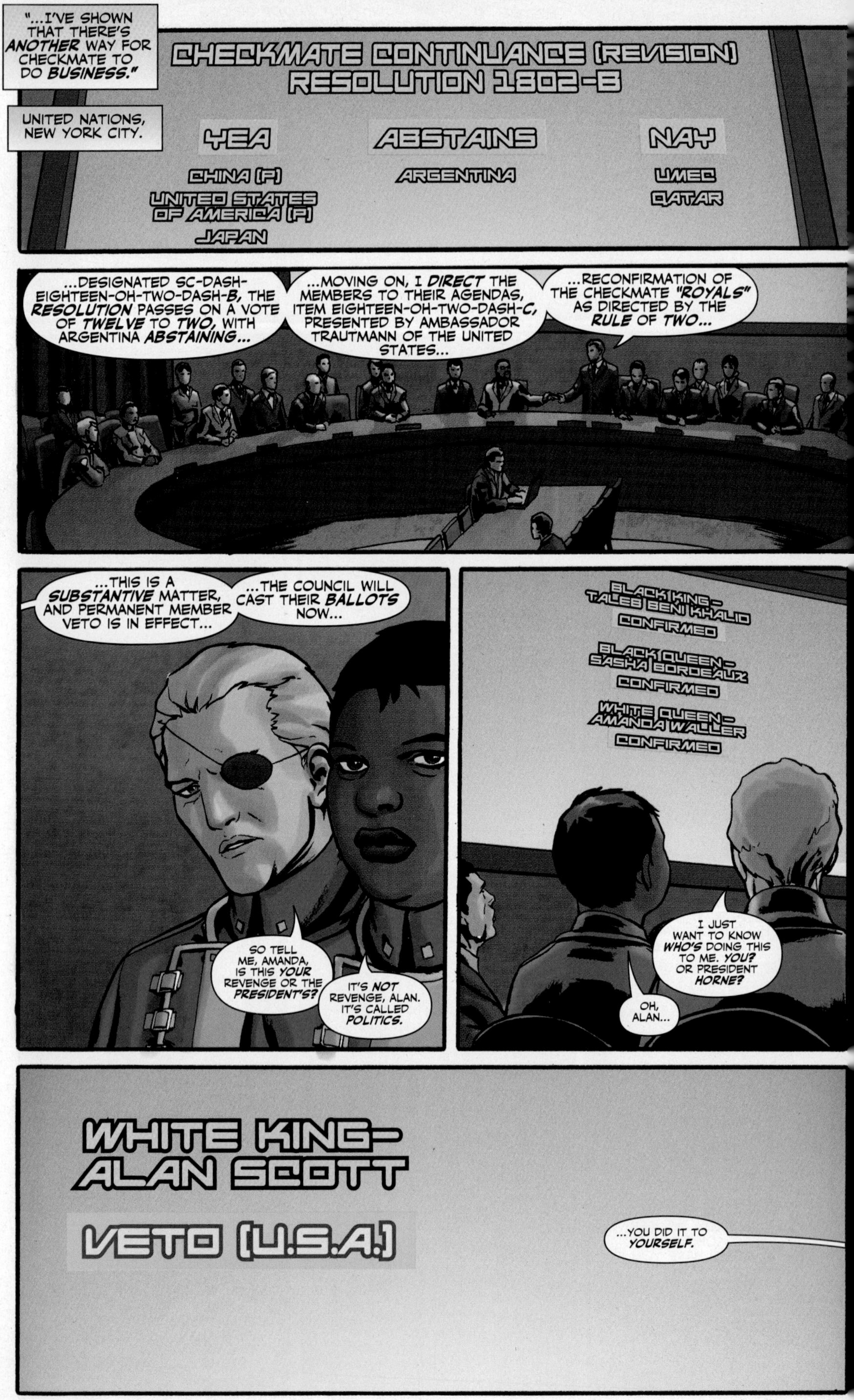
"...I'VE SHOWN THAT THERE'S ANOTHER WAY FOR CHECKMATE TO DO BUSINESS."
UNITED NATIONS, NEW YORK CITY.
CHECKMATE CONTINUANCE (REVISION) RESOLUTION 1802-B
YEA
CHINA (P)
UNITED STATES OF AMERICA (P)
JAPAN
ABSTAINS
ARGENTINA
NAY
UMEC
QATAR
...DESIGNATED SC-DASH-EIGHTEEN-OH-TWO-DASH-B, THE RESOLUTION PASSES ON A VOTE OF TWELVE TO TWO, WITH ARGENTINA ABSTAINING...
...MOVING ON, I DIRECT THE MEMBERS TO THEIR AGENDAS, ITEM EIGHTEEN-OH-TWO-DASH-C, PRESENTED BY AMBASSADOR TRAUTMANN OF THE UNITED STATES...
...RECONFIRMATION OF THE CHECKMATE "ROYALS" AS DIRECTED BY THE RULE OF TWO...
...THIS IS A SUBSTANTIVE MATTER, AND PERMANENT MEMBER VETO IS IN EFFECT...
...THE COUNCIL WILL CAST THEIR BALLOTS NOW...
SO TELL ME, AMANDA, IS THIS YOUR REVENGE OR THE PRESIDENT'S?
IT'S NOT REVENGE, ALAN. IT'S CALLED POLITICS.
BLACK KING— TALEB BENI KHALID
CONFIRMED
BLACK QUEEN— SASHA BORDEAUX
CONFIRMED
WHITE QUEEN— AMANDA WALLER
CONFIRMED
I JUST WANT TO KNOW WHO'S DOING THIS TO ME. YOU? OR PRESIDENT HORNE?
OH, ALAN...
WHITE KING— ALAN SCOTT
VETO (U.S.A.)
...YOU DID IT TO YOURSELF.

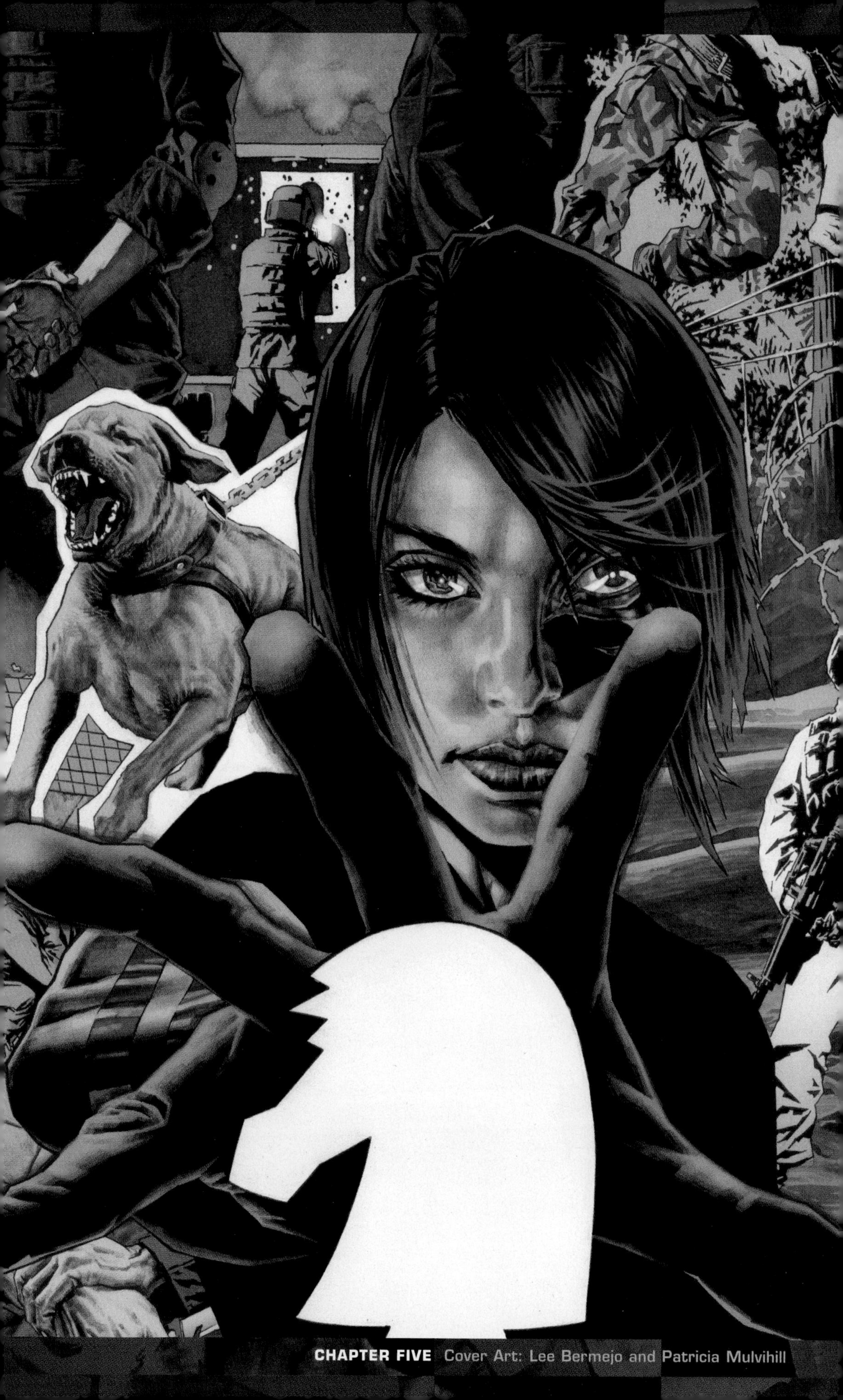

CHAPTER FIVE Cover Art: Lee Bermejo and Patricia Mulvihill

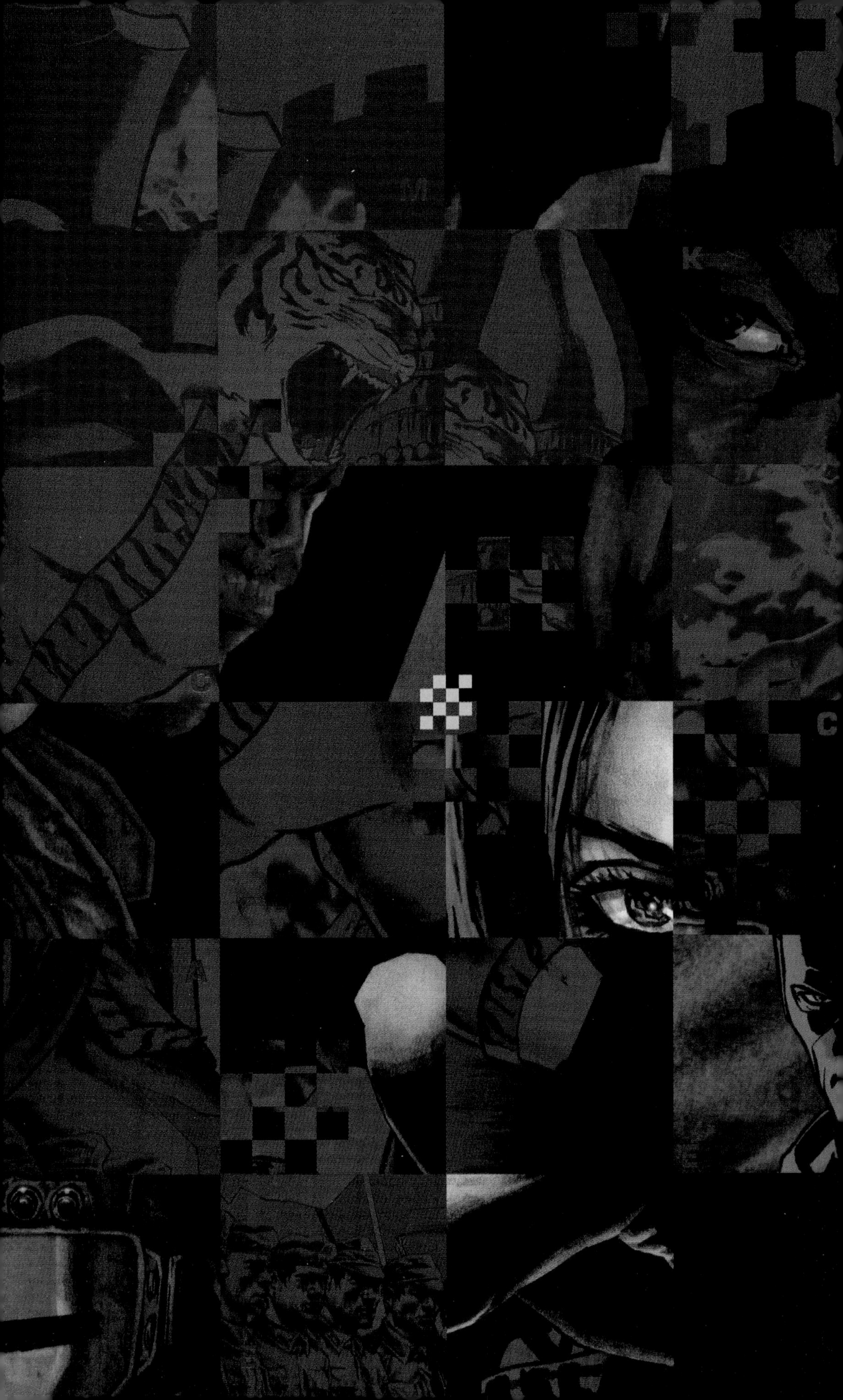

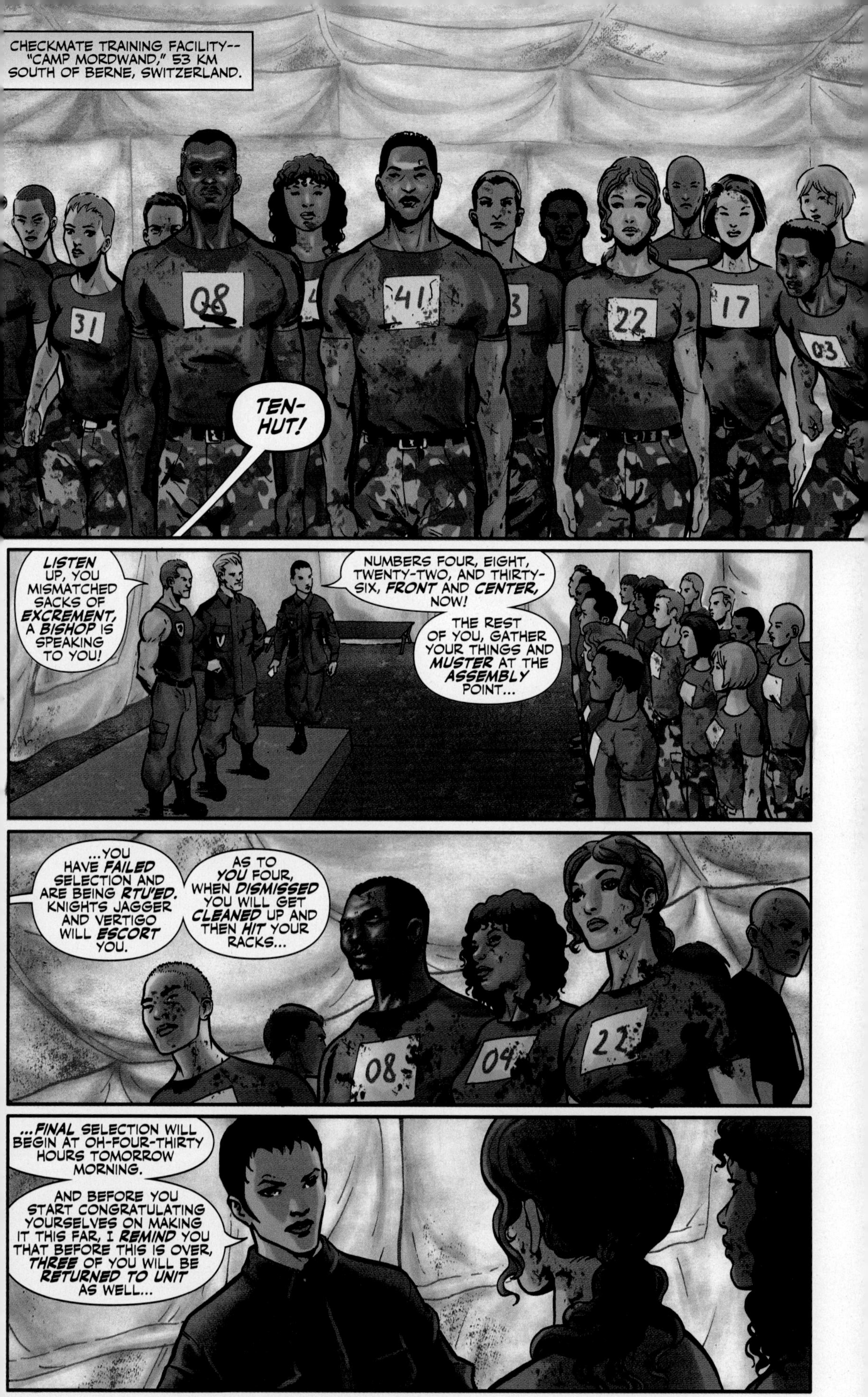

CHECKMATE TRAINING FACILITY-- "CAMP MORDWAND," 53 KM SOUTH OF BERNE, SWITZERLAND.
TEN-HUT!
LISTEN UP, YOU MISMATCHED SACKS OF EXCREMENT, A BISHOP IS SPEAKING TO YOU!
NUMBERS FOUR, EIGHT, TWENTY-TWO, AND THIRTY-SIX, FRONT AND CENTER, NOW!
THE REST OF YOU, GATHER YOUR THINGS AND MUSTER AT THE ASSEMBLY POINT...
...YOU HAVE FAILED SELECTION AND ARE BEING RTU'ED. KNIGHTS JAGGER AND VERTIGO WILL ESCORT YOU.
AS TO YOU FOUR, WHEN DISMISSED YOU WILL GET CLEANED UP AND THEN HIT YOUR RACKS...
...FINAL SELECTION WILL BEGIN AT OH-FOUR-THIRTY HOURS TOMORROW MORNING.
AND BEFORE YOU START CONGRATULATING YOURSELVES ON MAKING IT THIS FAR, I REMIND YOU THAT BEFORE THIS IS OVER, THREE OF YOU WILL BE RETURNED TO UNIT AS WELL...

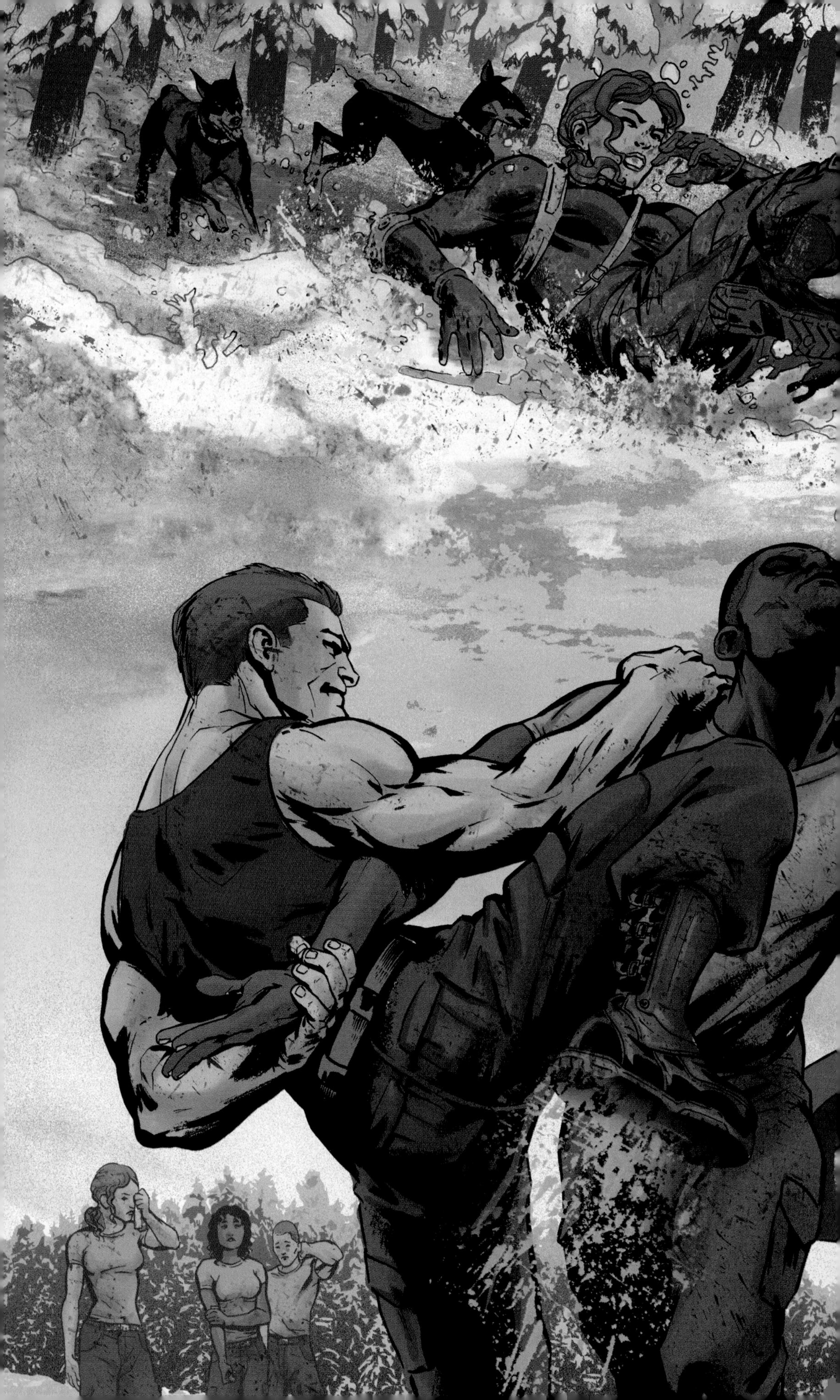

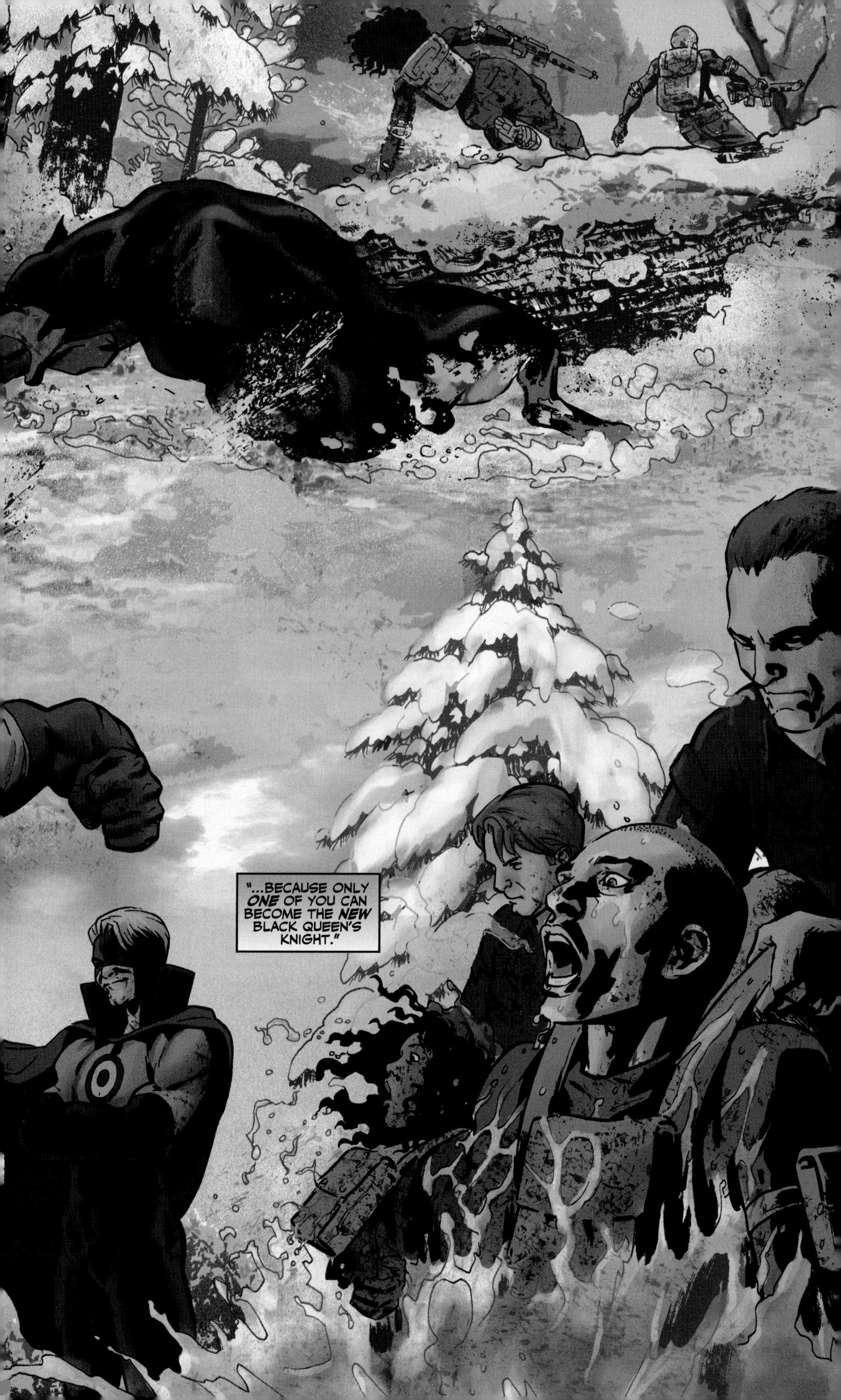
"...BECAUSE ONLY *ONE* OF YOU CAN BECOME THE *NEW* BLACK QUEEN'S KNIGHT."

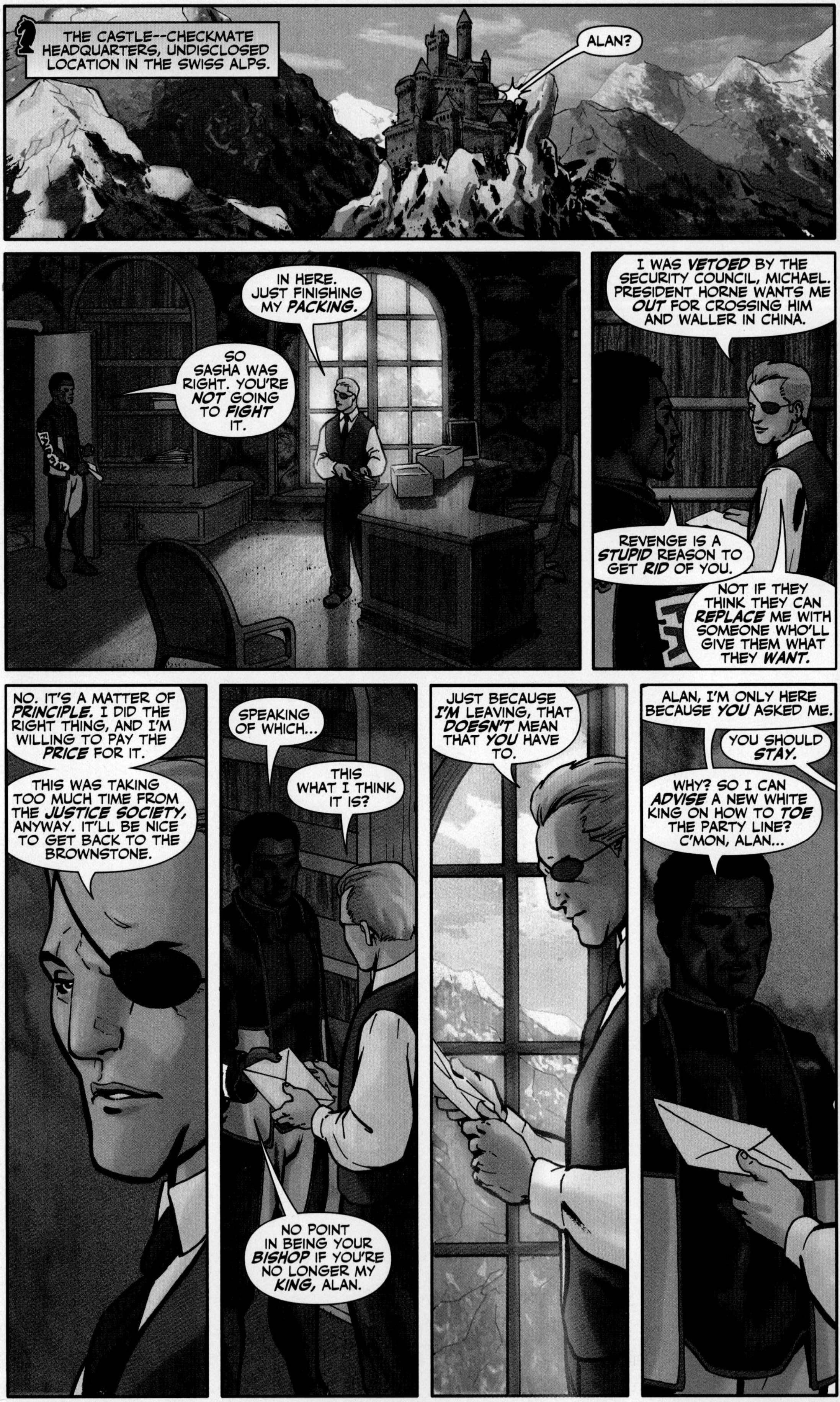
THE CASTLE--CHECKMATE HEADQUARTERS, UNDISCLOSED LOCATION IN THE SWISS ALPS.
ALAN?
IN HERE. JUST FINISHING MY PACKING.
SO SASHA WAS RIGHT. YOU'RE NOT GOING TO FIGHT IT.
I WAS VETOED BY THE SECURITY COUNCIL, MICHAEL. PRESIDENT HORNE WANTS ME OUT FOR CROSSING HIM AND WALLER IN CHINA.
REVENGE IS A STUPID REASON TO GET RID OF YOU.
NOT IF THEY THINK THEY CAN REPLACE ME WITH SOMEONE WHO'LL GIVE THEM WHAT THEY WANT.
NO. IT'S A MATTER OF PRINCIPLE. I DID THE RIGHT THING, AND I'M WILLING TO PAY THE PRICE FOR IT.
THIS WAS TAKING TOO MUCH TIME FROM THE JUSTICE SOCIETY, ANYWAY. IT'LL BE NICE TO GET BACK TO THE BROWNSTONE.
SPEAKING OF WHICH...
THIS WHAT I THINK IT IS?
NO POINT IN BEING YOUR BISHOP IF YOU'RE NO LONGER MY KING, ALAN.
JUST BECAUSE I'M LEAVING, THAT DOESN'T MEAN THAT YOU HAVE TO.
ALAN, I'M ONLY HERE BECAUSE YOU ASKED ME.
YOU SHOULD STAY.
WHY? SO I CAN ADVISE A NEW WHITE KING ON HOW TO TOE THE PARTY LINE? C'MON, ALAN...

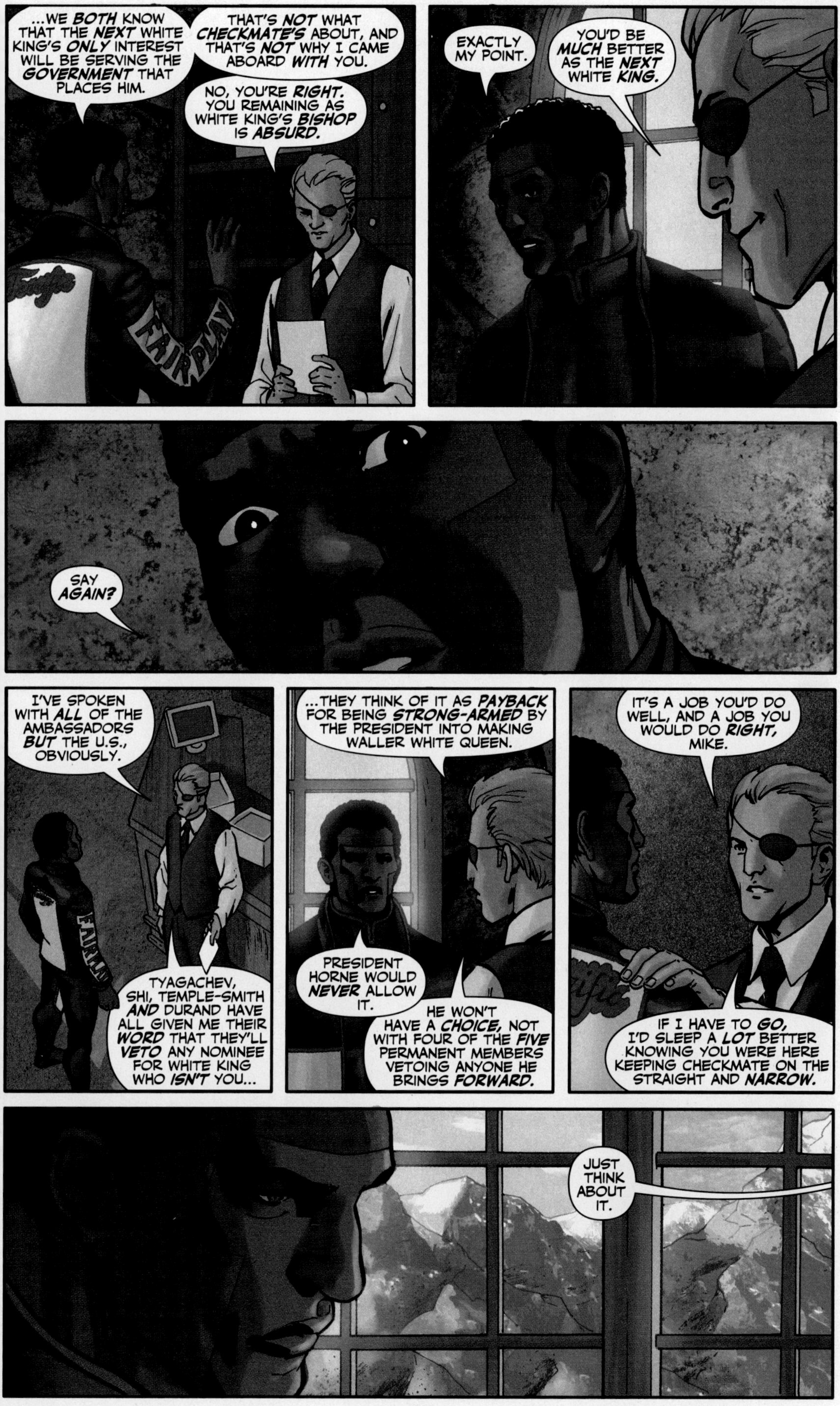
...WE BOTH KNOW THAT THE NEXT WHITE KING'S ONLY INTEREST WILL BE SERVING THE GOVERNMENT THAT PLACES HIM.
THAT'S NOT WHAT CHECKMATE'S ABOUT, AND THAT'S NOT WHY I CAME ABOARD WITH YOU.
NO, YOU'RE RIGHT. YOU REMAINING AS WHITE KING'S BISHOP IS ABSURD.
FAIR PLAY
EXACTLY MY POINT.
YOU'D BE MUCH BETTER AS THE NEXT WHITE KING.
SAY AGAIN?
I'VE SPOKEN WITH ALL OF THE AMBASSADORS BUT THE U.S., OBVIOUSLY.
TYAGACHEV, SHI, TEMPLE-SMITH AND DURAND HAVE ALL GIVEN ME THEIR WORD THAT THEY'LL VETO ANY NOMINEE FOR WHITE KING WHO ISN'T YOU...
...THEY THINK OF IT AS PAYBACK FOR BEING STRONG-ARMED BY THE PRESIDENT INTO MAKING WALLER WHITE QUEEN.
PRESIDENT HORNE WOULD NEVER ALLOW IT.
HE WON'T HAVE A CHOICE, NOT WITH FOUR OF THE FIVE PERMANENT MEMBERS VETOING ANYONE HE BRINGS FORWARD.
IT'S A JOB YOU'D DO WELL, AND A JOB YOU WOULD DO RIGHT, MIKE.
IF I HAVE TO GO, I'D SLEEP A LOT BETTER KNOWING YOU WERE HERE KEEPING CHECKMATE ON THE STRAIGHT AND NARROW.
JUST THINK ABOUT IT.

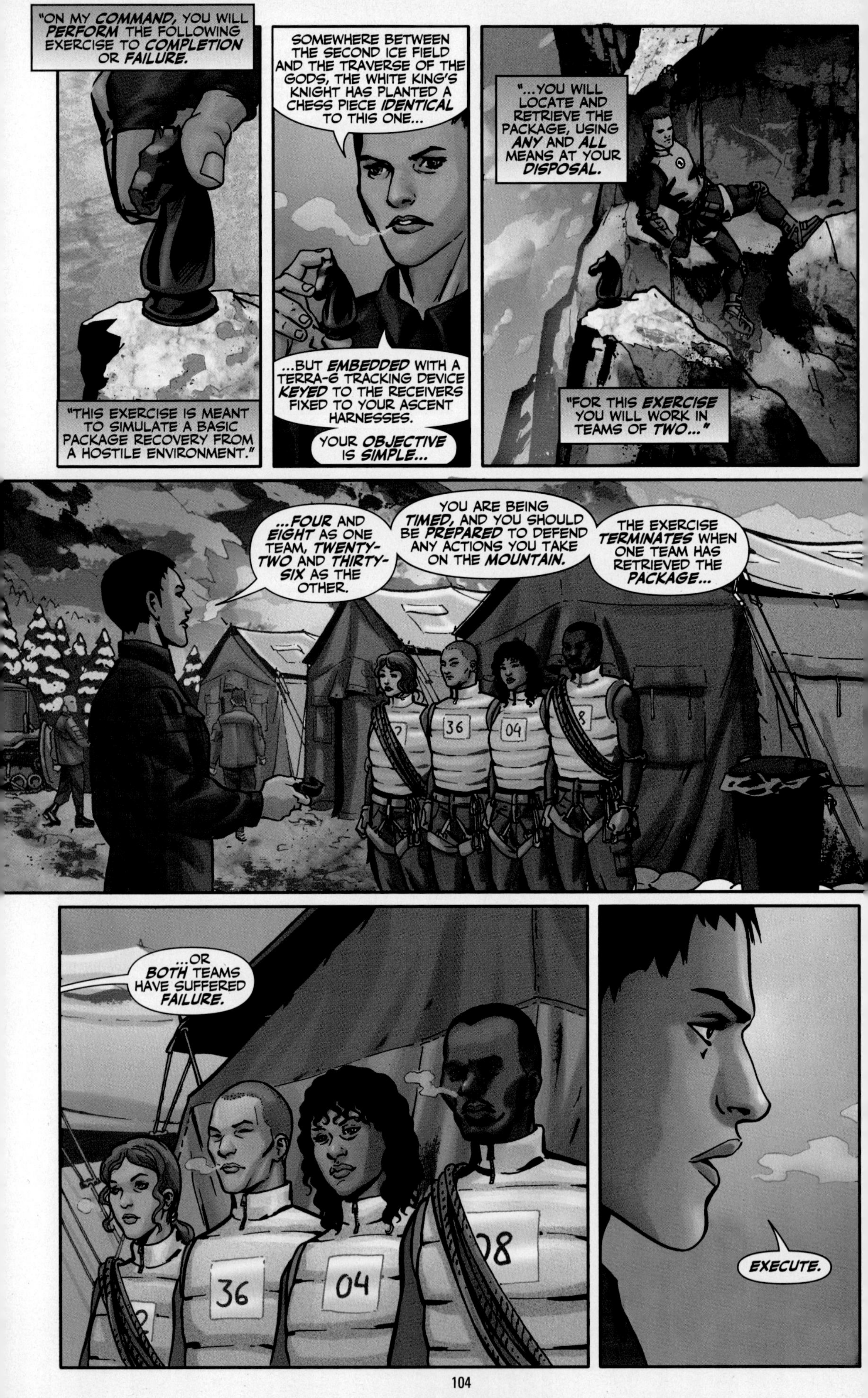
"ON MY COMMAND, YOU WILL PERFORM THE FOLLOWING EXERCISE TO COMPLETION OR FAILURE.
"THIS EXERCISE IS MEANT TO SIMULATE A BASIC PACKAGE RECOVERY FROM A HOSTILE ENVIRONMENT."
SOMEWHERE BETWEEN THE SECOND ICE FIELD AND THE TRAVERSE OF THE GODS, THE WHITE KING'S KNIGHT HAS PLANTED A CHESS PIECE IDENTICAL TO THIS ONE...
...BUT EMBEDDED WITH A TERRA-6 TRACKING DEVICE KEYED TO THE RECEIVERS FIXED TO YOUR ASCENT HARNESSES.
YOUR OBJECTIVE IS SIMPLE...
"...YOU WILL LOCATE AND RETRIEVE THE PACKAGE, USING ANY AND ALL MEANS AT YOUR DISPOSAL.
"FOR THIS EXERCISE YOU WILL WORK IN TEAMS OF TWO..."
...FOUR AND EIGHT AS ONE TEAM, TWENTY-TWO AND THIRTY-SIX AS THE OTHER.
YOU ARE BEING TIMED, AND YOU SHOULD BE PREPARED TO DEFEND ANY ACTIONS YOU TAKE ON THE MOUNTAIN.
THE EXERCISE TERMINATES WHEN ONE TEAM HAS RETRIEVED THE PACKAGE...
36
04
...OR BOTH TEAMS HAVE SUFFERED FAILURE.
36
04
08
EXECUTE.

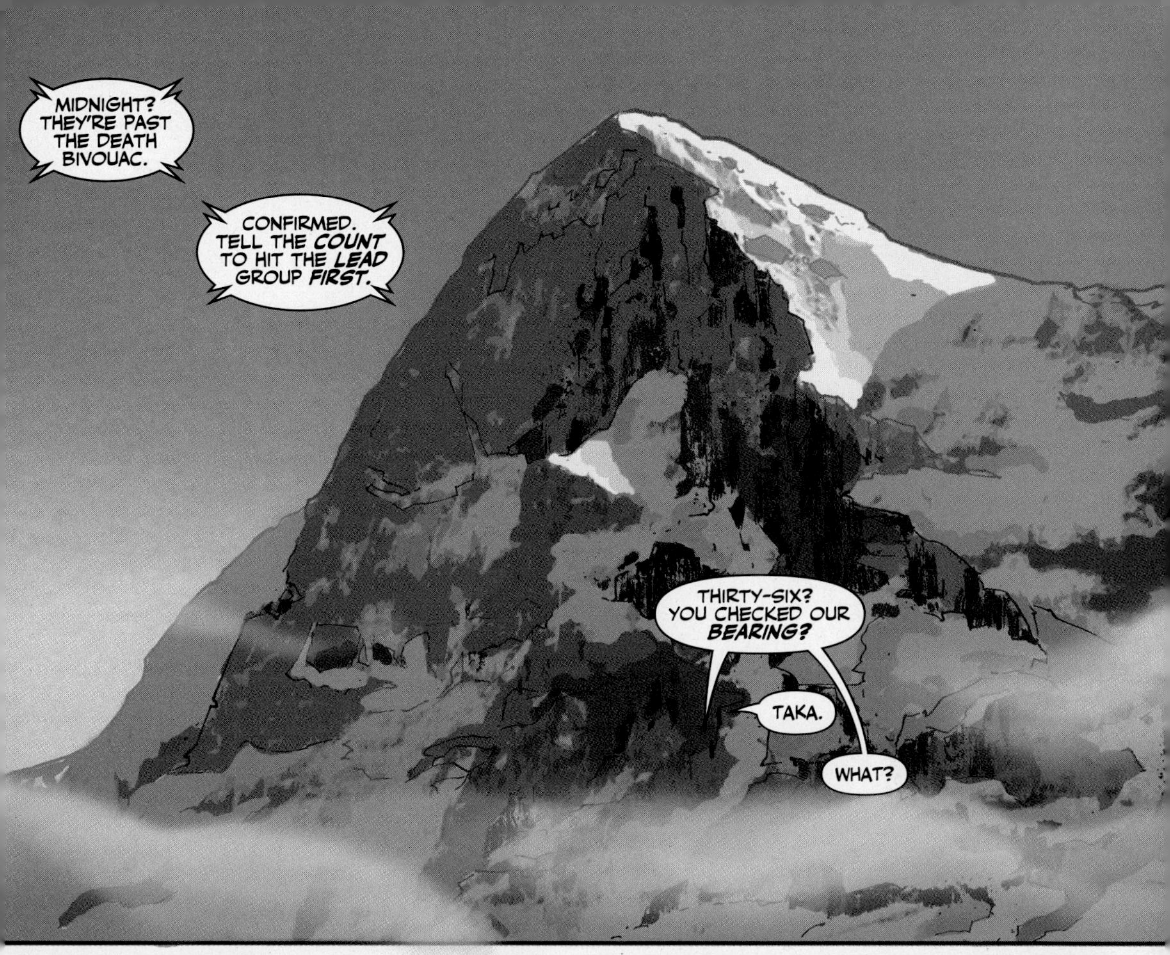

MIDNIGHT? THEY'RE PAST THE DEATH BIVOUAC.
CONFIRMED. TELL THE COUNT TO HIT THE LEAD GROUP FIRST.
THIRTY-SIX? YOU CHECKED OUR BEARING?
TAKA.
WHAT?

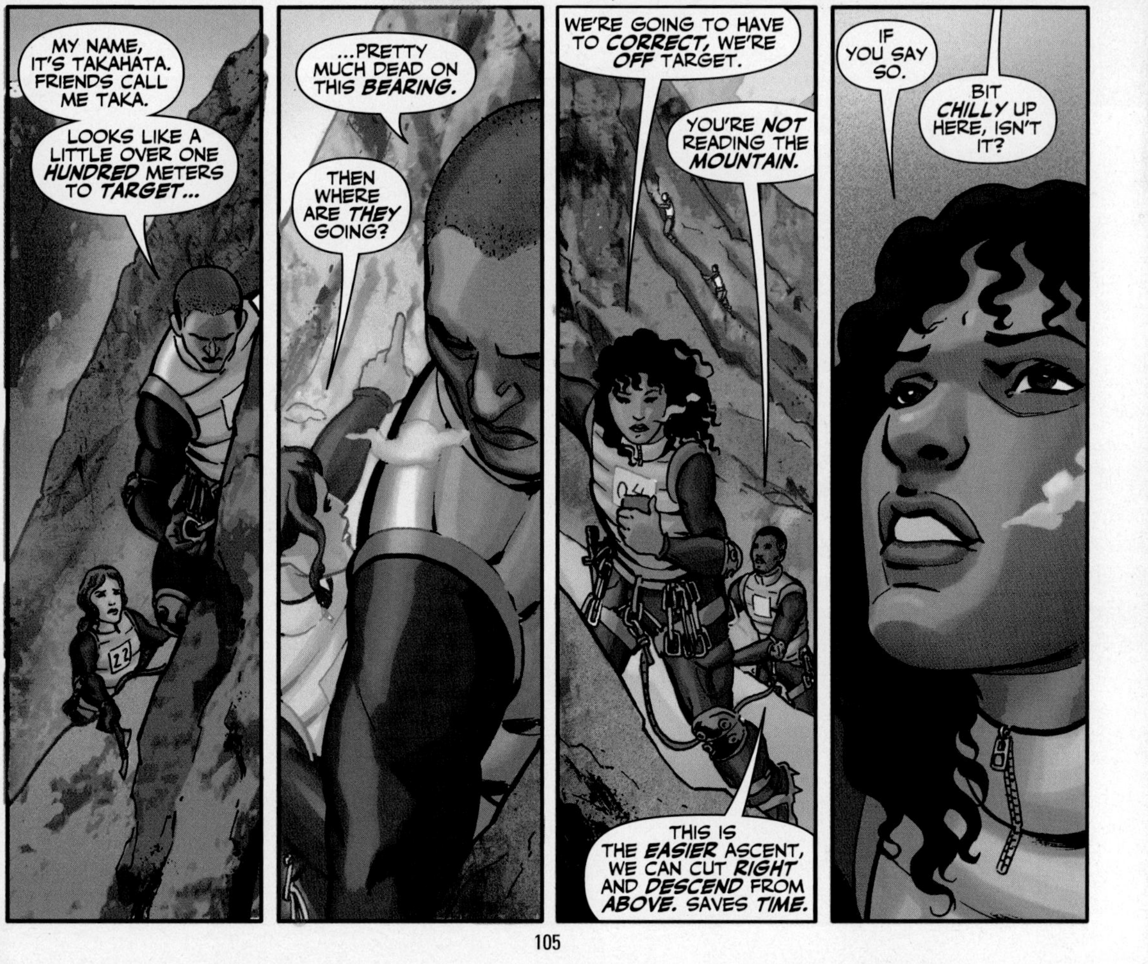

MY NAME, IT'S TAKAHATA. FRIENDS CALL ME TAKA.
LOOKS LIKE A LITTLE OVER ONE HUNDRED METERS TO TARGET...
...PRETTY MUCH DEAD ON THIS BEARING.
THEN WHERE ARE THEY GOING?
WE'RE GOING TO HAVE TO CORRECT, WE'RE OFF TARGET.
YOU'RE NOT READING THE MOUNTAIN.
THIS IS THE EASIER ASCENT, WE CAN CUT RIGHT AND DESCEND FROM ABOVE. SAVES TIME.
IF YOU SAY SO.
BIT CHILLY UP HERE, ISN'T IT?

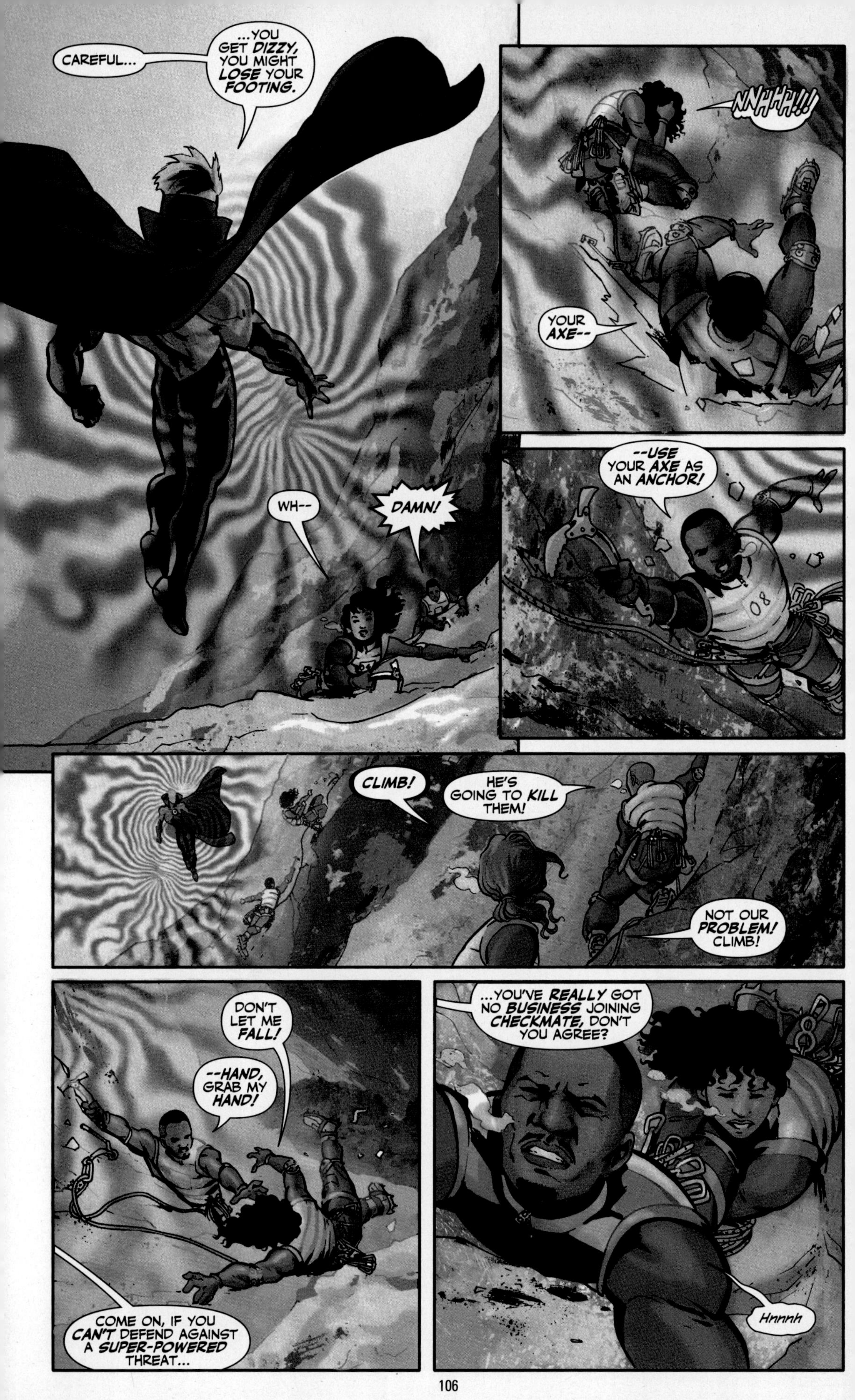
CAREFUL...
...YOU GET DIZZY, YOU MIGHT LOSE YOUR FOOTING.
NNHHH!!!
YOUR AXE--
--USE YOUR AXE AS AN ANCHOR!
WH--
DAMN!
CLIMB!
HE'S GOING TO KILL THEM!
NOT OUR PROBLEM! CLIMB!
DON'T LET ME FALL!
--HAND, GRAB MY HAND!
COME ON, IF YOU CAN'T DEFEND AGAINST A SUPER-POWERED THREAT...
...YOU'VE REALLY GOT NO BUSINESS JOINING CHECKMATE, DON'T YOU AGREE?
Hnnnh

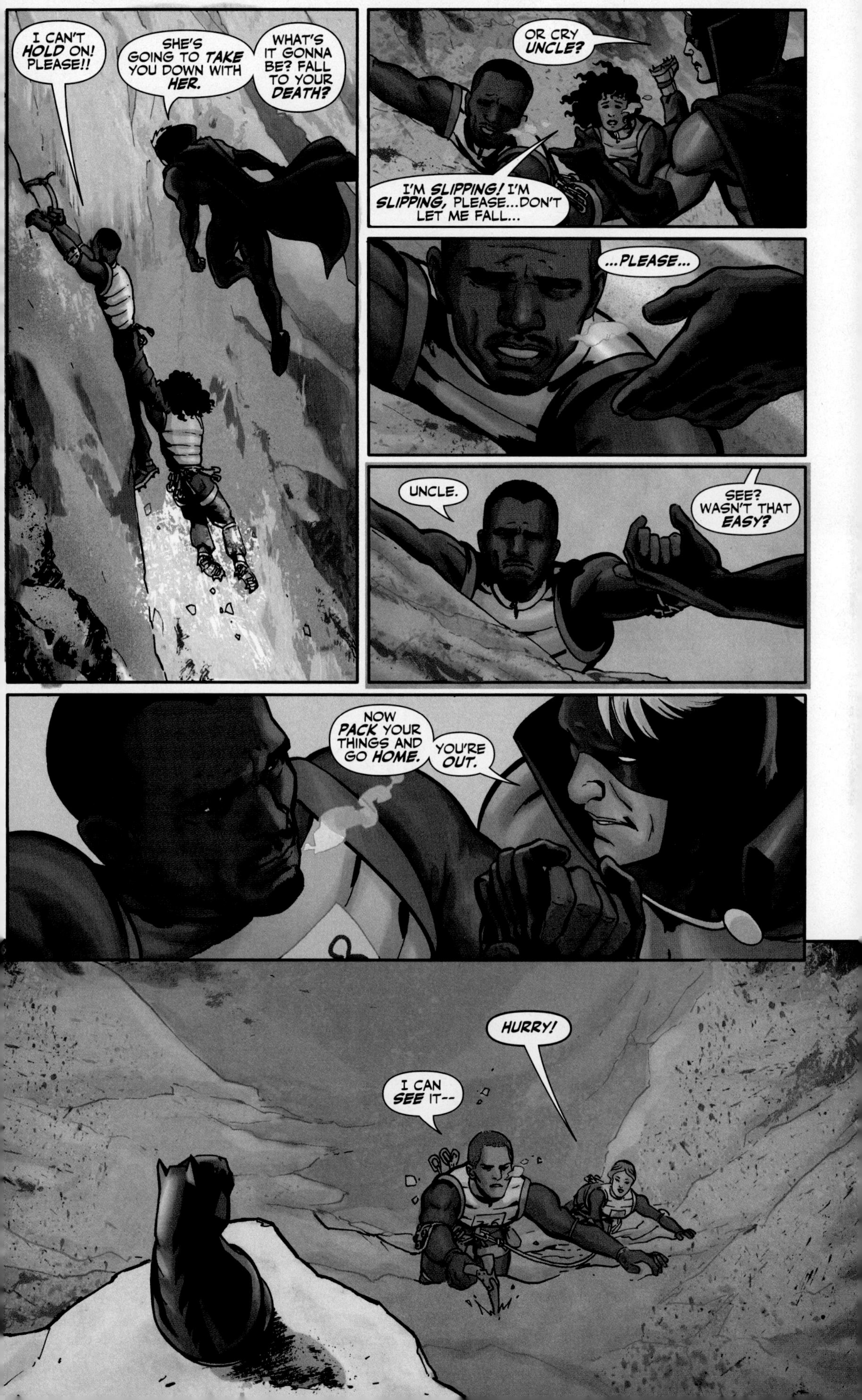
I CAN'T *HOLD* ON! PLEASE!!
SHE'S GOING TO *TAKE* YOU DOWN WITH *HER.*
WHAT'S IT GONNA BE? FALL TO YOUR *DEATH?*
OR CRY *UNCLE?*
I'M *SLIPPING!* I'M *SLIPPING,* PLEASE...DON'T LET ME FALL...
...*PLEASE*...
UNCLE.
SEE? WASN'T THAT *EASY?*
NOW *PACK* YOUR THINGS AND GO *HOME.*
YOU'RE *OUT.*
HURRY!
I CAN *SEE* IT--

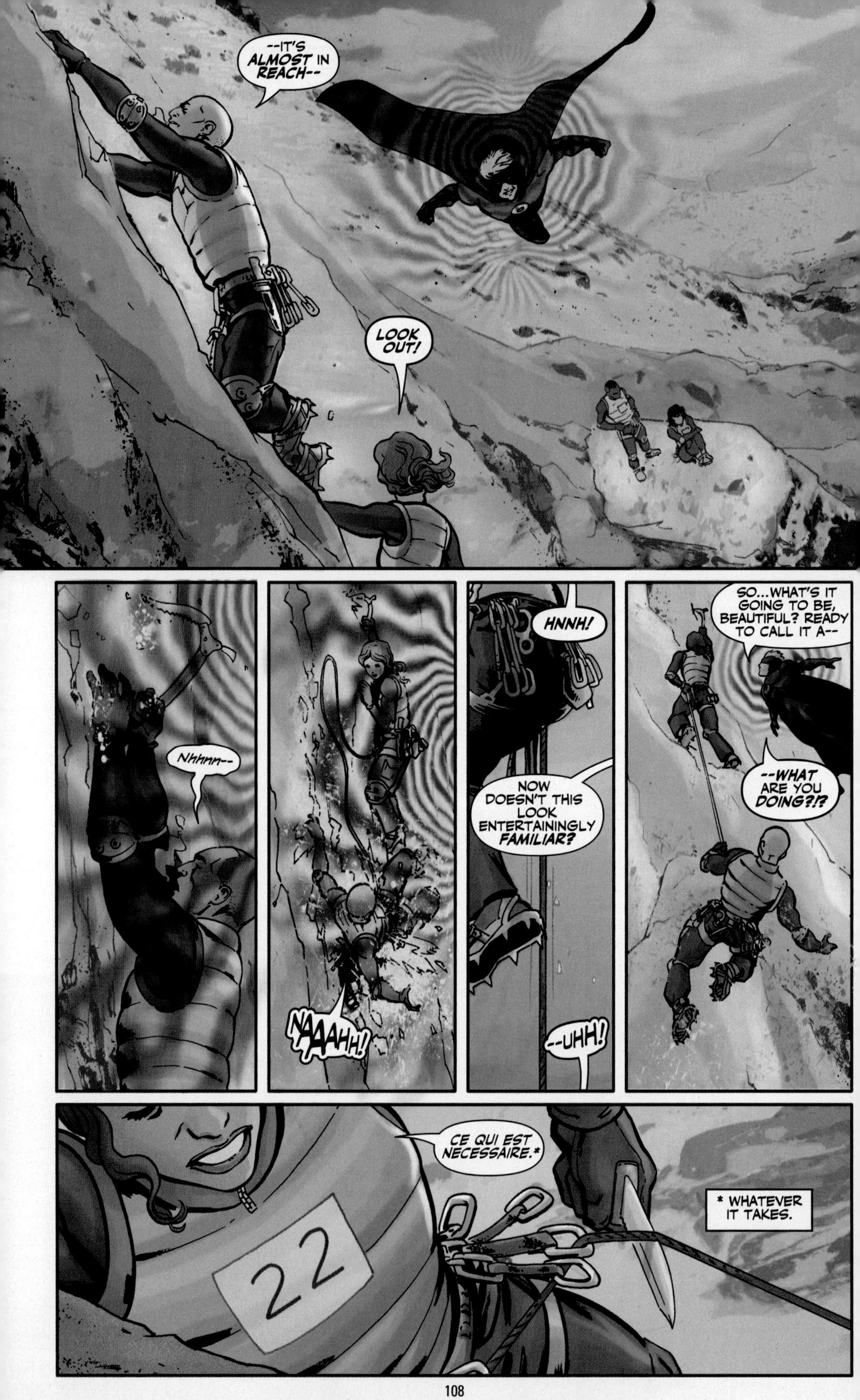

--IT'S ALMOST IN REACH--
LOOK OUT!
Nhhnn--
NAAAHH!
HNNH!
NOW DOESN'T THIS LOOK ENTERTAININGLY FAMILIAR?
--UHH!
SO...WHAT'S IT GOING TO BE, BEAUTIFUL? READY TO CALL IT A--
--WHAT ARE YOU DOING?!?
CE QUI EST NECESSAIRE.*
* WHATEVER IT TAKES.
22

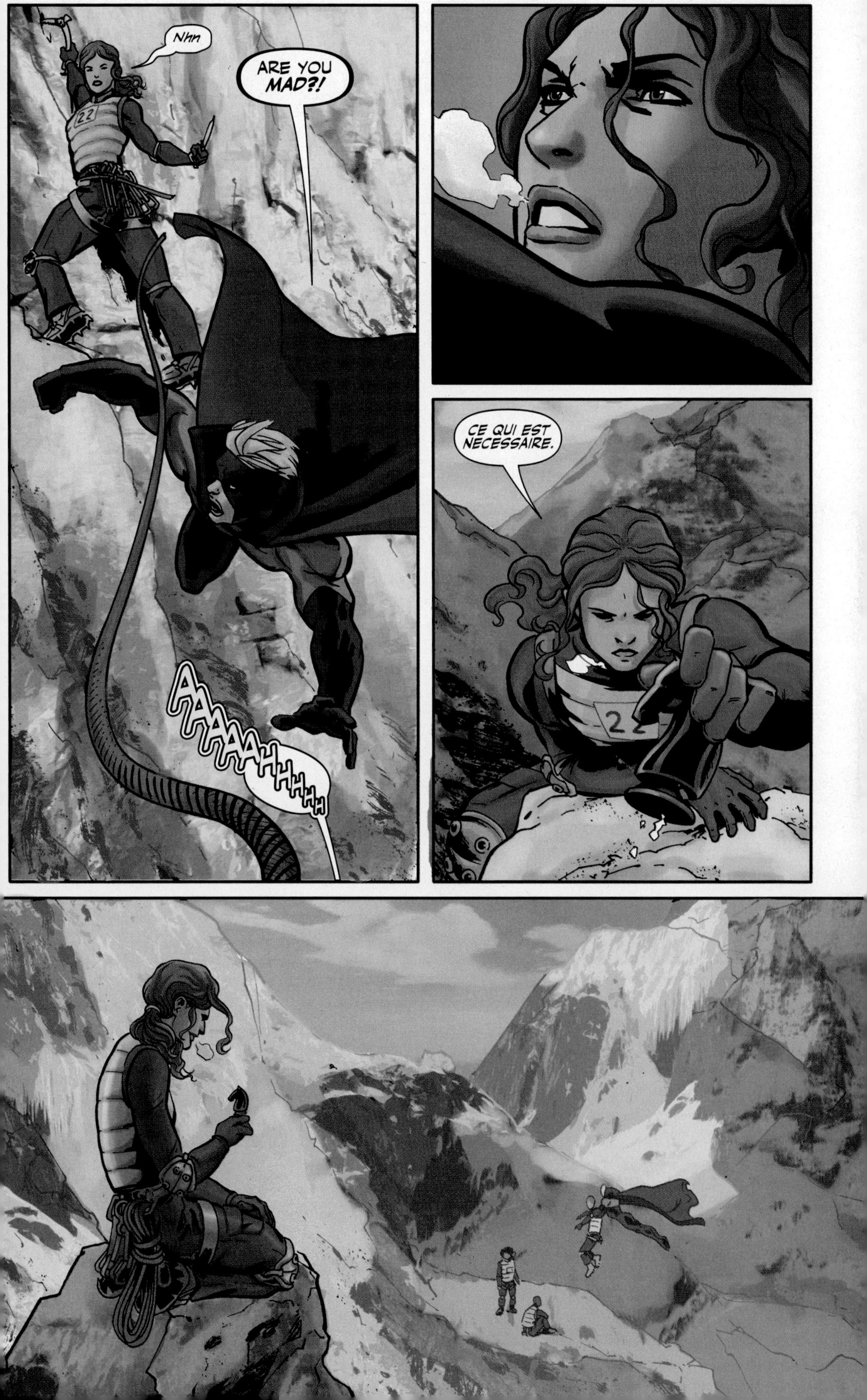
Nhn
ARE YOU MAD?!
AAAAAAHHHHH
CE QUI EST NECESSAIRE.

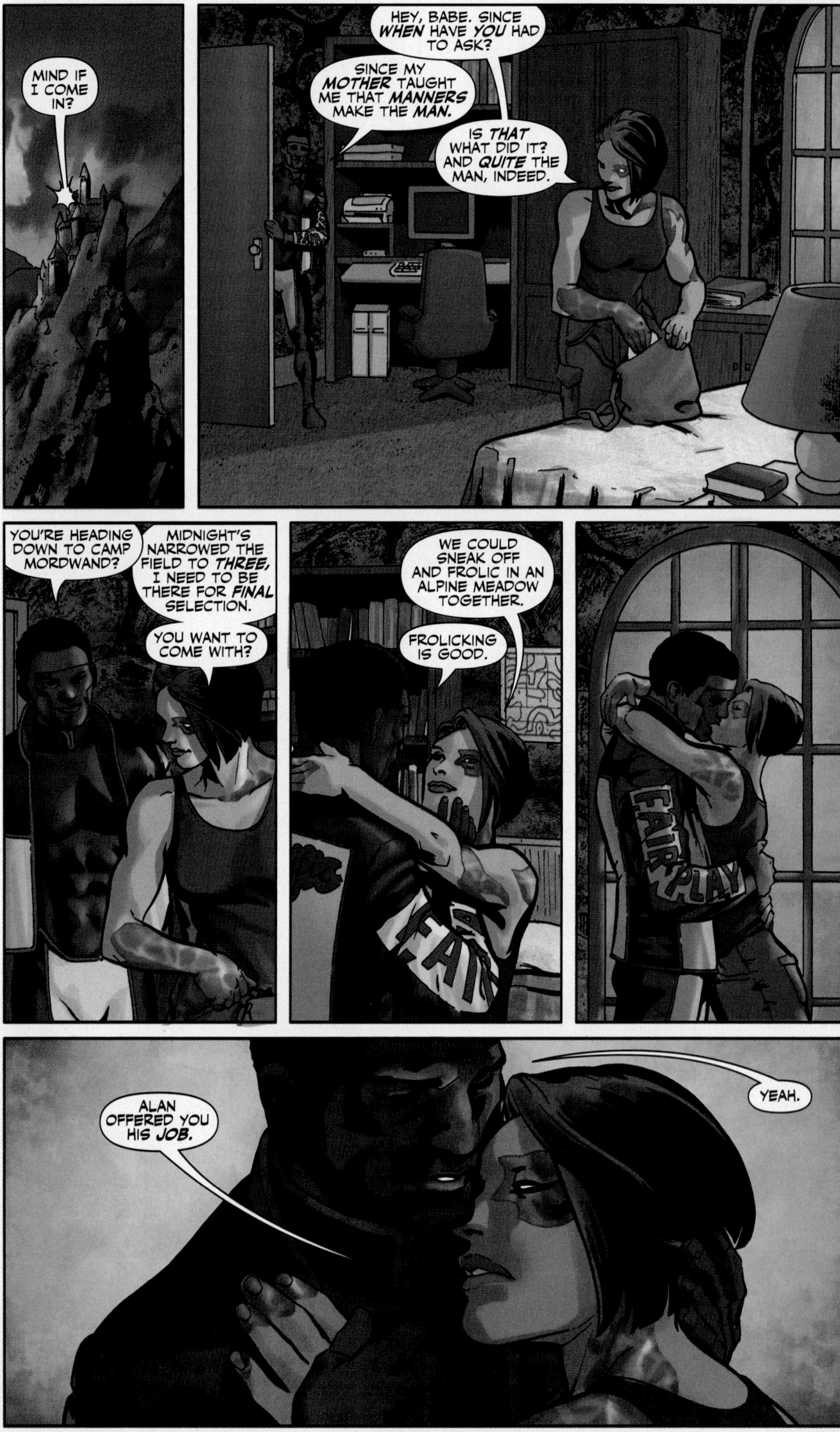
MIND IF I COME IN?
HEY, BABE. SINCE WHEN HAVE YOU HAD TO ASK?
SINCE MY MOTHER TAUGHT ME THAT MANNERS MAKE THE MAN.
IS THAT WHAT DID IT? AND QUITE THE MAN, INDEED.
YOU'RE HEADING DOWN TO CAMP MORDWAND?
MIDNIGHT'S NARROWED THE FIELD TO THREE, I NEED TO BE THERE FOR FINAL SELECTION.
YOU WANT TO COME WITH?
WE COULD SNEAK OFF AND FROLIC IN AN ALPINE MEADOW TOGETHER.
FROLICKING IS GOOD.
FAIR PLAY
ALAN OFFERED YOU HIS JOB.
YEAH.

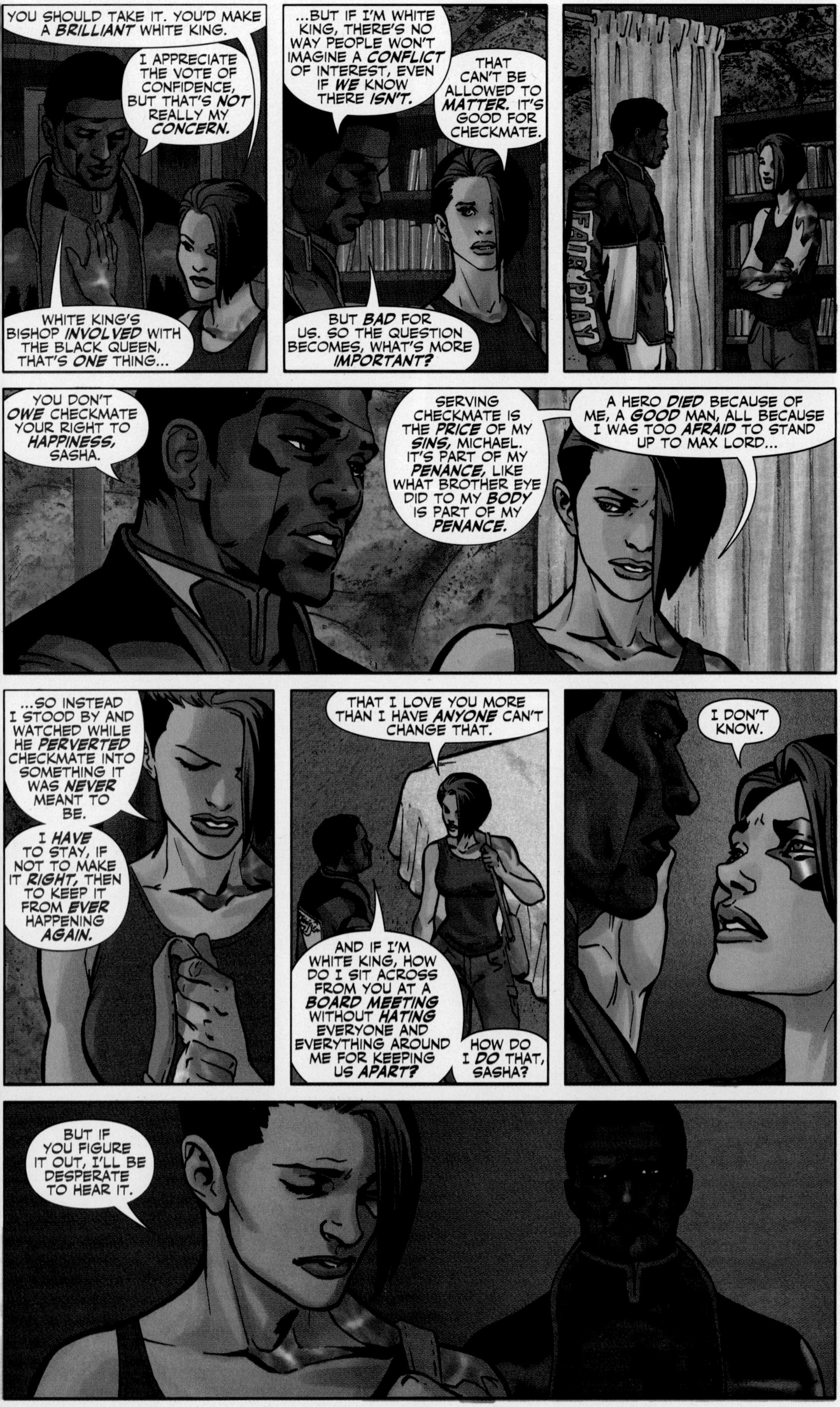

YOU SHOULD TAKE IT. YOU'D MAKE A BRILLIANT WHITE KING.
I APPRECIATE THE VOTE OF CONFIDENCE, BUT THAT'S NOT REALLY MY CONCERN.
WHITE KING'S BISHOP INVOLVED WITH THE BLACK QUEEN, THAT'S ONE THING...
...BUT IF I'M WHITE KING, THERE'S NO WAY PEOPLE WON'T IMAGINE A CONFLICT OF INTEREST, EVEN IF WE KNOW THERE ISN'T.
THAT CAN'T BE ALLOWED TO MATTER. IT'S GOOD FOR CHECKMATE.
BUT BAD FOR US. SO THE QUESTION BECOMES, WHAT'S MORE IMPORTANT?
FAIR PLAY
YOU DON'T OWE CHECKMATE YOUR RIGHT TO HAPPINESS, SASHA.
SERVING CHECKMATE IS THE PRICE OF MY SINS, MICHAEL. IT'S PART OF MY PENANCE, LIKE WHAT BROTHER EYE DID TO MY BODY IS PART OF MY PENANCE.
A HERO DIED BECAUSE OF ME, A GOOD MAN, ALL BECAUSE I WAS TOO AFRAID TO STAND UP TO MAX LORD...
...SO INSTEAD I STOOD BY AND WATCHED WHILE HE PERVERTED CHECKMATE INTO SOMETHING IT WAS NEVER MEANT TO BE.
I HAVE TO STAY, IF NOT TO MAKE IT RIGHT, THEN TO KEEP IT FROM EVER HAPPENING AGAIN.
THAT I LOVE YOU MORE THAN I HAVE ANYONE CAN'T CHANGE THAT.
AND IF I'M WHITE KING, HOW DO I SIT ACROSS FROM YOU AT A BOARD MEETING WITHOUT HATING EVERYONE AND EVERYTHING AROUND ME FOR KEEPING US APART?
HOW DO I DO THAT, SASHA?
I DON'T KNOW.
BUT IF YOU FIGURE IT OUT, I'LL BE DESPERATE TO HEAR IT.

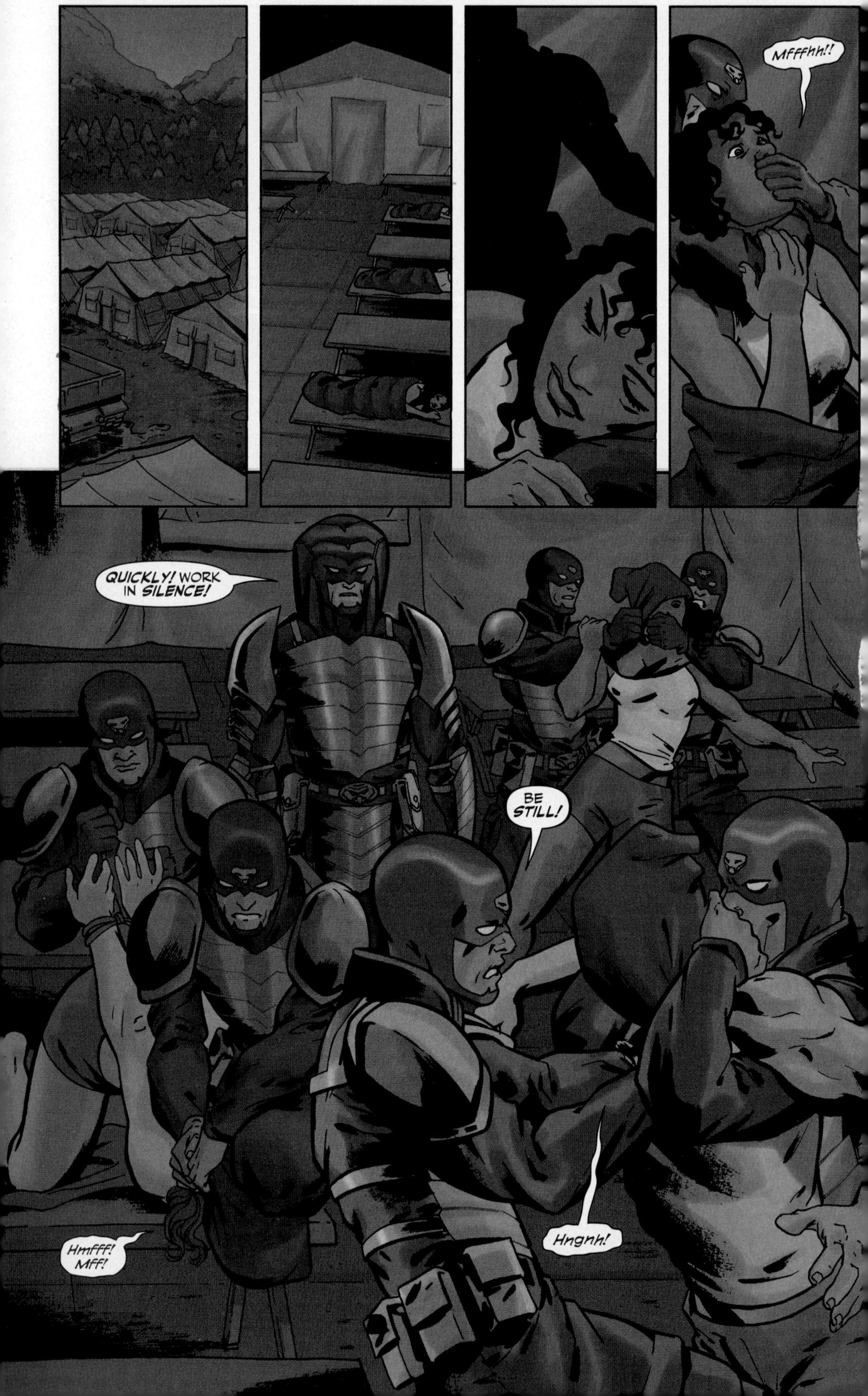
Mfffhh!!
QUICKLY! WORK IN SILENCE!
BE STILL!
Hmfff! Mff!
Hngnh!

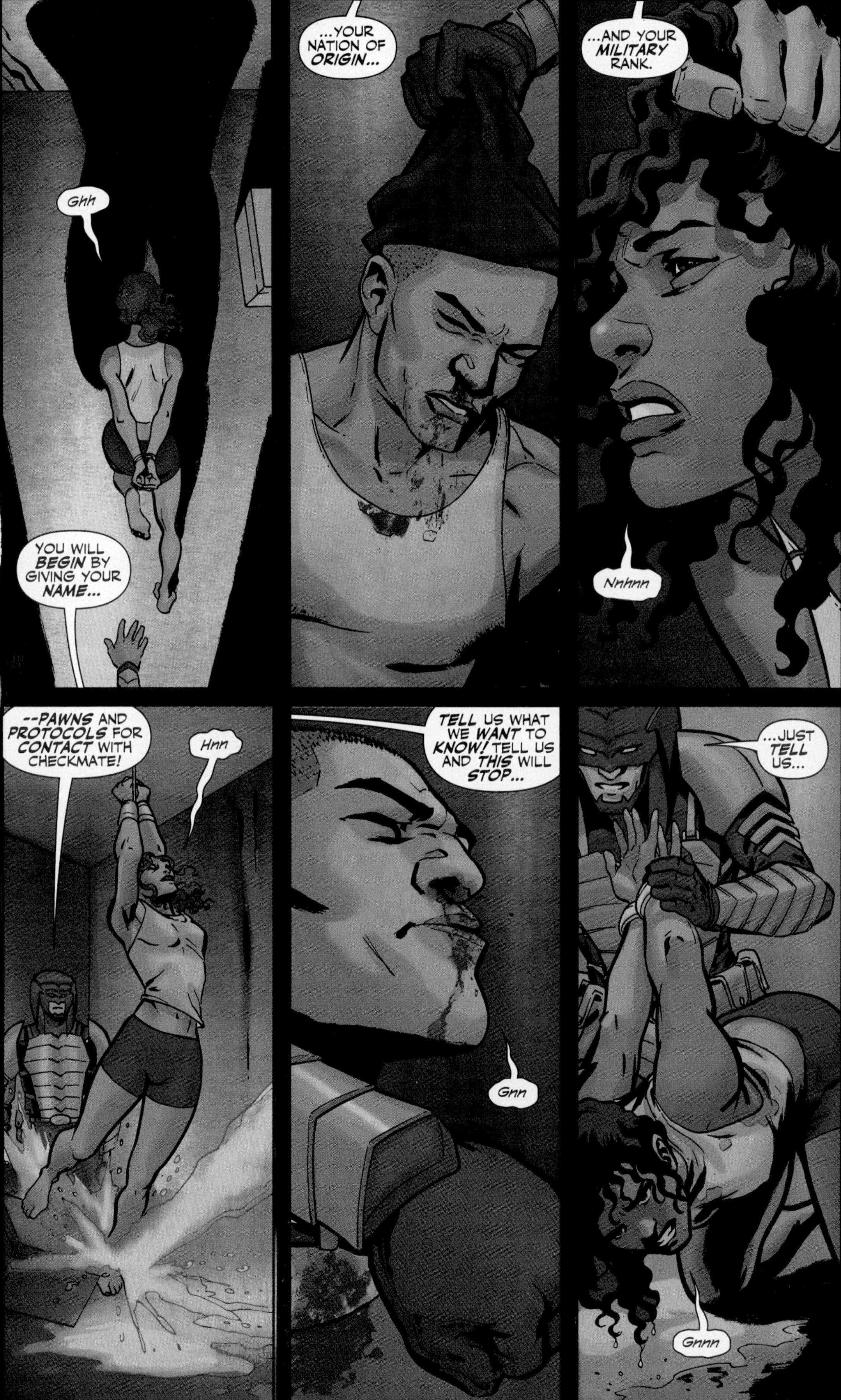
Ghh
YOU WILL BEGIN BY GIVING YOUR NAME...
...YOUR NATION OF ORIGIN...
...AND YOUR MILITARY RANK.
Nnhnn
--PAWNS AND PROTOCOLS FOR CONTACT WITH CHECKMATE!
Hnn
TELL US WHAT WE WANT TO KNOW! TELL US AND THIS WILL STOP...
Gnn
...JUST TELL US...
Gnnn

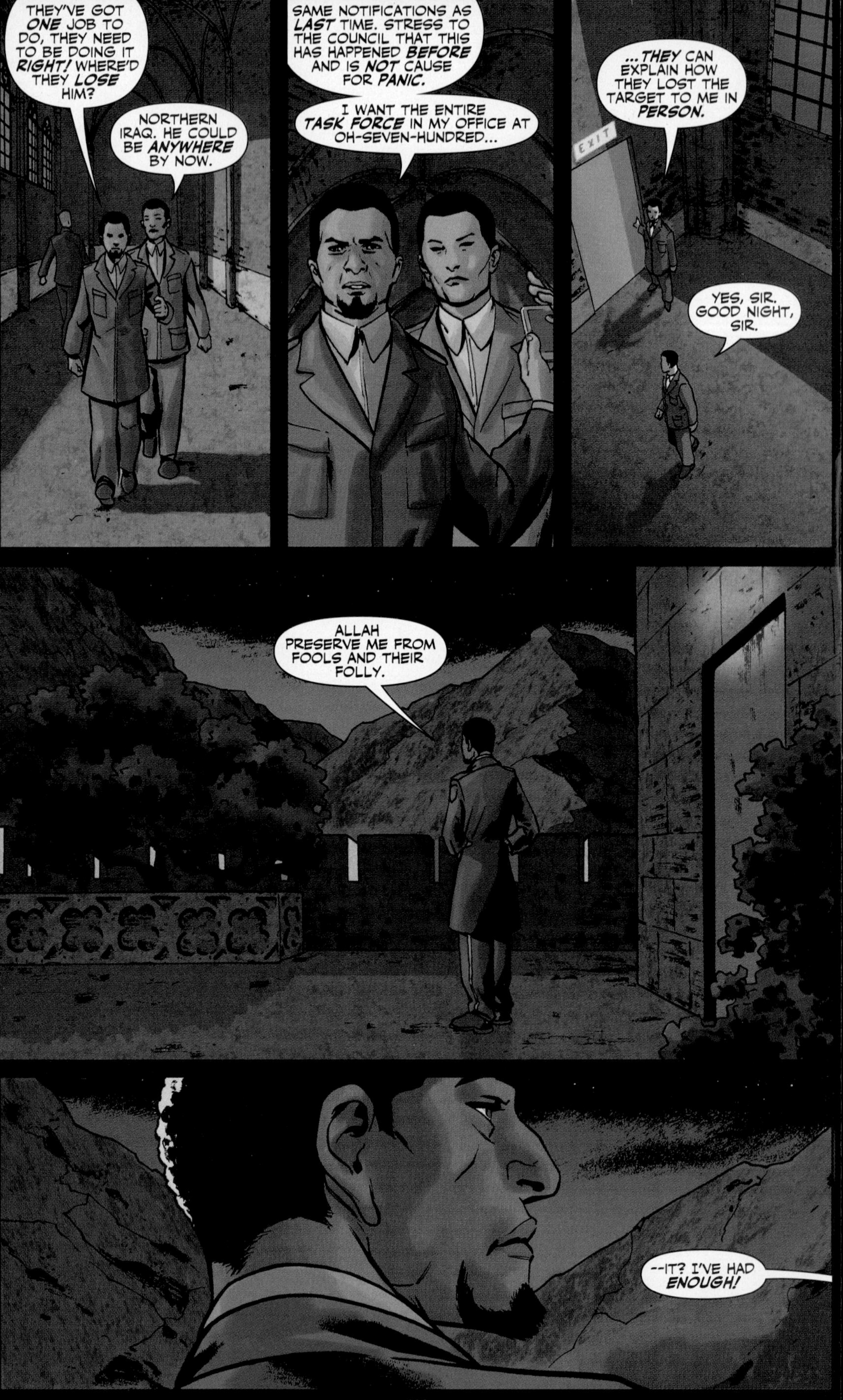
THEY'VE GOT ONE JOB TO DO, THEY NEED TO BE DOING IT RIGHT! WHERE'D THEY LOSE HIM?
NORTHERN IRAQ. HE COULD BE ANYWHERE BY NOW.
SAME NOTIFICATIONS AS LAST TIME. STRESS TO THE COUNCIL THAT THIS HAS HAPPENED BEFORE AND IS NOT CAUSE FOR PANIC.
I WANT THE ENTIRE TASK FORCE IN MY OFFICE AT OH-SEVEN-HUNDRED...
...THEY CAN EXPLAIN HOW THEY LOST THE TARGET TO ME IN PERSON.
EXIT
YES, SIR. GOOD NIGHT, SIR.
ALLAH PRESERVE ME FROM FOOLS AND THEIR FOLLY.
--IT? I'VE HAD ENOUGH!

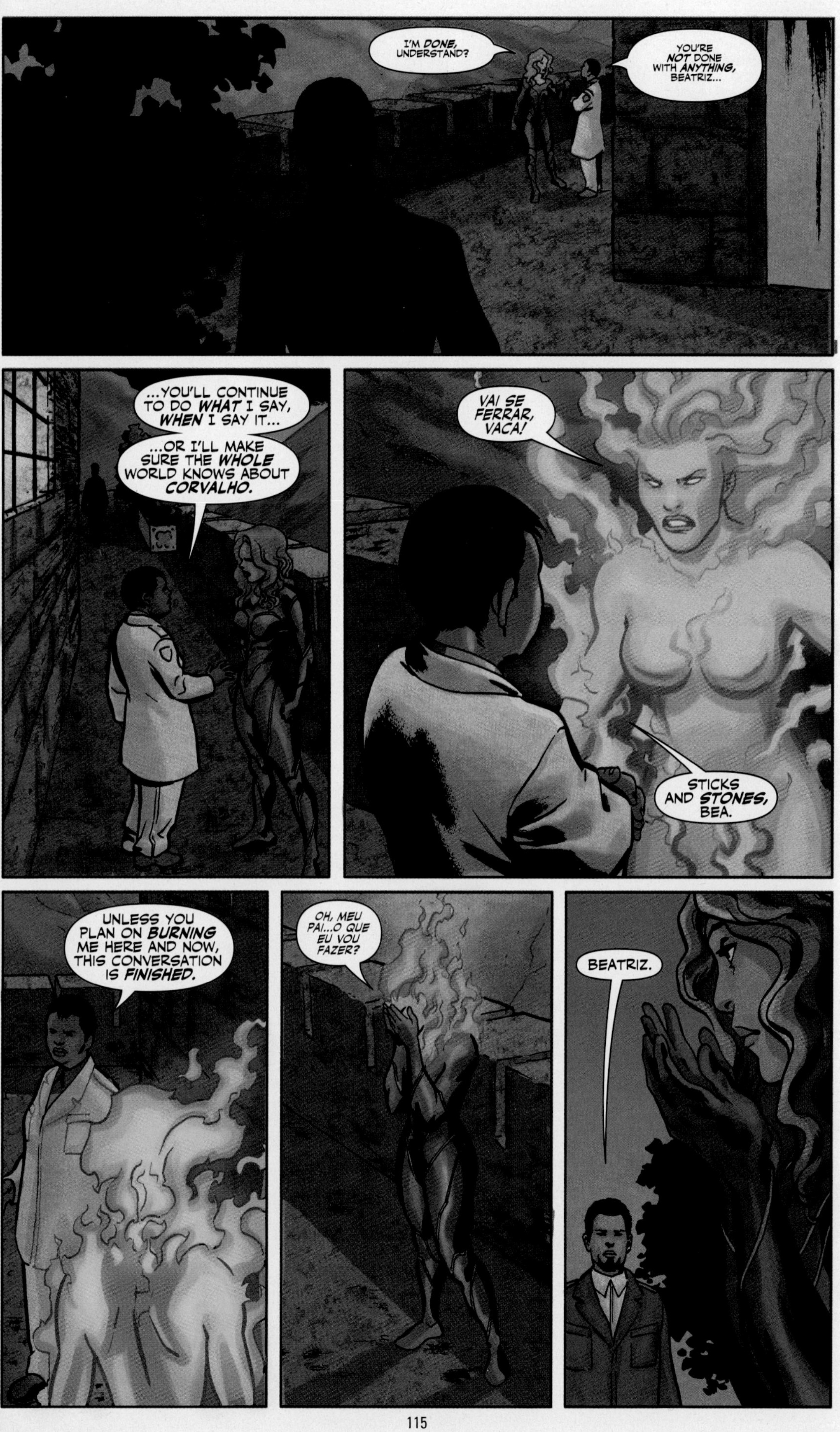

I'M DONE, UNDERSTAND?
YOU'RE NOT DONE WITH ANYTHING, BEATRIZ...
...YOU'LL CONTINUE TO DO WHAT I SAY, WHEN I SAY IT...
...OR I'LL MAKE SURE THE WHOLE WORLD KNOWS ABOUT CORVALHO.
VAI SE FERRAR, VACA!
STICKS AND STONES, BEA.
UNLESS YOU PLAN ON BURNING ME HERE AND NOW, THIS CONVERSATION IS FINISHED.
OH, MEU PAI...O QUE EU VOU FAZER?
BEATRIZ.

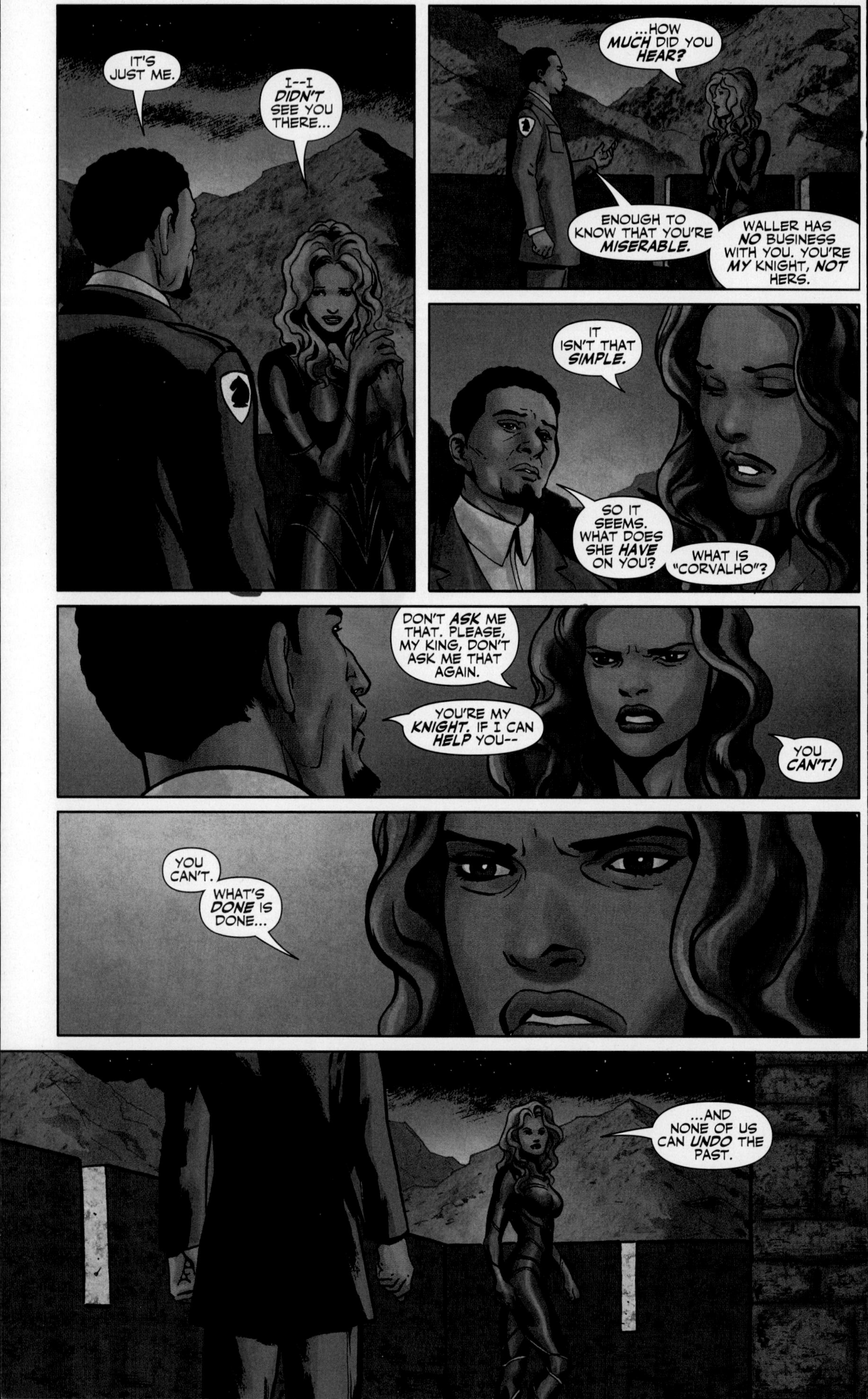
IT'S JUST ME.
I--I DIDN'T SEE YOU THERE...
...HOW MUCH DID YOU HEAR?
ENOUGH TO KNOW THAT YOU'RE MISERABLE.
WALLER HAS NO BUSINESS WITH YOU. YOU'RE MY KNIGHT, NOT HERS.
IT ISN'T THAT SIMPLE.
SO IT SEEMS. WHAT DOES SHE HAVE ON YOU?
WHAT IS "CORVALHO"?
DON'T ASK ME THAT. PLEASE, MY KING, DON'T ASK ME THAT AGAIN.
YOU'RE MY KNIGHT. IF I CAN HELP YOU--
YOU CAN'T!
YOU CAN'T.
WHAT'S DONE IS DONE...
...AND NONE OF US CAN UNDO THE PAST.

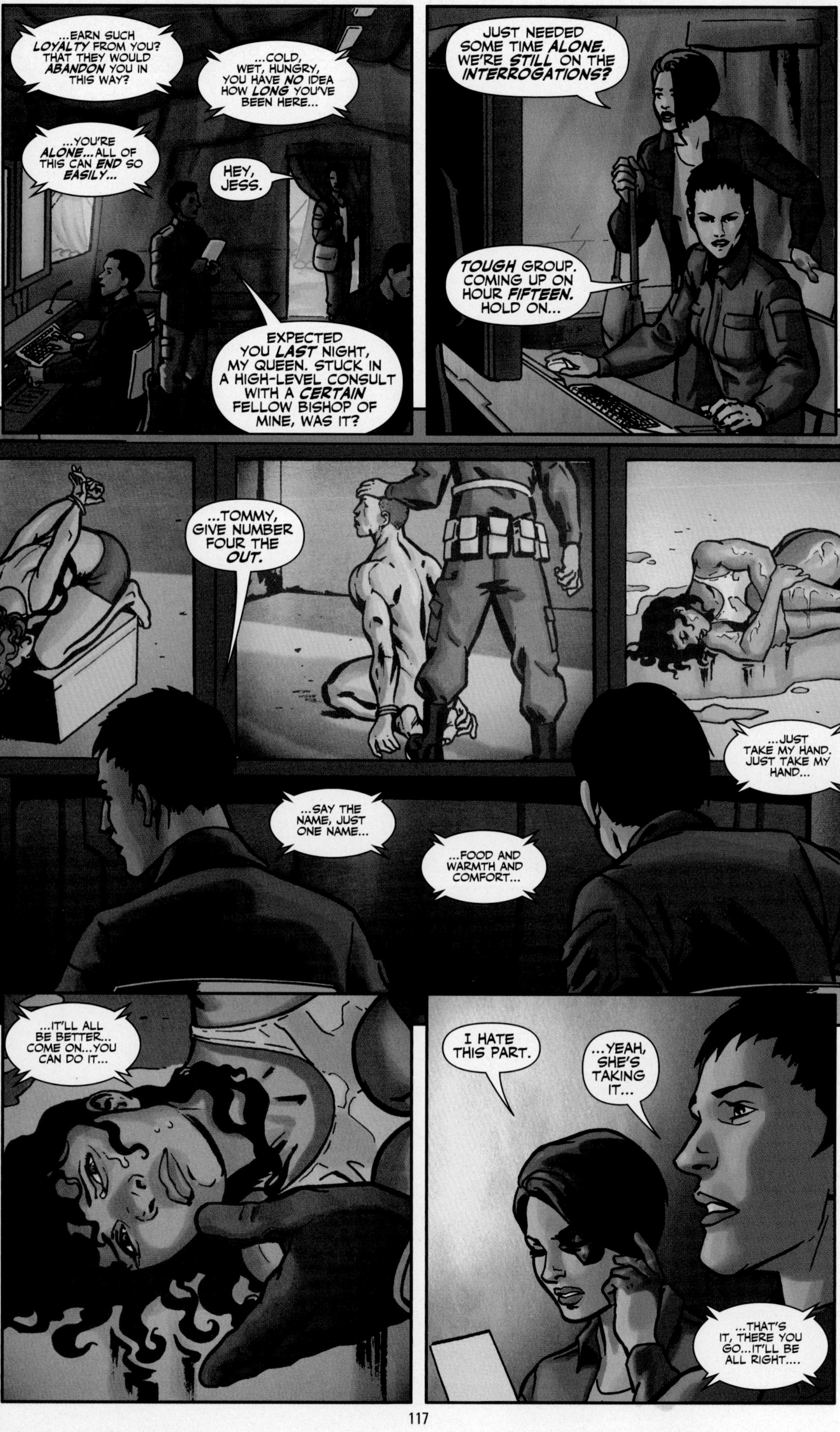
...EARN SUCH LOYALTY FROM YOU? THAT THEY WOULD ABANDON YOU IN THIS WAY?
...COLD, WET, HUNGRY, YOU HAVE NO IDEA HOW LONG YOU'VE BEEN HERE...
...YOU'RE ALONE...ALL OF THIS CAN END SO EASILY...
HEY, JESS.
EXPECTED YOU LAST NIGHT, MY QUEEN. STUCK IN A HIGH-LEVEL CONSULT WITH A CERTAIN FELLOW BISHOP OF MINE, WAS IT?
JUST NEEDED SOME TIME ALONE. WE'RE STILL ON THE INTERROGATIONS?
TOUGH GROUP. COMING UP ON HOUR FIFTEEN. HOLD ON...
...TOMMY, GIVE NUMBER FOUR THE OUT.
...JUST TAKE MY HAND. JUST TAKE MY HAND...
...SAY THE NAME, JUST ONE NAME...
...FOOD AND WARMTH AND COMFORT...
...IT'LL ALL BE BETTER...COME ON...YOU CAN DO IT...
I HATE THIS PART.
...YEAH, SHE'S TAKING IT...
...THAT'S IT, THERE YOU GO...IT'LL BE ALL RIGHT....

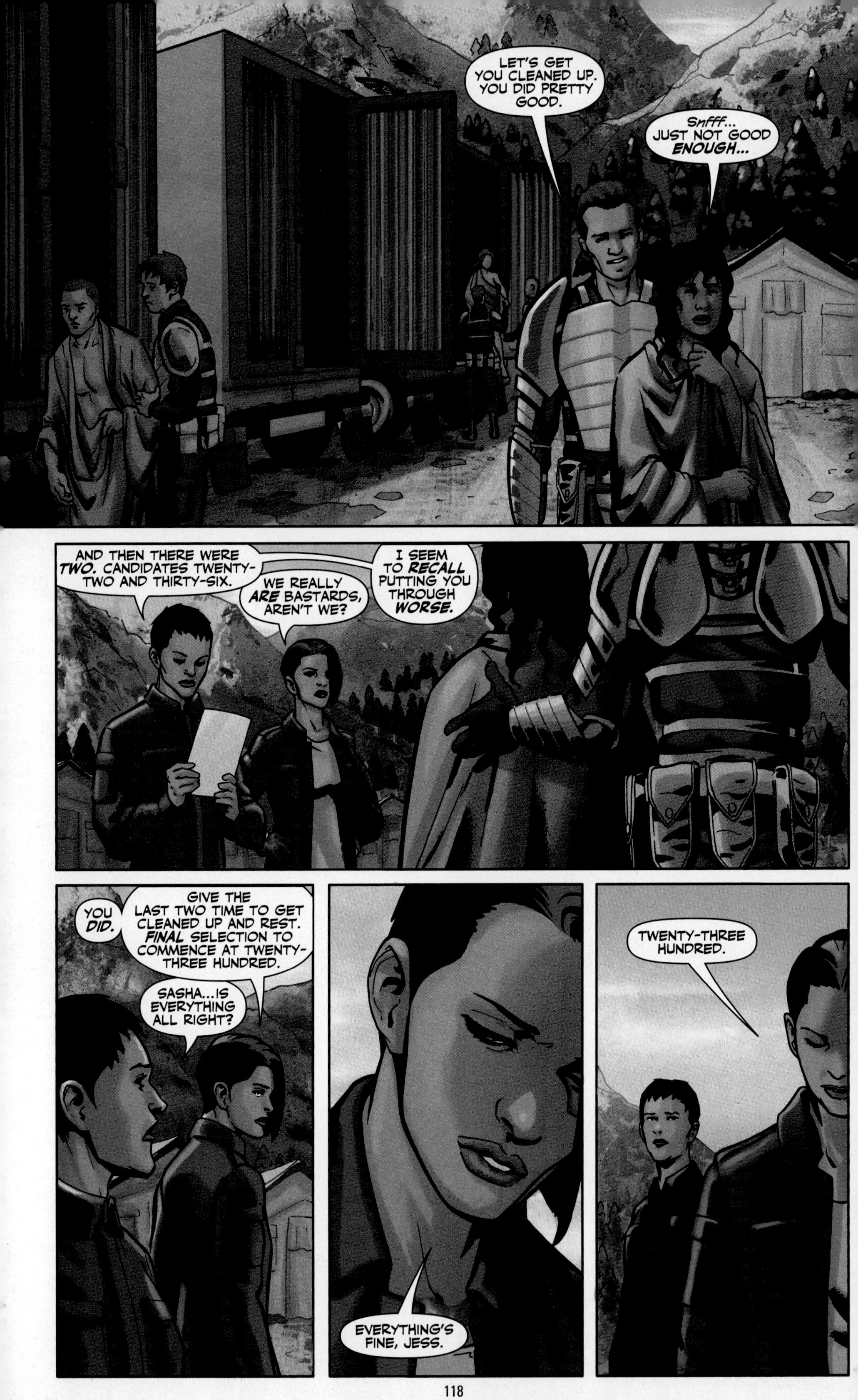
LET'S GET YOU CLEANED UP. YOU DID PRETTY GOOD.
Snfff... JUST NOT GOOD ENOUGH...
AND THEN THERE WERE TWO. CANDIDATES TWENTY-TWO AND THIRTY-SIX.
WE REALLY ARE BASTARDS, AREN'T WE?
I SEEM TO RECALL PUTTING YOU THROUGH WORSE.
YOU DID.
GIVE THE LAST TWO TIME TO GET CLEANED UP AND REST. FINAL SELECTION TO COMMENCE AT TWENTY-THREE HUNDRED.
SASHA...IS EVERYTHING ALL RIGHT?
EVERYTHING'S FINE, JESS.
TWENTY-THREE HUNDRED.

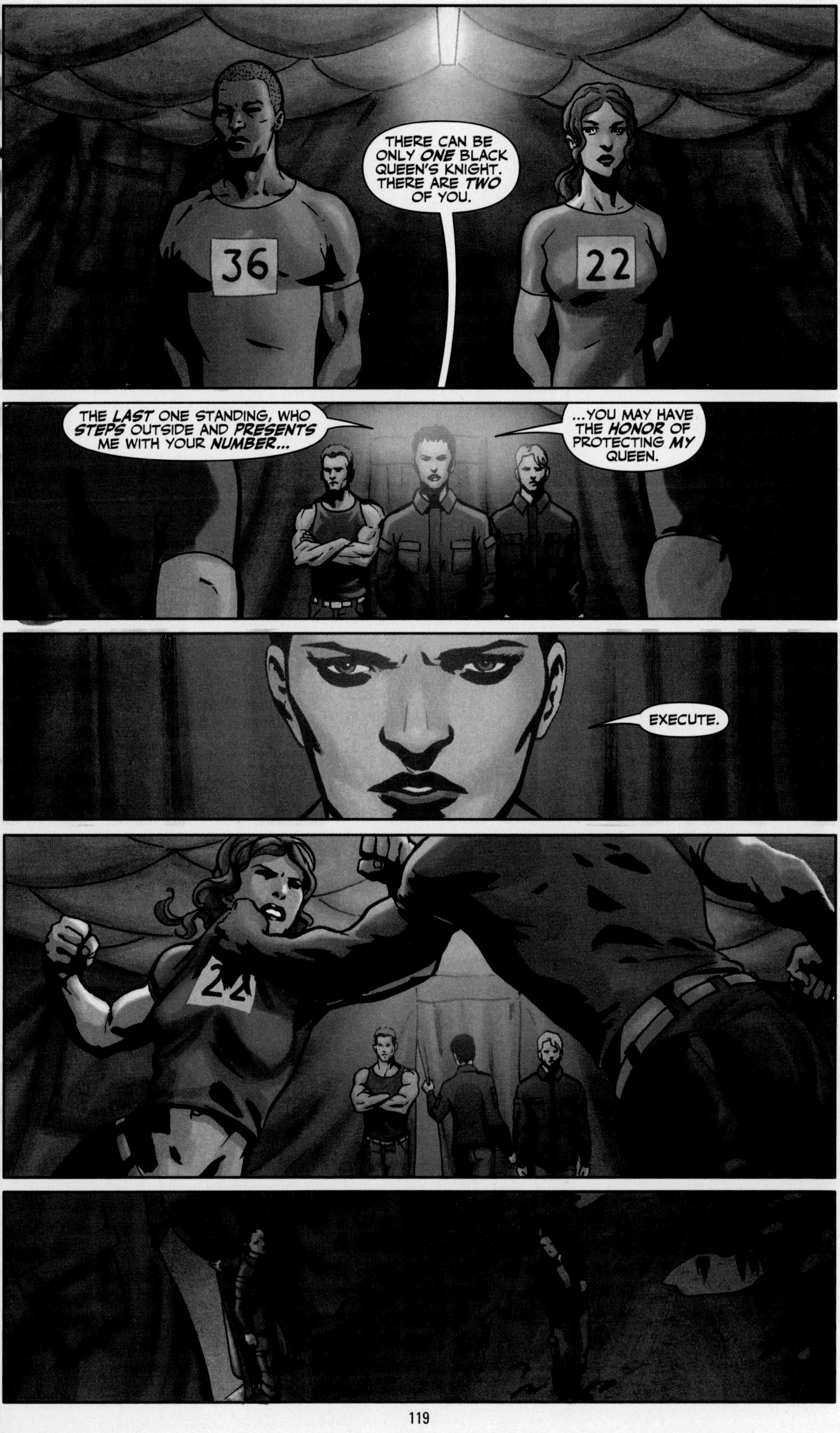

THERE CAN BE ONLY ONE BLACK QUEEN'S KNIGHT. THERE ARE TWO OF YOU.
36
22
THE LAST ONE STANDING, WHO STEPS OUTSIDE AND PRESENTS ME WITH YOUR NUMBER...
...YOU MAY HAVE THE HONOR OF PROTECTING MY QUEEN.
EXECUTE.
22

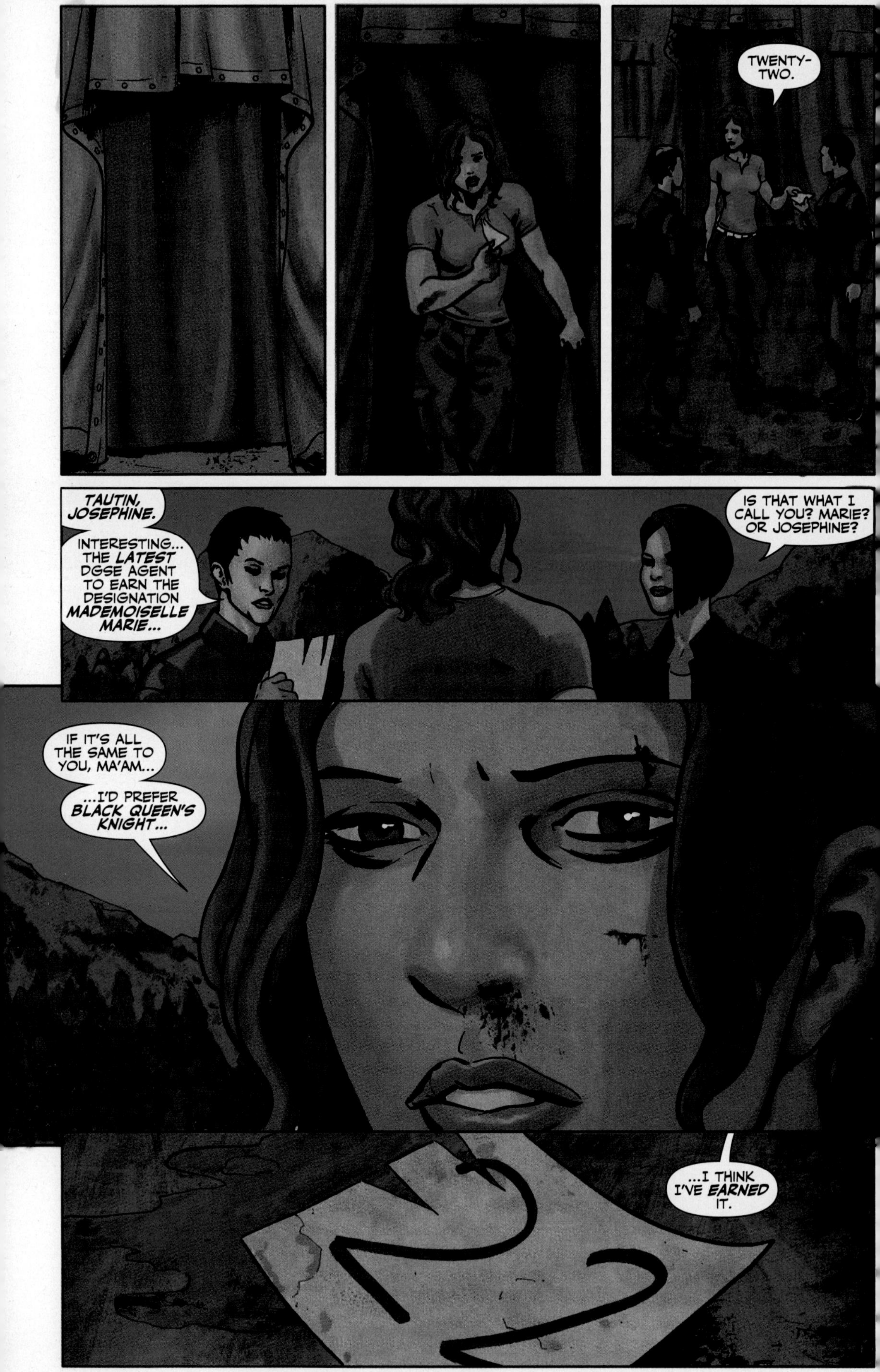

TWENTY-TWO.
TAUTIN, JOSEPHINE.
INTERESTING... THE LATEST DGSE AGENT TO EARN THE DESIGNATION MADEMOISELLE MARIE...
IS THAT WHAT I CALL YOU? MARIE? OR JOSEPHINE?
IF IT'S ALL THE SAME TO YOU, MA'AM...
...I'D PREFER BLACK QUEEN'S KNIGHT...
...I THINK I'VE EARNED IT.

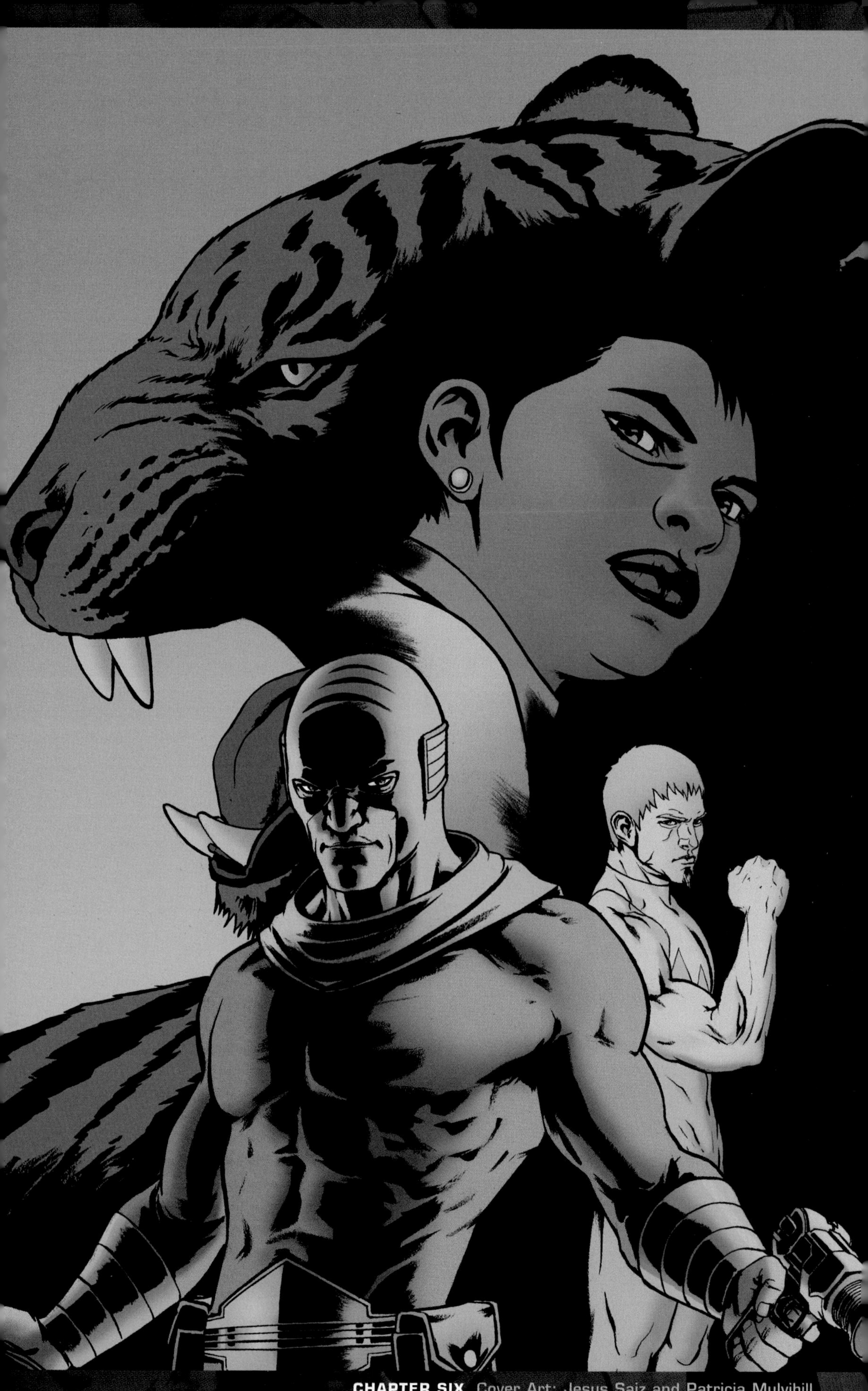

CHAPTER SIX Cover Art: Jesus Saiz and Patricia Mulvihill

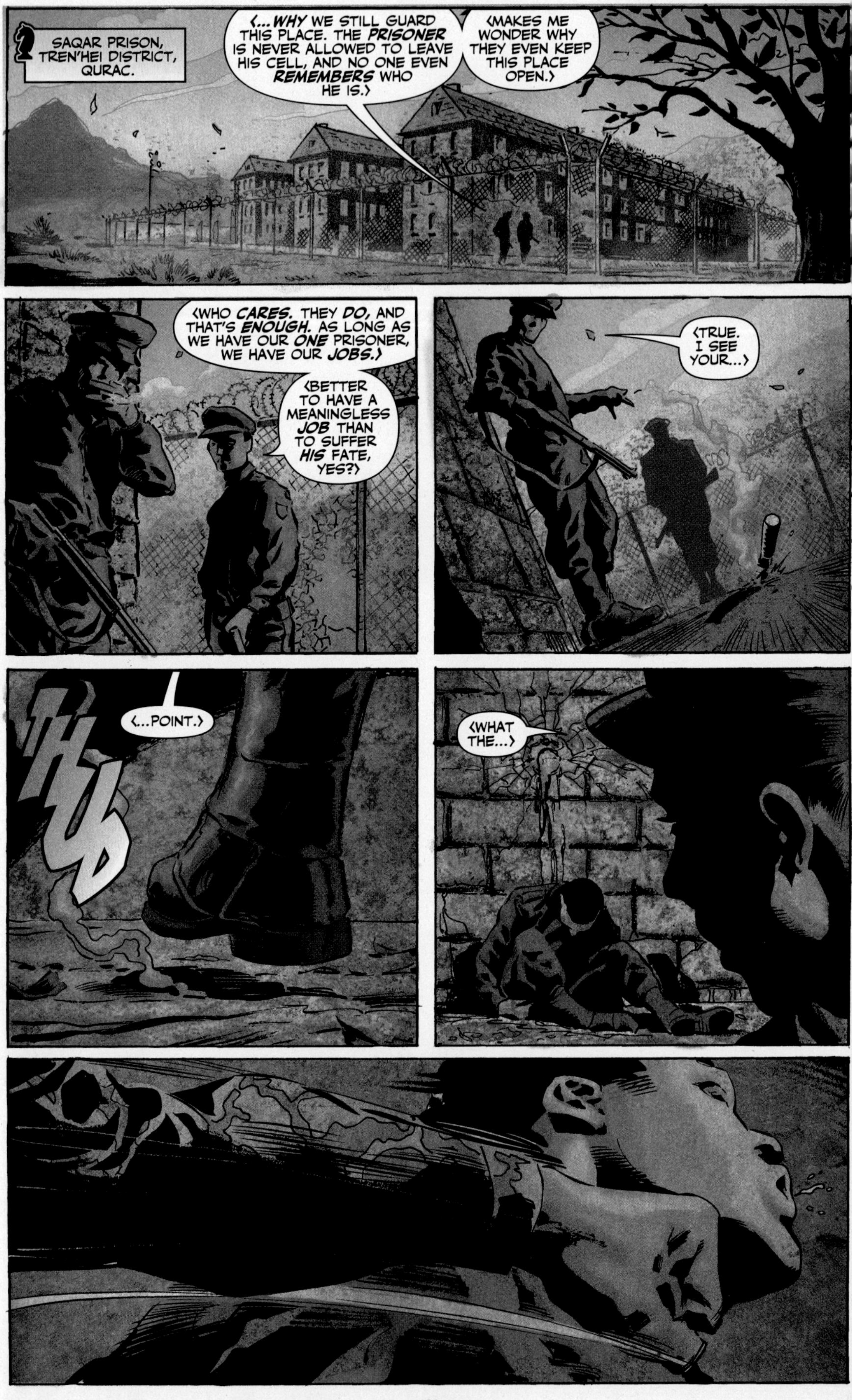

SAQAR PRISON, TREN'HEI DISTRICT, QURAC.
‹...WHY WE STILL GUARD THIS PLACE. THE PRISONER IS NEVER ALLOWED TO LEAVE HIS CELL, AND NO ONE EVEN REMEMBERS WHO HE IS.›
‹MAKES ME WONDER WHY THEY EVEN KEEP THIS PLACE OPEN.›
‹WHO CARES. THEY DO, AND THAT'S ENOUGH. AS LONG AS WE HAVE OUR ONE PRISONER, WE HAVE OUR JOBS.›
‹BETTER TO HAVE A MEANINGLESS JOB THAN TO SUFFER HIS FATE, YES?›
‹TRUE. I SEE YOUR...›
THUD
‹...POINT.›
‹WHAT THE...›

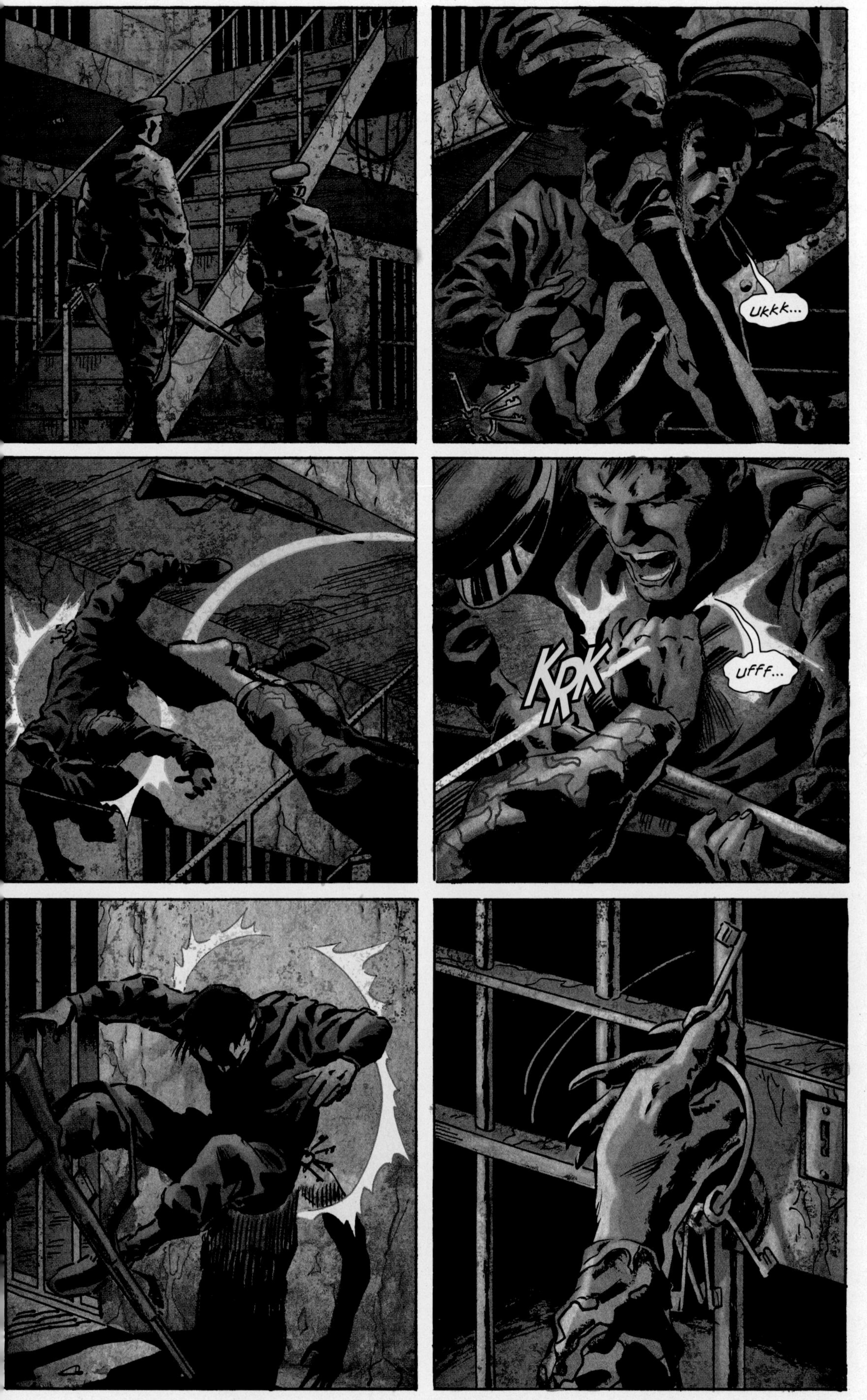
UKKK...
KRK
UFFF...

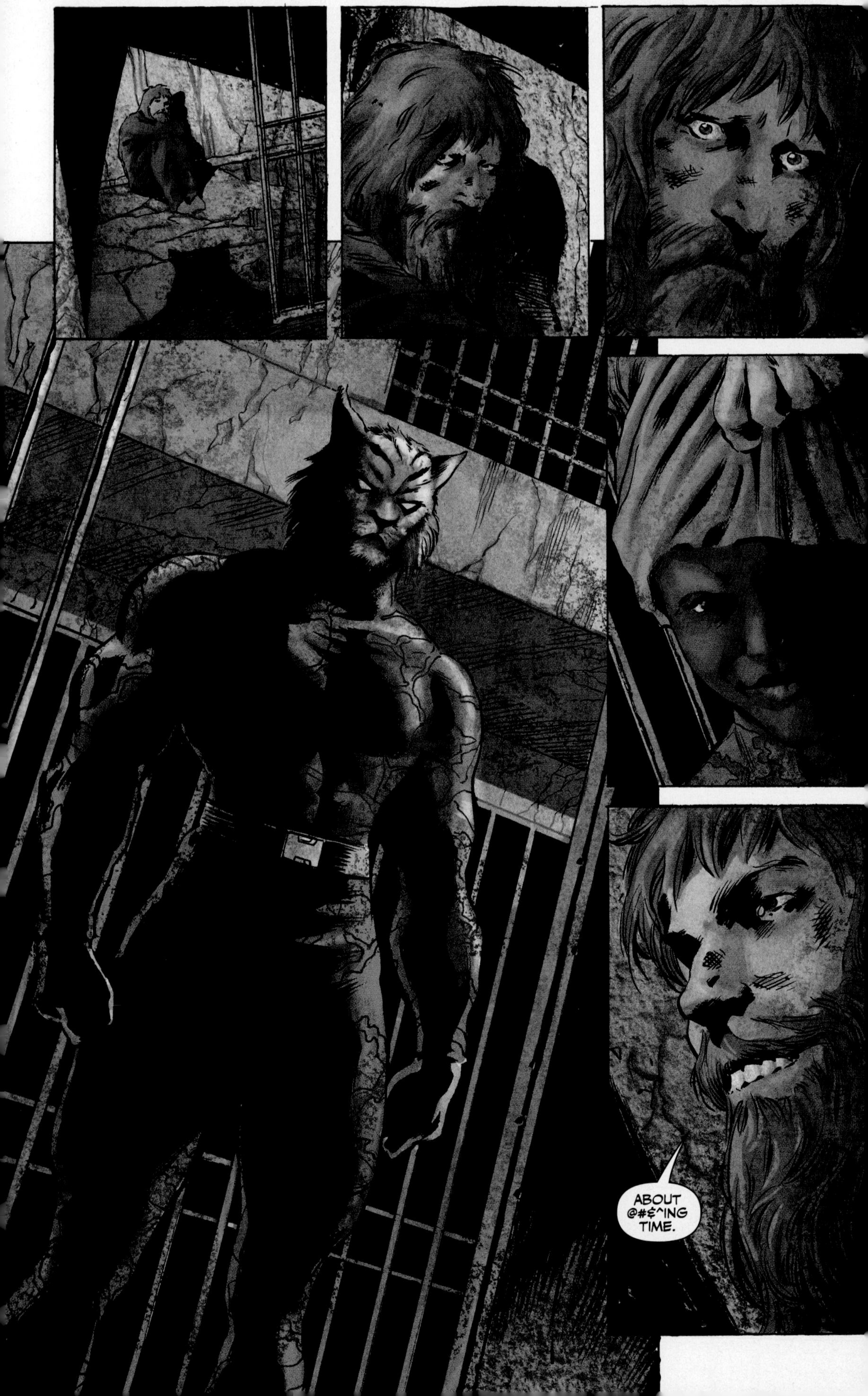
ABOUT @#&^ING TIME.

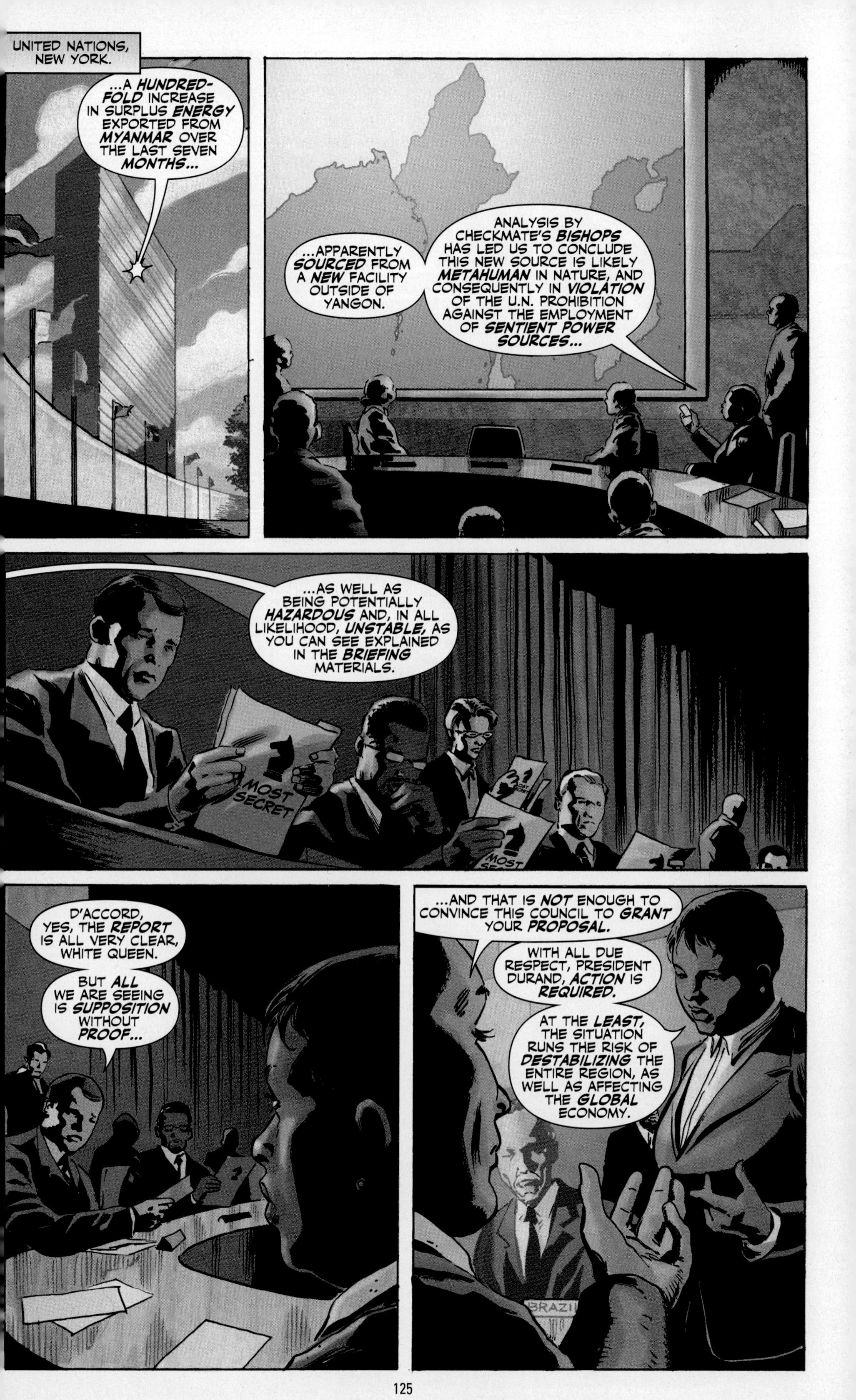
UNITED NATIONS, NEW YORK.
...A HUNDRED-FOLD INCREASE IN SURPLUS ENERGY EXPORTED FROM MYANMAR OVER THE LAST SEVEN MONTHS...
...APPARENTLY SOURCED FROM A NEW FACILITY OUTSIDE OF YANGON.
ANALYSIS BY CHECKMATE'S BISHOPS HAS LED US TO CONCLUDE THIS NEW SOURCE IS LIKELY METAHUMAN IN NATURE, AND CONSEQUENTLY IN VIOLATION OF THE U.N. PROHIBITION AGAINST THE EMPLOYMENT OF SENTIENT POWER SOURCES...
...AS WELL AS BEING POTENTIALLY HAZARDOUS AND, IN ALL LIKELIHOOD, UNSTABLE, AS YOU CAN SEE EXPLAINED IN THE BRIEFING MATERIALS.
MOST SECRET
D'ACCORD, YES, THE REPORT IS ALL VERY CLEAR, WHITE QUEEN.
BUT ALL WE ARE SEEING IS SUPPOSITION WITHOUT PROOF...
...AND THAT IS NOT ENOUGH TO CONVINCE THIS COUNCIL TO GRANT YOUR PROPOSAL.
WITH ALL DUE RESPECT, PRESIDENT DURAND, ACTION IS REQUIRED.
AT THE LEAST, THE SITUATION RUNS THE RISK OF DESTABILIZING THE ENTIRE REGION, AS WELL AS AFFECTING THE GLOBAL ECONOMY.
BRAZIL

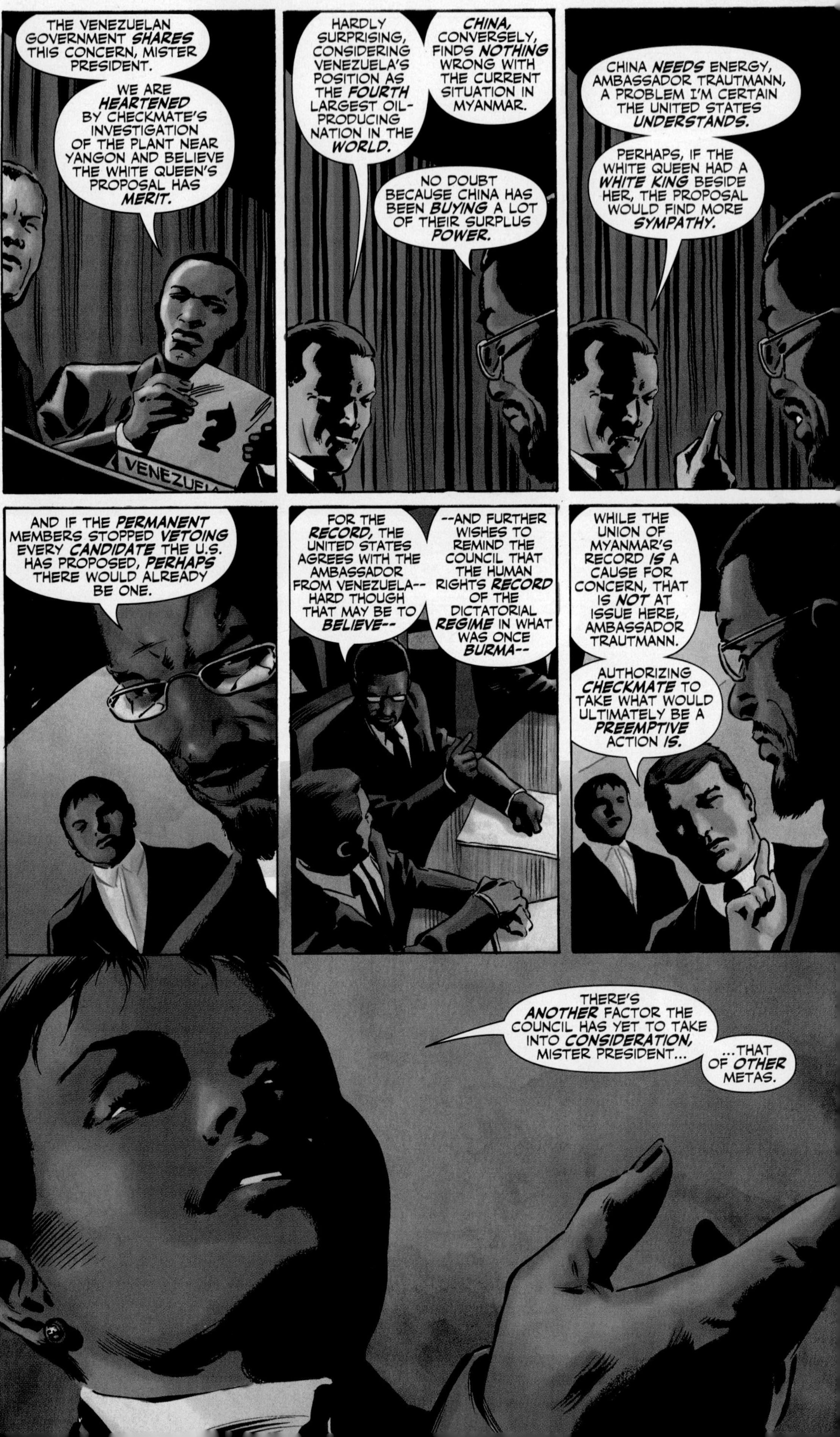

THE VENEZUELAN GOVERNMENT SHARES THIS CONCERN, MISTER PRESIDENT.
WE ARE HEARTENED BY CHECKMATE'S INVESTIGATION OF THE PLANT NEAR YANGON AND BELIEVE THE WHITE QUEEN'S PROPOSAL HAS MERIT.
VENEZUELA
HARDLY SURPRISING, CONSIDERING VENEZUELA'S POSITION AS THE FOURTH LARGEST OIL-PRODUCING NATION IN THE WORLD.
CHINA, CONVERSELY, FINDS NOTHING WRONG WITH THE CURRENT SITUATION IN MYANMAR.
NO DOUBT BECAUSE CHINA HAS BEEN BUYING A LOT OF THEIR SURPLUS POWER.
CHINA NEEDS ENERGY, AMBASSADOR TRAUTMANN, A PROBLEM I'M CERTAIN THE UNITED STATES UNDERSTANDS.
PERHAPS, IF THE WHITE QUEEN HAD A WHITE KING BESIDE HER, THE PROPOSAL WOULD FIND MORE SYMPATHY.
AND IF THE PERMANENT MEMBERS STOPPED VETOING EVERY CANDIDATE THE U.S. HAS PROPOSED, PERHAPS THERE WOULD ALREADY BE ONE.
FOR THE RECORD, THE UNITED STATES AGREES WITH THE AMBASSADOR FROM VENEZUELA--HARD THOUGH THAT MAY BE TO BELIEVE--
--AND FURTHER WISHES TO REMIND THE COUNCIL THAT THE HUMAN RIGHTS RECORD OF THE DICTATORIAL REGIME IN WHAT WAS ONCE BURMA--
WHILE THE UNION OF MYANMAR'S RECORD IS A CAUSE FOR CONCERN, THAT IS NOT AT ISSUE HERE, AMBASSADOR TRAUTMANN.
AUTHORIZING CHECKMATE TO TAKE WHAT WOULD ULTIMATELY BE A PREEMPTIVE ACTION IS.
THERE'S ANOTHER FACTOR THE COUNCIL HAS YET TO TAKE INTO CONSIDERATION, MISTER PRESIDENT...
...THAT OF OTHER METAS.

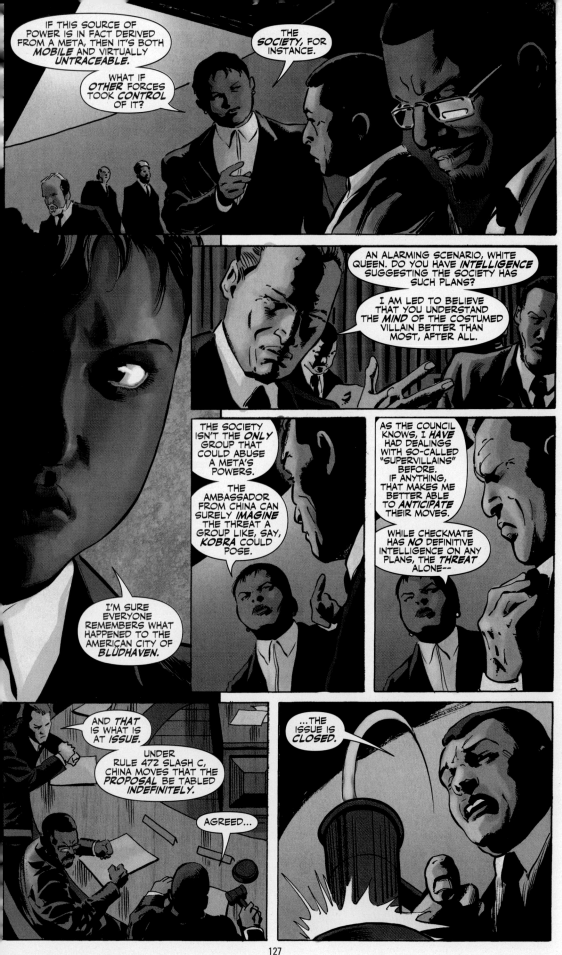

IF THIS SOURCE OF POWER IS IN FACT DERIVED FROM A META, THEN IT'S BOTH *MOBILE* AND VIRTUALLY *UNTRACEABLE.*

WHAT IF *OTHER* FORCES TOOK *CONTROL* OF IT?

THE *SOCIETY,* FOR INSTANCE.

AN ALARMING SCENARIO, WHITE QUEEN. DO YOU HAVE *INTELLIGENCE* SUGGESTING THE SOCIETY HAS SUCH PLANS?

I AM LED TO BELIEVE THAT YOU UNDERSTAND THE *MIND* OF THE COSTUMED VILLAIN BETTER THAN MOST, AFTER ALL.

THE SOCIETY ISN'T THE *ONLY* GROUP THAT COULD ABUSE A META'S POWERS.

THE AMBASSADOR FROM CHINA CAN SURELY *IMAGINE* THE THREAT A GROUP LIKE, SAY, *KOBRA* COULD POSE.

I'M SURE EVERYONE REMEMBERS WHAT HAPPENED TO THE AMERICAN CITY OF *BLÜDHAVEN.*

AS THE COUNCIL KNOWS, I *HAVE* HAD DEALINGS WITH SO-CALLED "SUPERVILLAINS" BEFORE. IF ANYTHING, THAT MAKES ME BETTER ABLE TO *ANTICIPATE* THEIR MOVES.

WHILE CHECKMATE HAS *NO* DEFINITIVE INTELLIGENCE ON ANY PLANS, THE *THREAT* ALONE--

AND *THAT* IS WHAT IS AT *ISSUE.*

UNDER RULE 472 SLASH C, CHINA MOVES THAT THE *PROPOSAL* BE TABLED *INDEFINITELY.*

AGREED...

...THE ISSUE IS *CLOSED.*

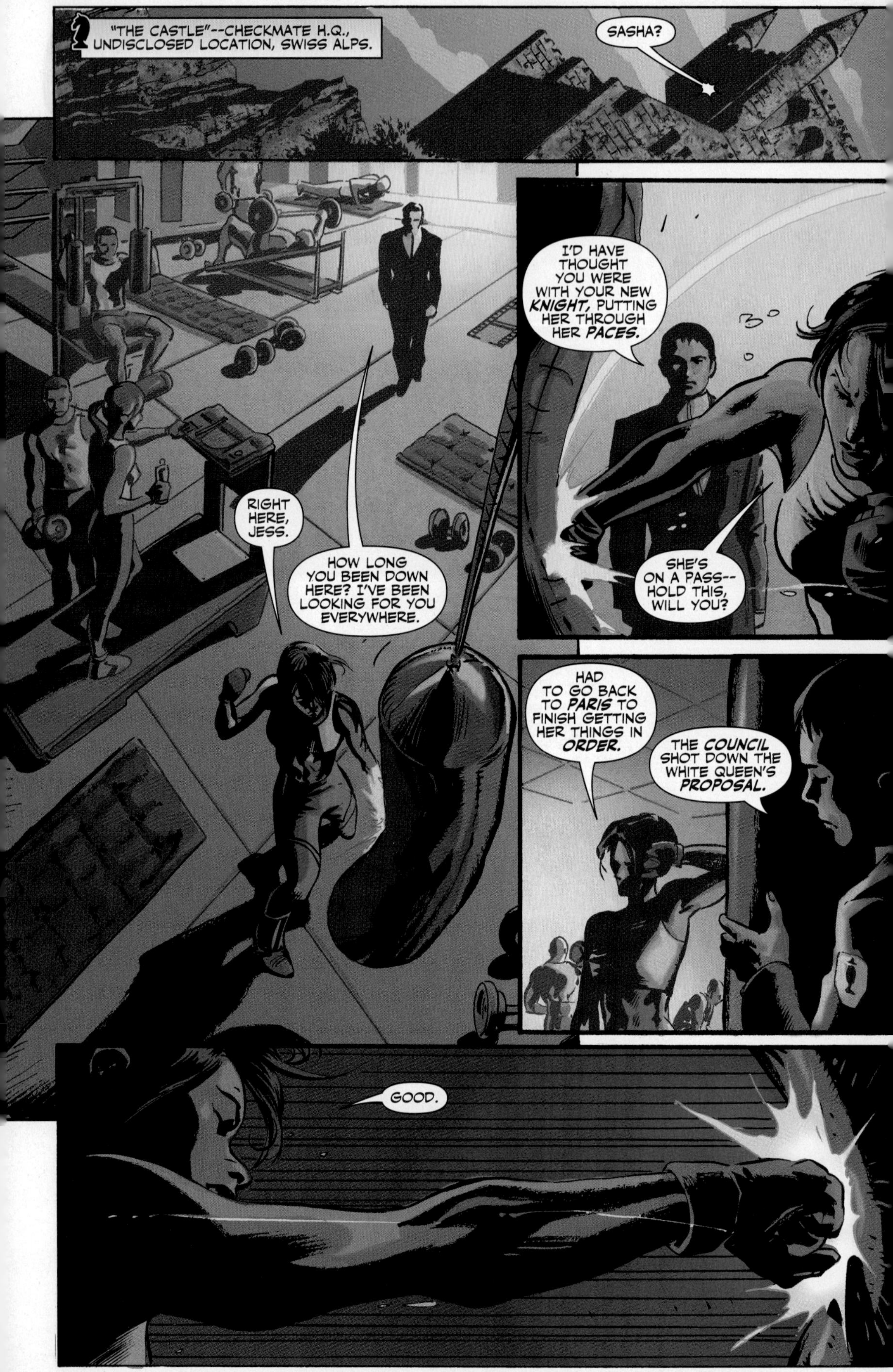
"THE CASTLE"--CHECKMATE H.Q., UNDISCLOSED LOCATION, SWISS ALPS.
SASHA?
RIGHT HERE, JESS.
HOW LONG YOU BEEN DOWN HERE? I'VE BEEN LOOKING FOR YOU EVERYWHERE.
I'D HAVE THOUGHT YOU WERE WITH YOUR NEW *KNIGHT*, PUTTING HER THROUGH HER *PACES*.
SHE'S ON A PASS--HOLD THIS, WILL YOU?
HAD TO GO BACK TO *PARIS* TO FINISH GETTING HER THINGS IN *ORDER*.
THE *COUNCIL* SHOT DOWN THE WHITE QUEEN'S *PROPOSAL*.
GOOD.

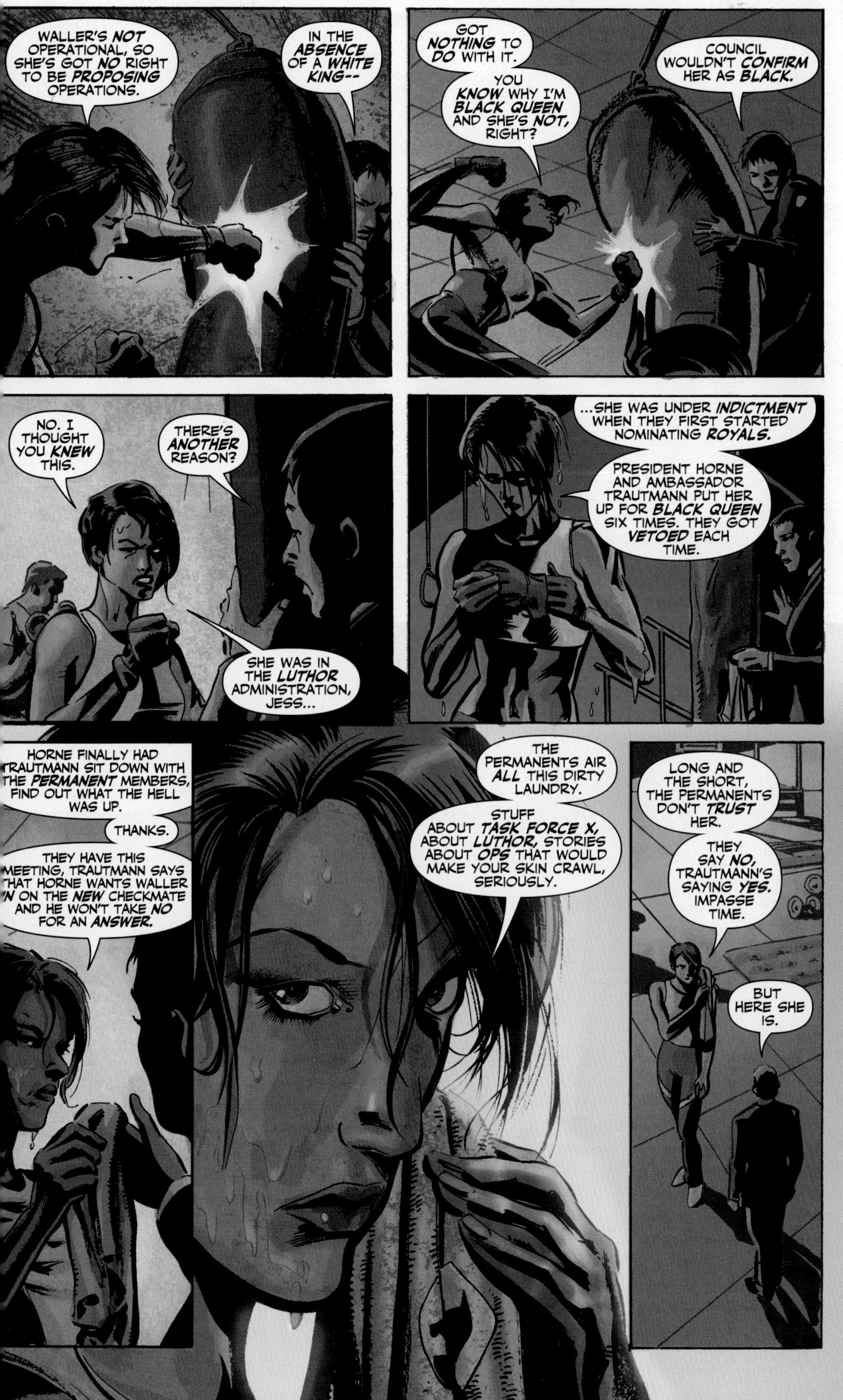

WALLER'S NOT OPERATIONAL, SO SHE'S GOT NO RIGHT TO BE PROPOSING OPERATIONS.
IN THE ABSENCE OF A WHITE KING--
GOT NOTHING TO DO WITH IT.
YOU KNOW WHY I'M BLACK QUEEN AND SHE'S NOT, RIGHT?
COUNCIL WOULDN'T CONFIRM HER AS BLACK.
NO. I THOUGHT YOU KNEW THIS.
THERE'S ANOTHER REASON?
SHE WAS IN THE LUTHOR ADMINISTRATION, JESS...
...SHE WAS UNDER INDICTMENT WHEN THEY FIRST STARTED NOMINATING ROYALS.
PRESIDENT HORNE AND AMBASSADOR TRAUTMANN PUT HER UP FOR BLACK QUEEN SIX TIMES. THEY GOT VETOED EACH TIME.
HORNE FINALLY HAD TRAUTMANN SIT DOWN WITH THE PERMANENT MEMBERS, FIND OUT WHAT THE HELL WAS UP.
THANKS.
THEY HAVE THIS MEETING, TRAUTMANN SAYS THAT HORNE WANTS WALLER IN ON THE NEW CHECKMATE AND HE WON'T TAKE NO FOR AN ANSWER.
THE PERMANENTS AIR ALL THIS DIRTY LAUNDRY.
STUFF ABOUT TASK FORCE X, ABOUT LUTHOR, STORIES ABOUT OPS THAT WOULD MAKE YOUR SKIN CRAWL, SERIOUSLY.
LONG AND THE SHORT, THE PERMANENTS DON'T TRUST HER.
THEY SAY NO, TRAUTMANN'S SAYING YES. IMPASSE TIME.
BUT HERE SHE IS.

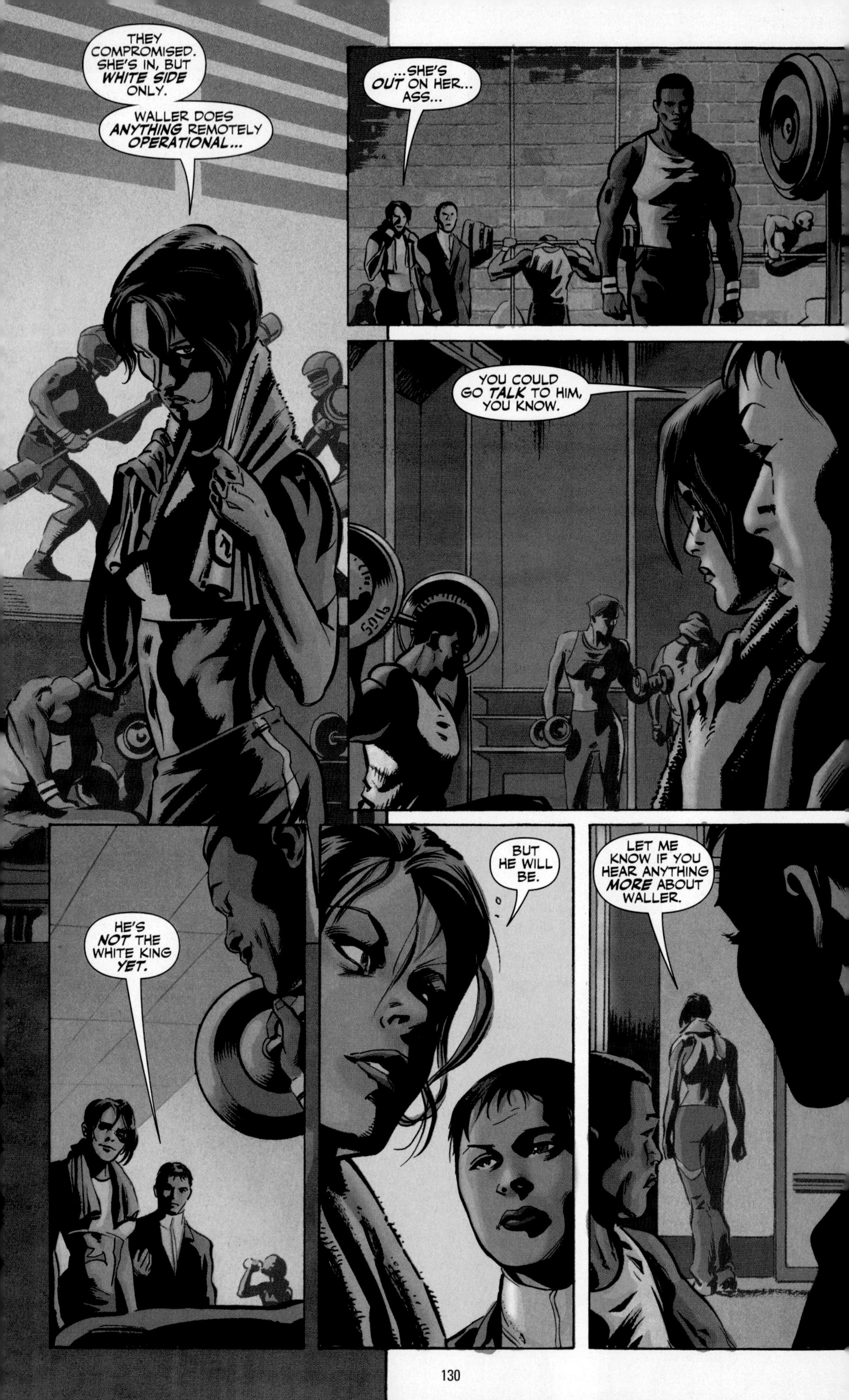
THEY COMPROMISED. SHE'S IN, BUT WHITE SIDE ONLY.
WALLER DOES ANYTHING REMOTELY OPERATIONAL...
...SHE'S OUT ON HER... ASS...
YOU COULD GO TALK TO HIM, YOU KNOW.
HE'S NOT THE WHITE KING YET.
BUT HE WILL BE.
LET ME KNOW IF YOU HEAR ANYTHING MORE ABOUT WALLER.

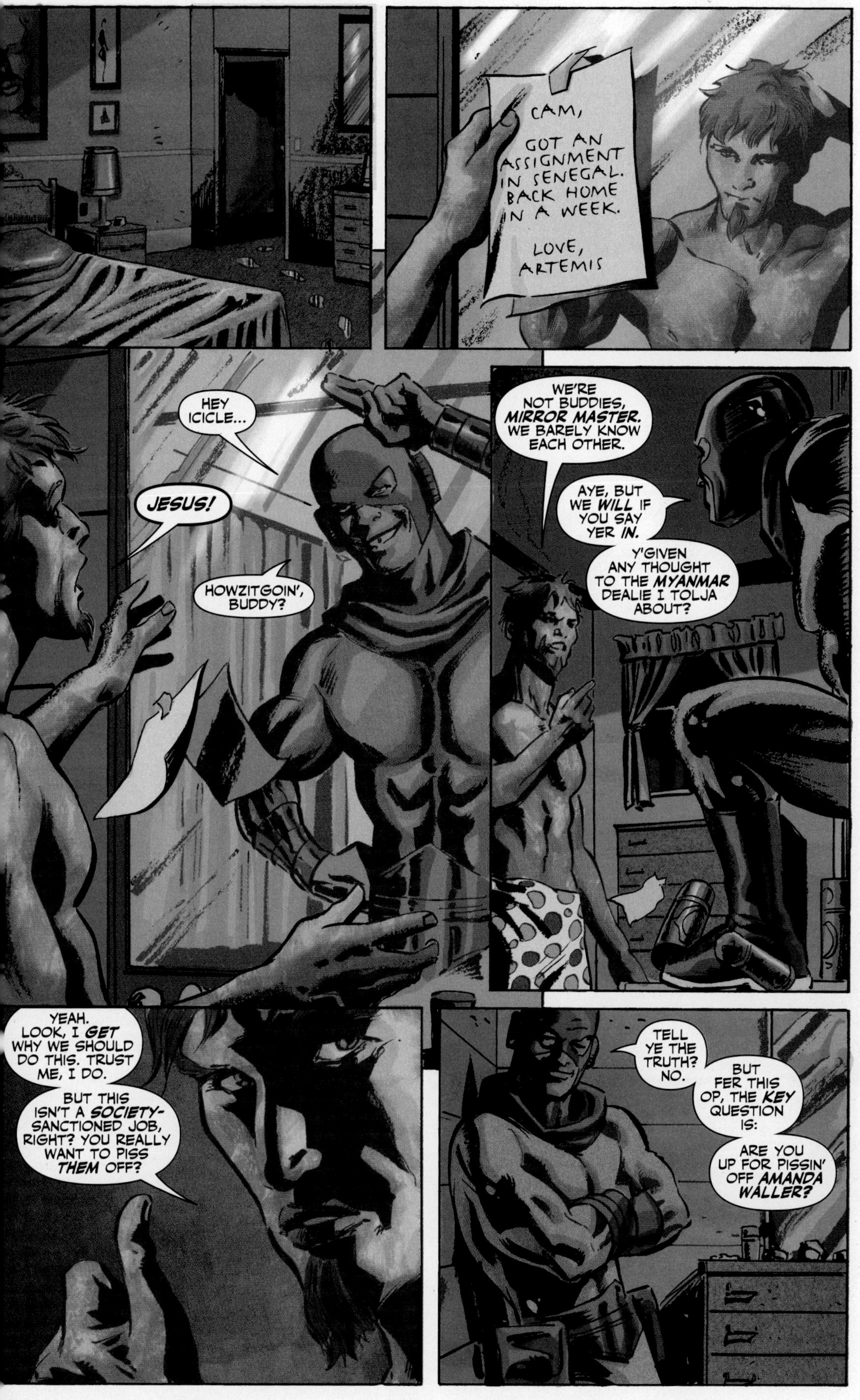
CAM,
GOT AN ASSIGNMENT IN SENEGAL. BACK HOME IN A WEEK.
LOVE, ARTEMIS
HEY ICICLE...
JESUS!
HOWZITGOIN', BUDDY?
WE'RE NOT BUDDIES, MIRROR MASTER. WE BARELY KNOW EACH OTHER.
AYE, BUT WE WILL IF YOU SAY YER IN.
Y'GIVEN ANY THOUGHT TO THE MYANMAR DEALIE I TOLJA ABOUT?
YEAH. LOOK, I GET WHY WE SHOULD DO THIS. TRUST ME, I DO.
BUT THIS ISN'T A SOCIETY-SANCTIONED JOB, RIGHT? YOU REALLY WANT TO PISS THEM OFF?
TELL YE THE TRUTH? NO.
BUT FER THIS OP, THE KEY QUESTION IS:
ARE YOU UP FOR PISSIN' OFF AMANDA WALLER?

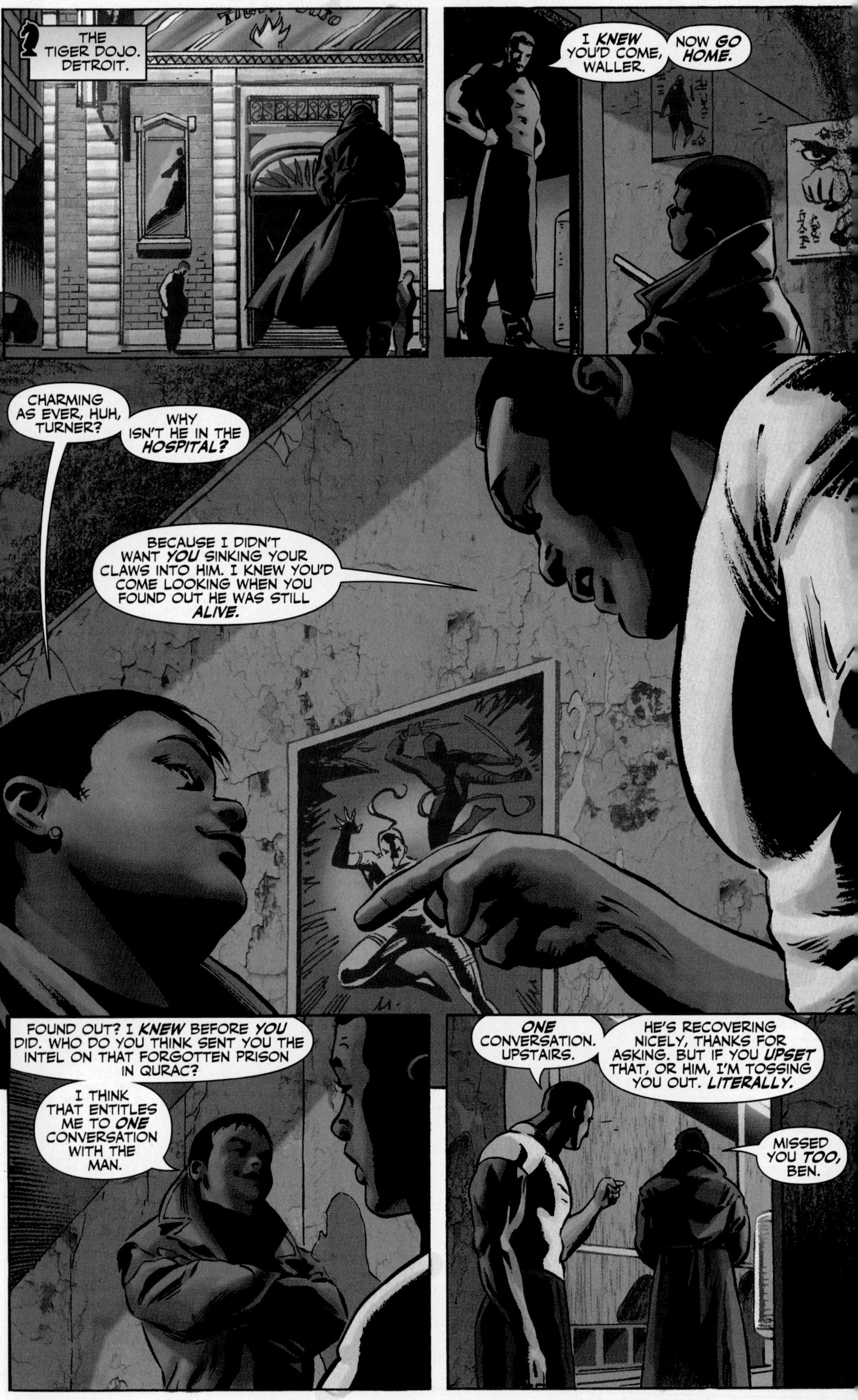
THE TIGER DOJO. DETROIT.
I KNEW YOU'D COME, WALLER.
NOW GO HOME.
CHARMING AS EVER, HUH, TURNER?
WHY ISN'T HE IN THE HOSPITAL?
BECAUSE I DIDN'T WANT YOU SINKING YOUR CLAWS INTO HIM. I KNEW YOU'D COME LOOKING WHEN YOU FOUND OUT HE WAS STILL ALIVE.
FOUND OUT? I KNEW BEFORE YOU DID. WHO DO YOU THINK SENT YOU THE INTEL ON THAT FORGOTTEN PRISON IN QURAC?
I THINK THAT ENTITLES ME TO ONE CONVERSATION WITH THE MAN.
ONE CONVERSATION. UPSTAIRS.
HE'S RECOVERING NICELY, THANKS FOR ASKING. BUT IF YOU UPSET THAT, OR HIM, I'M TOSSING YOU OUT. LITERALLY.
MISSED YOU TOO, BEN.

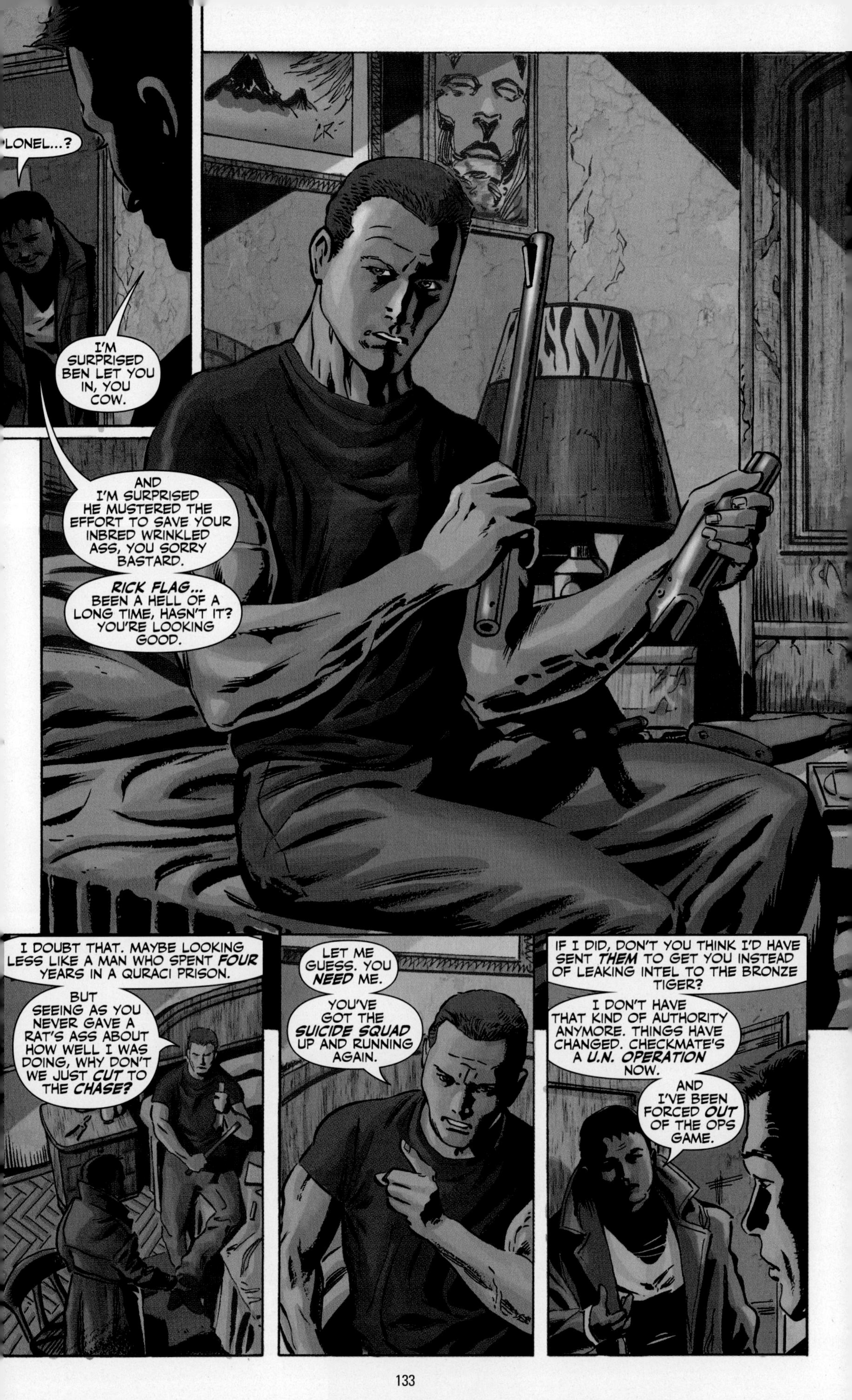

-LONEL...?
I'M SURPRISED BEN LET YOU IN, YOU COW.
AND I'M SURPRISED HE MUSTERED THE EFFORT TO SAVE YOUR INBRED WRINKLED ASS, YOU SORRY BASTARD.
RICK FLAG... BEEN A HELL OF A LONG TIME, HASN'T IT? YOU'RE LOOKING GOOD.
I DOUBT THAT. MAYBE LOOKING LESS LIKE A MAN WHO SPENT FOUR YEARS IN A QURACI PRISON.
BUT SEEING AS YOU NEVER GAVE A RAT'S ASS ABOUT HOW WELL I WAS DOING, WHY DON'T WE JUST CUT TO THE CHASE?
LET ME GUESS. YOU NEED ME.
YOU'VE GOT THE SUICIDE SQUAD UP AND RUNNING AGAIN.
IF I DID, DON'T YOU THINK I'D HAVE SENT THEM TO GET YOU INSTEAD OF LEAKING INTEL TO THE BRONZE TIGER?
I DON'T HAVE THAT KIND OF AUTHORITY ANYMORE. THINGS HAVE CHANGED. CHECKMATE'S A U.N. OPERATION NOW.
AND I'VE BEEN FORCED OUT OF THE OPS GAME.

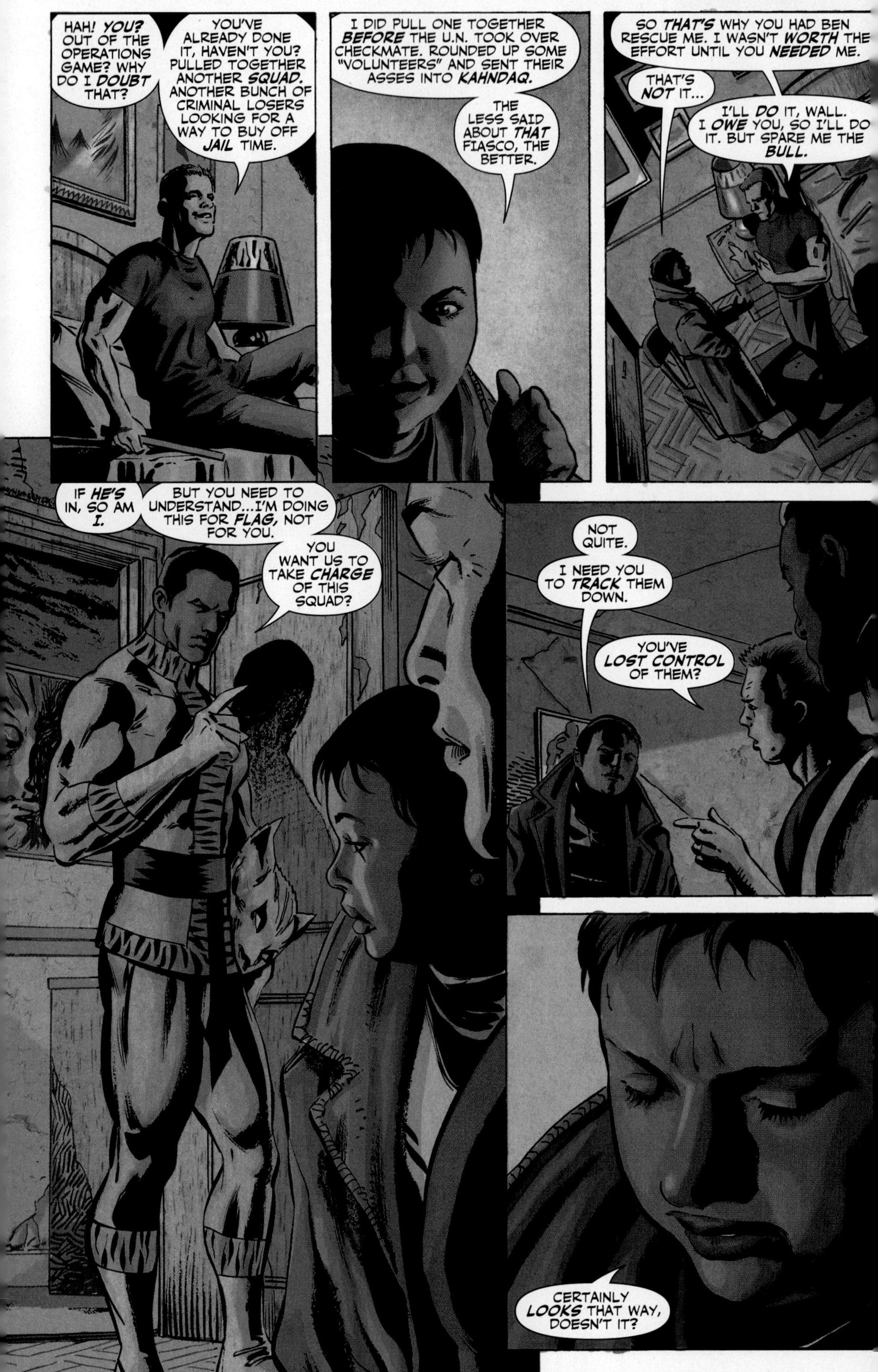
HAH! YOU? OUT OF THE OPERATIONS GAME? WHY DO I DOUBT THAT?
YOU'VE ALREADY DONE IT, HAVEN'T YOU? PULLED TOGETHER ANOTHER SQUAD. ANOTHER BUNCH OF CRIMINAL LOSERS LOOKING FOR A WAY TO BUY OFF JAIL TIME.
I DID PULL ONE TOGETHER BEFORE THE U.N. TOOK OVER CHECKMATE. ROUNDED UP SOME "VOLUNTEERS" AND SENT THEIR ASSES INTO KAHNDAQ.
THE LESS SAID ABOUT THAT FIASCO, THE BETTER.
SO THAT'S WHY YOU HAD BEN RESCUE ME. I WASN'T WORTH THE EFFORT UNTIL YOU NEEDED ME.
THAT'S NOT IT...
I'LL DO IT, WALL. I OWE YOU, SO I'LL DO IT. BUT SPARE ME THE BULL.
IF HE'S IN, SO AM I.
BUT YOU NEED TO UNDERSTAND...I'M DOING THIS FOR FLAG, NOT FOR YOU.
YOU WANT US TO TAKE CHARGE OF THIS SQUAD?
NOT QUITE.
I NEED YOU TO TRACK THEM DOWN.
YOU'VE LOST CONTROL OF THEM?
CERTAINLY LOOKS THAT WAY, DOESN'T IT?

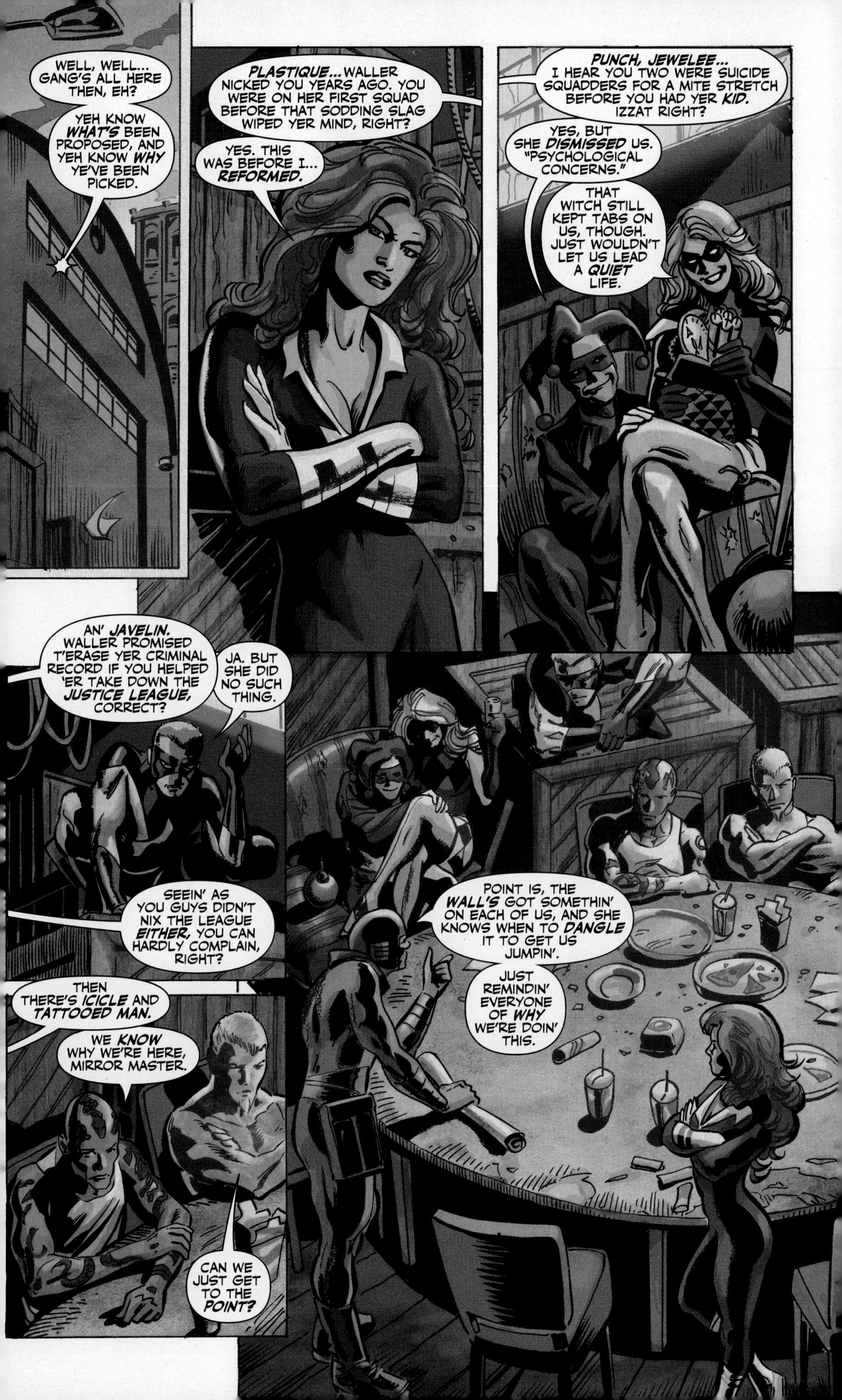

WELL, WELL... GANG'S ALL HERE THEN, EH?
YEH KNOW WHAT'S BEEN PROPOSED, AND YEH KNOW WHY YE'VE BEEN PICKED.
PLASTIQUE... WALLER NICKED YOU YEARS AGO. YOU WERE ON HER FIRST SQUAD BEFORE THAT SODDING SLAG WIPED YER MIND, RIGHT?
YES. THIS WAS BEFORE I... REFORMED.
PUNCH, JEWELEE... I HEAR YOU TWO WERE SUICIDE SQUADDERS FOR A MITE STRETCH BEFORE YOU HAD YER KID. IZZAT RIGHT?
YES, BUT SHE DISMISSED US. "PSYCHOLOGICAL CONCERNS."
THAT WITCH STILL KEPT TABS ON US, THOUGH. JUST WOULDN'T LET US LEAD A QUIET LIFE.
AN' JAVELIN. WALLER PROMISED T'ERASE YER CRIMINAL RECORD IF YOU HELPED 'ER TAKE DOWN THE JUSTICE LEAGUE, CORRECT?
JA. BUT SHE DID NO SUCH THING.
SEEIN' AS YOU GUYS DIDN'T NIX THE LEAGUE EITHER, YOU CAN HARDLY COMPLAIN, RIGHT?
THEN THERE'S ICICLE AND TATTOOED MAN.
WE KNOW WHY WE'RE HERE, MIRROR MASTER.
CAN WE JUST GET TO THE POINT?
POINT IS, THE WALL'S GOT SOMETHIN' ON EACH OF US, AND SHE KNOWS WHEN TO DANGLE IT TO GET US JUMPIN'.
JUST REMINDIN' EVERYONE OF WHY WE'RE DOIN' THIS.

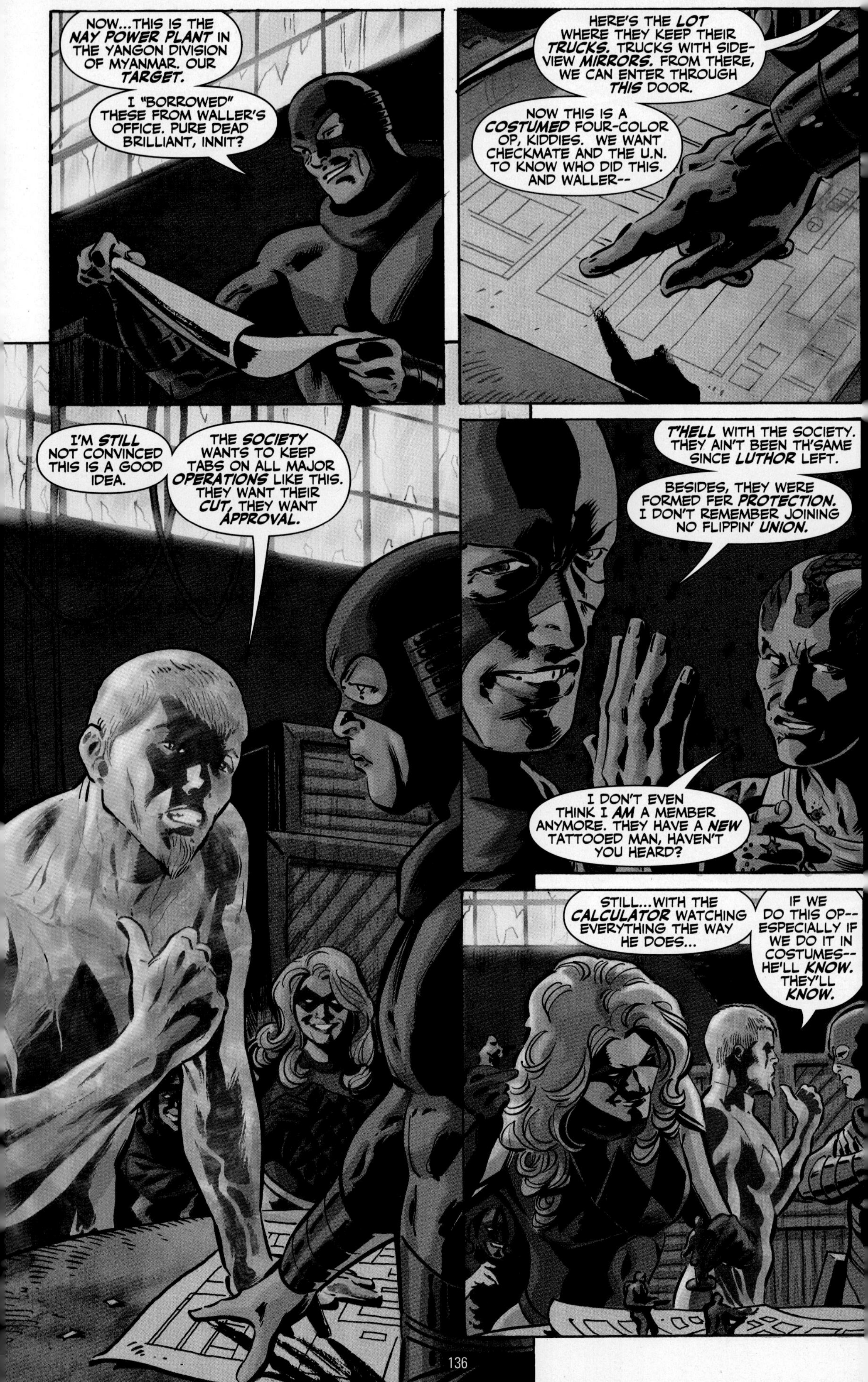
NOW...THIS IS THE NAY POWER PLANT IN THE YANGON DIVISION OF MYANMAR. OUR TARGET.
I "BORROWED" THESE FROM WALLER'S OFFICE. PURE DEAD BRILLIANT, INNIT?
HERE'S THE LOT WHERE THEY KEEP THEIR TRUCKS. TRUCKS WITH SIDE-VIEW MIRRORS. FROM THERE, WE CAN ENTER THROUGH THIS DOOR.
NOW THIS IS A COSTUMED FOUR-COLOR OP, KIDDIES. WE WANT CHECKMATE AND THE U.N. TO KNOW WHO DID THIS. AND WALLER--
I'M STILL NOT CONVINCED THIS IS A GOOD IDEA.
THE SOCIETY WANTS TO KEEP TABS ON ALL MAJOR OPERATIONS LIKE THIS. THEY WANT THEIR CUT, THEY WANT APPROVAL.
T'HELL WITH THE SOCIETY. THEY AIN'T BEEN TH'SAME SINCE LUTHOR LEFT.
BESIDES, THEY WERE FORMED FER PROTECTION. I DON'T REMEMBER JOINING NO FLIPPIN' UNION.
I DON'T EVEN THINK I AM A MEMBER ANYMORE. THEY HAVE A NEW TATTOOED MAN, HAVEN'T YOU HEARD?
STILL...WITH THE CALCULATOR WATCHING EVERYTHING THE WAY HE DOES...
IF WE DO THIS OP--ESPECIALLY IF WE DO IT IN COSTUMES--HE'LL KNOW. THEY'LL KNOW.

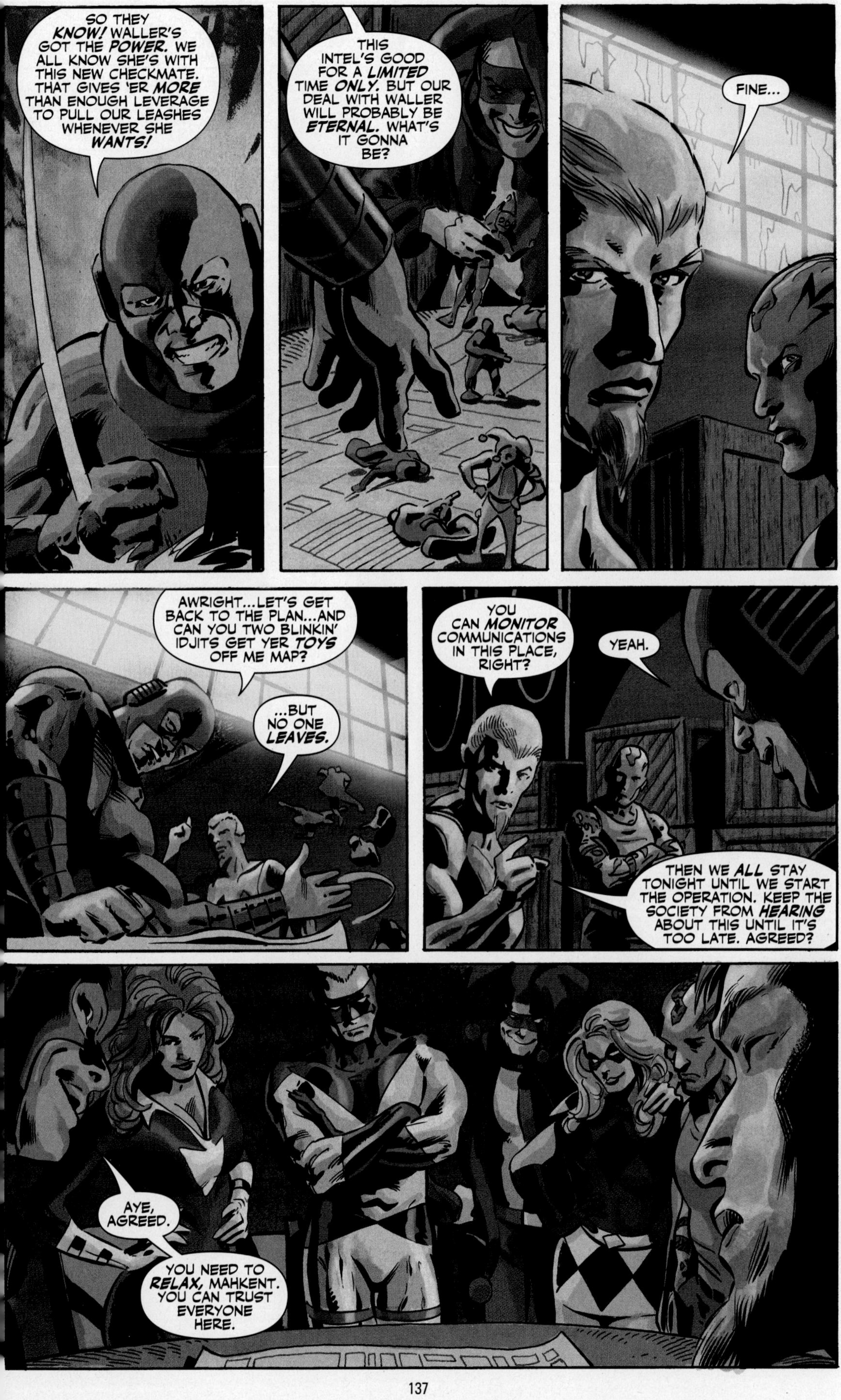

SO THEY KNOW! WALLER'S GOT THE POWER. WE ALL KNOW SHE'S WITH THIS NEW CHECKMATE. THAT GIVES 'ER MORE THAN ENOUGH LEVERAGE TO PULL OUR LEASHES WHENEVER SHE WANTS!
THIS INTEL'S GOOD FOR A LIMITED TIME ONLY. BUT OUR DEAL WITH WALLER WILL PROBABLY BE ETERNAL. WHAT'S IT GONNA BE?
FINE...
...BUT NO ONE LEAVES.
AWRIGHT...LET'S GET BACK TO THE PLAN...AND CAN YOU TWO BLINKIN' IDJITS GET YER TOYS OFF ME MAP?
YOU CAN MONITOR COMMUNICATIONS IN THIS PLACE, RIGHT?
YEAH.
THEN WE ALL STAY TONIGHT UNTIL WE START THE OPERATION. KEEP THE SOCIETY FROM HEARING ABOUT THIS UNTIL IT'S TOO LATE. AGREED?
AYE, AGREED.
YOU NEED TO RELAX, MAHKENT. YOU CAN TRUST EVERYONE HERE.

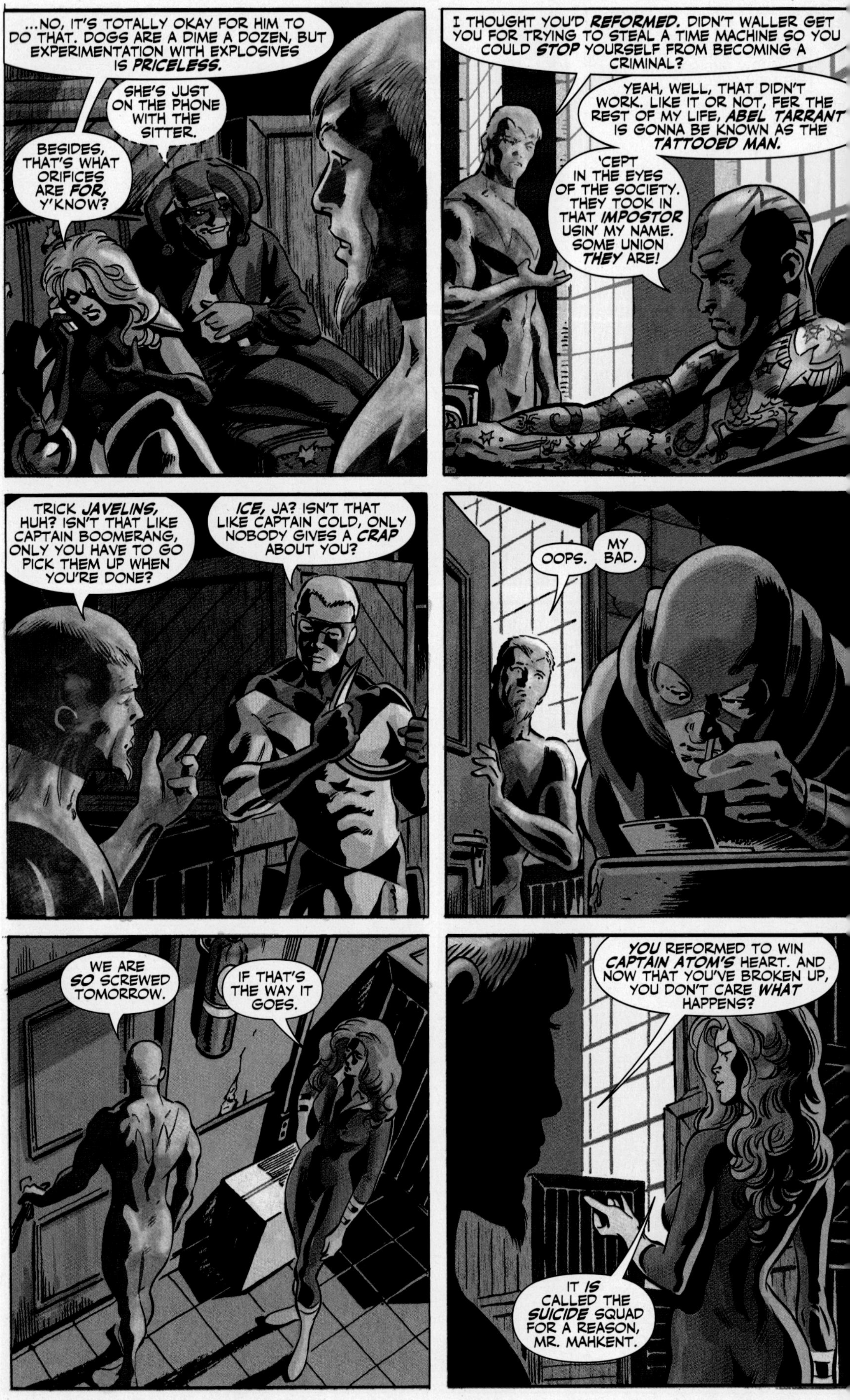

...NO, IT'S TOTALLY OKAY FOR HIM TO DO THAT. DOGS ARE A DIME A DOZEN, BUT EXPERIMENTATION WITH EXPLOSIVES IS PRICELESS.
SHE'S JUST ON THE PHONE WITH THE SITTER.
BESIDES, THAT'S WHAT ORIFICES ARE FOR, Y'KNOW?
I THOUGHT YOU'D REFORMED. DIDN'T WALLER GET YOU FOR TRYING TO STEAL A TIME MACHINE SO YOU COULD STOP YOURSELF FROM BECOMING A CRIMINAL?
YEAH, WELL, THAT DIDN'T WORK. LIKE IT OR NOT, FER THE REST OF MY LIFE, ABEL TARRANT IS GONNA BE KNOWN AS THE TATTOOED MAN.
'CEPT IN THE EYES OF THE SOCIETY. THEY TOOK IN THAT IMPOSTOR USIN' MY NAME. SOME UNION THEY ARE!
TRICK JAVELINS, HUH? ISN'T THAT LIKE CAPTAIN BOOMERANG, ONLY YOU HAVE TO GO PICK THEM UP WHEN YOU'RE DONE?
ICE, JA? ISN'T THAT LIKE CAPTAIN COLD, ONLY NOBODY GIVES A CRAP ABOUT YOU?
OOPS.
MY BAD.
WE ARE SO SCREWED TOMORROW.
IF THAT'S THE WAY IT GOES.
YOU REFORMED TO WIN CAPTAIN ATOM'S HEART. AND NOW THAT YOU'VE BROKEN UP, YOU DON'T CARE WHAT HAPPENS?
IT IS CALLED THE SUICIDE SQUAD FOR A REASON, MR. MAHKENT.

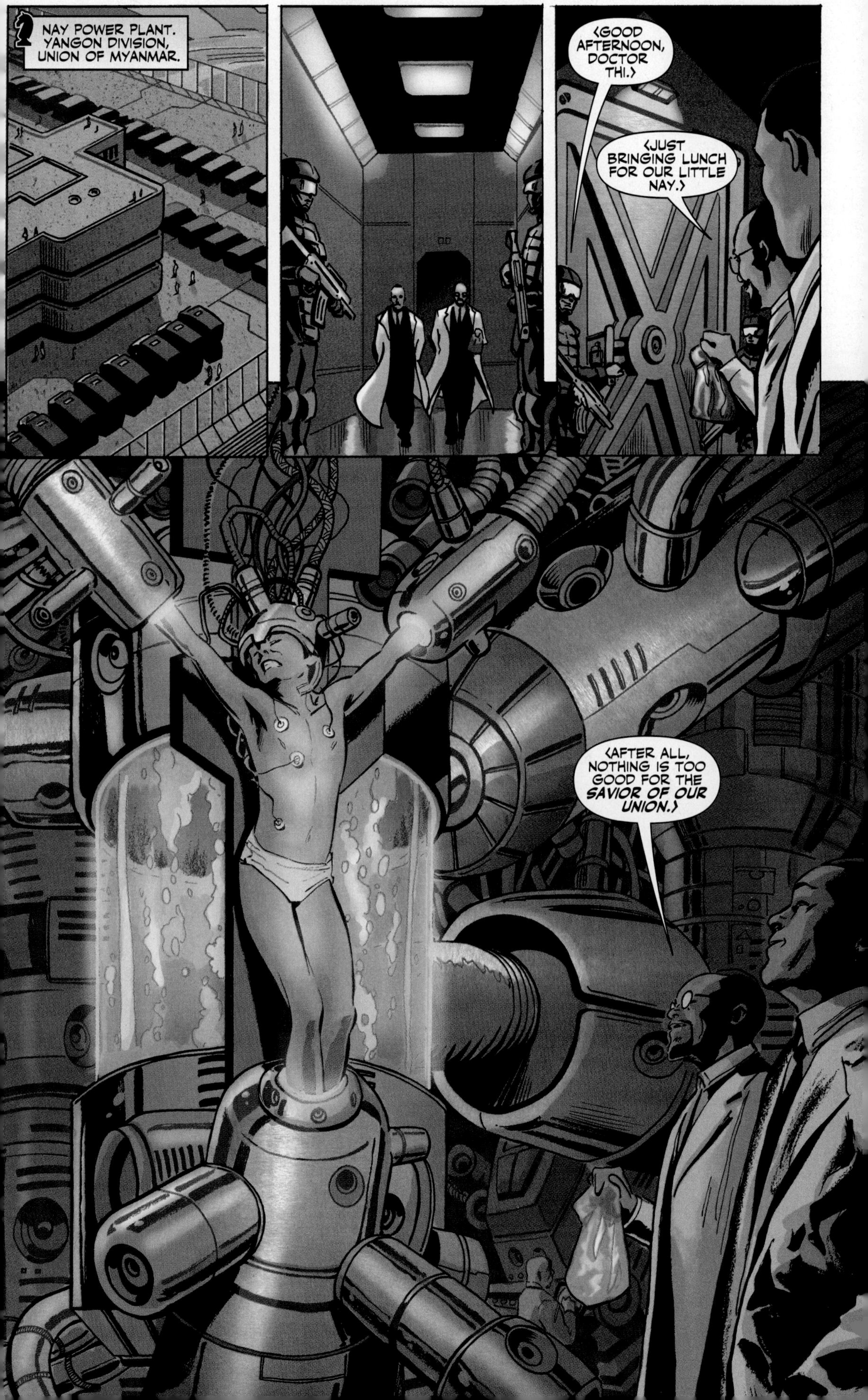
NAY POWER PLANT. YANGON DIVISION, UNION OF MYANMAR.
‹GOOD AFTERNOON, DOCTOR THI.›
‹JUST BRINGING LUNCH FOR OUR LITTLE NAY.›
‹AFTER ALL, NOTHING IS TOO GOOD FOR THE SAVIOR OF OUR UNION.›

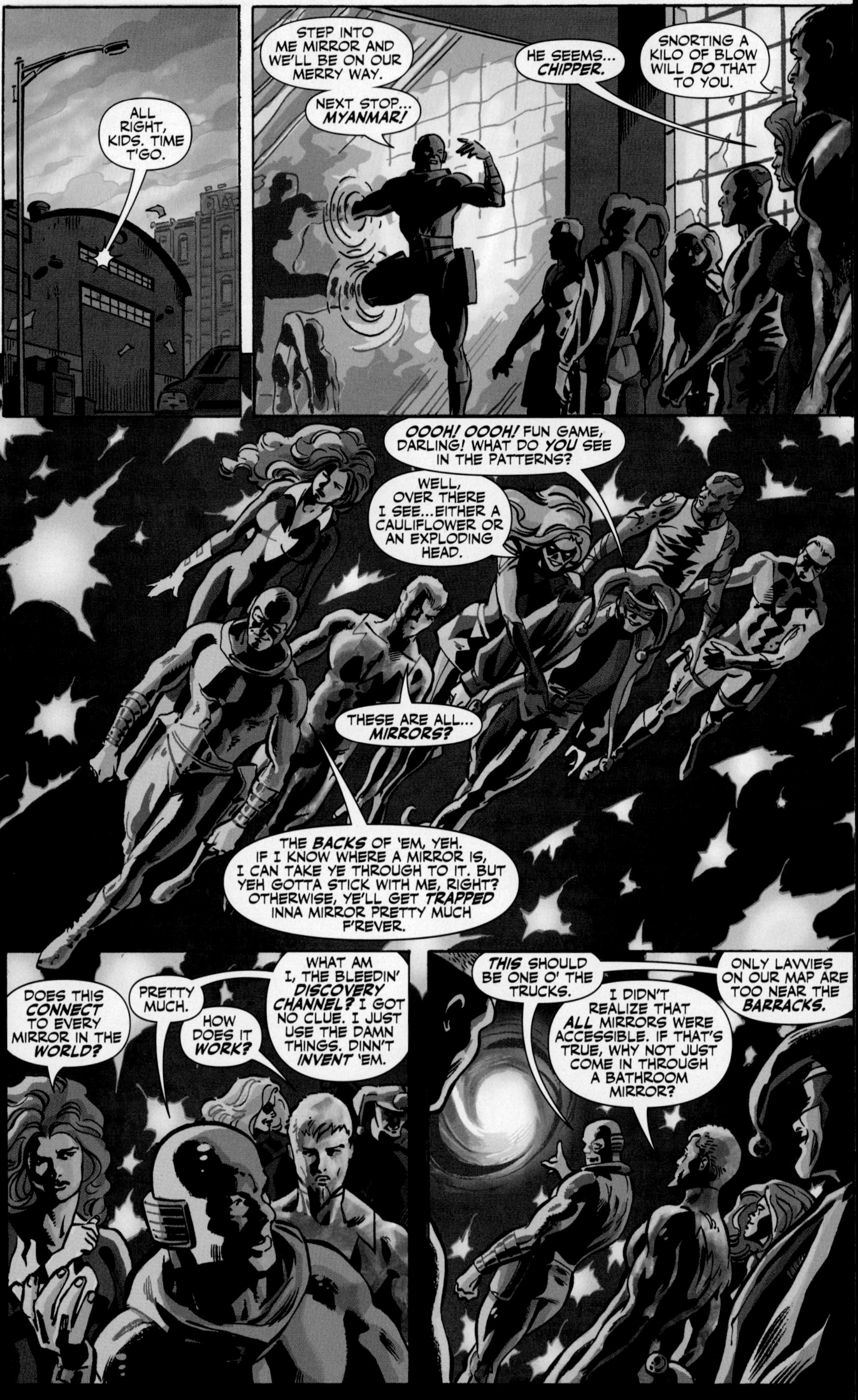
ALL RIGHT, KIDS. TIME T'GO.
STEP INTO ME MIRROR AND WE'LL BE ON OUR MERRY WAY.
NEXT STOP... MYANMAR!
HE SEEMS... CHIPPER.
SNORTING A KILO OF BLOW WILL DO THAT TO YOU.
OOOH! OOOH! FUN GAME, DARLING! WHAT DO YOU SEE IN THE PATTERNS?
WELL, OVER THERE I SEE...EITHER A CAULIFLOWER OR AN EXPLODING HEAD.
THESE ARE ALL... MIRRORS?
THE BACKS OF 'EM, YEH. IF I KNOW WHERE A MIRROR IS, I CAN TAKE YE THROUGH TO IT. BUT YEH GOTTA STICK WITH ME, RIGHT? OTHERWISE, YE'LL GET TRAPPED INNA MIRROR PRETTY MUCH F'REVER.
DOES THIS CONNECT TO EVERY MIRROR IN THE WORLD?
PRETTY MUCH.
HOW DOES IT WORK?
WHAT AM I, THE BLEEDIN' DISCOVERY CHANNEL? I GOT NO CLUE. I JUST USE THE DAMN THINGS. DINN'T INVENT 'EM.
THIS SHOULD BE ONE O' THE TRUCKS.
ONLY LAVVIES ON OUR MAP ARE TOO NEAR THE BARRACKS.
I DIDN'T REALIZE THAT ALL MIRRORS WERE ACCESSIBLE. IF THAT'S TRUE, WHY NOT JUST COME IN THROUGH A BATHROOM MIRROR?

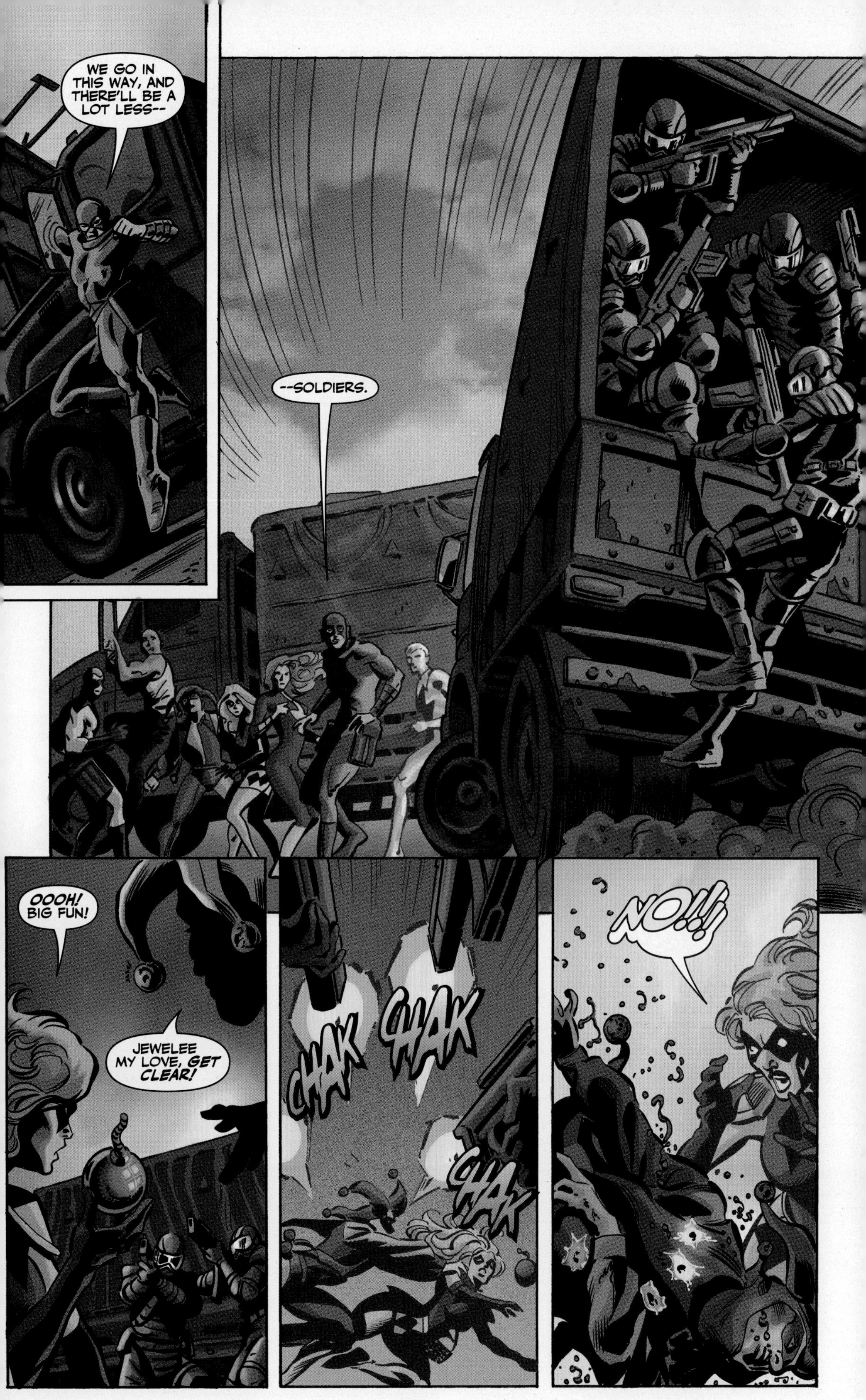
WE GO IN THIS WAY, AND THERE'LL BE A LOT LESS--
--SOLDIERS.
OOOH! BIG FUN!
JEWELEE MY LOVE, GET CLEAR!
CHAK
CHAK
CHAK
NO!!!

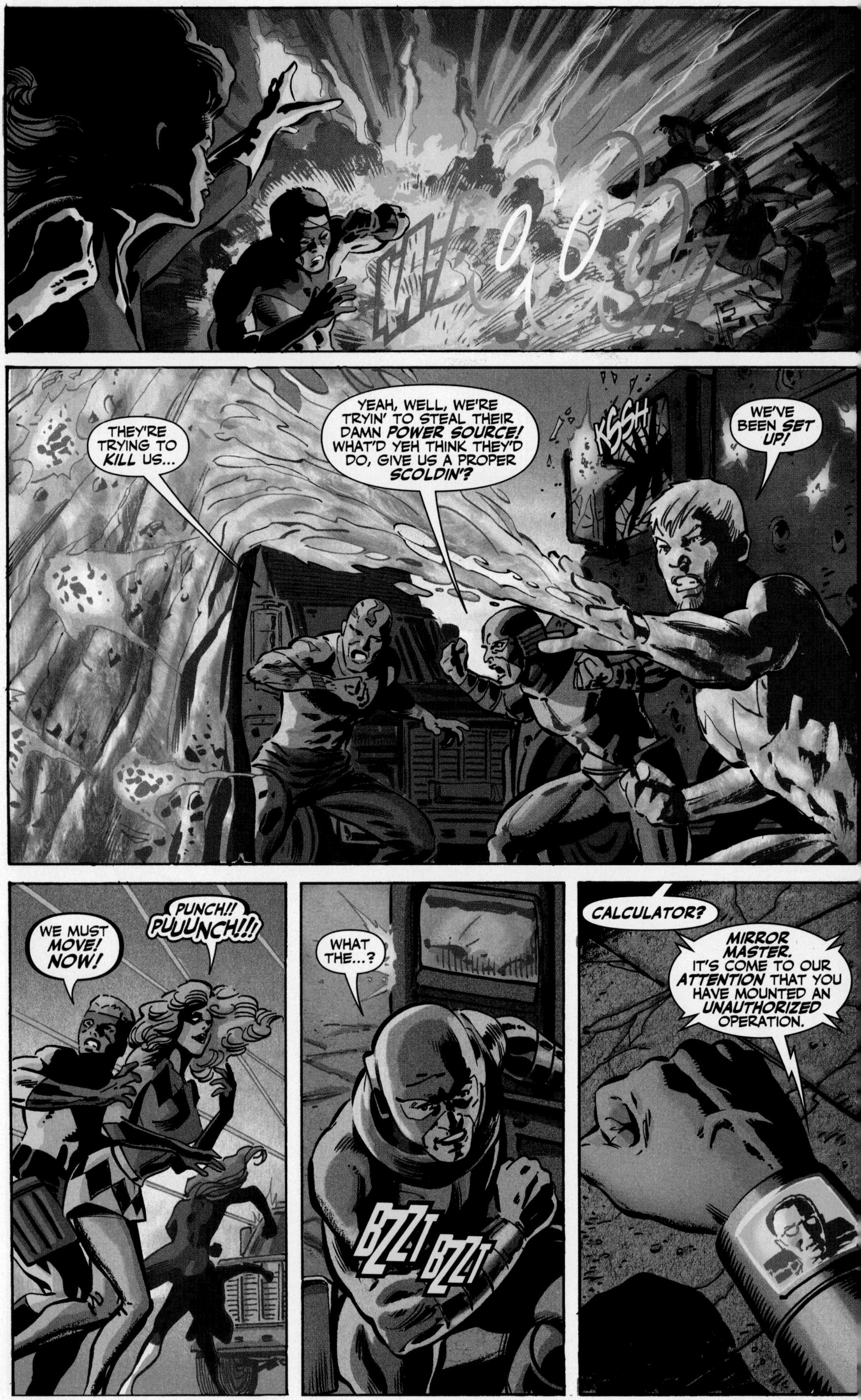
THEY'RE TRYING TO *KILL* US...
YEAH, WELL, WE'RE TRYIN' TO STEAL THEIR DAMN ***POWER SOURCE!*** WHAT'D YEH THINK THEY'D DO, GIVE US A PROPER ***SCOLDIN'?***
KSSH
WE'VE BEEN ***SET UP!***
WE MUST ***MOVE! NOW!***
PUNCH!! PUUUNCH!!!
WHAT THE...?
BZZT BZZT
CALCULATOR?
MIRROR MASTER. IT'S COME TO OUR ***ATTENTION*** THAT YOU HAVE MOUNTED AN ***UNAUTHORIZED*** OPERATION.

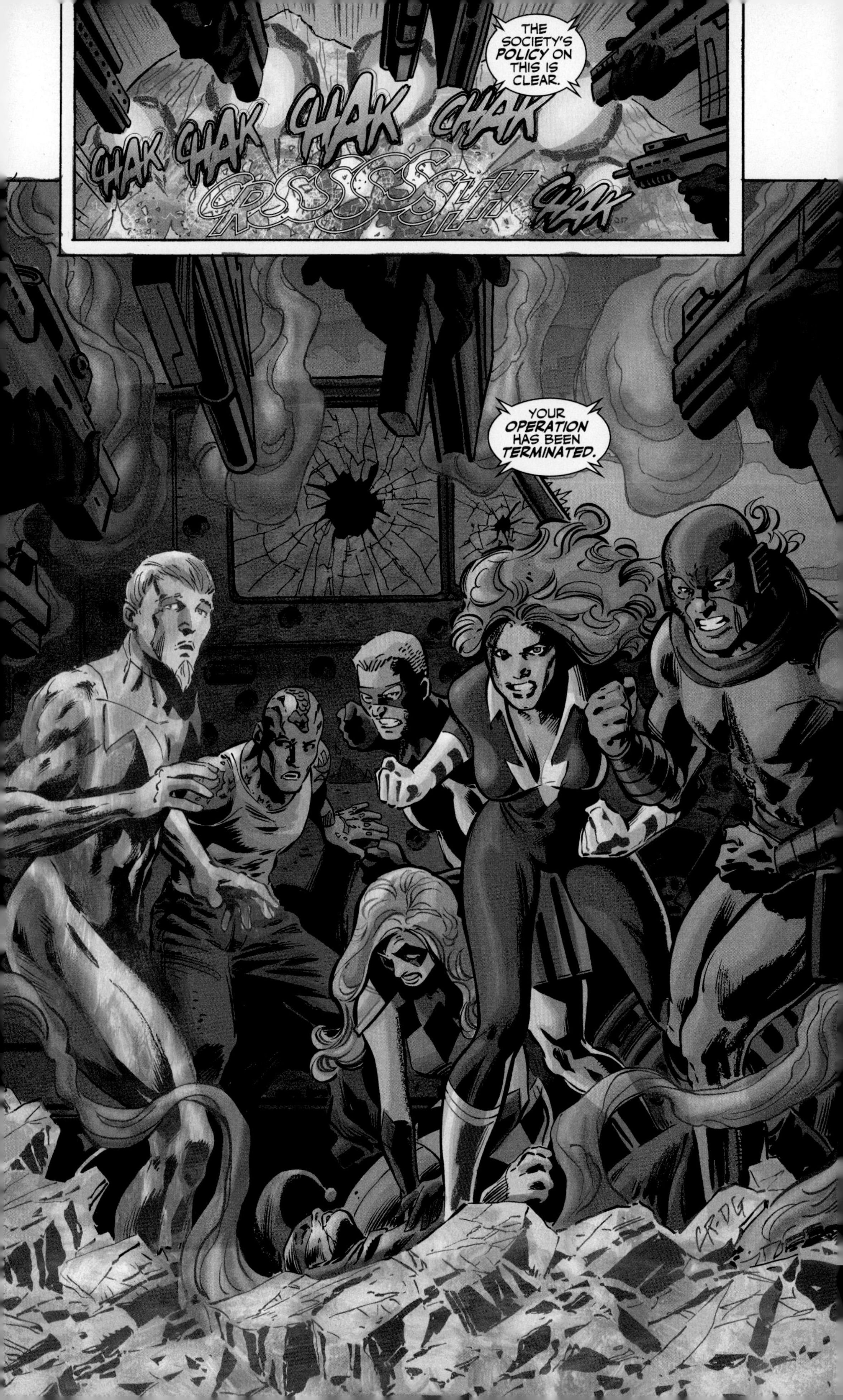
THE SOCIETY'S *POLICY* ON THIS IS CLEAR.
CHAK CHAK CHAK CHAK
CRSSSSSHH CHAK
YOUR *OPERATION* HAS BEEN *TERMINATED.*
CR-DG

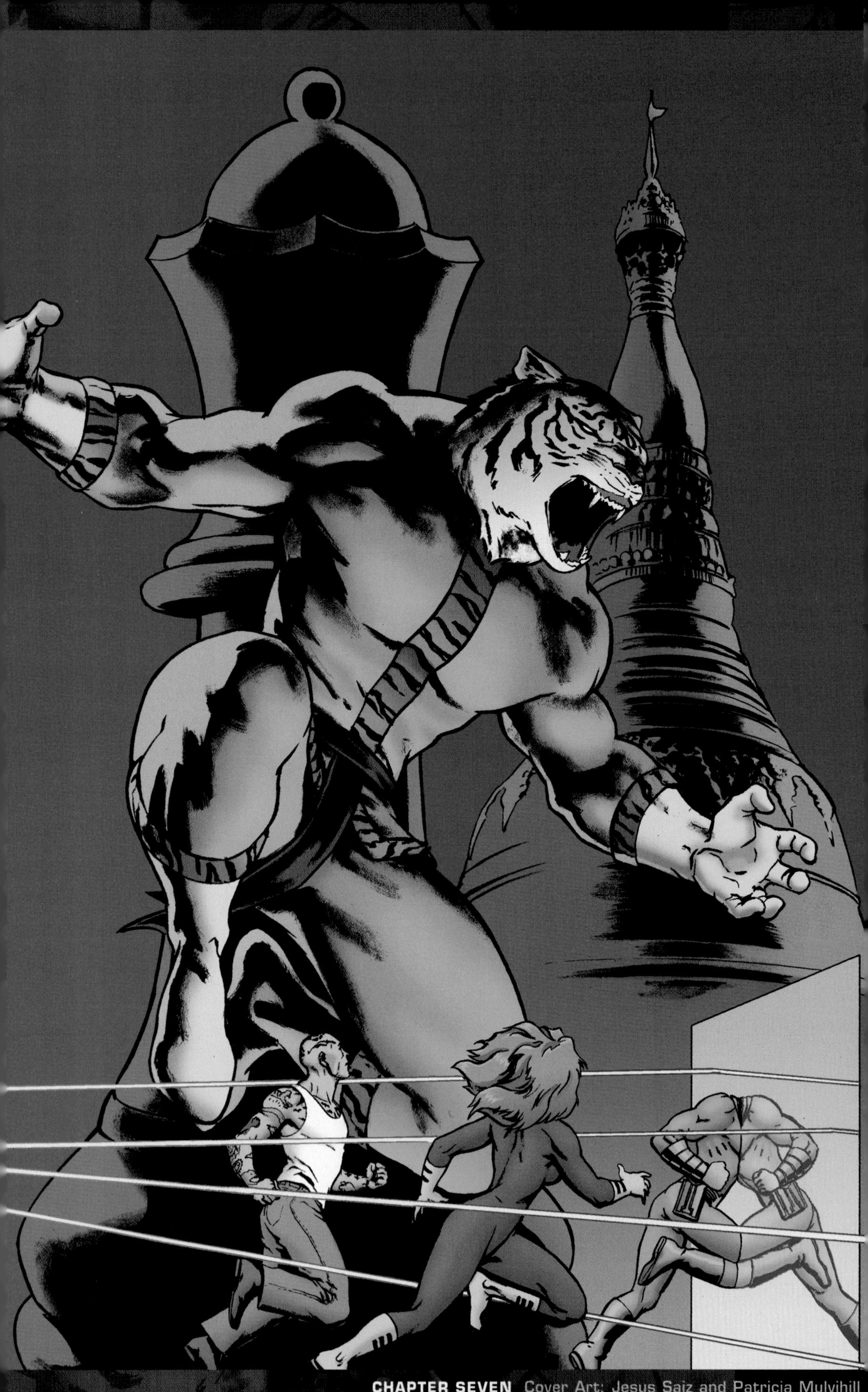

CHAPTER SEVEN Cover Art: Jesus Saiz and Patricia Mulvihill

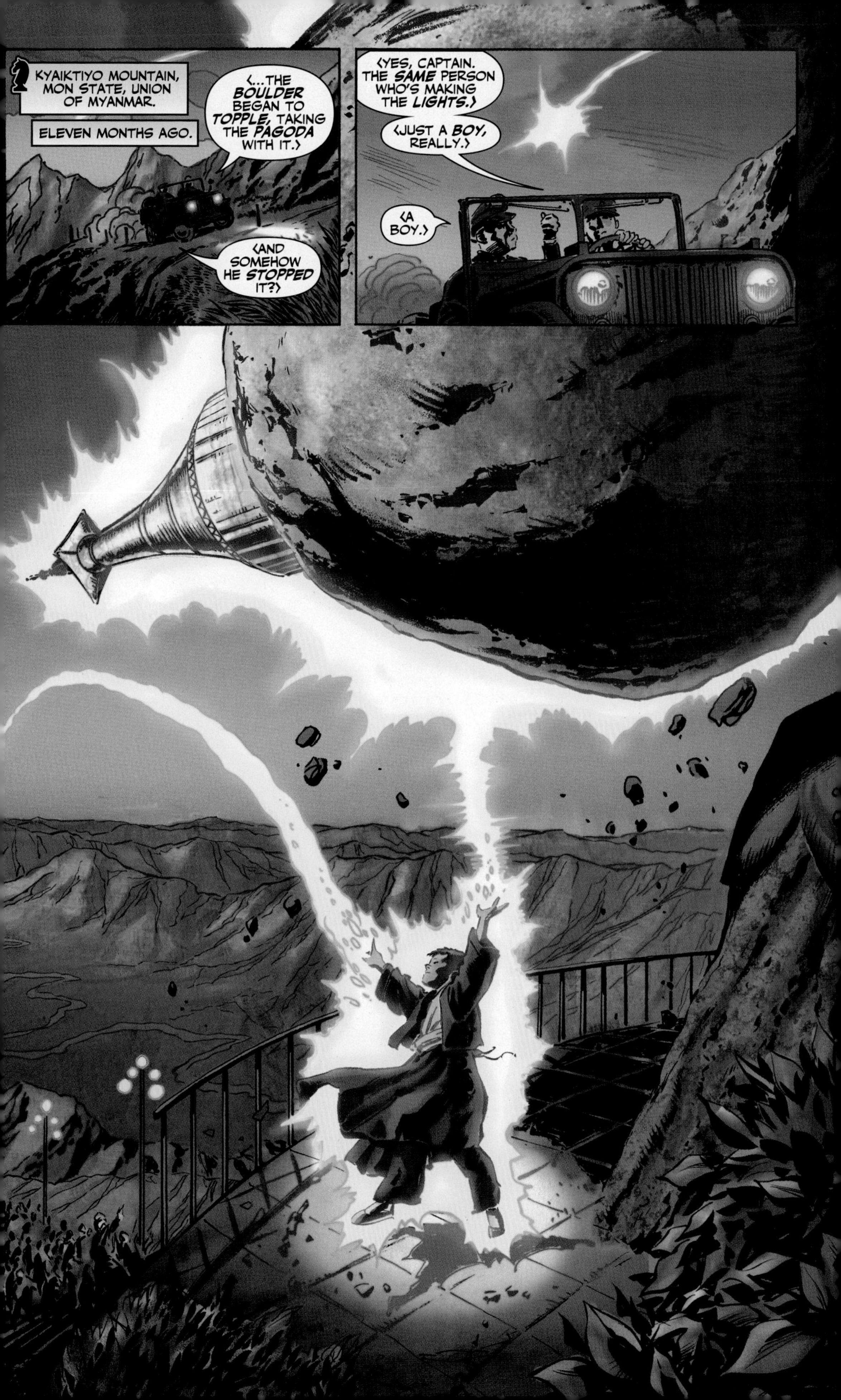
KYAIKTIYO MOUNTAIN, MON STATE, UNION OF MYANMAR.
ELEVEN MONTHS AGO.
<...THE BOULDER BEGAN TO TOPPLE, TAKING THE PAGODA WITH IT.>
<AND SOMEHOW HE STOPPED IT?>
<YES, CAPTAIN. THE SAME PERSON WHO'S MAKING THE LIGHTS.>
<JUST A BOY, REALLY.>
<A BOY.>

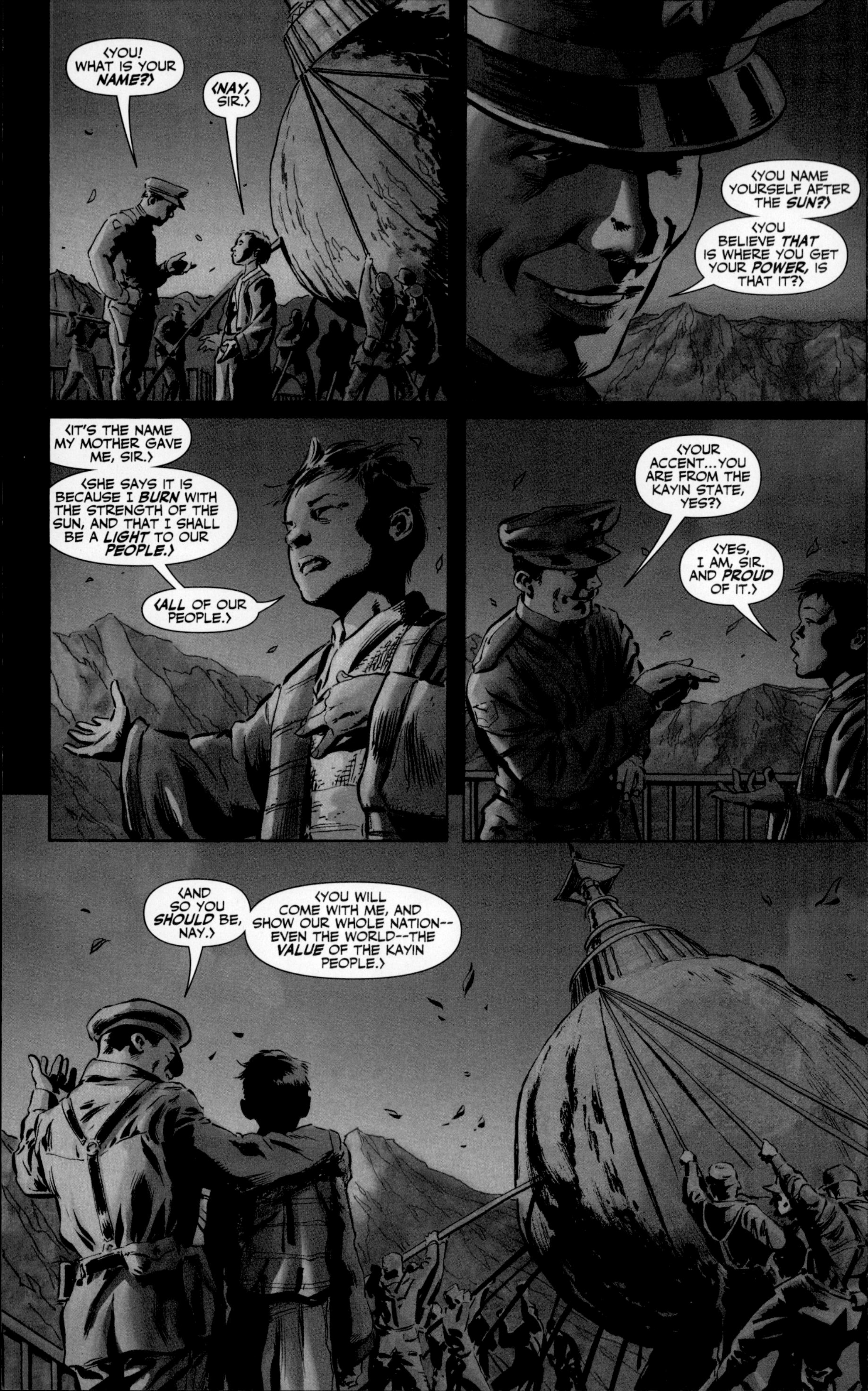

‹YOU! WHAT IS YOUR NAME?›
‹NAY, SIR.›
‹YOU NAME YOURSELF AFTER THE SUN?›
‹YOU BELIEVE THAT IS WHERE YOU GET YOUR POWER, IS THAT IT?›
‹IT'S THE NAME MY MOTHER GAVE ME, SIR.›
‹SHE SAYS IT IS BECAUSE I BURN WITH THE STRENGTH OF THE SUN, AND THAT I SHALL BE A LIGHT TO OUR PEOPLE.›
‹ALL OF OUR PEOPLE.›
‹YOUR ACCENT...YOU ARE FROM THE KAYIN STATE, YES?›
‹YES, I AM, SIR. AND PROUD OF IT.›
‹AND SO YOU SHOULD BE, NAY.›
‹YOU WILL COME WITH ME, AND SHOW OUR WHOLE NATION--EVEN THE WORLD--THE VALUE OF THE KAYIN PEOPLE.›

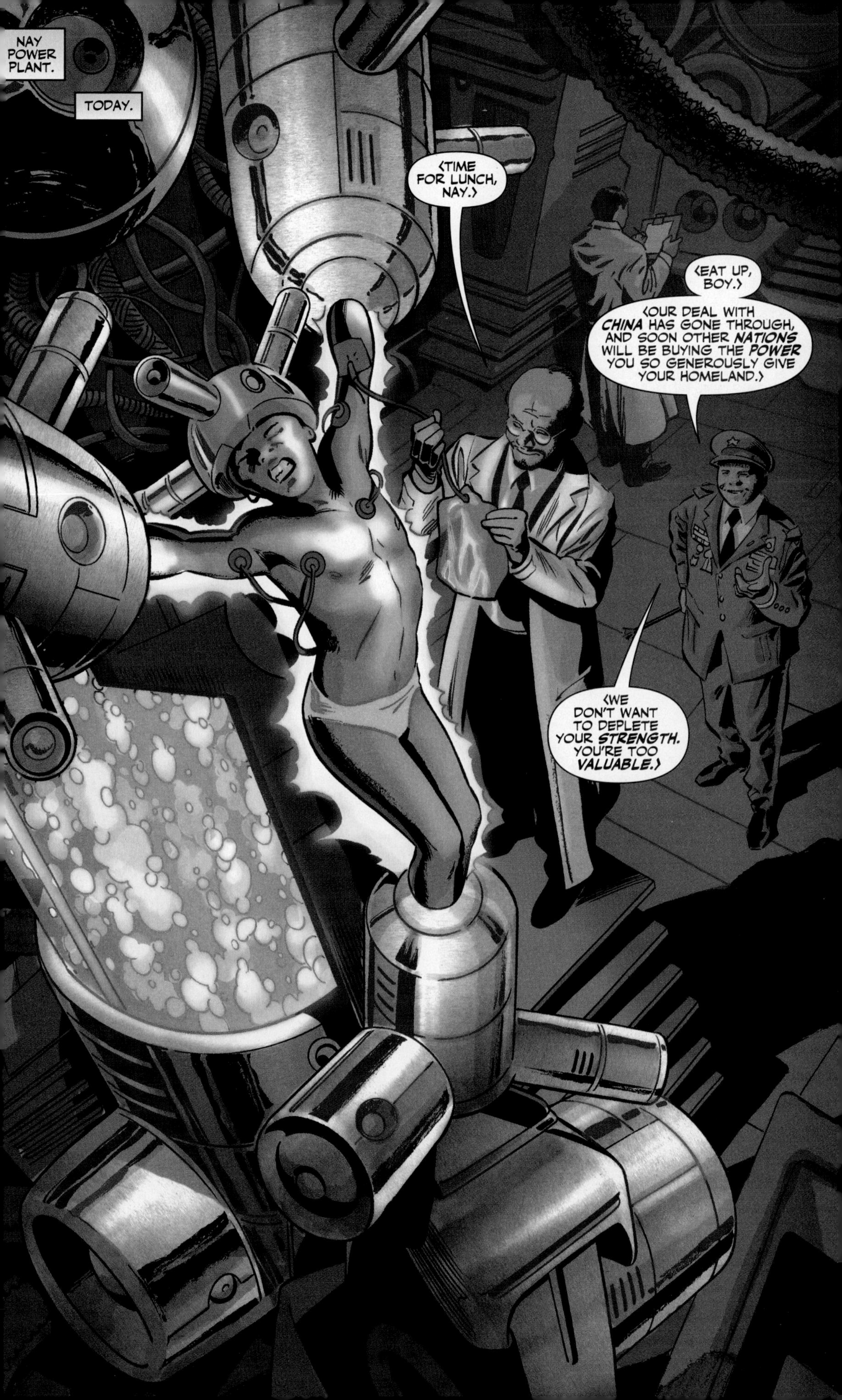
NAY POWER PLANT.
TODAY.
‹TIME FOR LUNCH, NAY.›
‹EAT UP, BOY.›
‹OUR DEAL WITH CHINA HAS GONE THROUGH, AND SOON OTHER NATIONS WILL BE BUYING THE POWER YOU SO GENEROUSLY GIVE YOUR HOMELAND.›
‹WE DON'T WANT TO DEPLETE YOUR STRENGTH. YOU'RE TOO VALUABLE.›

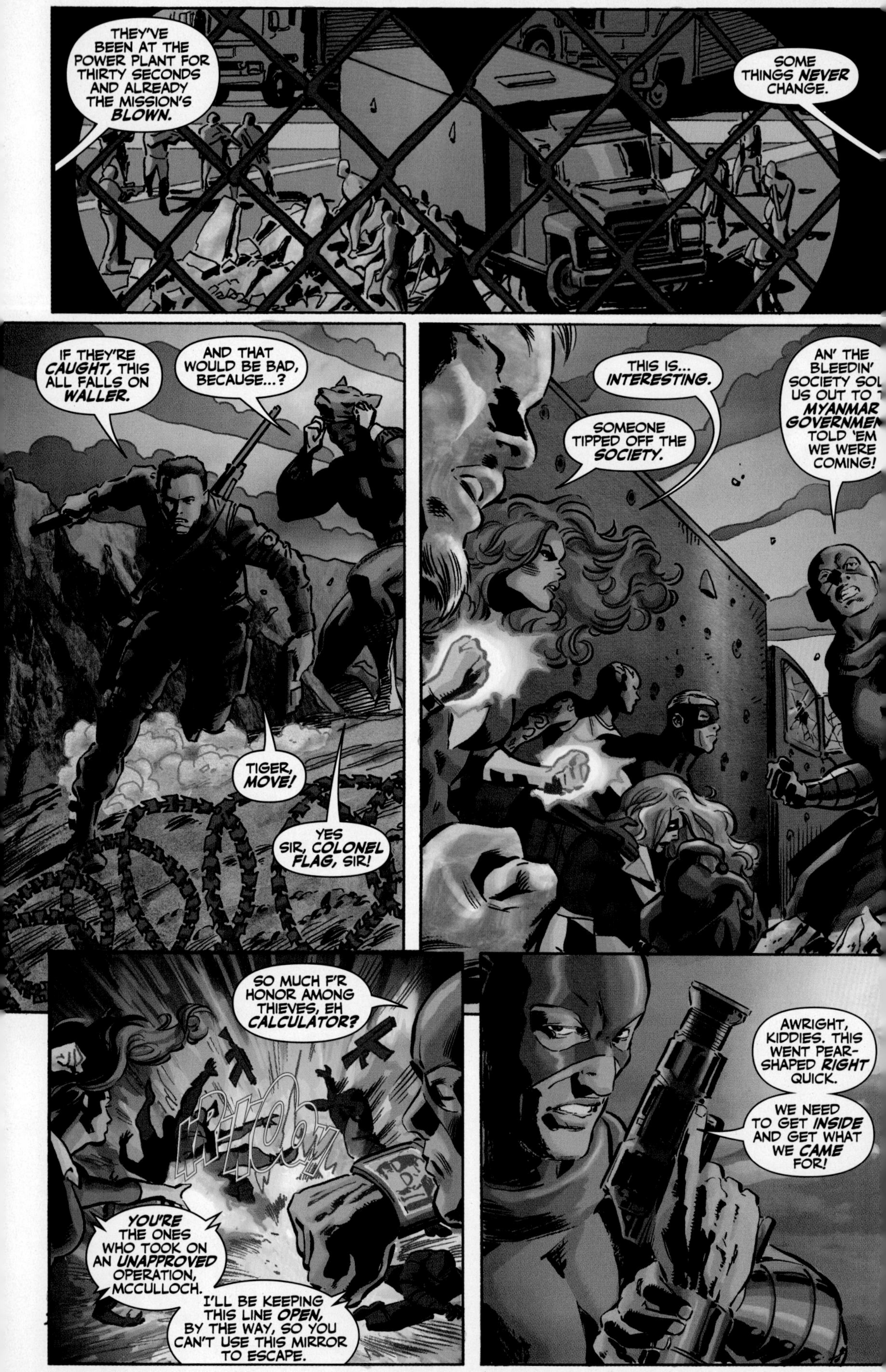
THEY'VE BEEN AT THE POWER PLANT FOR THIRTY SECONDS AND ALREADY THE MISSION'S BLOWN.
SOME THINGS NEVER CHANGE.
IF THEY'RE CAUGHT, THIS ALL FALLS ON WALLER.
AND THAT WOULD BE BAD, BECAUSE...?
TIGER, MOVE!
YES SIR, COLONEL FLAG, SIR!
THIS IS... INTERESTING.
SOMEONE TIPPED OFF THE SOCIETY.
AN' THE BLEEDIN' SOCIETY SOL US OUT TO T MYANMAR GOVERNME TOLD 'EM WE WERE COMING!
SO MUCH F'R HONOR AMONG THIEVES, EH CALCULATOR?
KA-THOOM
YOU'RE THE ONES WHO TOOK ON AN UNAPPROVED OPERATION, MCCULLOCH.
I'LL BE KEEPING THIS LINE OPEN, BY THE WAY, SO YOU CAN'T USE THIS MIRROR TO ESCAPE.
AWRIGHT, KIDDIES. THIS WENT PEAR-SHAPED RIGHT QUICK.
WE NEED TO GET INSIDE AND GET WHAT WE CAME FOR!

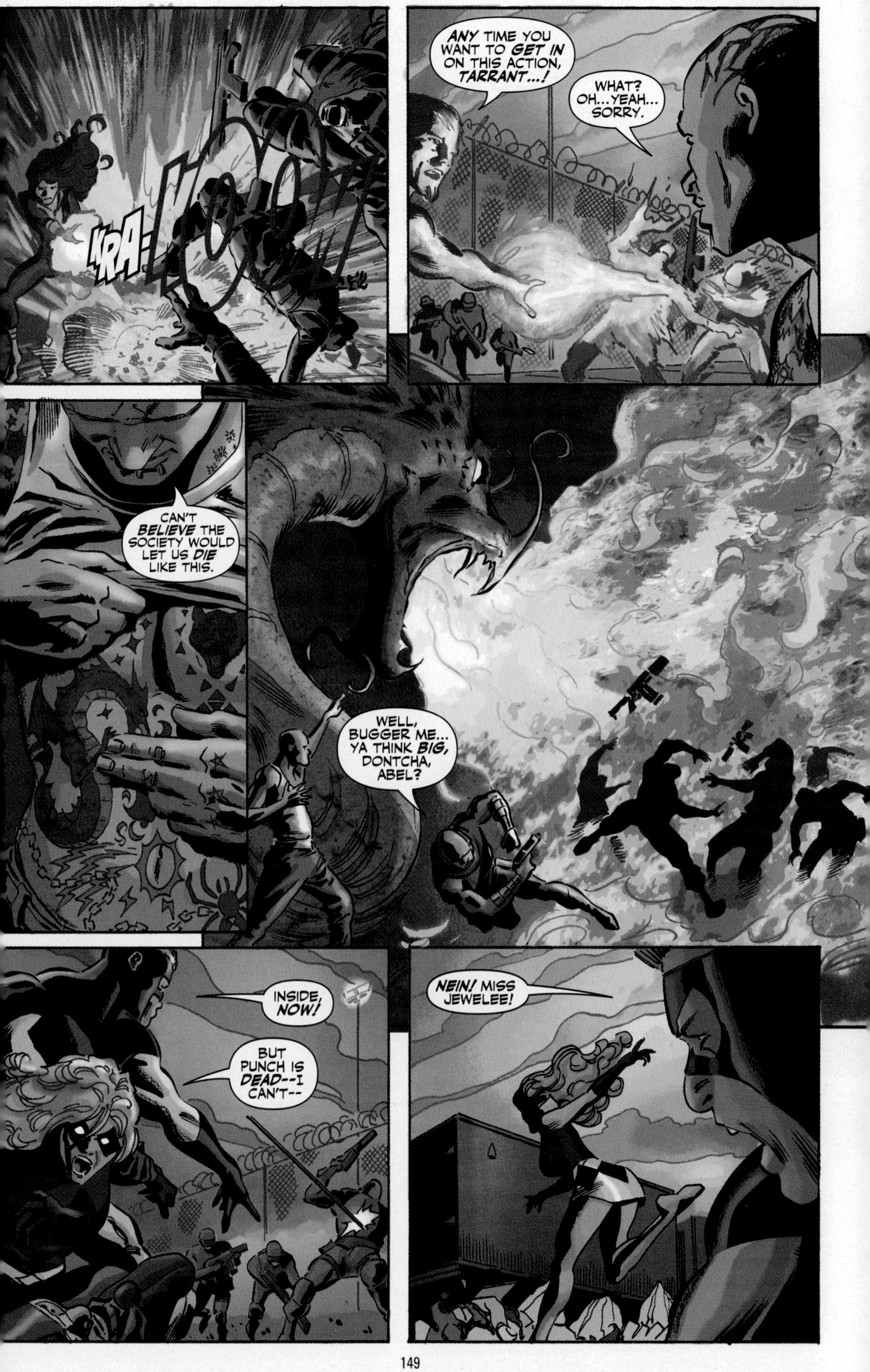
KRA-KOOOM
ANY TIME YOU WANT TO GET IN ON THIS ACTION, TARRANT...!
WHAT? OH...YEAH... SORRY.
CAN'T BELIEVE THE SOCIETY WOULD LET US DIE LIKE THIS.
WELL, BUGGER ME... YA THINK BIG, DONTCHA, ABEL?
INSIDE, NOW!
BUT PUNCH IS DEAD--I CAN'T--
NEIN! MISS JEWELEE!

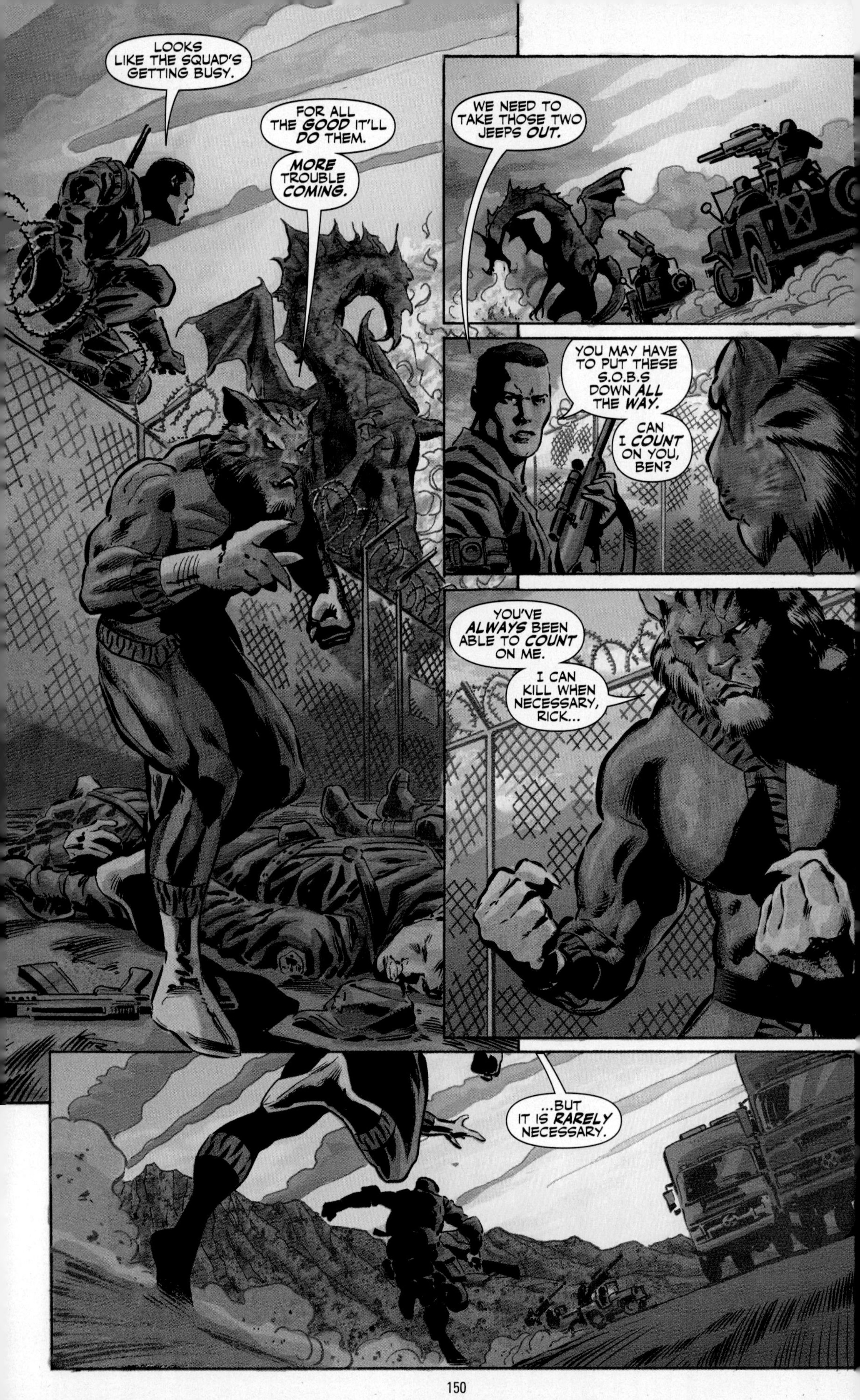

LOOKS LIKE THE SQUAD'S GETTING BUSY.
FOR ALL THE GOOD IT'LL DO THEM.
MORE TROUBLE COMING.
WE NEED TO TAKE THOSE TWO JEEPS OUT.
YOU MAY HAVE TO PUT THESE S.O.B.S DOWN ALL THE WAY.
CAN I COUNT ON YOU, BEN?
YOU'VE ALWAYS BEEN ABLE TO COUNT ON ME.
I CAN KILL WHEN NECESSARY, RICK...
...BUT IT IS RARELY NECESSARY.

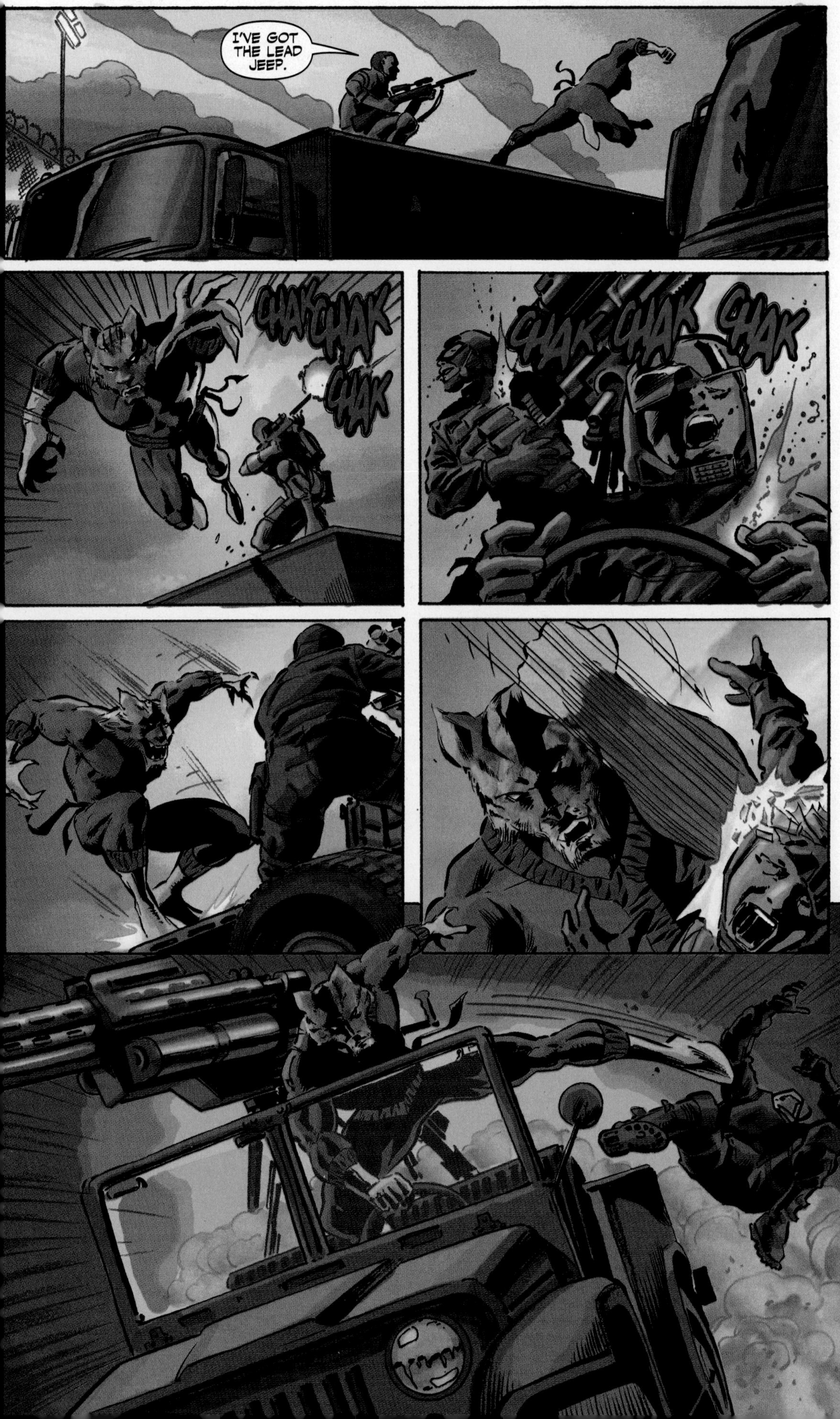
I'VE GOT THE LEAD JEEP.
CHAK CHAK CHAK
CHAK CHAK CHAK

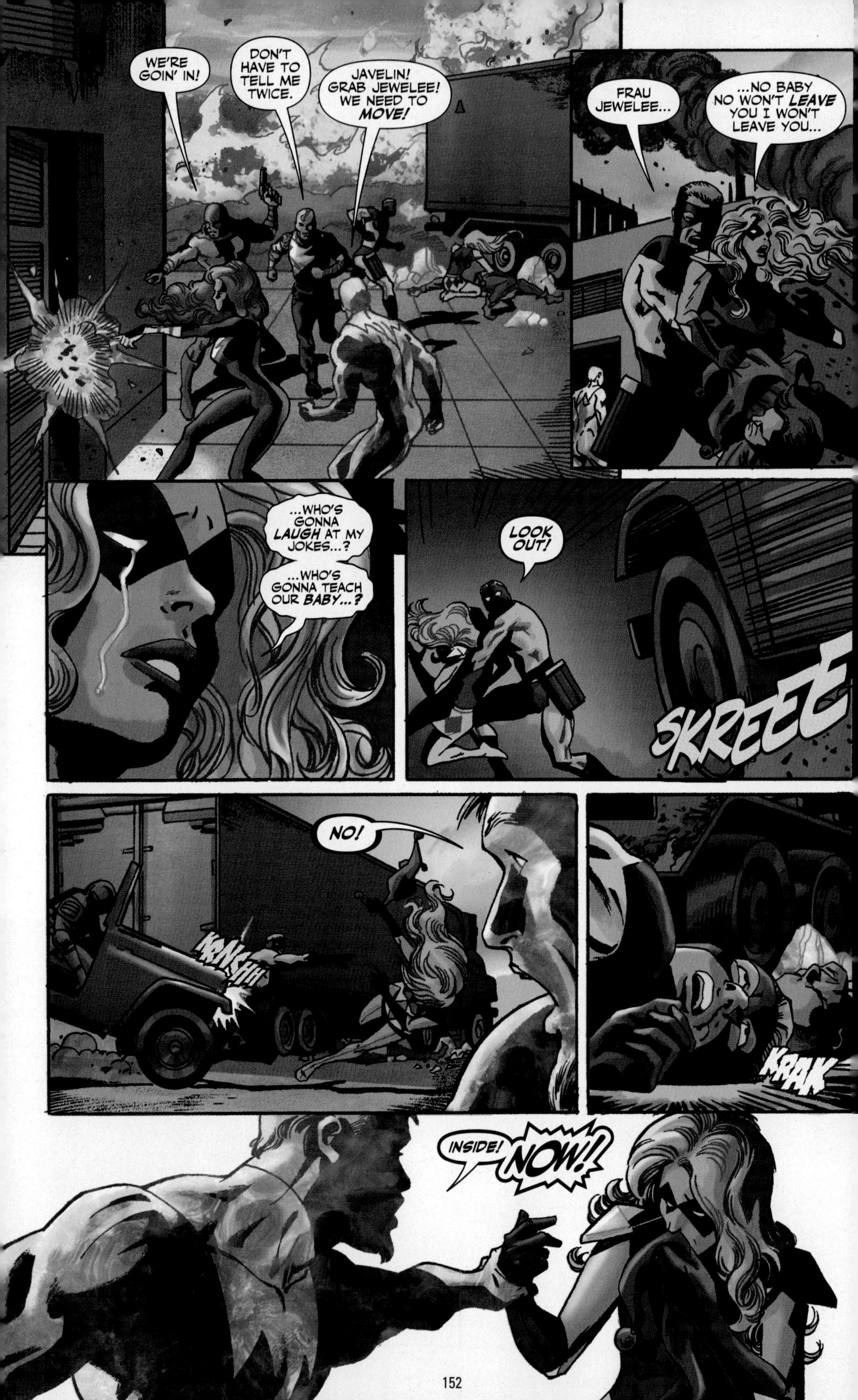

WE'RE GOIN' IN!
DON'T HAVE TO TELL ME TWICE.
JAVELIN! GRAB JEWELEE! WE NEED TO *MOVE!*
FRAU JEWELEE...
...NO BABY NO WON'T *LEAVE* YOU I WON'T LEAVE YOU...
...WHO'S GONNA *LAUGH* AT MY JOKES...?
...WHO'S GONNA TEACH OUR *BABY*...?
LOOK OUT!
SKREEE
NO!
KRNSHH
KRAK
INSIDE! NOW!!

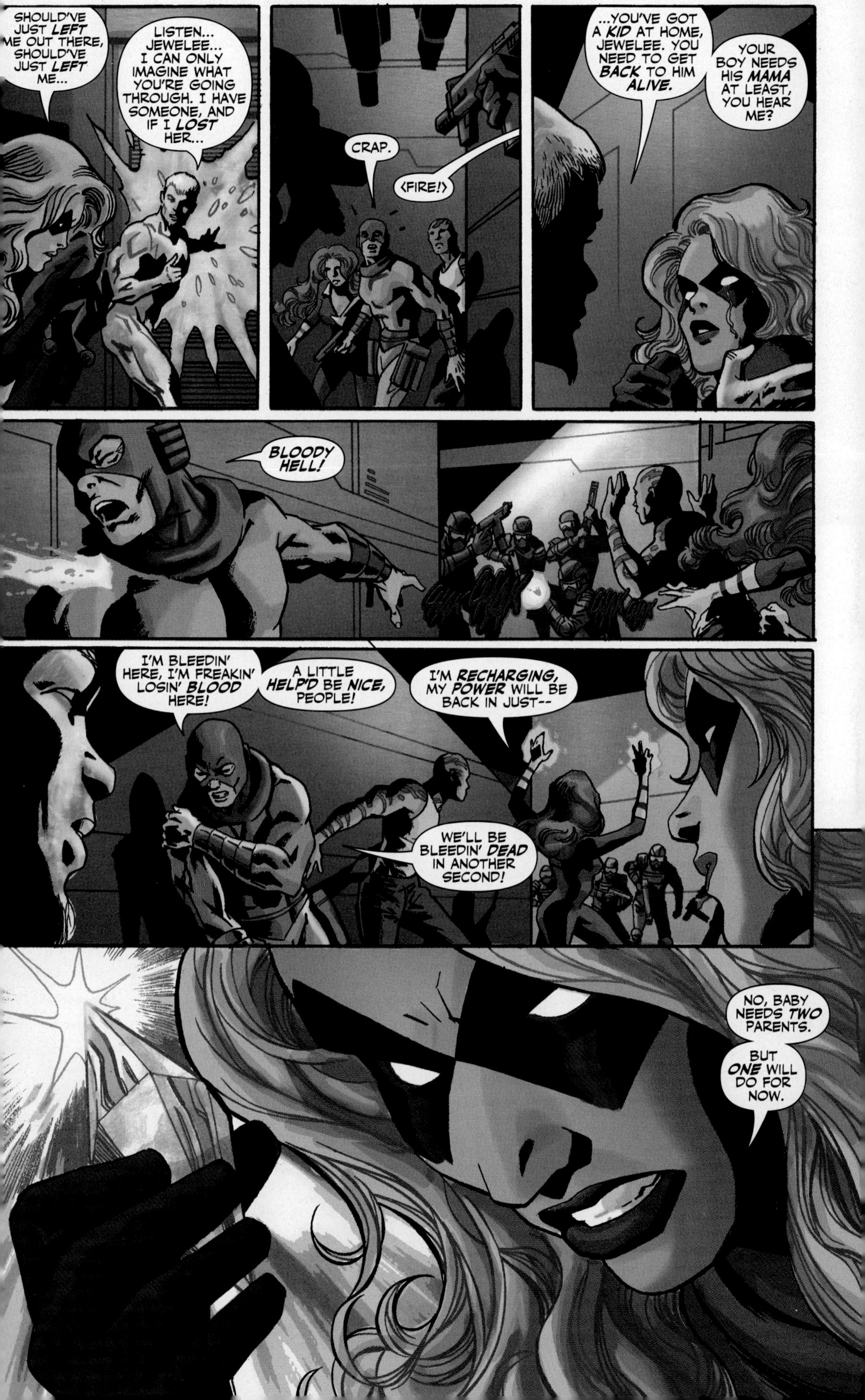
SHOULD'VE JUST LEFT ME OUT THERE, SHOULD'VE JUST LEFT ME...
LISTEN... JEWELEE... I CAN ONLY IMAGINE WHAT YOU'RE GOING THROUGH. I HAVE SOMEONE, AND IF I LOST HER...
CRAP.
‹FIRE!›
...YOU'VE GOT A KID AT HOME, JEWELEE. YOU NEED TO GET BACK TO HIM ALIVE.
YOUR BOY NEEDS HIS MAMA AT LEAST, YOU HEAR ME?
BLOODY HELL!
I'M BLEEDIN' HERE, I'M FREAKIN' LOSIN' BLOOD HERE!
A LITTLE HELP'D BE NICE, PEOPLE!
I'M RECHARGING, MY POWER WILL BE BACK IN JUST--
WE'LL BE BLEEDIN' DEAD IN ANOTHER SECOND!
NO, BABY NEEDS TWO PARENTS.
BUT ONE WILL DO FOR NOW.

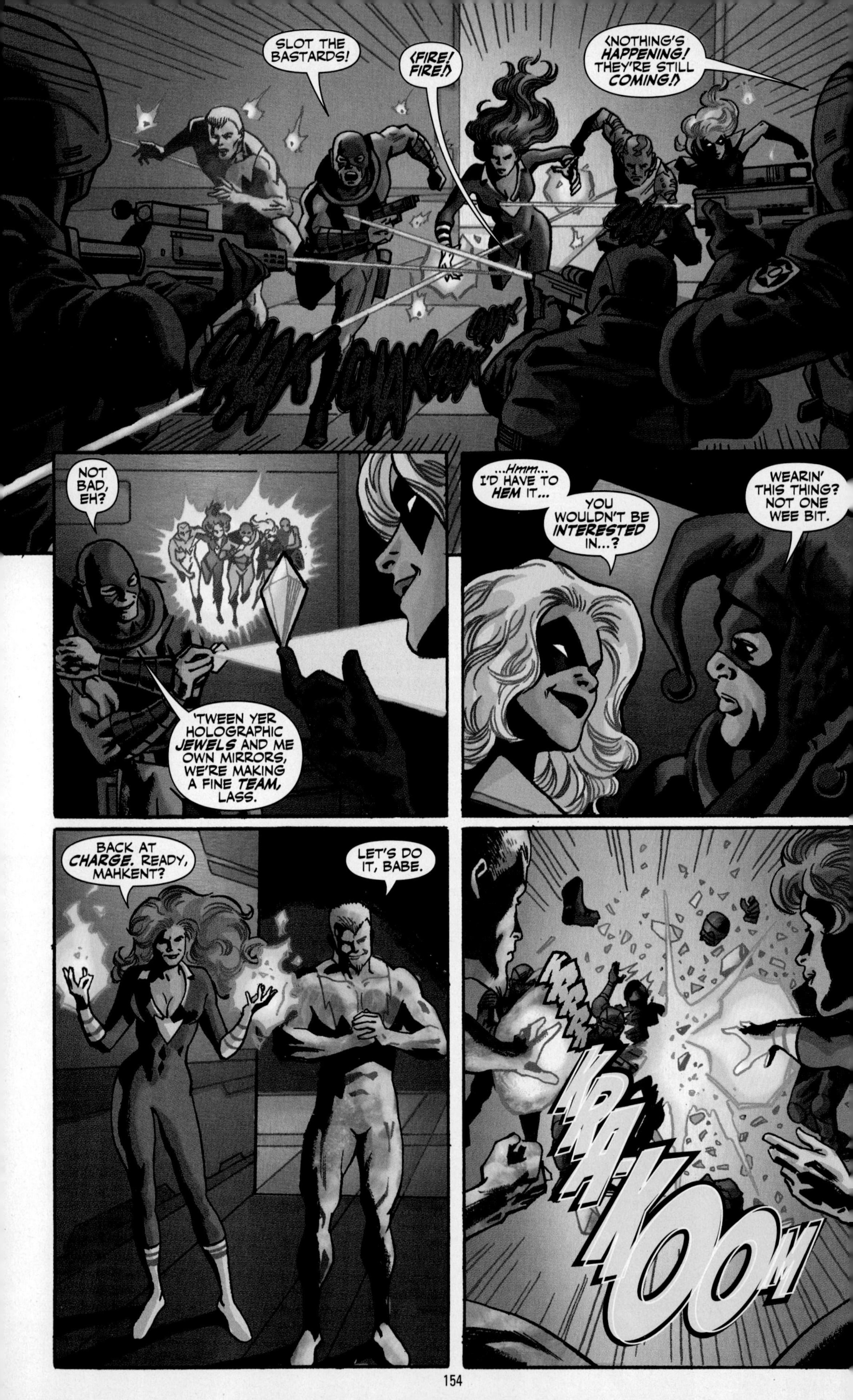

SLOT THE BASTARDS!
‹FIRE! FIRE!›
‹NOTHING'S HAPPENING! THEY'RE STILL COMING!›
NOT BAD, EH?
'TWEEN YER HOLOGRAPHIC JEWELS AND ME OWN MIRRORS, WE'RE MAKING A FINE TEAM, LASS.
...Hmm... I'D HAVE TO HEM IT...
YOU WOULDN'T BE INTERESTED IN...?
WEARIN' THIS THING? NOT ONE WEE BIT.
BACK AT CHARGE. READY, MAHKENT?
LET'S DO IT, BABE.
KA-KA-KROOOM

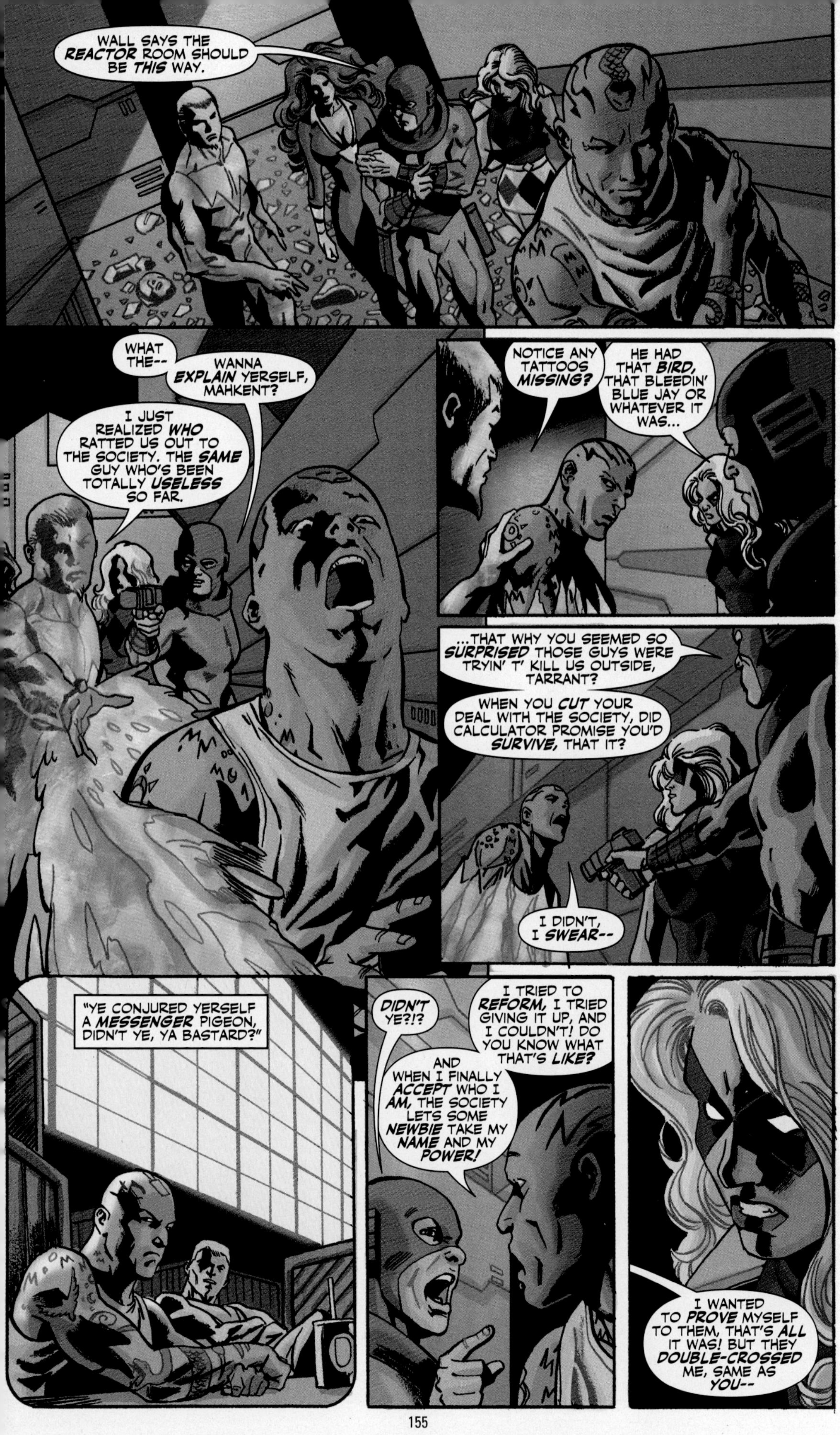
WALL SAYS THE REACTOR ROOM SHOULD BE THIS WAY.
WHAT THE--
WANNA EXPLAIN YERSELF, MAHKENT?
I JUST REALIZED WHO RATTED US OUT TO THE SOCIETY. THE SAME GUY WHO'S BEEN TOTALLY USELESS SO FAR.
NOTICE ANY TATTOOS MISSING?
HE HAD THAT BIRD, THAT BLEEDIN' BLUE JAY OR WHATEVER IT WAS...
...THAT WHY YOU SEEMED SO SURPRISED THOSE GUYS WERE TRYIN' T' KILL US OUTSIDE, TARRANT?
WHEN YOU CUT YOUR DEAL WITH THE SOCIETY, DID CALCULATOR PROMISE YOU'D SURVIVE, THAT IT?
I DIDN'T, I SWEAR--
"YE CONJURED YERSELF A MESSENGER PIGEON, DIDN'T YE, YA BASTARD?"
DIDN'T YE?!?
I TRIED TO REFORM, I TRIED GIVING IT UP, AND I COULDN'T! DO YOU KNOW WHAT THAT'S LIKE?
AND WHEN I FINALLY ACCEPT WHO I AM, THE SOCIETY LETS SOME NEWBIE TAKE MY NAME AND MY POWER!
I WANTED TO PROVE MYSELF TO THEM, THAT'S ALL IT WAS! BUT THEY DOUBLE-CROSSED ME, SAME AS YOU--

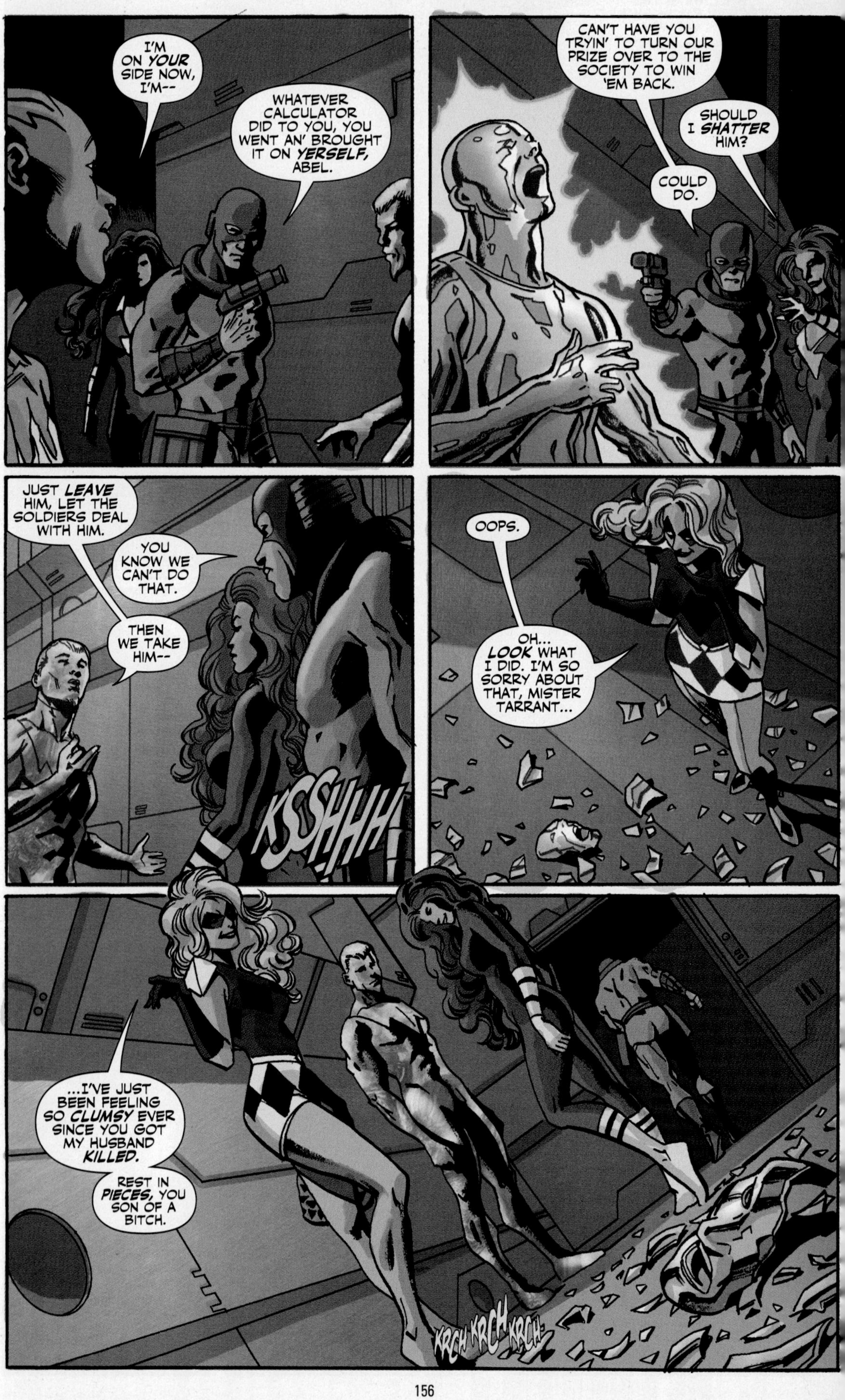
I'M ON YOUR SIDE NOW, I'M--
WHATEVER CALCULATOR DID TO YOU, YOU WENT AN' BROUGHT IT ON YERSELF, ABEL.
CAN'T HAVE YOU TRYIN' TO TURN OUR PRIZE OVER TO THE SOCIETY TO WIN 'EM BACK.
SHOULD I SHATTER HIM?
COULD DO.
JUST LEAVE HIM, LET THE SOLDIERS DEAL WITH HIM.
YOU KNOW WE CAN'T DO THAT.
THEN WE TAKE HIM--
KSSHHH
OOPS.
OH... LOOK WHAT I DID. I'M SO SORRY ABOUT THAT, MISTER TARRANT...
...I'VE JUST BEEN FEELING SO CLUMSY EVER SINCE YOU GOT MY HUSBAND KILLED.
REST IN PIECES, YOU SON OF A BITCH.
KRCH KRCH KRCH

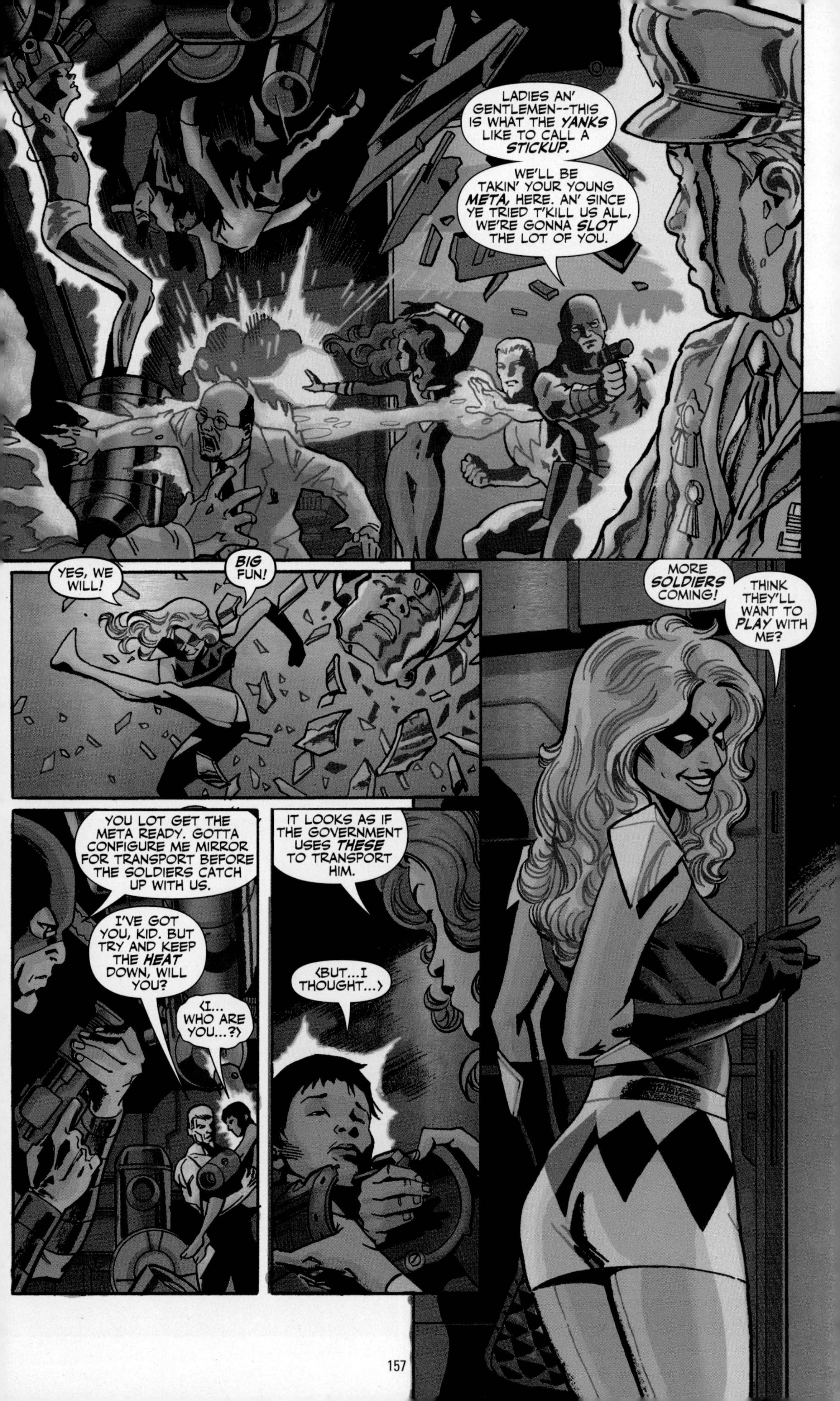

LADIES AN' GENTLEMEN--THIS IS WHAT THE YANKS LIKE TO CALL A STICKUP.
WE'LL BE TAKIN' YOUR YOUNG META, HERE. AN' SINCE YE TRIED T'KILL US ALL, WE'RE GONNA SLOT THE LOT OF YOU.
YES, WE WILL!
BIG FUN!
MORE SOLDIERS COMING!
THINK THEY'LL WANT TO PLAY WITH ME?
YOU LOT GET THE META READY. GOTTA CONFIGURE ME MIRROR FOR TRANSPORT BEFORE THE SOLDIERS CATCH UP WITH US.
I'VE GOT YOU, KID. BUT TRY AND KEEP THE HEAT DOWN, WILL YOU?
<I... WHO ARE YOU...?>
IT LOOKS AS IF THE GOVERNMENT USES THESE TO TRANSPORT HIM.
<BUT...I THOUGHT...>

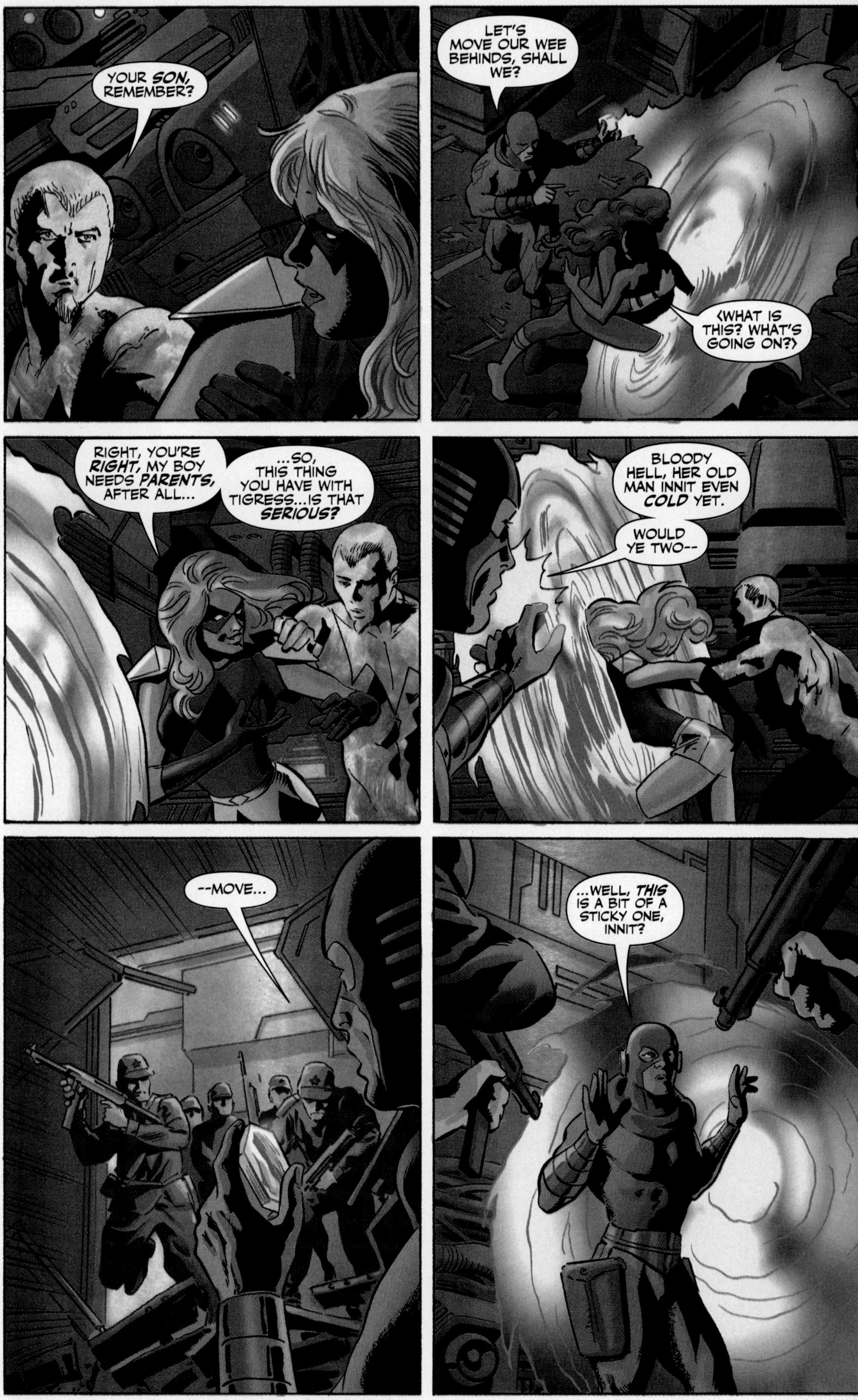
YOUR SON, REMEMBER?
LET'S MOVE OUR WEE BEHINDS, SHALL WE?
<WHAT IS THIS? WHAT'S GOING ON?>
RIGHT, YOU'RE RIGHT, MY BOY NEEDS PARENTS, AFTER ALL...
...SO, THIS THING YOU HAVE WITH TIGRESS...IS THAT SERIOUS?
BLOODY HELL, HER OLD MAN INNIT EVEN COLD YET.
WOULD YE TWO--
--MOVE...
...WELL, THIS IS A BIT OF A STICKY ONE, INNIT?

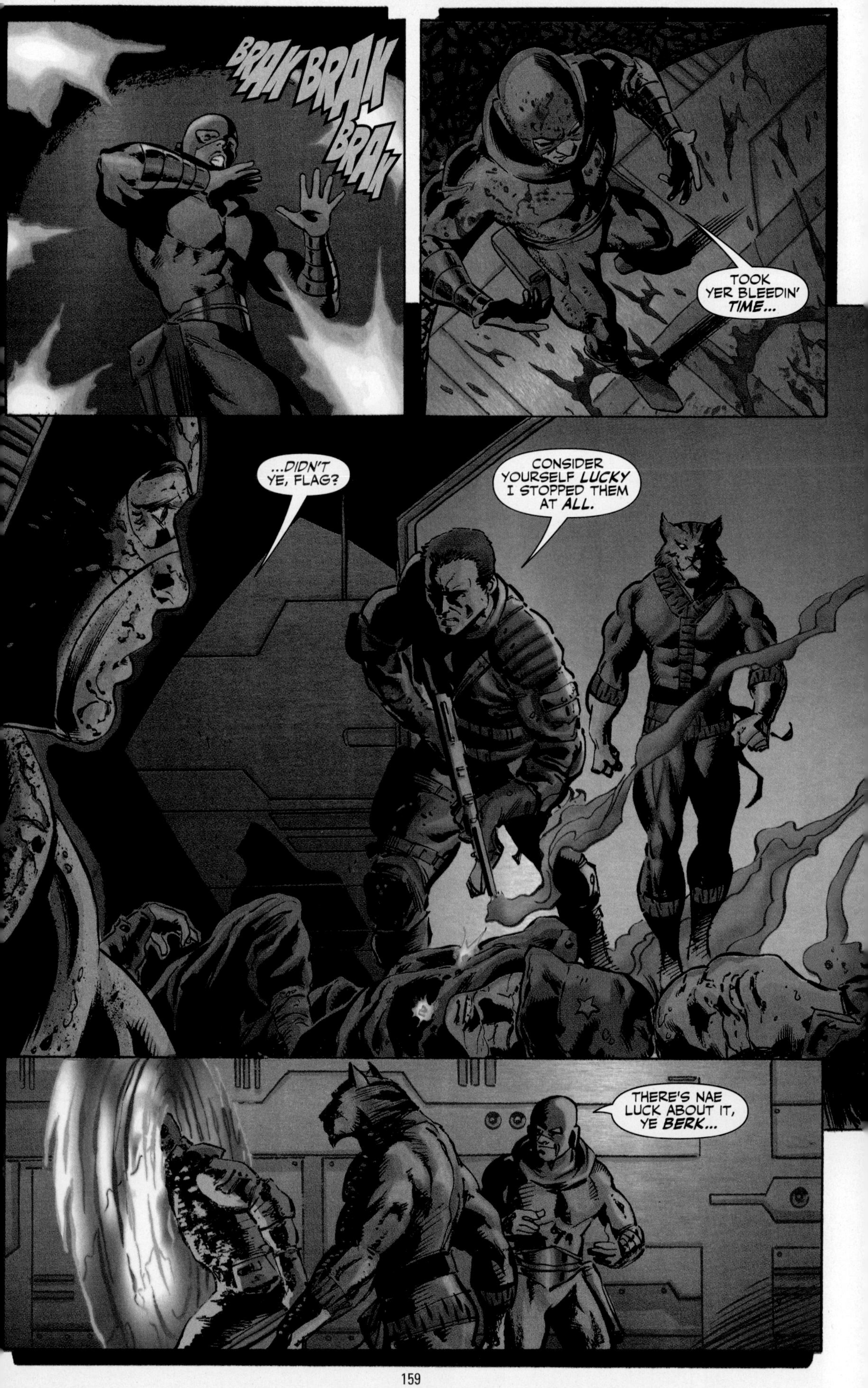
BRAK BRAK BRAK BRAK
TOOK YER BLEEDIN' TIME...
...DIDN'T YE, FLAG?
CONSIDER YOURSELF LUCKY I STOPPED THEM AT ALL.
THERE'S NAE LUCK ABOUT IT, YE BERK...

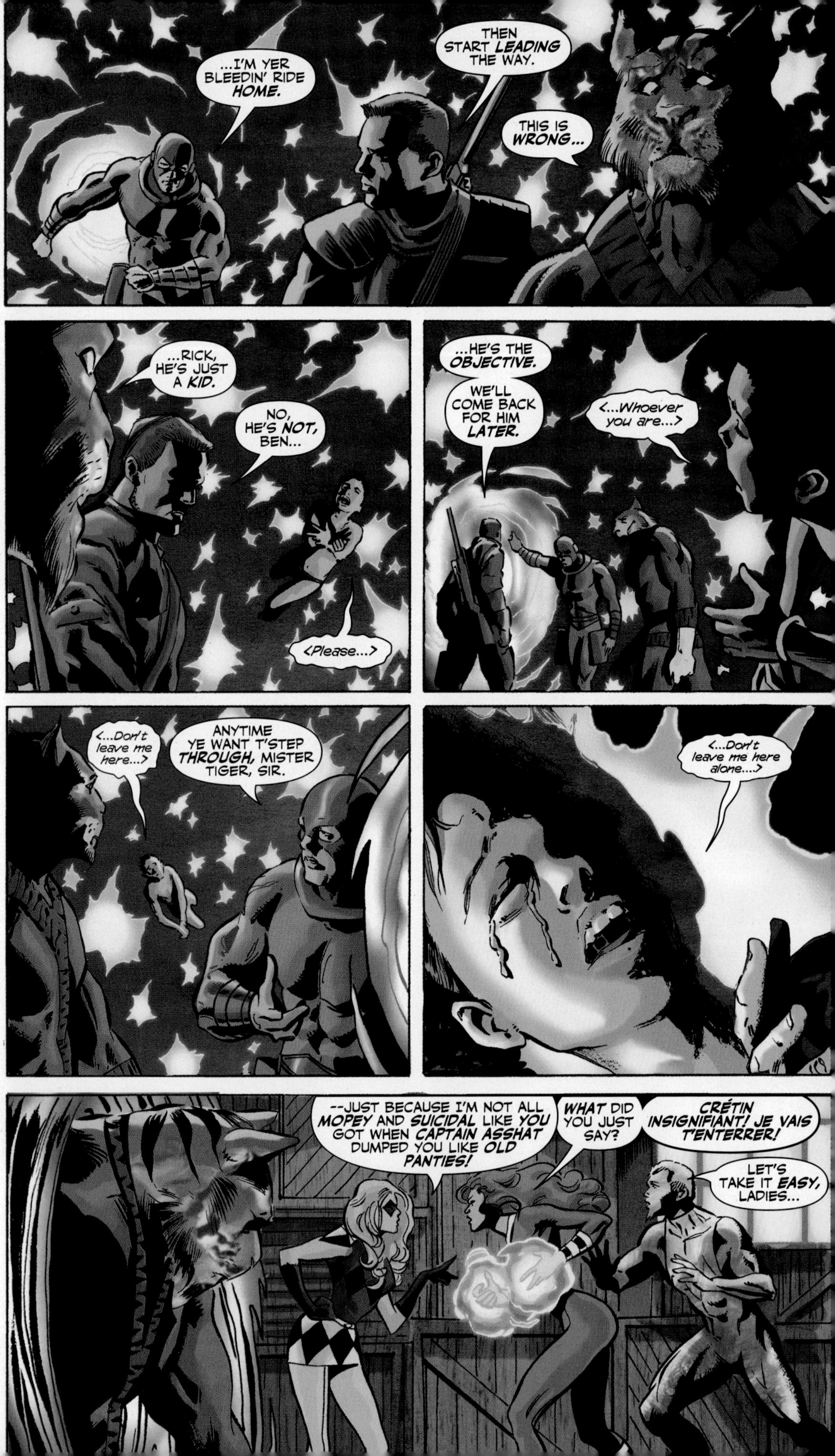
...I'M YER BLEEDIN' RIDE HOME.
THEN START LEADING THE WAY.
THIS IS WRONG...
...RICK, HE'S JUST A KID.
NO, HE'S NOT, BEN...
<Please...>
...HE'S THE OBJECTIVE.
WE'LL COME BACK FOR HIM LATER.
<...Whoever you are...>
<...Don't leave me here...>
ANYTIME YE WANT T'STEP THROUGH, MISTER TIGER, SIR.
<...Don't leave me here alone....>
--JUST BECAUSE I'M NOT ALL MOPEY AND SUICIDAL LIKE YOU GOT WHEN CAPTAIN ASSHAT DUMPED YOU LIKE OLD PANTIES!
WHAT DID YOU JUST SAY?
CRÉTIN INSIGNIFIANT! JE VAIS T'ENTERRER!
LET'S TAKE IT EASY, LADIES...

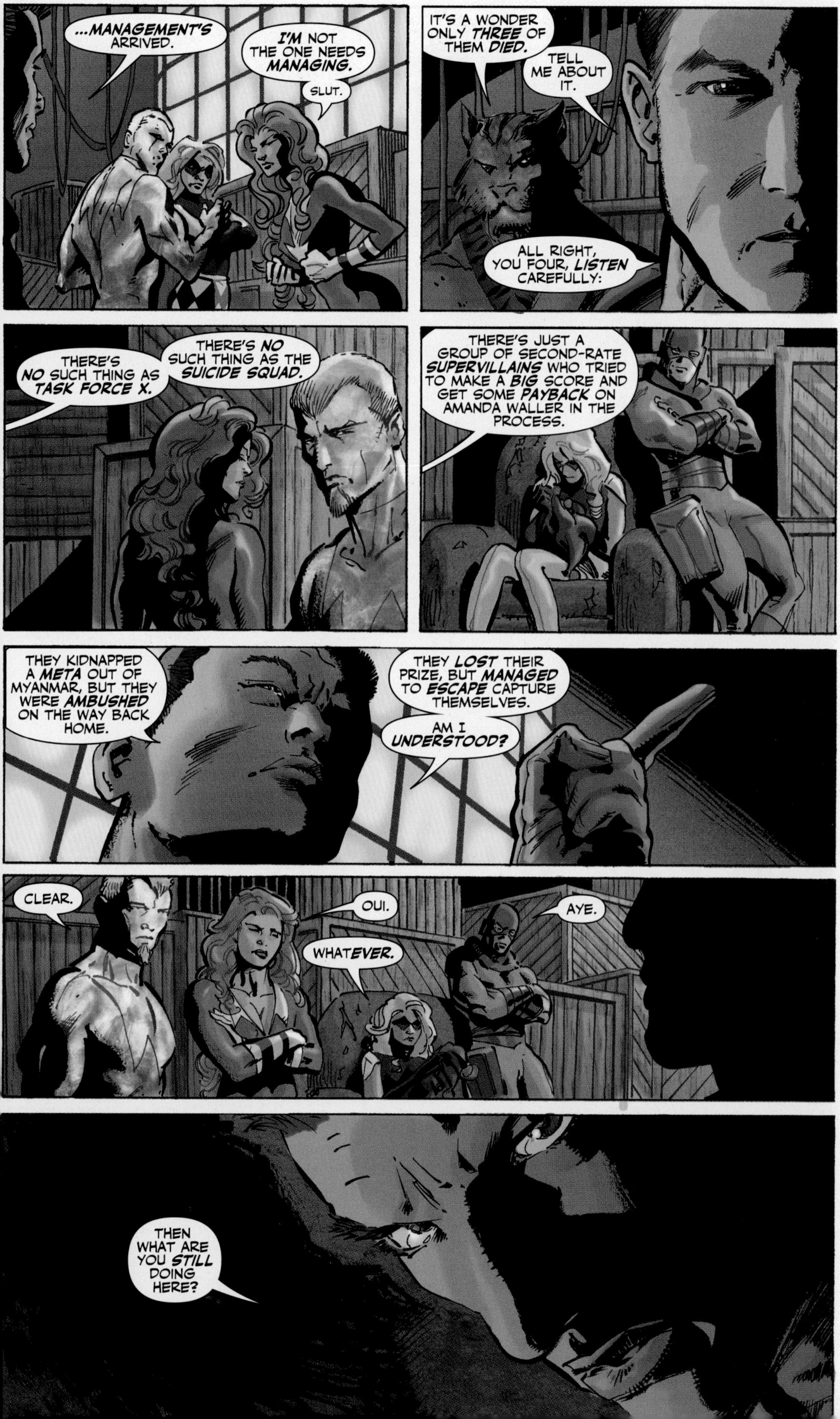
...MANAGEMENT'S ARRIVED.
I'M NOT THE ONE NEEDS MANAGING.
SLUT.
IT'S A WONDER ONLY THREE OF THEM DIED.
TELL ME ABOUT IT.
ALL RIGHT, YOU FOUR, LISTEN CAREFULLY:
THERE'S NO SUCH THING AS TASK FORCE X.
THERE'S NO SUCH THING AS THE SUICIDE SQUAD.
THERE'S JUST A GROUP OF SECOND-RATE SUPERVILLAINS WHO TRIED TO MAKE A BIG SCORE AND GET SOME PAYBACK ON AMANDA WALLER IN THE PROCESS.
THEY KIDNAPPED A META OUT OF MYANMAR, BUT THEY WERE AMBUSHED ON THE WAY BACK HOME.
THEY LOST THEIR PRIZE, BUT MANAGED TO ESCAPE CAPTURE THEMSELVES.
AM I UNDERSTOOD?
CLEAR.
OUI.
WHATEVER.
AYE.
THEN WHAT ARE YOU STILL DOING HERE?

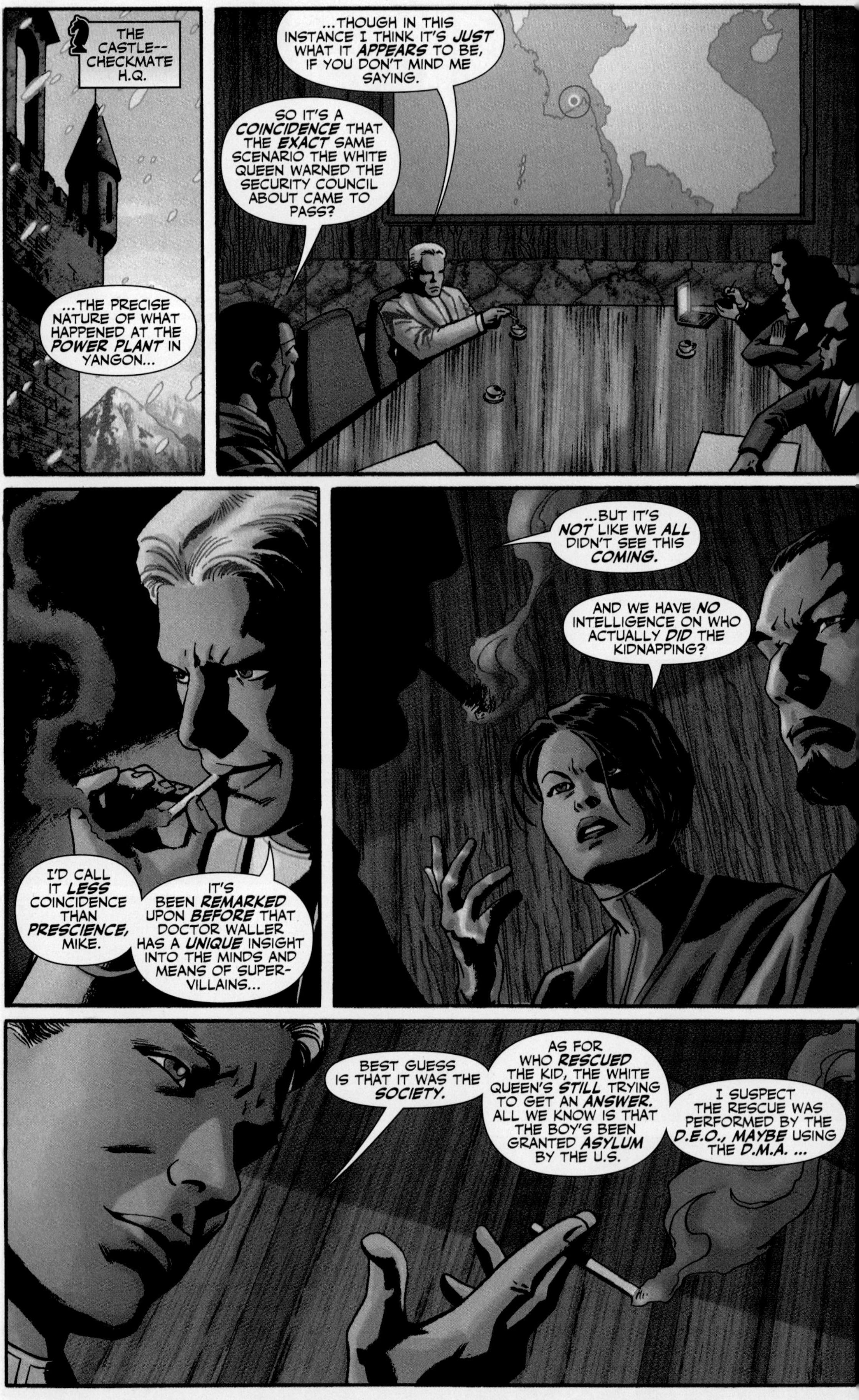
THE CASTLE-- CHECKMATE H.Q.
...THE PRECISE NATURE OF WHAT HAPPENED AT THE POWER PLANT IN YANGON...
...THOUGH IN THIS INSTANCE I THINK IT'S JUST WHAT IT APPEARS TO BE, IF YOU DON'T MIND ME SAYING.
SO IT'S A COINCIDENCE THAT THE EXACT SAME SCENARIO THE WHITE QUEEN WARNED THE SECURITY COUNCIL ABOUT CAME TO PASS?
IT'S BEEN REMARKED UPON BEFORE THAT DOCTOR WALLER HAS A UNIQUE INSIGHT INTO THE MINDS AND MEANS OF SUPER-VILLAINS...
I'D CALL IT LESS COINCIDENCE THAN PRESCIENCE, MIKE.
...BUT IT'S NOT LIKE WE ALL DIDN'T SEE THIS COMING.
AND WE HAVE NO INTELLIGENCE ON WHO ACTUALLY DID THE KIDNAPPING?
BEST GUESS IS THAT IT WAS THE SOCIETY.
AS FOR WHO RESCUED THE KID, THE WHITE QUEEN'S STILL TRYING TO GET AN ANSWER. ALL WE KNOW IS THAT THE BOY'S BEEN GRANTED ASYLUM BY THE U.S.
I SUSPECT THE RESCUE WAS PERFORMED BY THE D.E.O., MAYBE USING THE D.M.A. ...

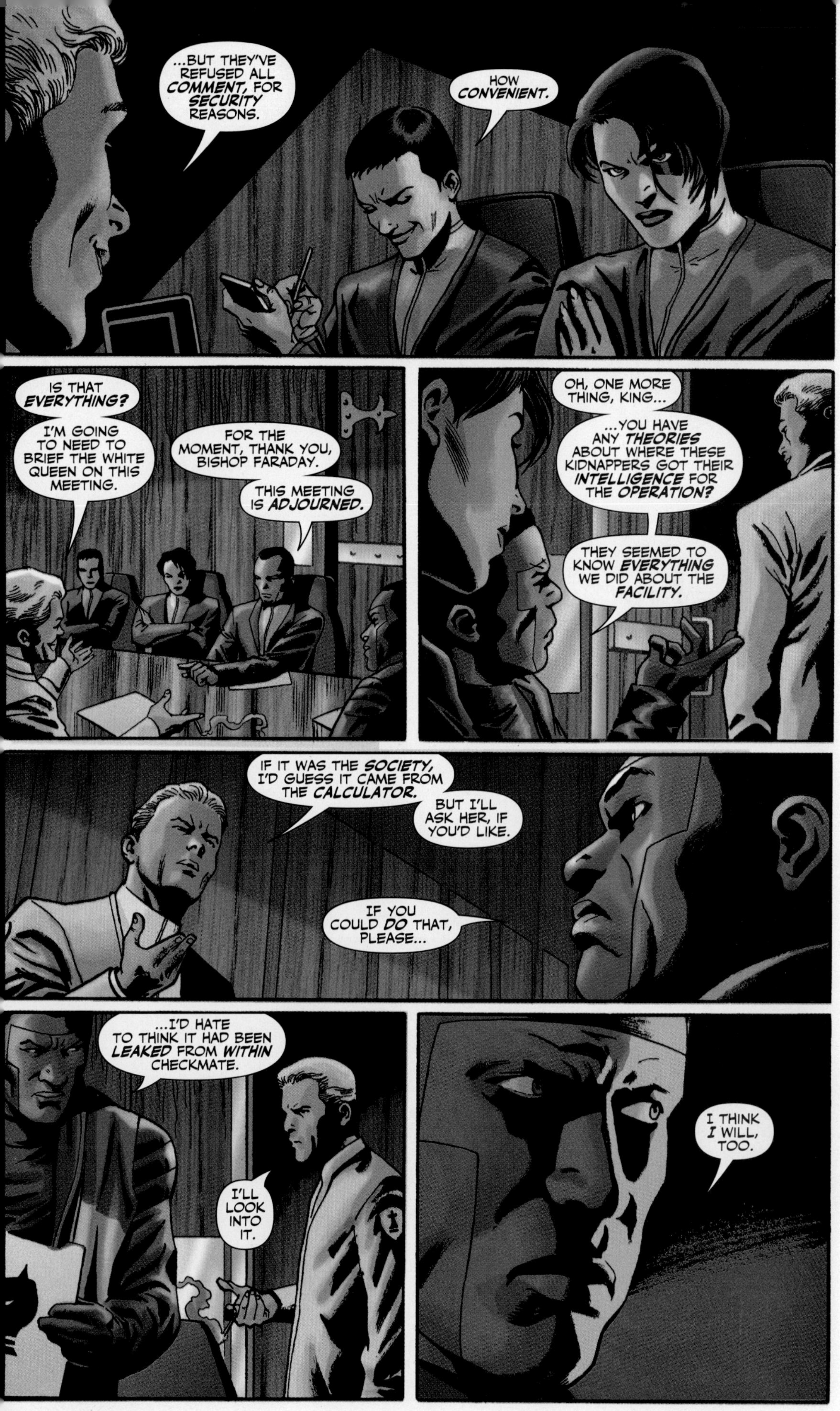
...BUT THEY'VE REFUSED ALL COMMENT, FOR SECURITY REASONS.
HOW CONVENIENT.
IS THAT EVERYTHING?
I'M GOING TO NEED TO BRIEF THE WHITE QUEEN ON THIS MEETING.
FOR THE MOMENT, THANK YOU, BISHOP FARADAY.
THIS MEETING IS ADJOURNED.
OH, ONE MORE THING, KING...
...YOU HAVE ANY THEORIES ABOUT WHERE THESE KIDNAPPERS GOT THEIR INTELLIGENCE FOR THE OPERATION?
THEY SEEMED TO KNOW EVERYTHING WE DID ABOUT THE FACILITY.
IF IT WAS THE SOCIETY, I'D GUESS IT CAME FROM THE CALCULATOR.
BUT I'LL ASK HER, IF YOU'D LIKE.
IF YOU COULD DO THAT, PLEASE...
...I'D HATE TO THINK IT HAD BEEN LEAKED FROM WITHIN CHECKMATE.
I'LL LOOK INTO IT.
I THINK I WILL, TOO.

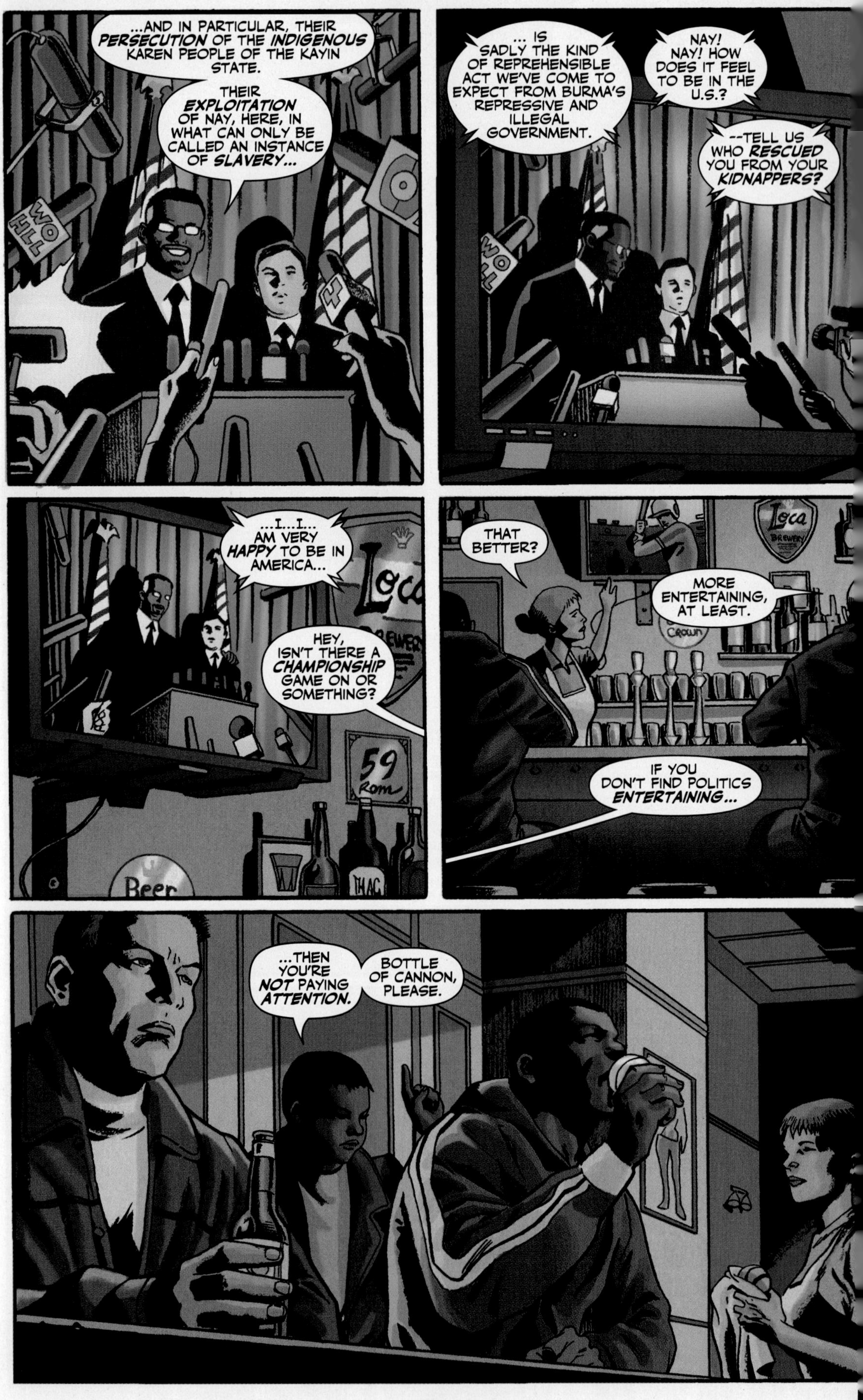
...AND IN PARTICULAR, THEIR PERSECUTION OF THE INDIGENOUS KAREN PEOPLE OF THE KAYIN STATE.
THEIR EXPLOITATION OF NAY, HERE, IN WHAT CAN ONLY BE CALLED AN INSTANCE OF SLAVERY...
... IS SADLY THE KIND OF REPREHENSIBLE ACT WE'VE COME TO EXPECT FROM BURMA'S REPRESSIVE AND ILLEGAL GOVERNMENT.
NAY! NAY! HOW DOES IT FEEL TO BE IN THE U.S.?
--TELL US WHO RESCUED YOU FROM YOUR KIDNAPPERS?
...I...I... AM VERY HAPPY TO BE IN AMERICA...
HEY, ISN'T THERE A CHAMPIONSHIP GAME ON OR SOMETHING?
THAT BETTER?
MORE ENTERTAINING, AT LEAST.
IF YOU DON'T FIND POLITICS ENTERTAINING...
...THEN YOU'RE NOT PAYING ATTENTION.
BOTTLE OF CANNON, PLEASE.

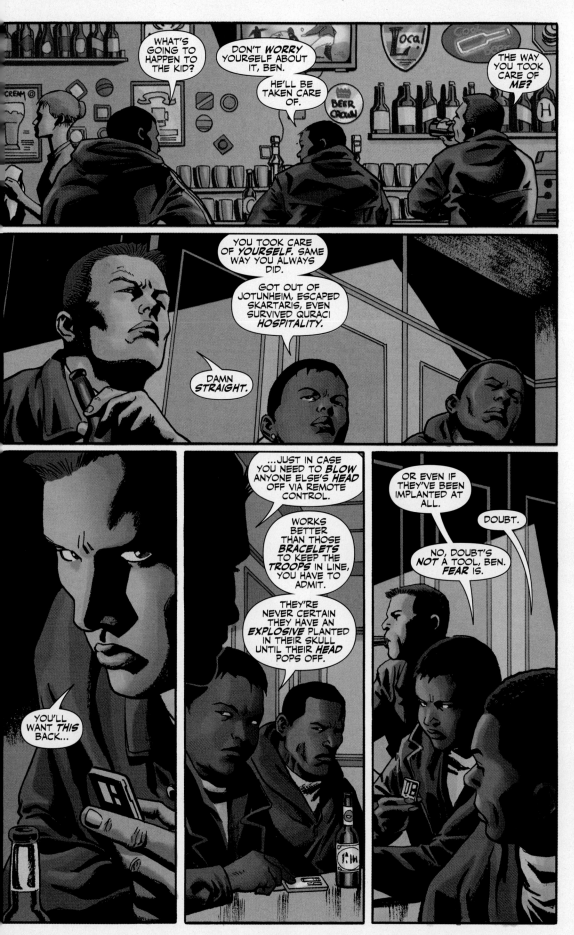

WHAT'S GOING TO HAPPEN TO THE KID?

DON'T *WORRY* YOURSELF ABOUT IT, BEN.

HE'LL BE TAKEN CARE OF.

THE WAY YOU TOOK CARE OF *ME?*

YOU TOOK CARE OF *YOURSELF.* SAME WAY YOU ALWAYS DID.

GOT OUT OF JOTUNHEIM, ESCAPED SKARTARIS, EVEN SURVIVED QURACI *HOSPITALITY.*

DAMN *STRAIGHT.*

...JUST IN CASE YOU NEED TO *BLOW* ANYONE ELSE'S *HEAD* OFF VIA REMOTE CONTROL.

WORKS BETTER THAN THOSE *BRACELETS* TO KEEP THE *TROOPS* IN LINE, YOU HAVE TO ADMIT.

THEY'RE NEVER CERTAIN THEY HAVE AN *EXPLOSIVE* PLANTED IN THEIR SKULL UNTIL THEIR *HEAD* POPS OFF.

OR EVEN IF THEY'VE BEEN IMPLANTED AT ALL.

DOUBT.

NO, DOUBT'S *NOT* A TOOL, BEN. *FEAR* IS.

YOU'LL WANT *THIS* BACK...

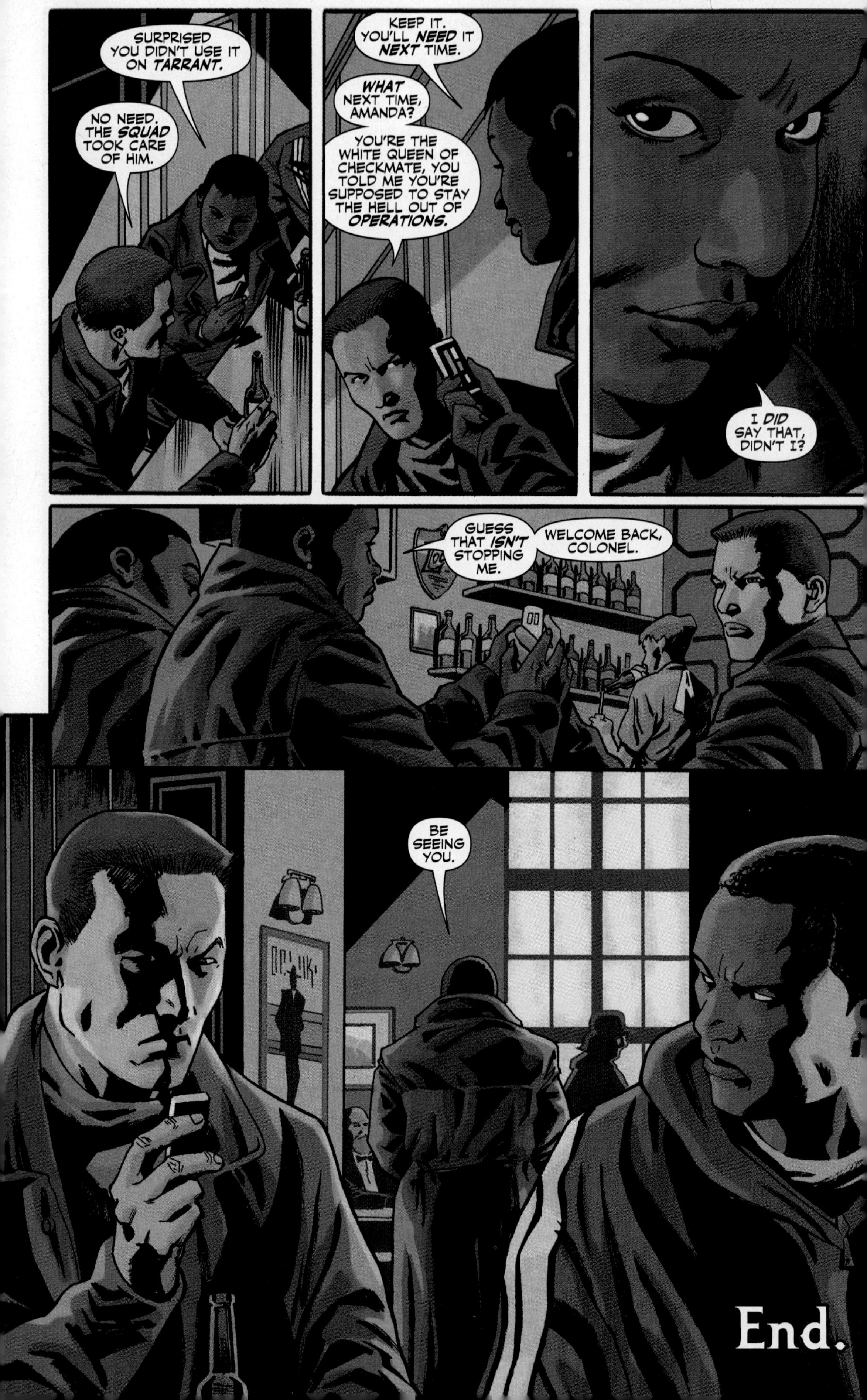
SURPRISED YOU DIDN'T USE IT ON *TARRANT.*
NO NEED. THE *SQUAD* TOOK CARE OF HIM.
KEEP IT. YOU'LL *NEED* IT *NEXT* TIME.
WHAT NEXT TIME, AMANDA?
YOU'RE THE WHITE QUEEN OF CHECKMATE, YOU TOLD ME YOU'RE SUPPOSED TO STAY THE HELL OUT OF *OPERATIONS.*
I *DID* SAY THAT, DIDN'T I?
GUESS THAT *ISN'T* STOPPING ME.
WELCOME BACK, COLONEL.
BE SEEING YOU.
End.

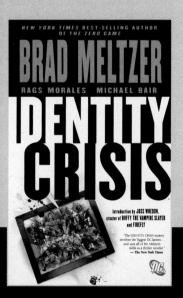

DON'T MISS THESE OTHER GREAT TITLES FROM AROUND THE **DCU!**